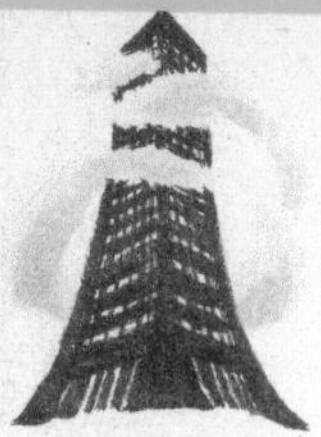

I moved. No, I had to move. After three years, I finally got bored of the workspace I loved so much. I had never even made it to two years in the past, so that means I liked this one 1.5 times more than the others. Wait. That's not as much as I thought. My new workspace is on the 34th floor! I'm not very good with heights, so how many years will I be able to stand it?! We'll see!!

-Tite Kubo

Bleach is author Tite Kubo's second title. Kubo made his debut with *ZOMBIEPOWDER.*, a four-volume series for *Weekly Shonen Jump*. To date, *Bleach* has been translated into numerous languages and has also inspired an animated TV series that began airing in the U.S. in 2006. Beginning its serialization in 2001, *Bleach* is still a mainstay in the pages of *Weekly Shonen Jump*. In 2005, *Bleach* was awarded the prestigious Shogakukan Manga Award in the *shonen* (boys) category.

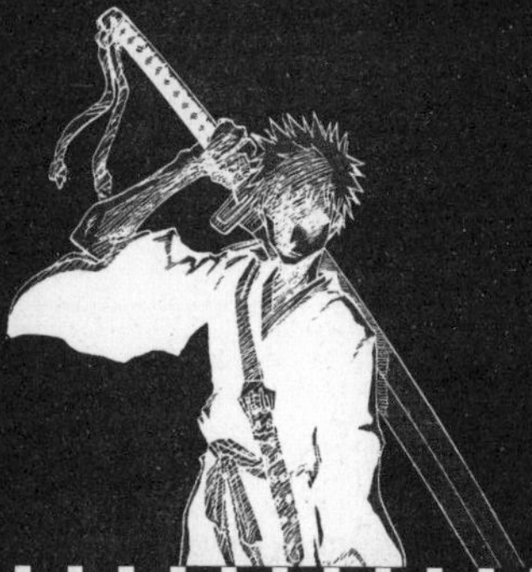

BLEACH
Vol. 41: HEART
SHONEN JUMP Manga Edition

STORY AND ART BY
TITE KUBO

English Adaptation/Lance Caselman
Translation/Joe Yamazaki
Touch-up Art & Lettering/Mark McMurray
Design/Yukiko Whitley, Kam Li
Editor/Alexis Kirsch

Printed in the U.S.A.

Published by VIZ Media, LLC
P.O. Box 77010
San Francisco, CA 94107

10 9 8 7 6 5 4 3 2 1
First printing, June 2012

Take back what was lost
Blood, flesh, bone, and one more thing

WITHDRAWN

STARS AND

Ulquiorra

Orihime Inoue

井上織姫

Ichigo Kurosaki

plot

When high school student Ichigo Kurosaki meets Soul Reaper Rukia Kuchiki his life is changed forever. Soon Ichigo is a soul-cleansing Soul Reaper too, and he finds himself having adventures, as well as problems, that he never would have imagined. Now Ichigo and his friends must stop renegade Soul Reaper Aizen and his army of Arrancars from destroying the Soul Society and wiping out Karakura as well.

In a long-awaited clash, the Thirteen Court Guard Companies do battle with the Espadas in Karakura Town. Meanwhile in Hueco Mundo, Ichigo fights Ulquiorra to save Orihime. But after the Espada's devastating second stage release, Orihime fears this might be Ichigo's final duel.

BLEACH ALL

朽木ルキア

Rukia Kuchiki

石田雨竜

Uryû Ishida

Yammy

ヤミー

STORIES

BLEACH41

HEART

Contents

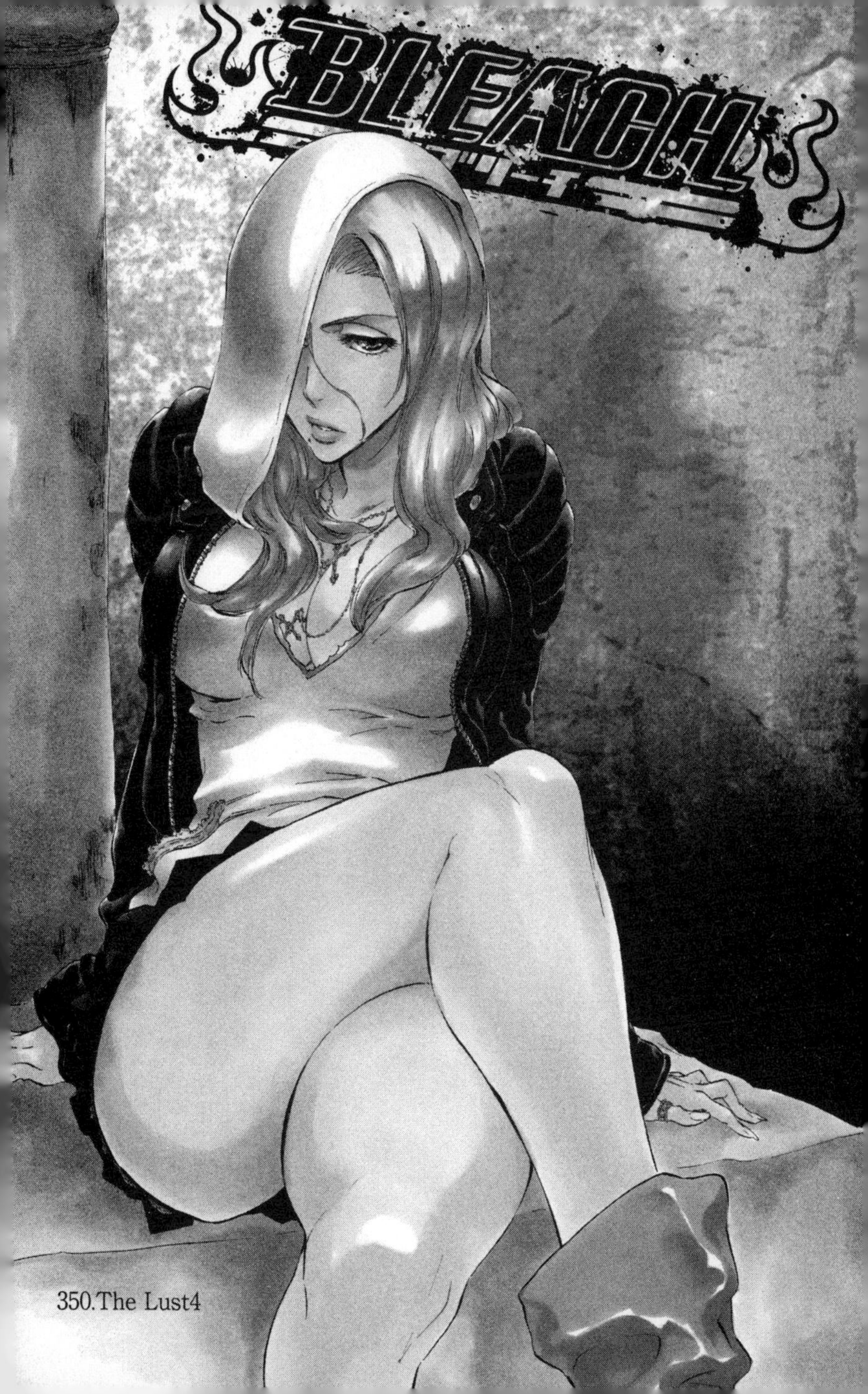
BLEACH
350.The Lust4

BLEACH
ブリーチ

READ THIS WAY

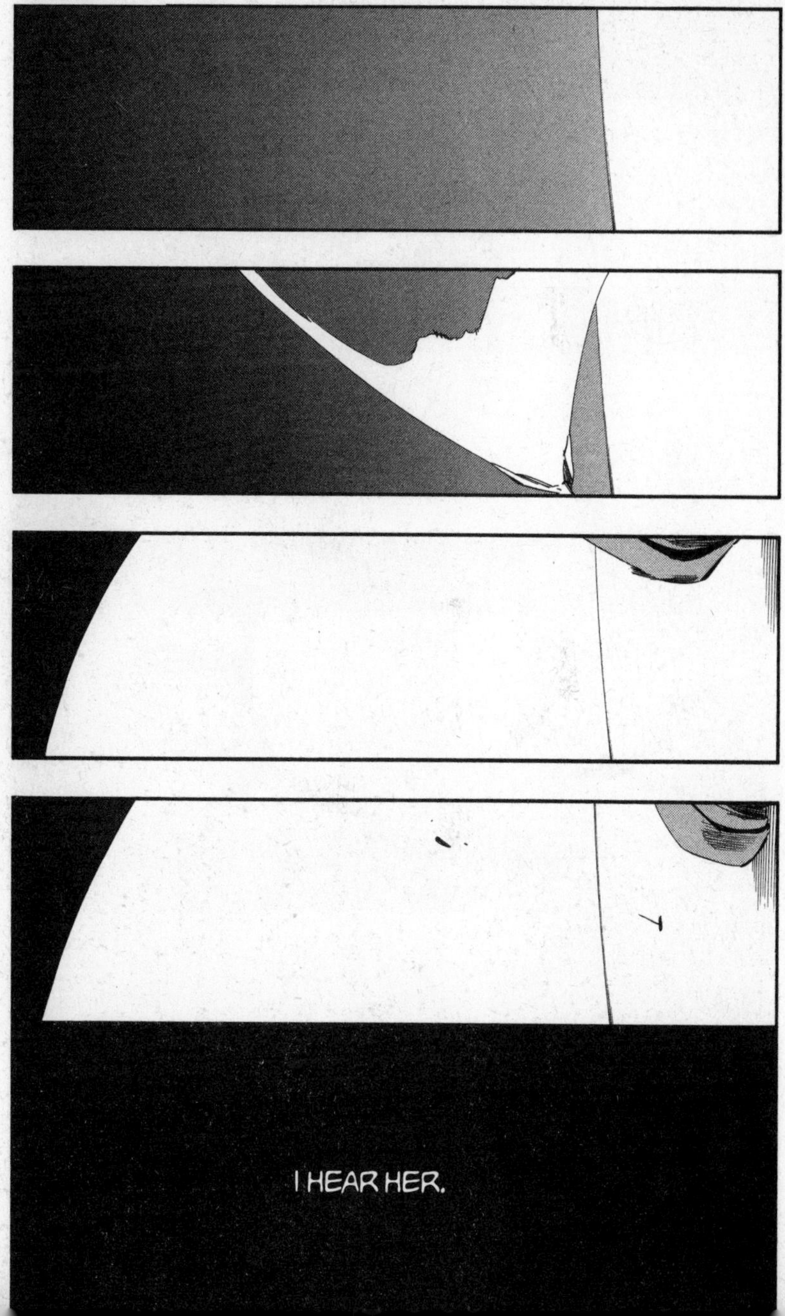
I HEAR HER.

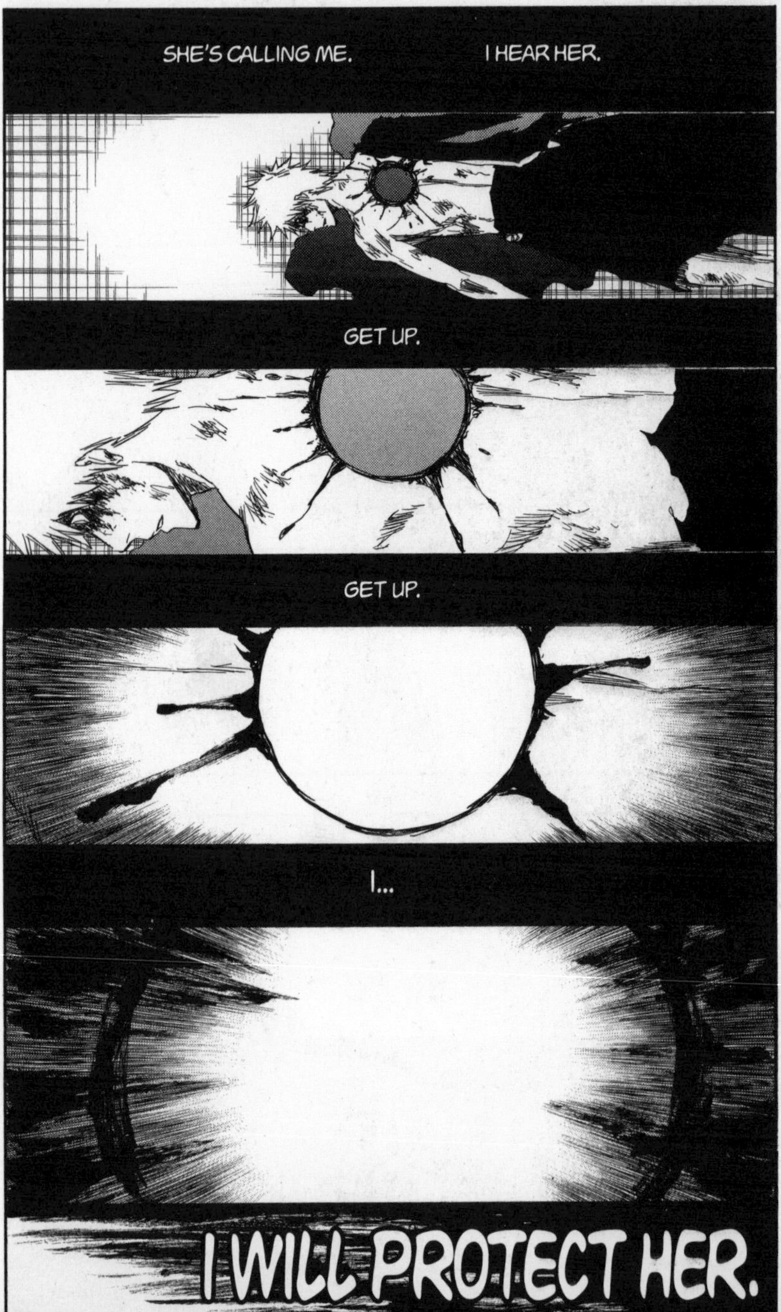
I HEAR HER.
SHE'S CALLING ME.
GET UP.
GET UP.
I...
I WILL PROTECT HER.

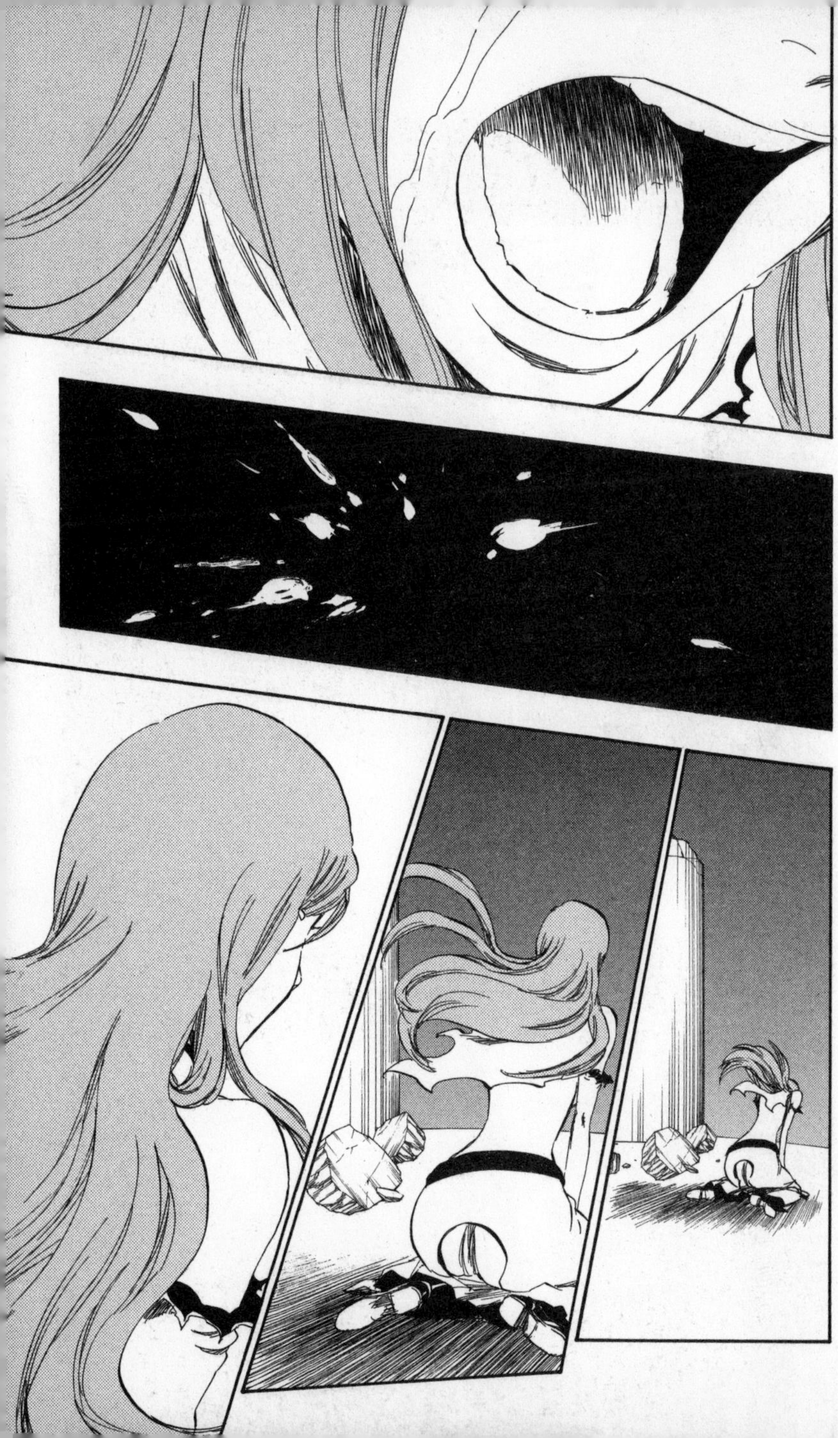

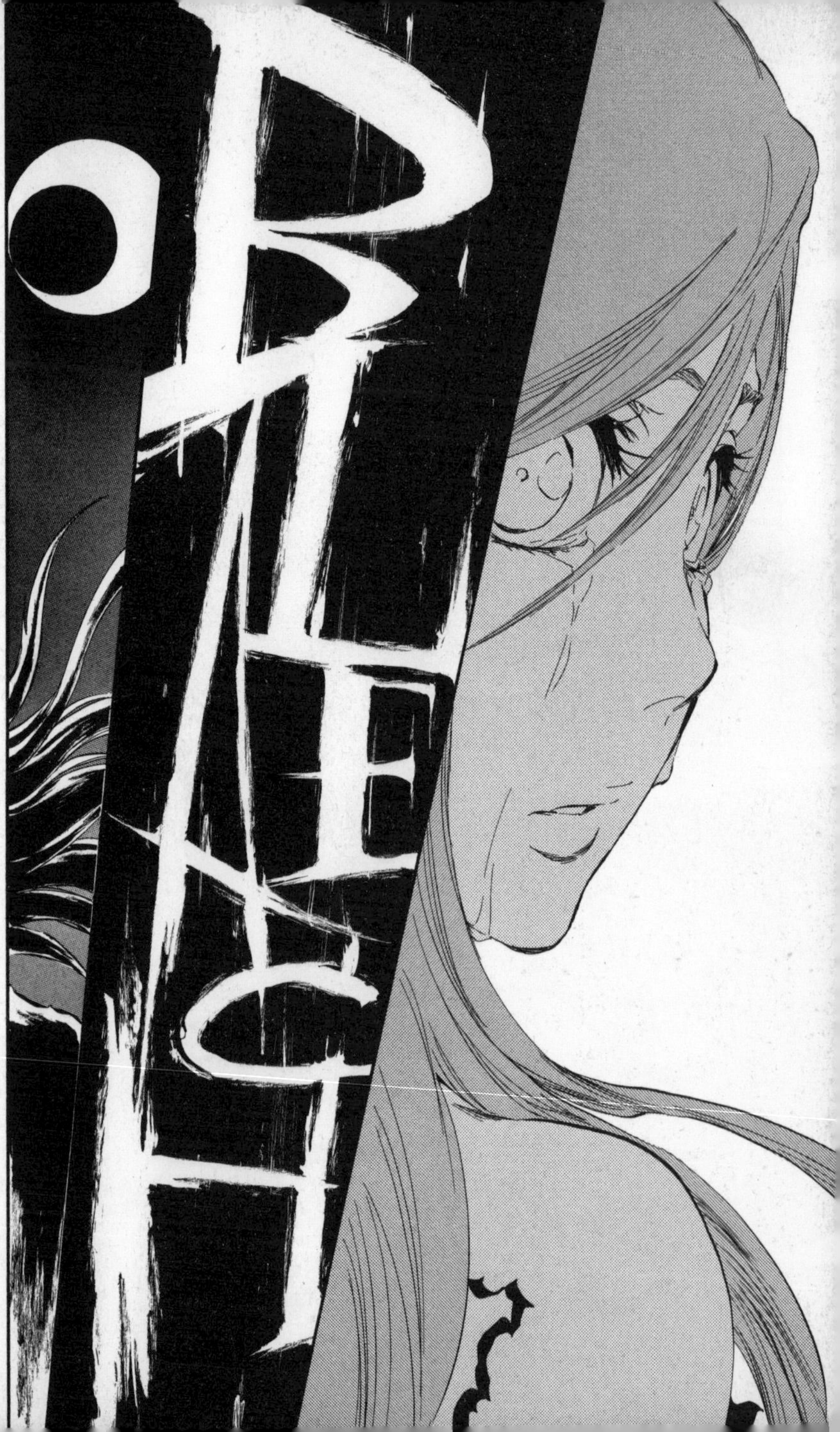

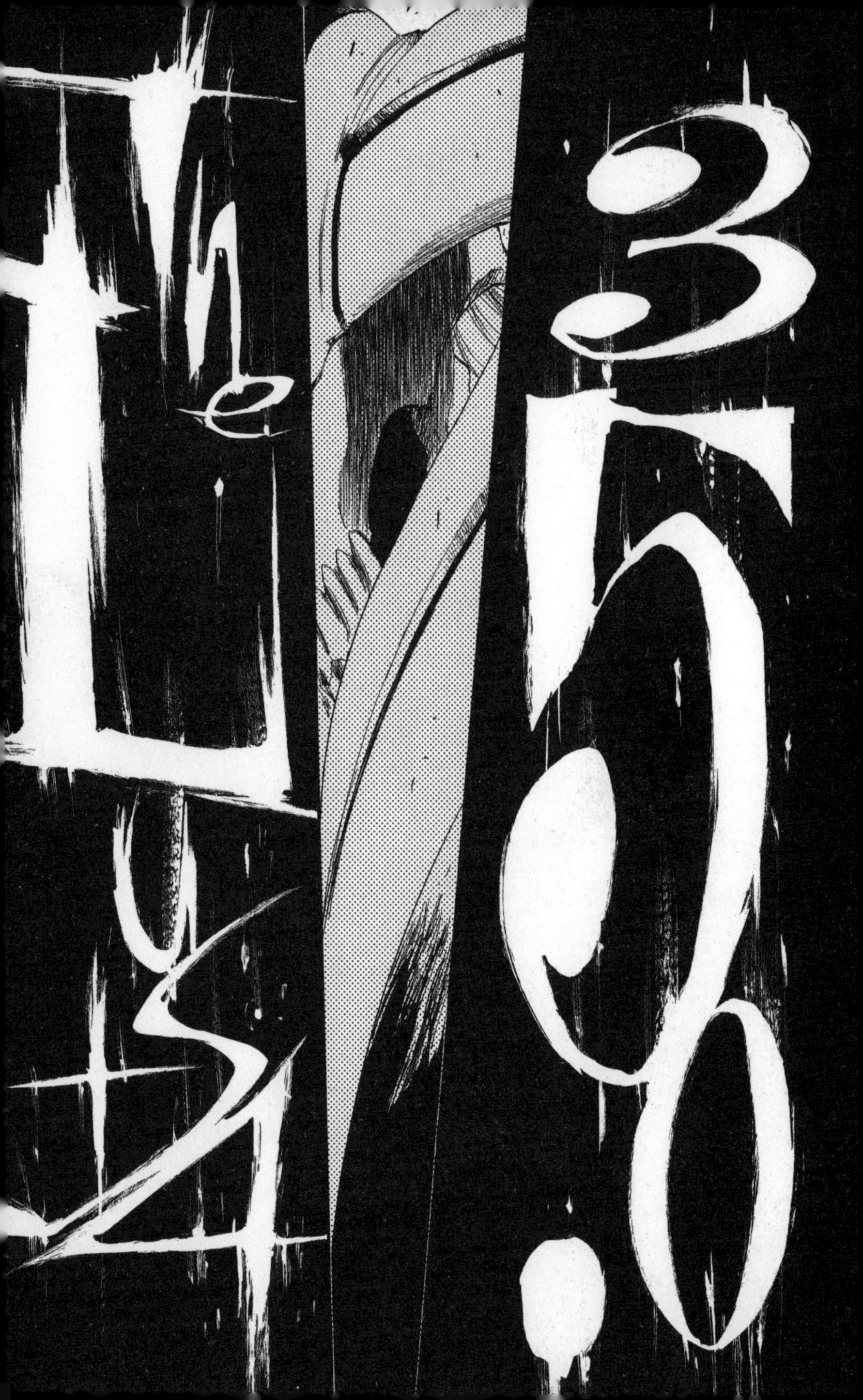
Let us

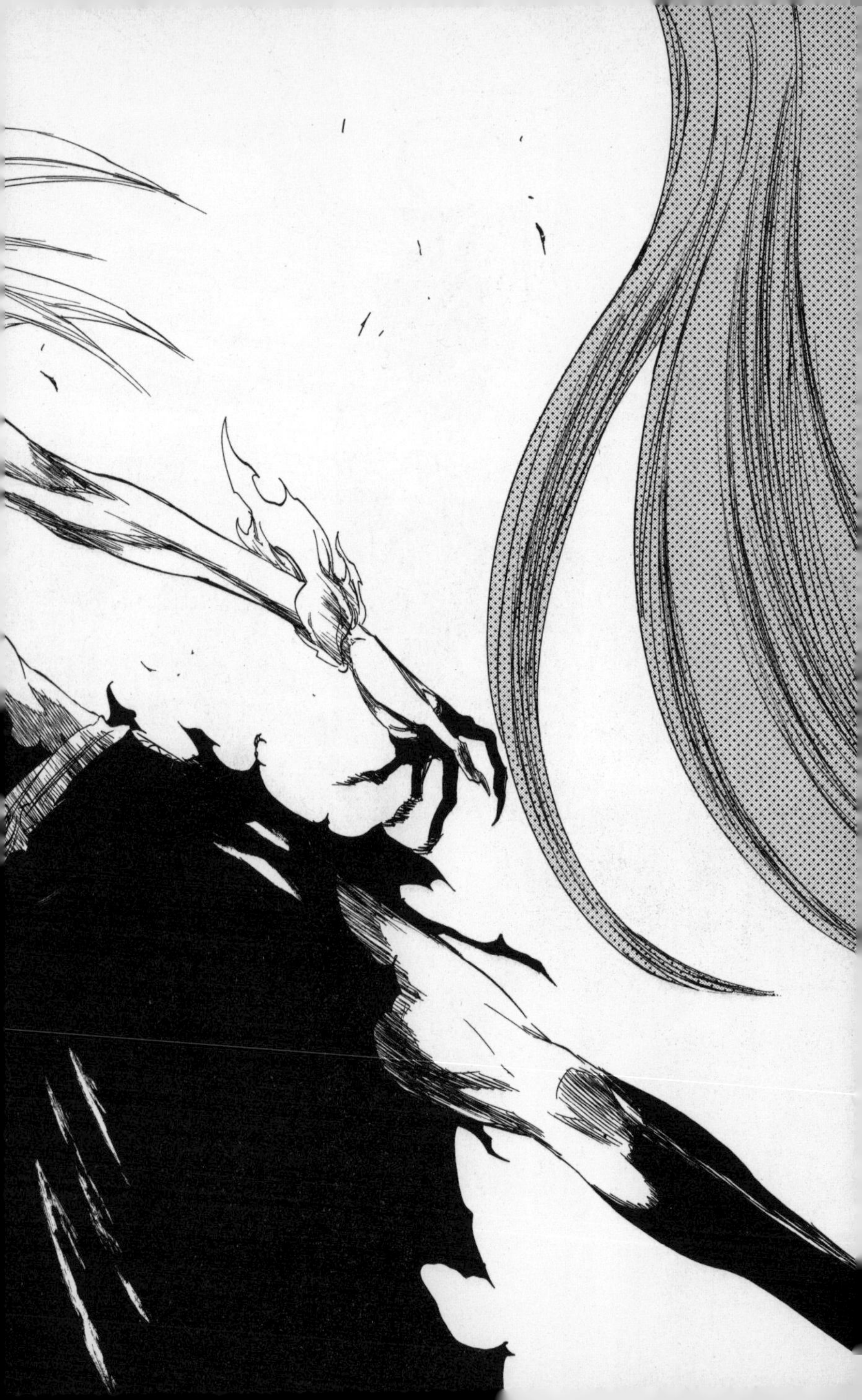

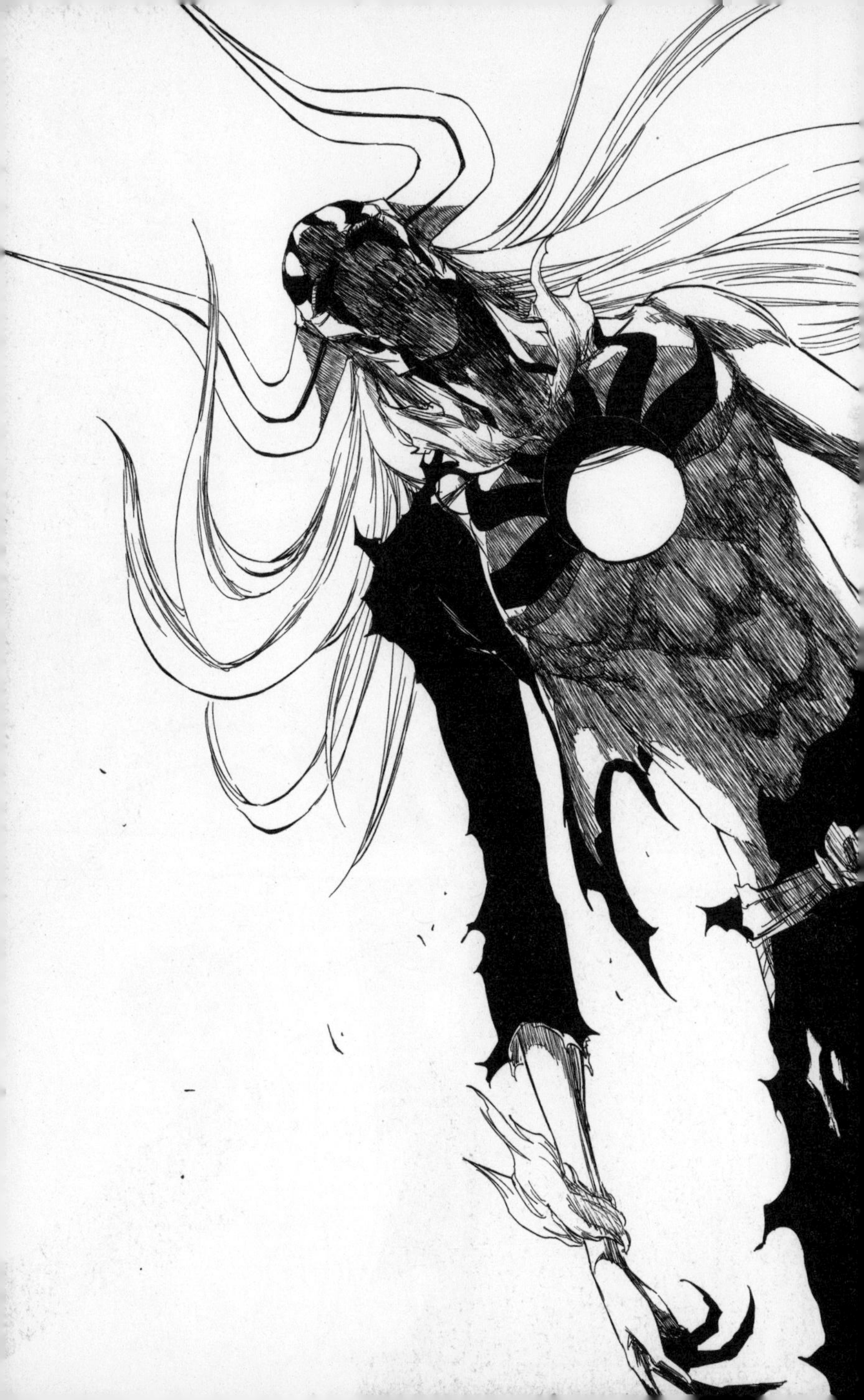

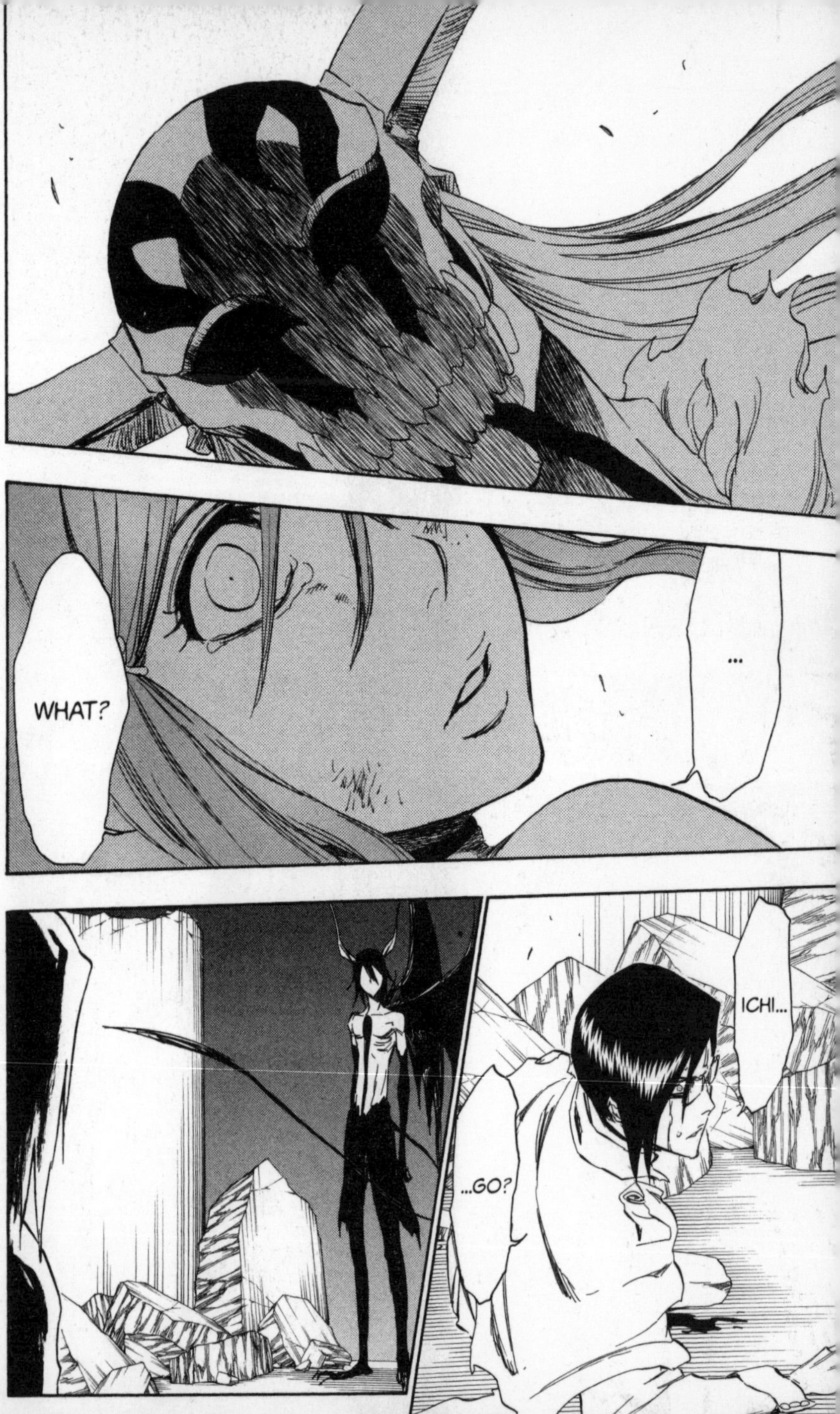
...
WHAT?
ICHI...
...GO?

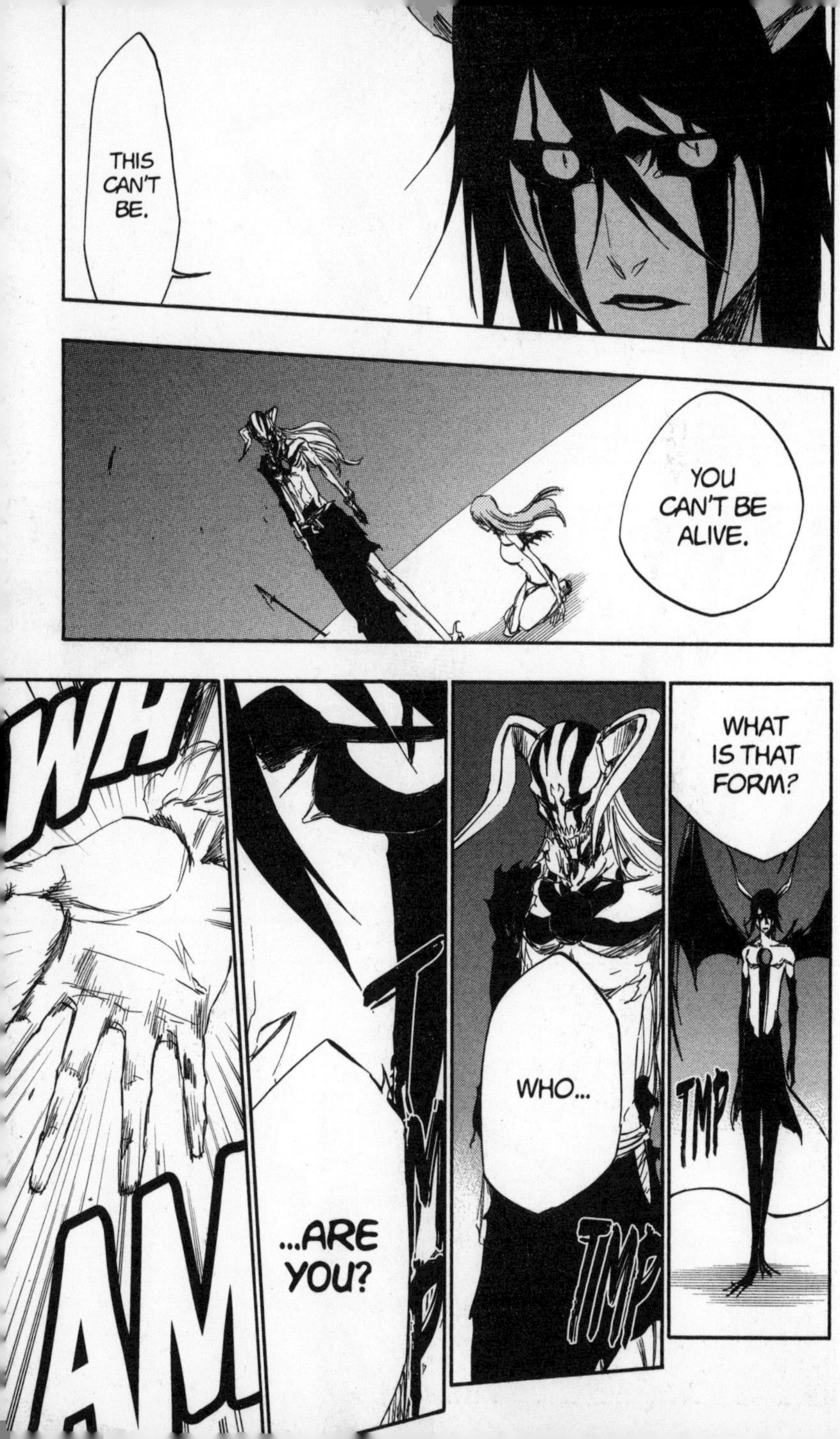
THIS CAN'T BE.
YOU CAN'T BE ALIVE.
WHAT IS THAT FORM?
TMP
WHO...
TMP
...ARE YOU?
WH
AM

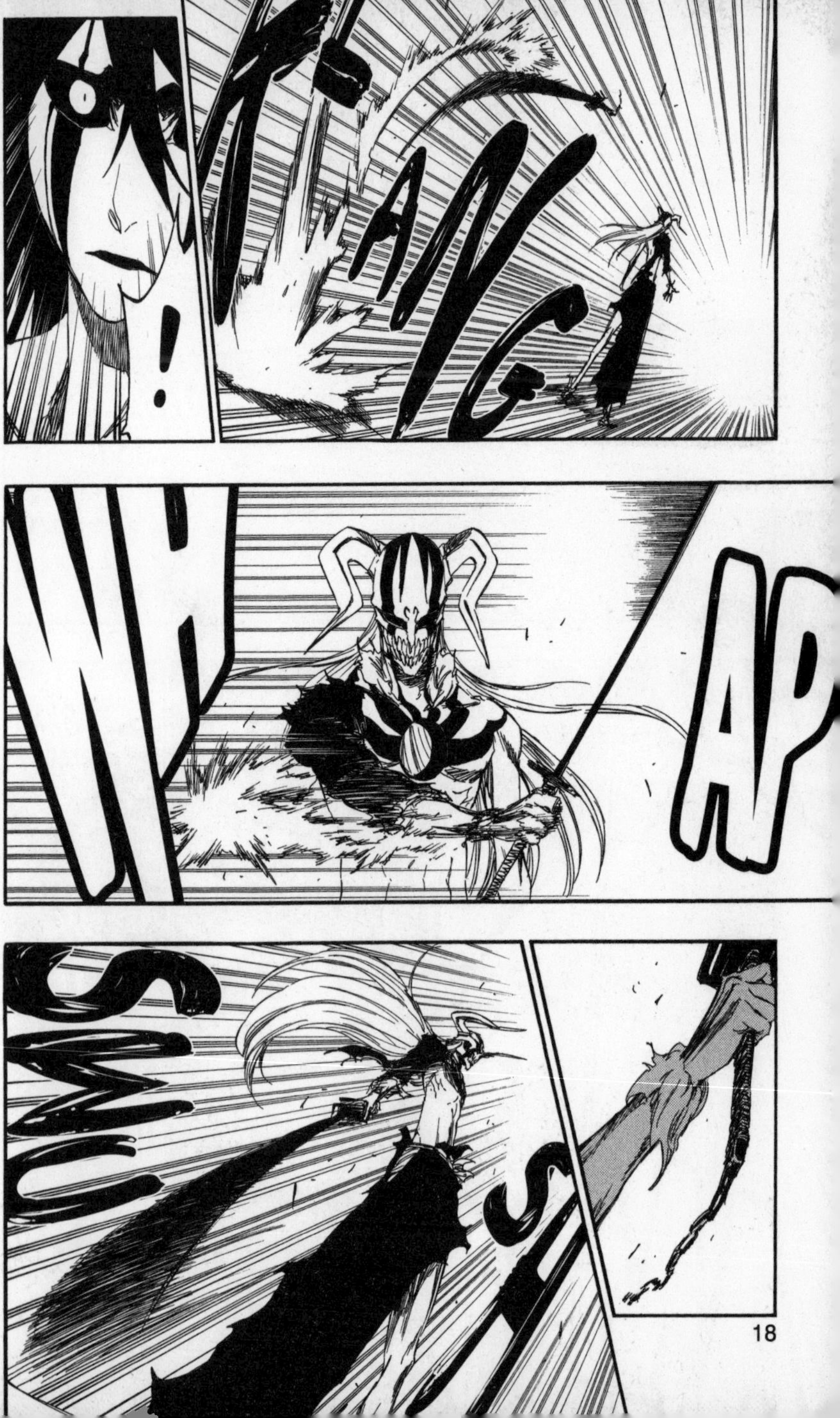
KLANG
!
WH
AP
SH
SWO

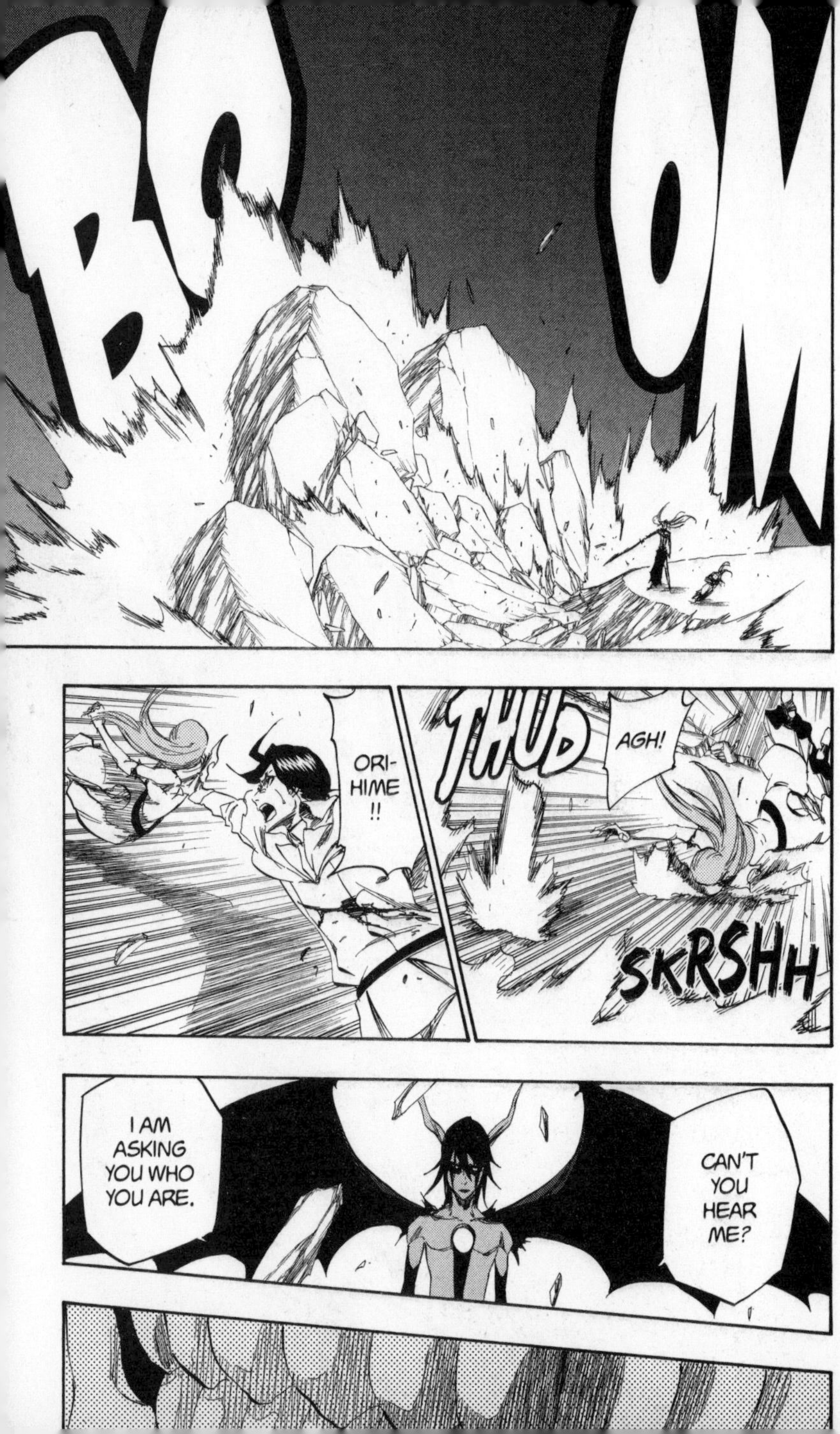
BOOM
THUD
AGH!
SKRSHH
ORI-HIME!!
CAN'T YOU HEAR ME?
I AM ASKING YOU WHO YOU ARE.

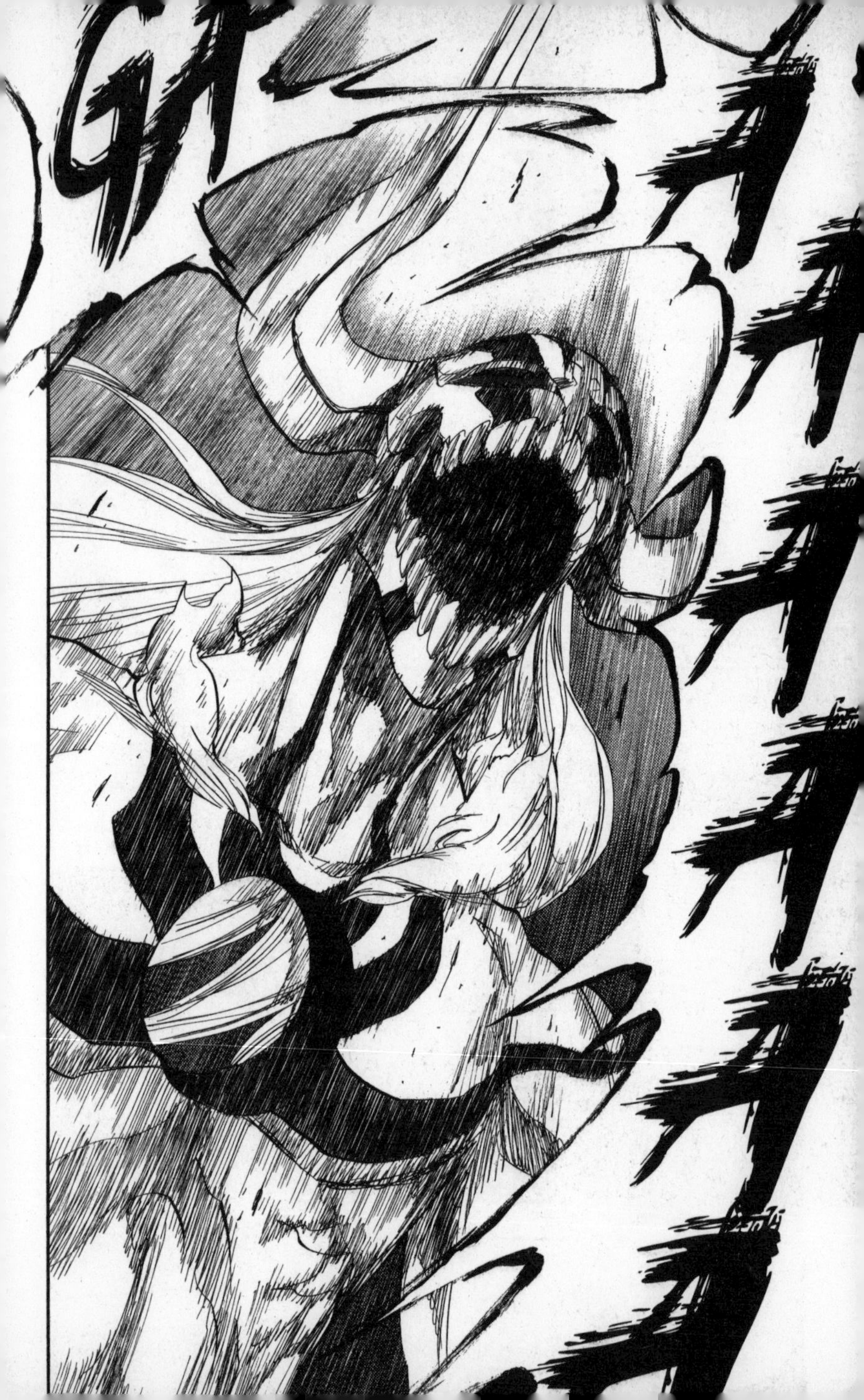

オオオオオ

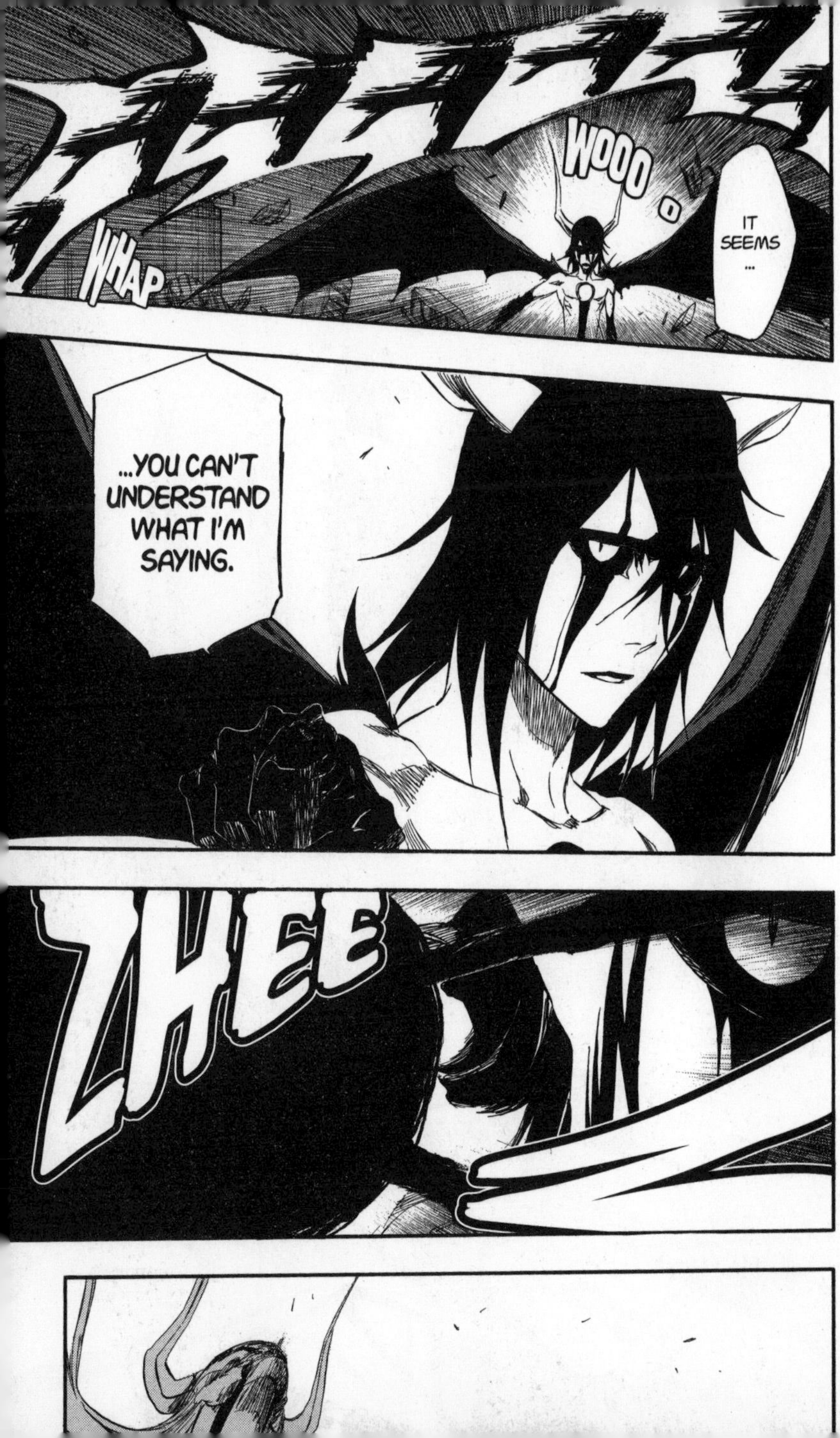
IT SEEMS ...
WOOO
WHAP
...YOU CAN'T UNDERSTAND WHAT I'M SAYING.
ZHEE

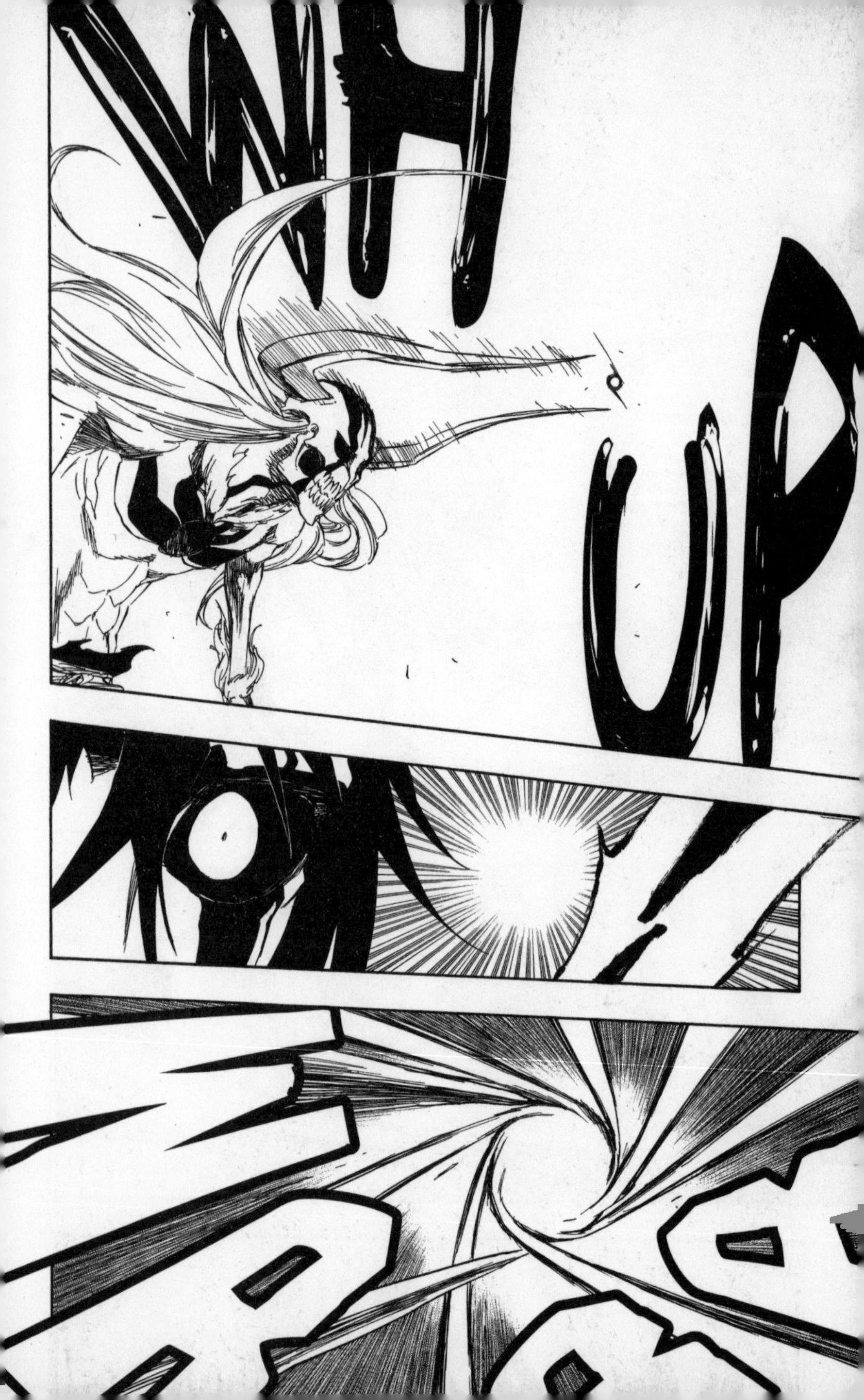
WHUP

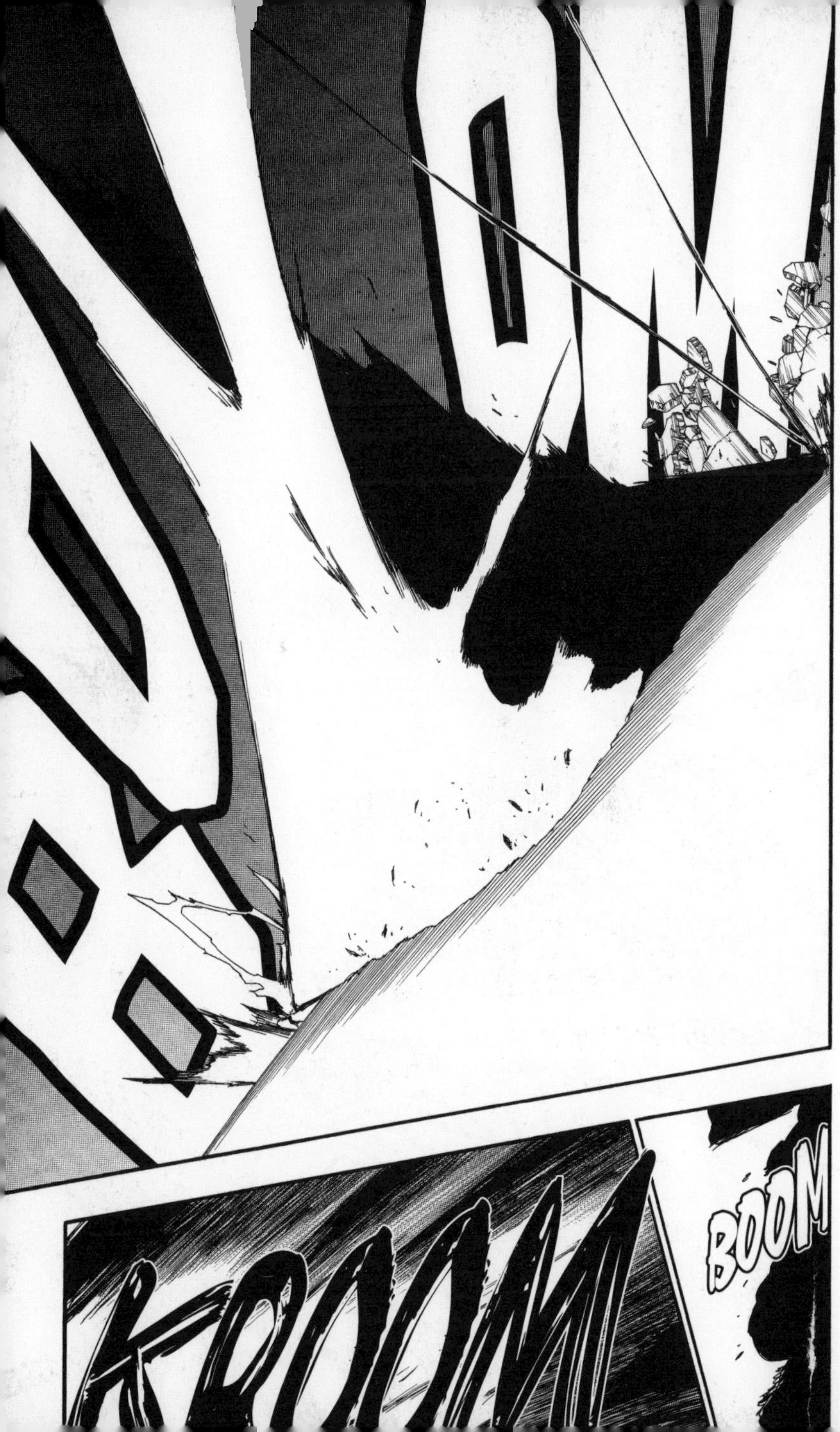
BOOM

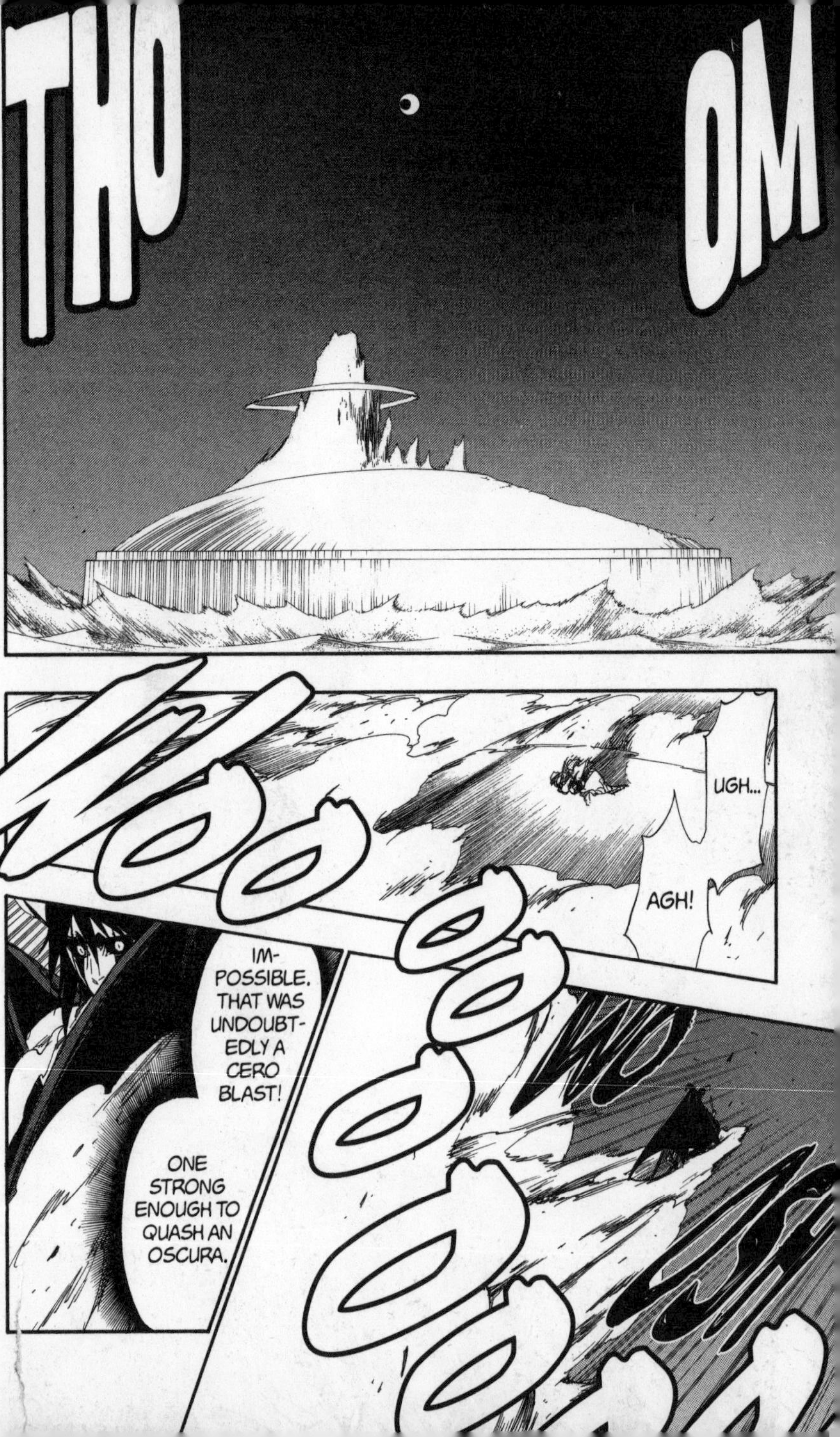
THO
OM
UGH...
AGH!
IM-POSSIBLE. THAT WAS UNDOUBT-EDLY A CERO BLAST!
ONE STRONG ENOUGH TO QUASH AN OSCURA.

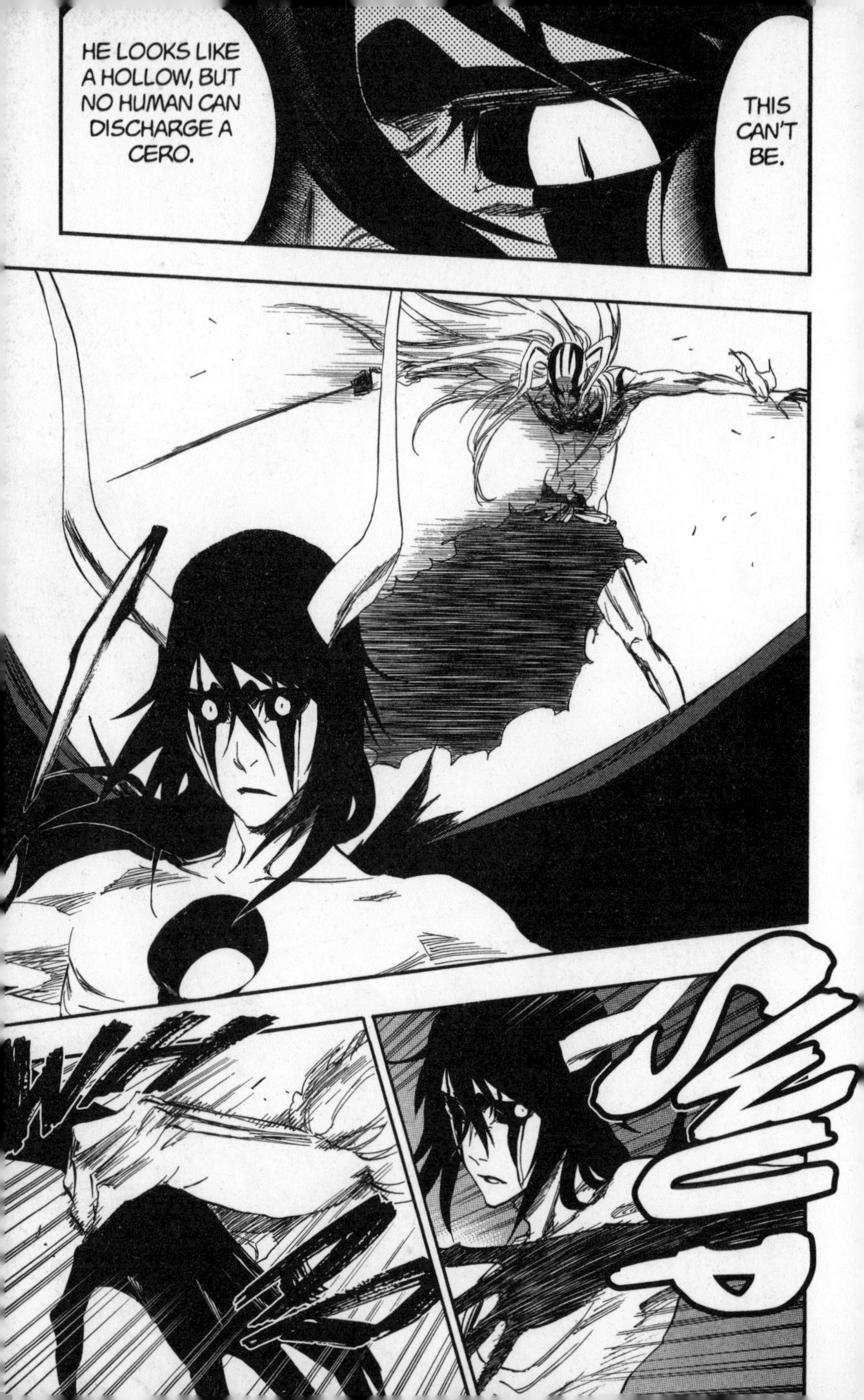
THIS CAN'T BE.
HE LOOKS LIKE A HOLLOW, BUT NO HUMAN CAN DISCHARGE A CERO.

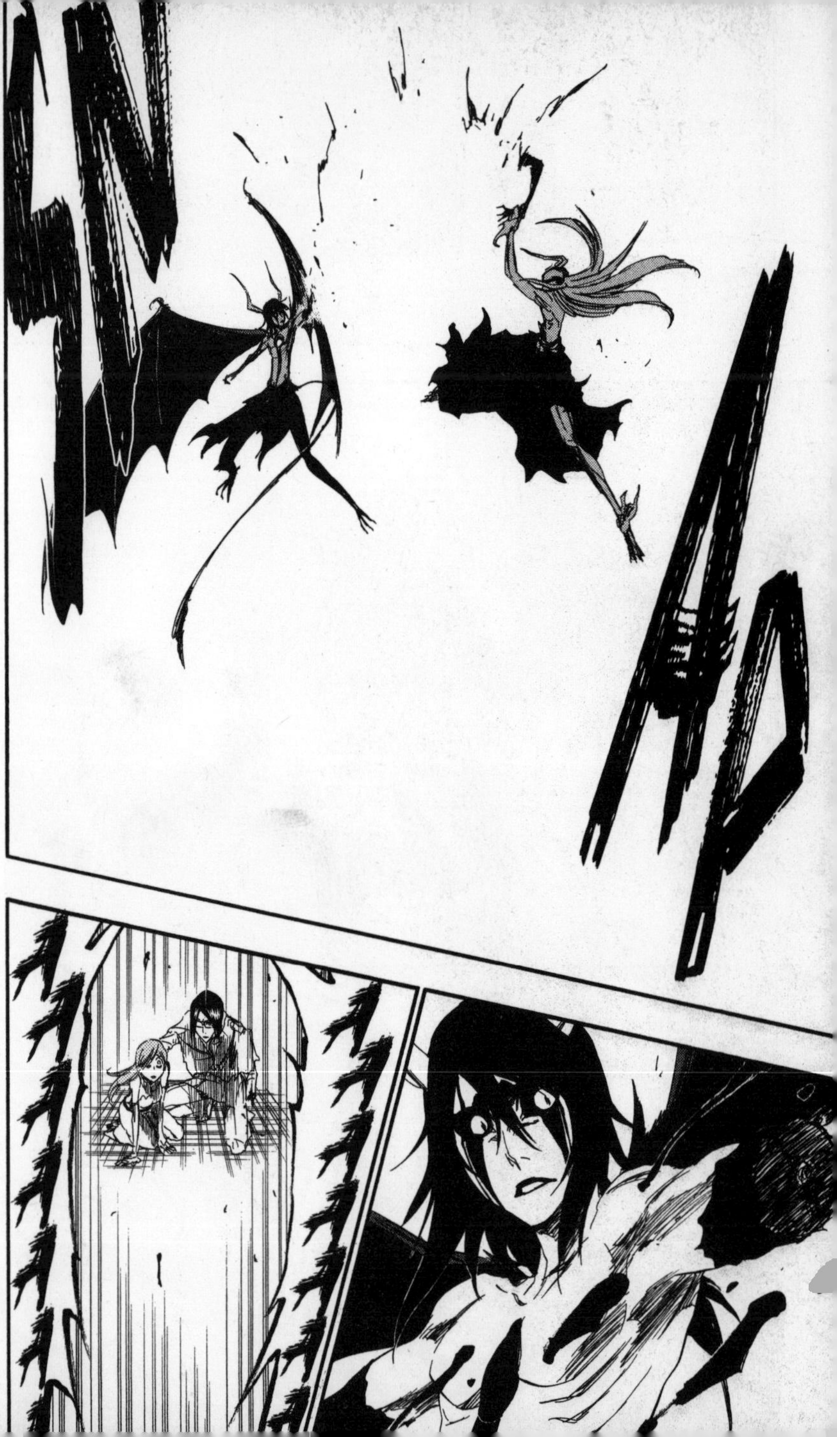
SNAP

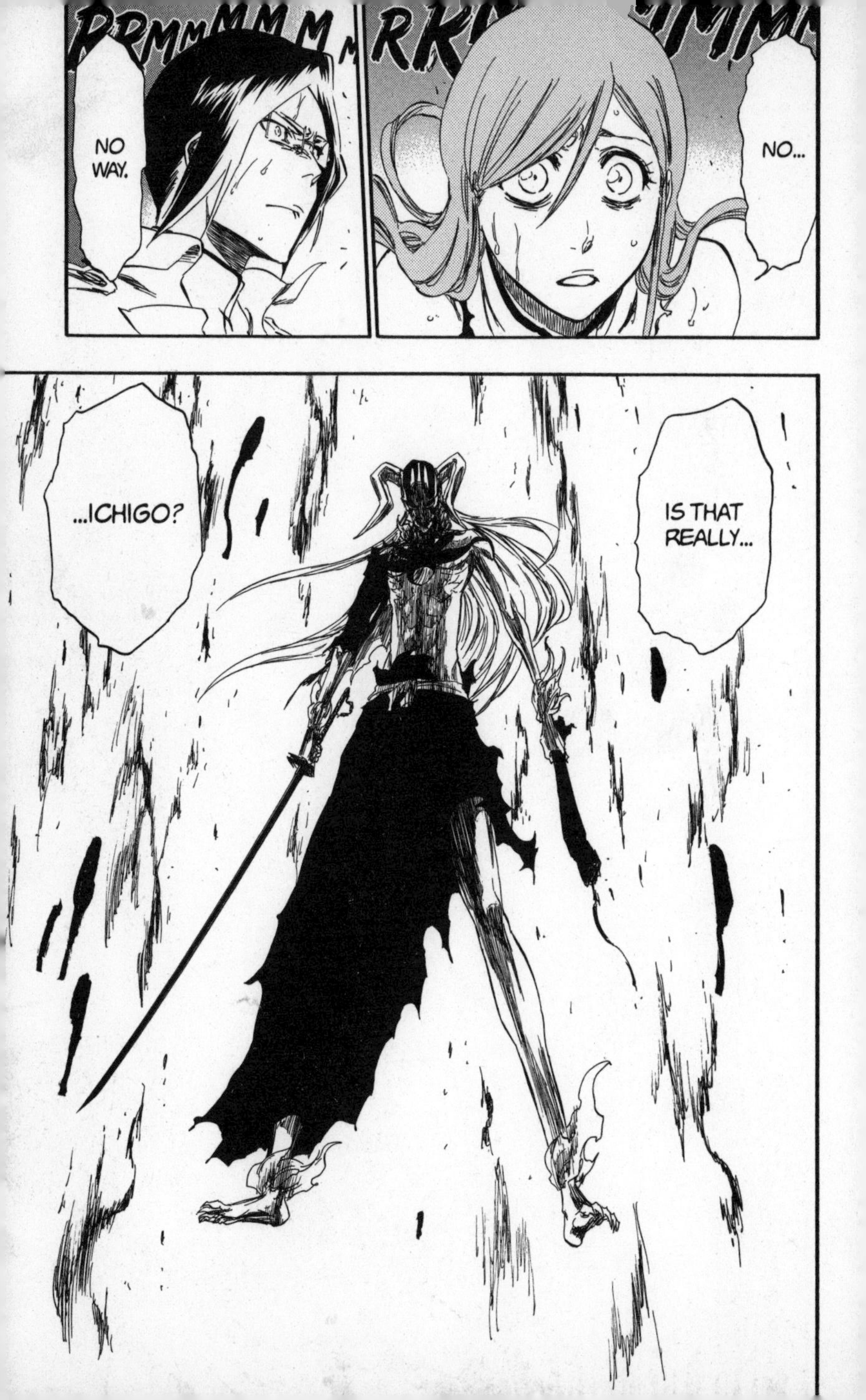
NO...
NO WAY.
IS THAT REALLY...
...ICHIGO?

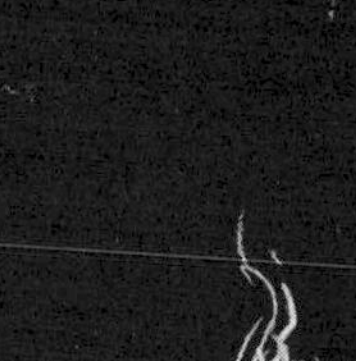

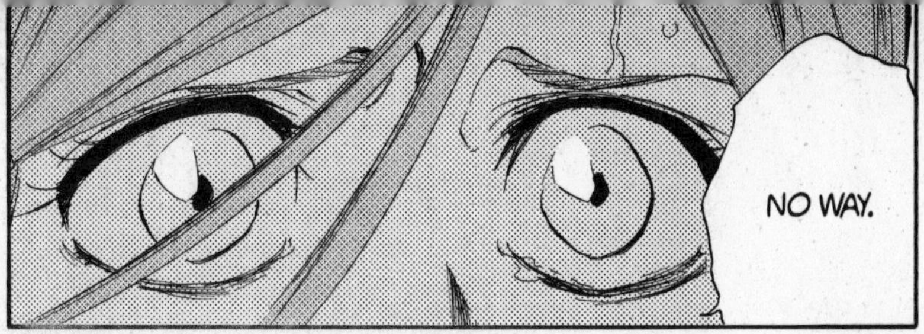
NO WAY.

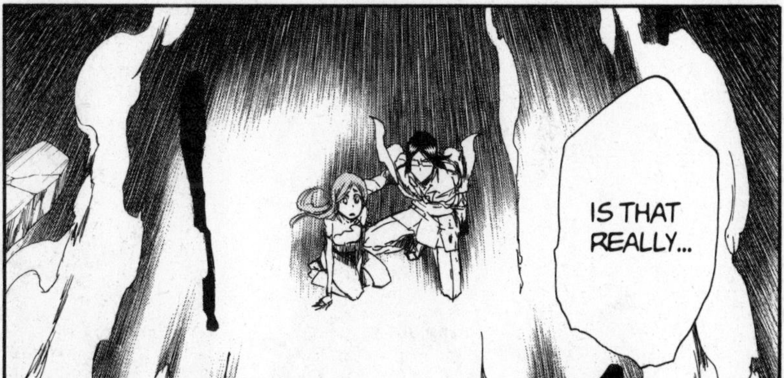
IS THAT REALLY...

351. The Lust 5

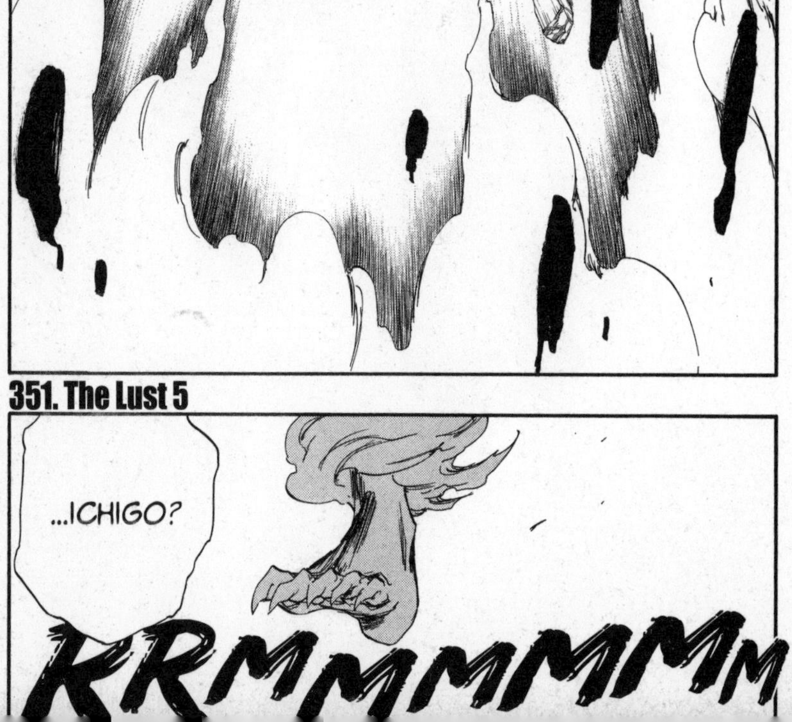
...ICHIGO?
KRMMMMMMm

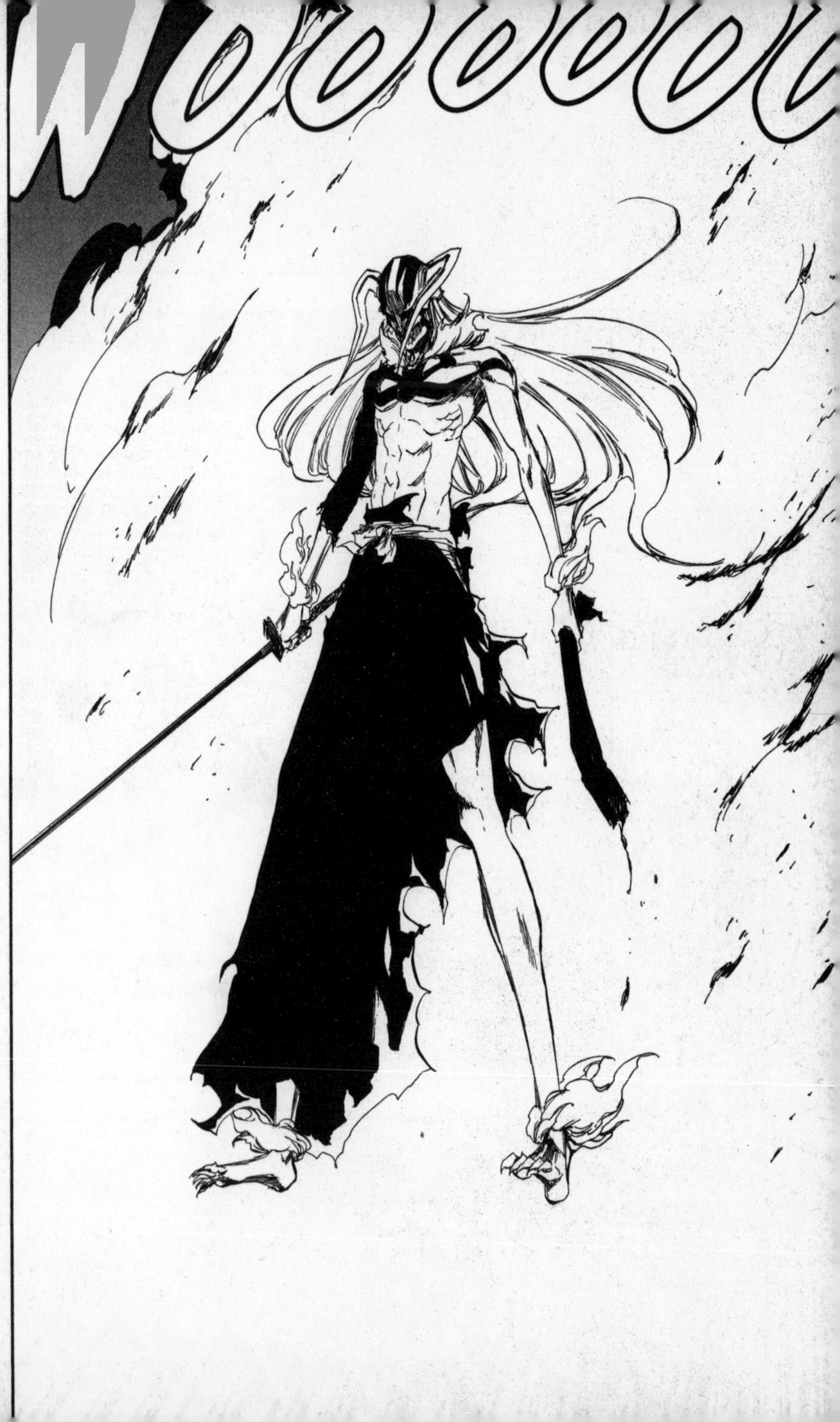
WOOOOOO

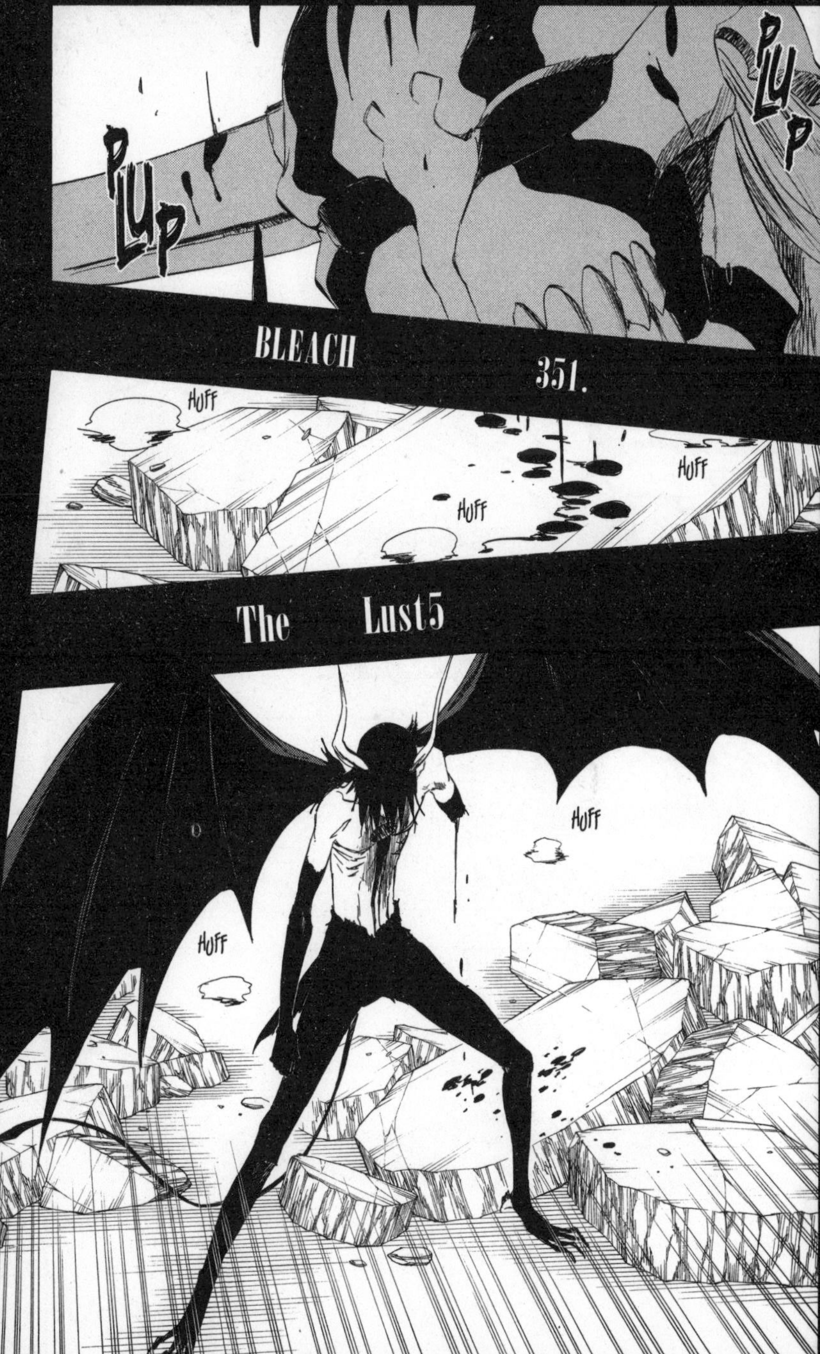

PLUP
PLUP
BLEACH 351. The Lust5
HUFF
HUFF
HUFF
HUFF
HUFF

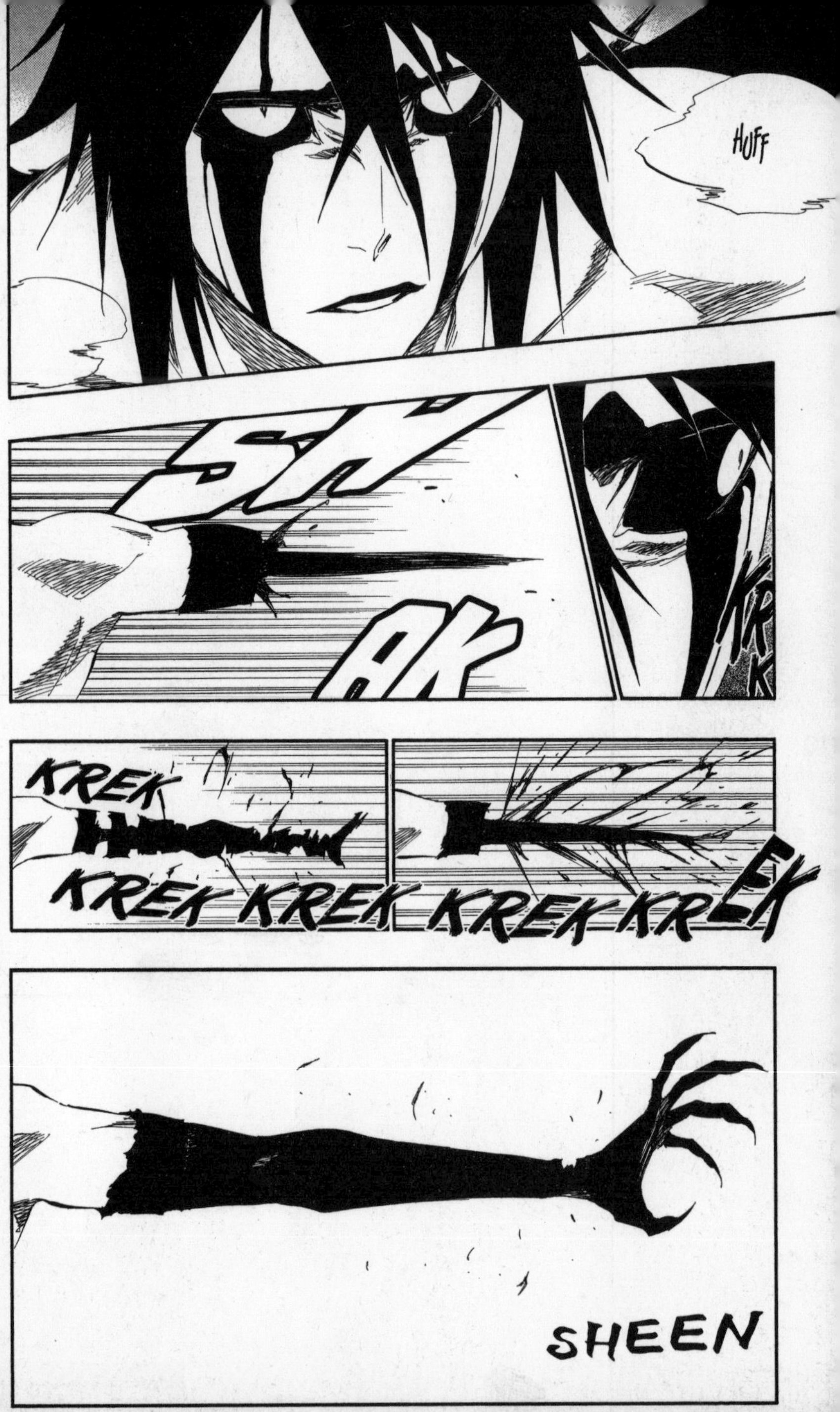
HUFF
KREK
SHAK
KREK
KREK KREK KREK KREK KRREK
SHEEN

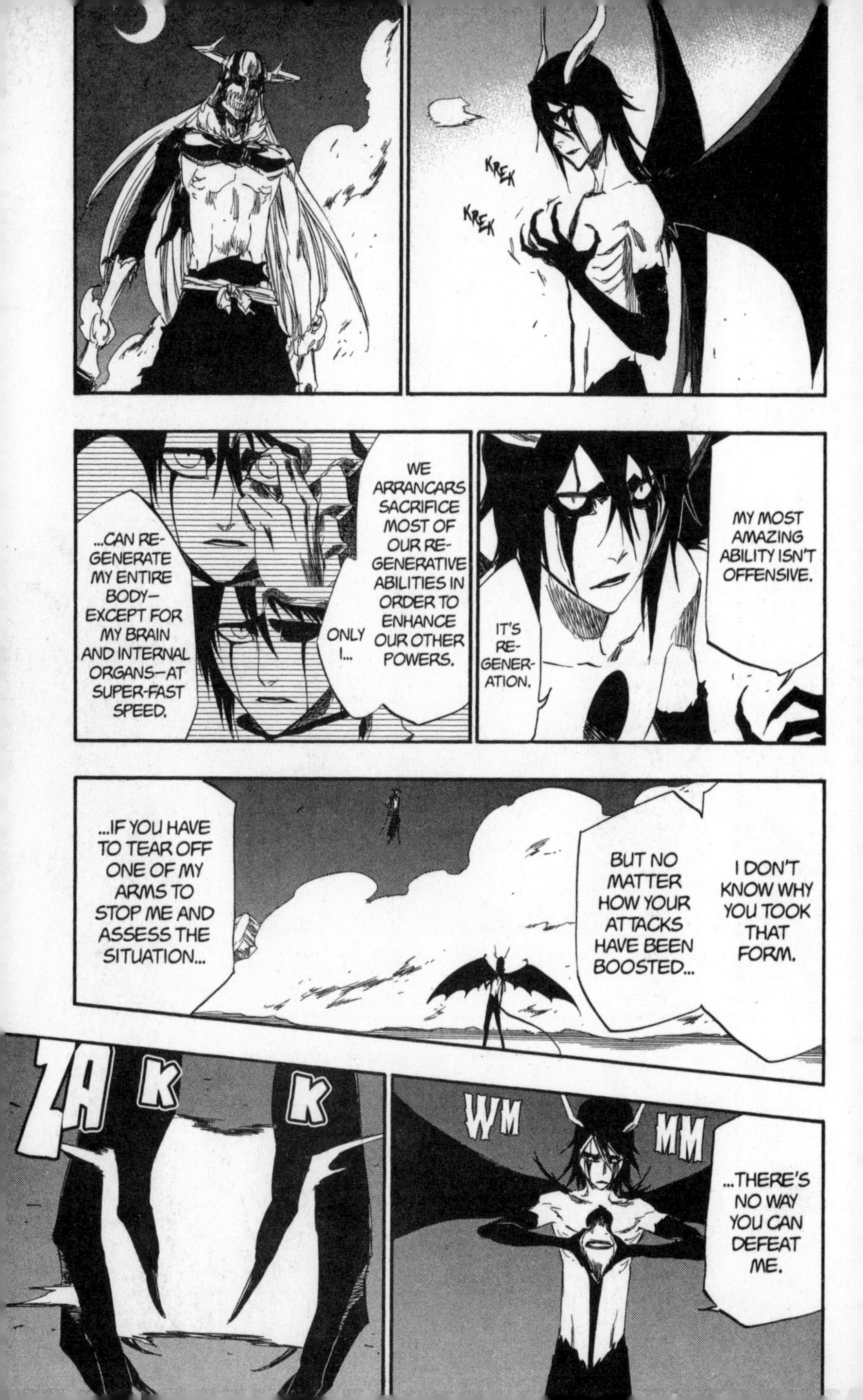
KREK
KREK
MY MOST AMAZING ABILITY ISN'T OFFENSIVE.
IT'S RE-GENERATION.
WE ARRANCARS SACRIFICE MOST OF OUR RE-GENERATIVE ABILITIES IN ORDER TO ENHANCE OUR OTHER POWERS.
ONLY I...
...CAN RE-GENERATE MY ENTIRE BODY—EXCEPT FOR MY BRAIN AND INTERNAL ORGANS—AT SUPER-FAST SPEED.
I DON'T KNOW WHY YOU TOOK THAT FORM.
BUT NO MATTER HOW YOUR ATTACKS HAVE BEEN BOOSTED...
...IF YOU HAVE TO TEAR OFF ONE OF MY ARMS TO STOP ME AND ASSESS THE SITUATION...
WMMM
...THERE'S NO WAY YOU CAN DEFEAT ME.
ZAKKK

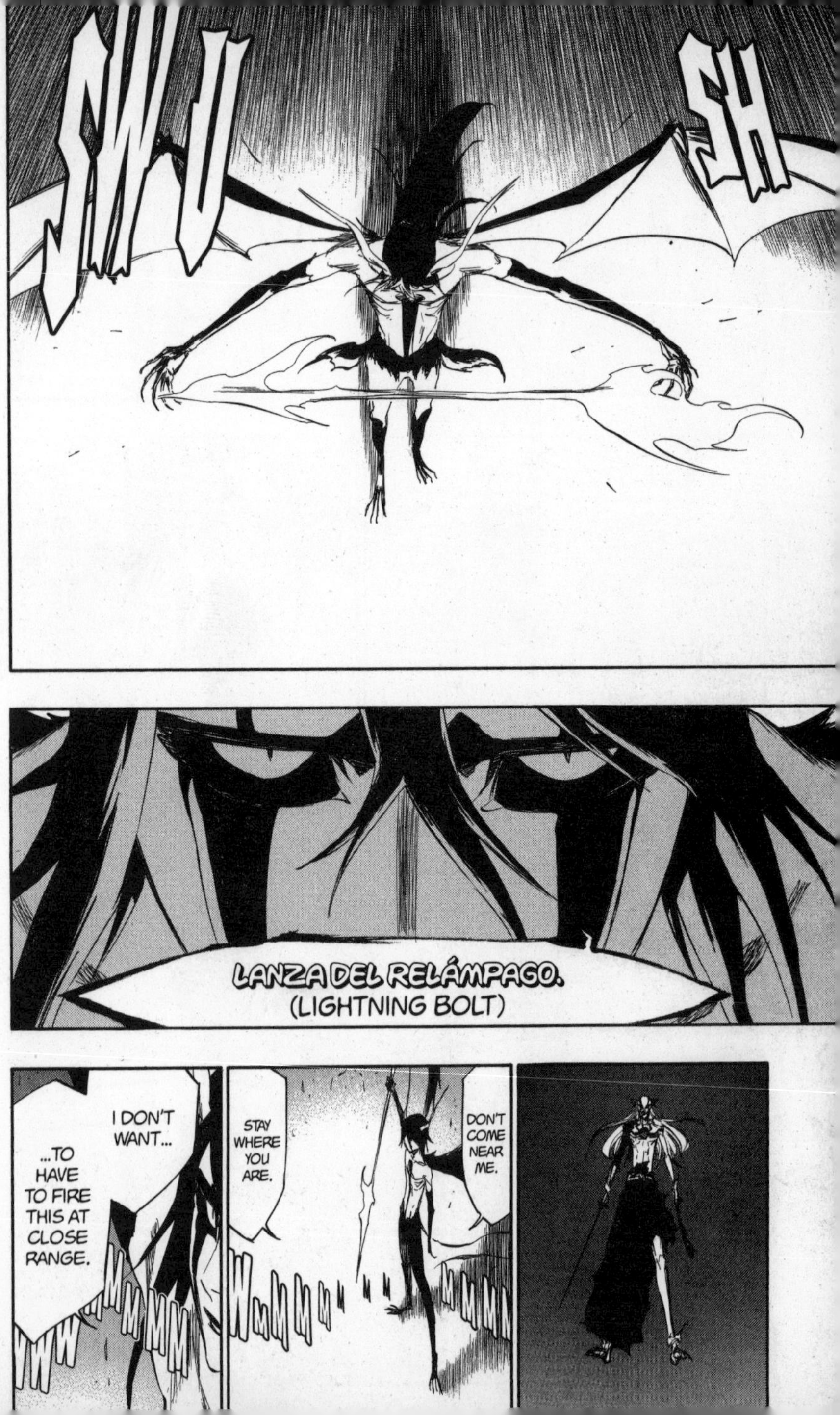
SWU
SH
LANZA DEL RELÁMPAGO.
(LIGHTNING BOLT)
DON'T COME NEAR ME.
STAY WHERE YOU ARE.
I DON'T WANT...
...TO HAVE TO FIRE THIS AT CLOSE RANGE.

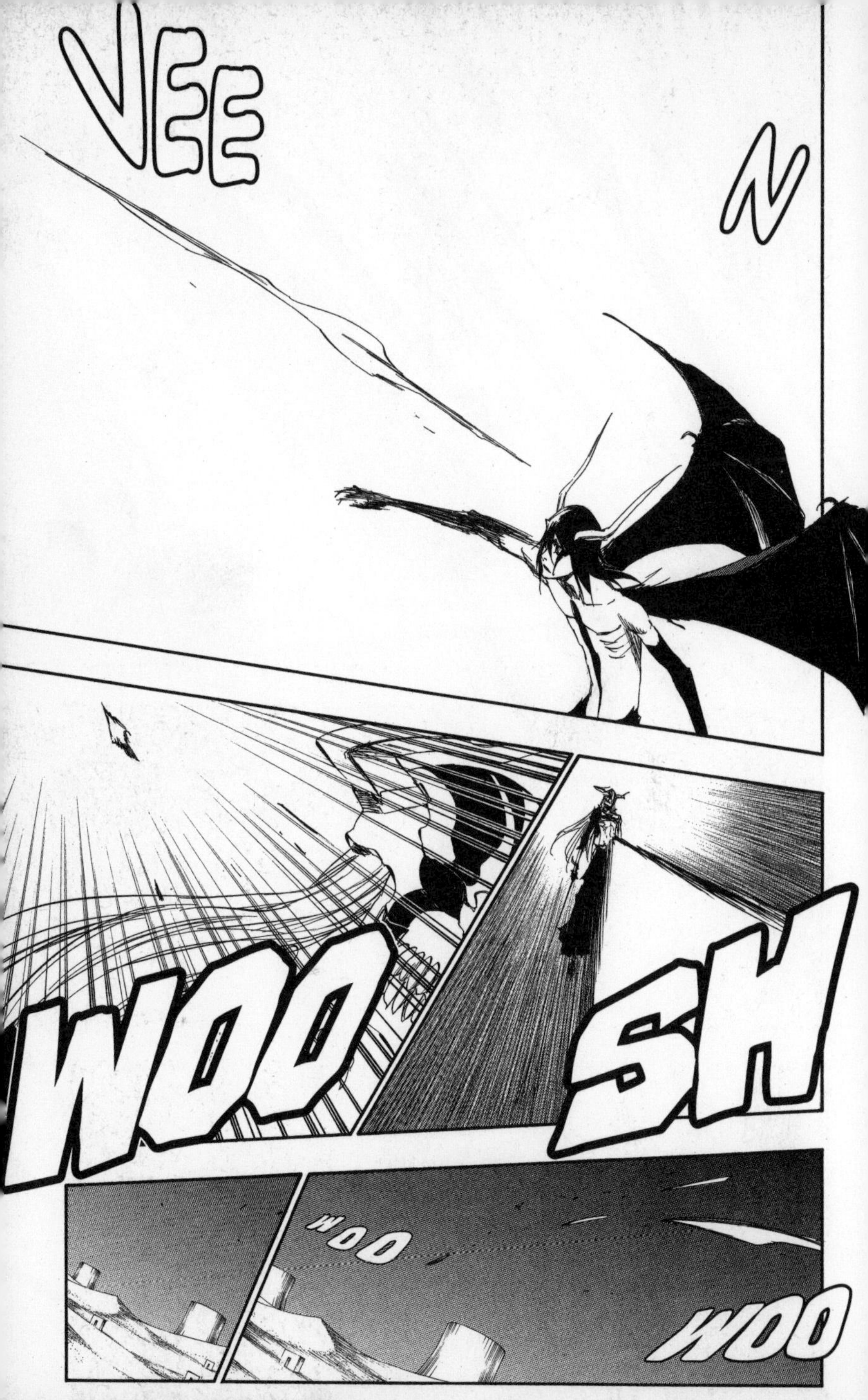
VEEN
WOOSH
WOO
WOO

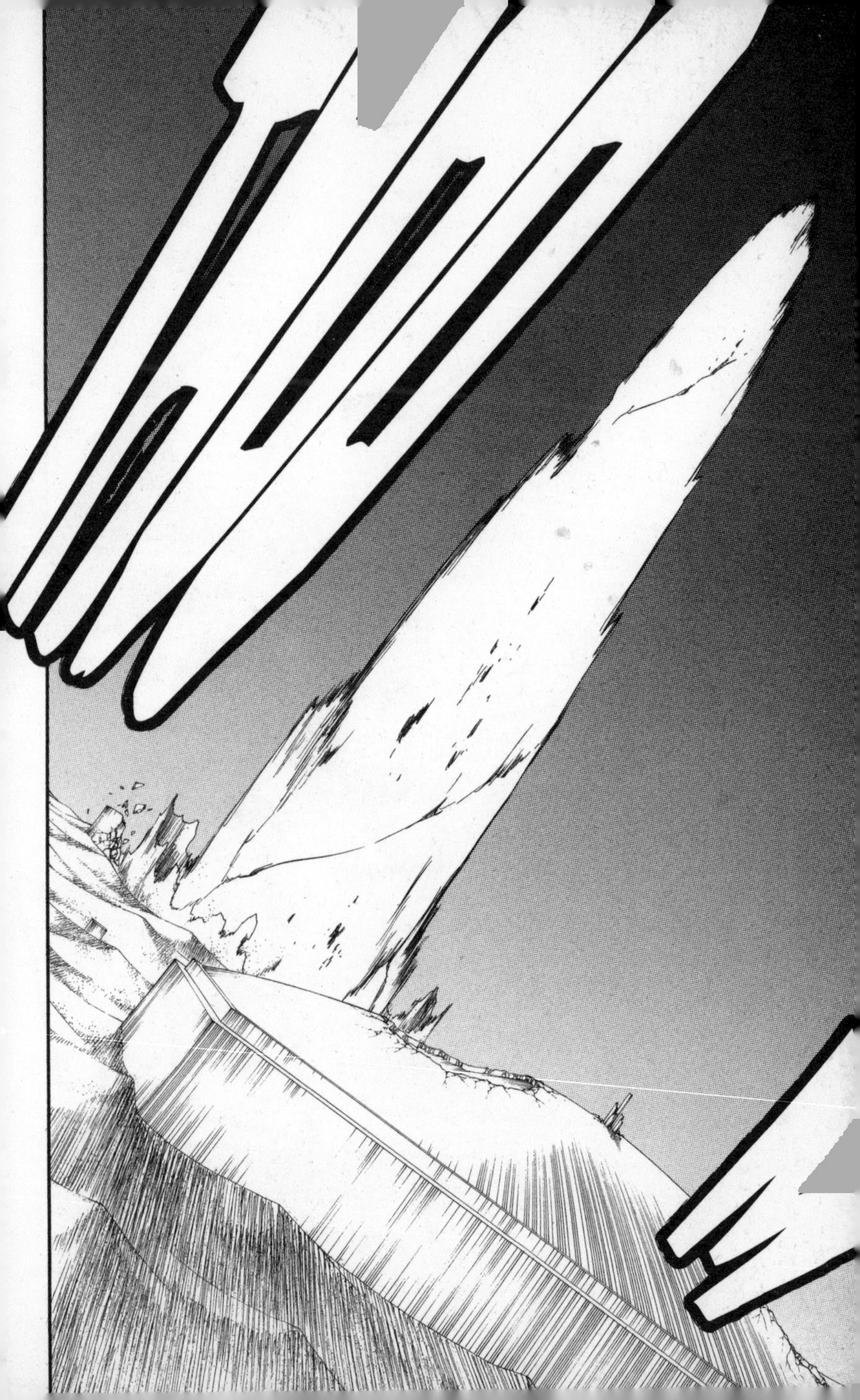

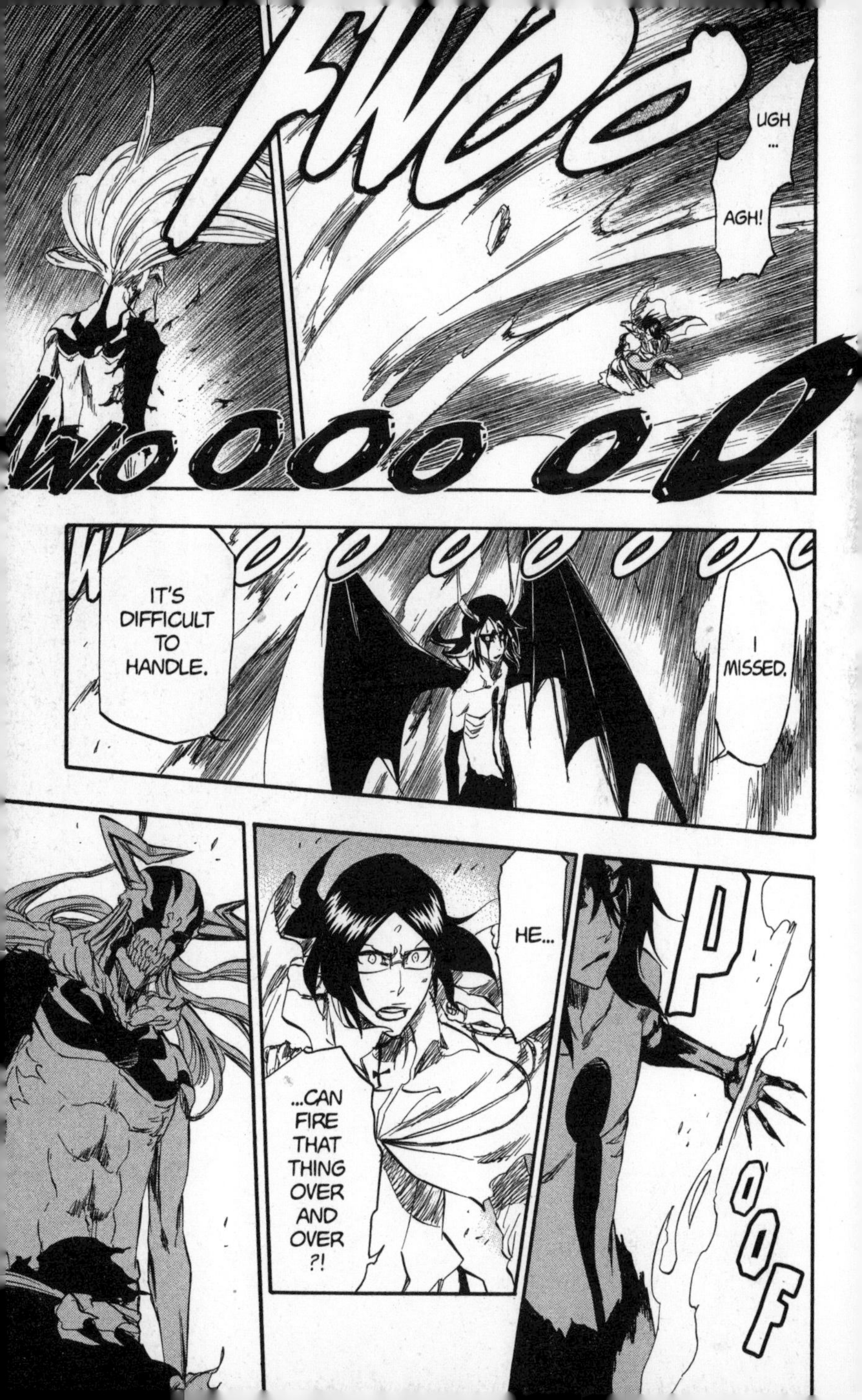
FWOO
UGH...
AGH!
WOOOOO OOO
WOOOOOOOO
I MISSED.
IT'S DIFFICULT TO HANDLE.
POOF
HE...
...CAN FIRE THAT THING OVER AND OVER?!

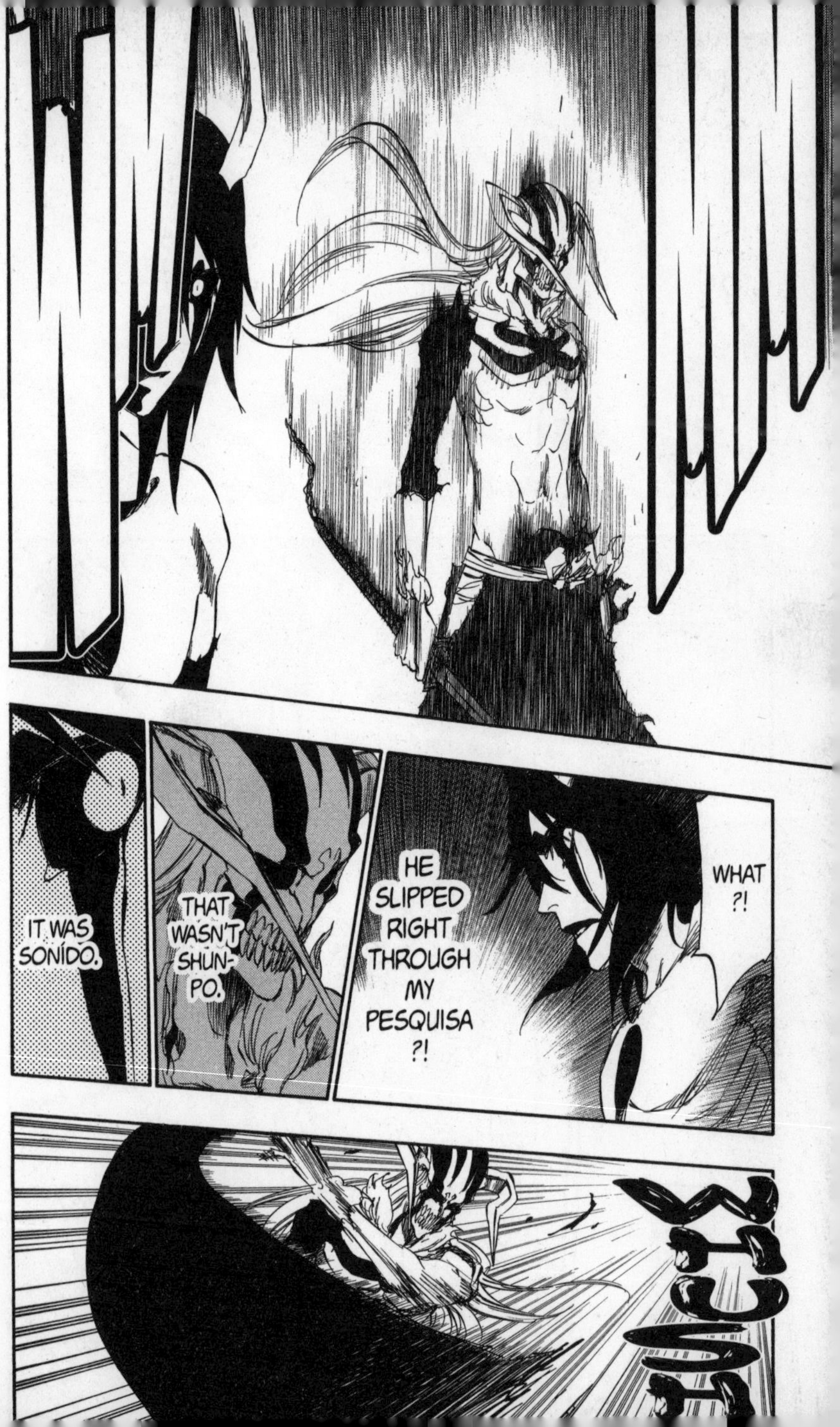
WHAT ?!
HE SLIPPED RIGHT THROUGH MY PESQUISA ?!
THAT WASN'T SHUN-PO.
IT WAS SONÍDO.

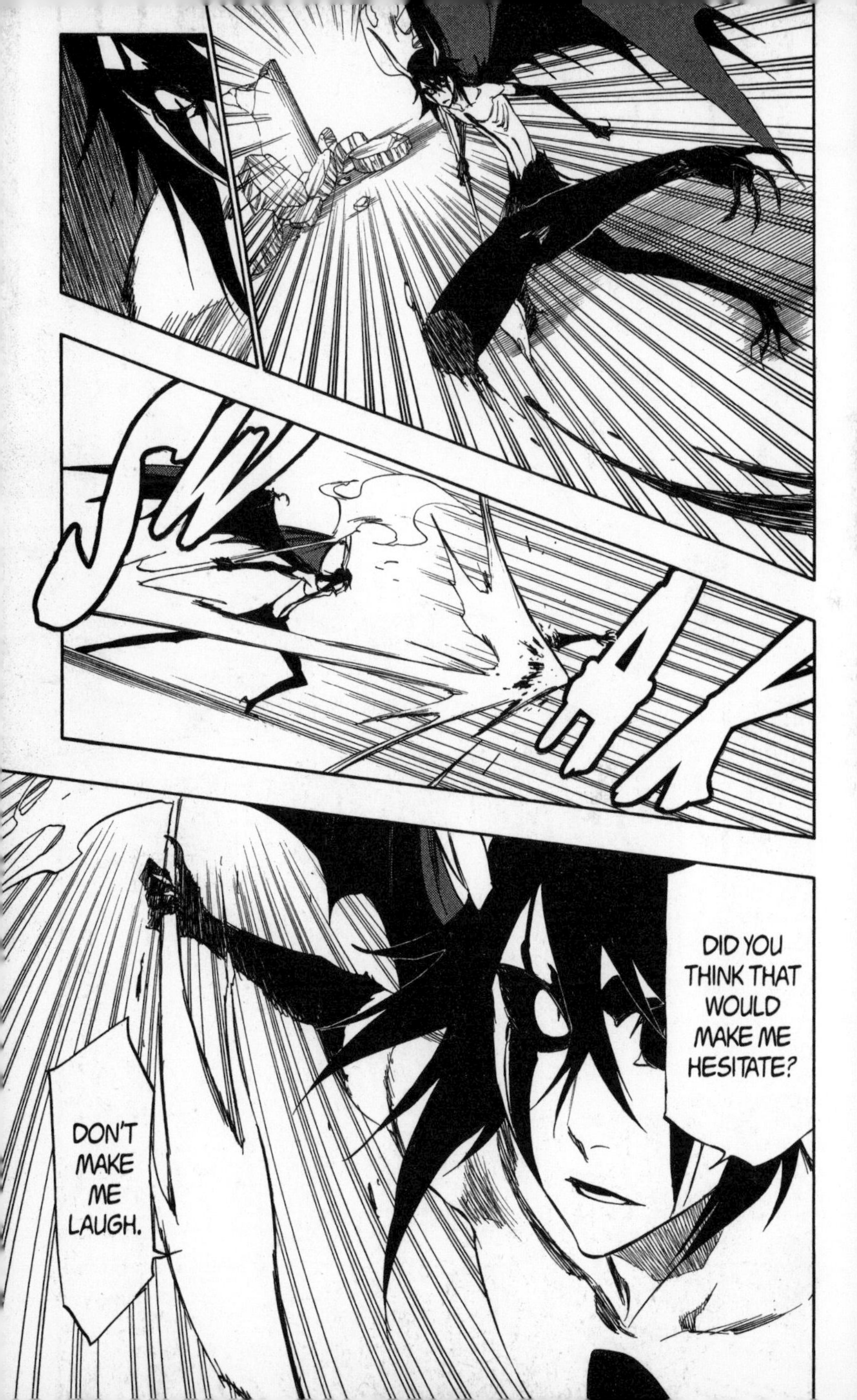
FW
HA
DID YOU THINK THAT WOULD MAKE ME HESITATE?
DON'T MAKE ME LAUGH.

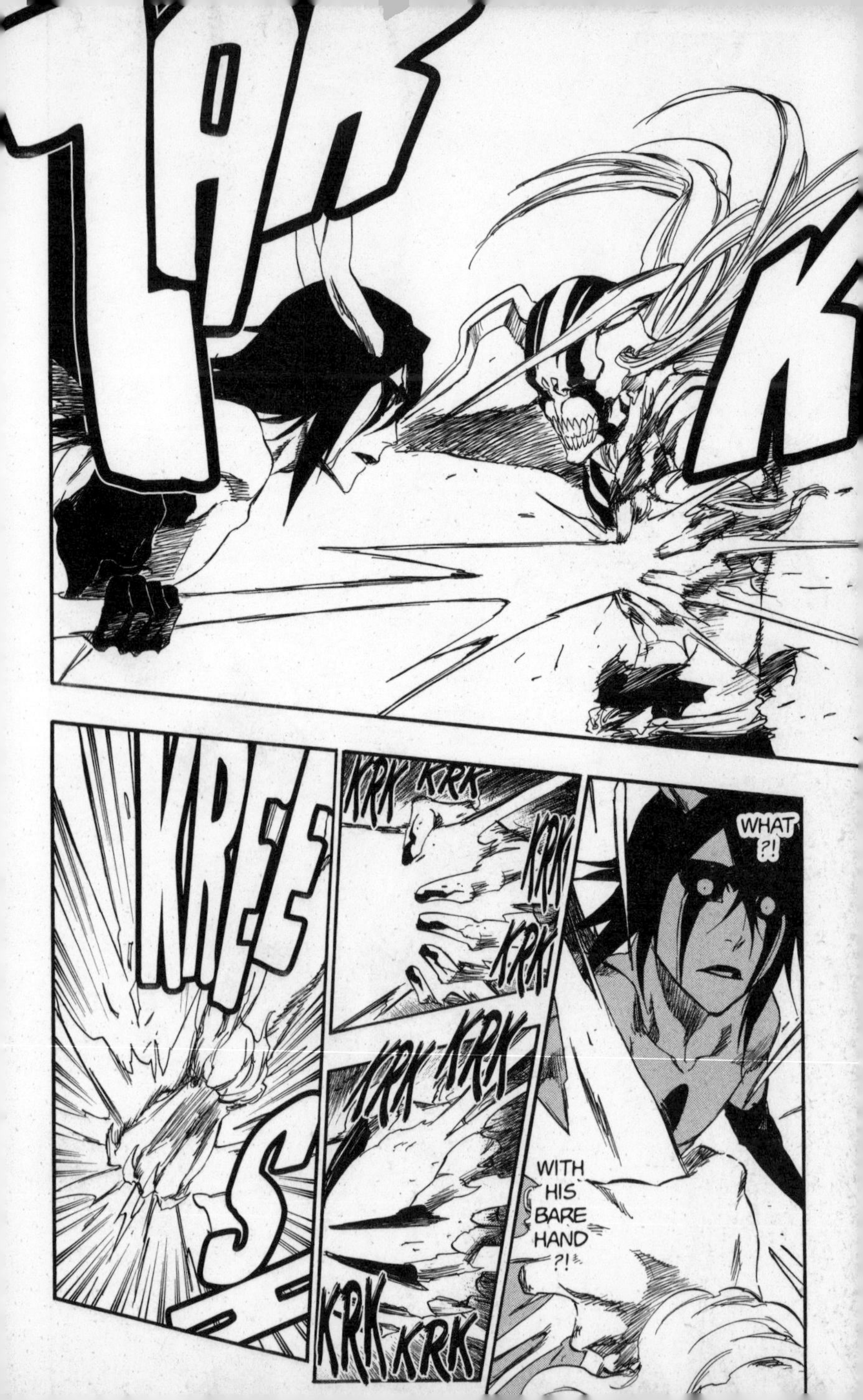
TAK
WHAT ?!
WITH HIS BARE HAND ?!
KRK KRK
KRK
KRK
KRK KRK
KRK KRK
KRE-E

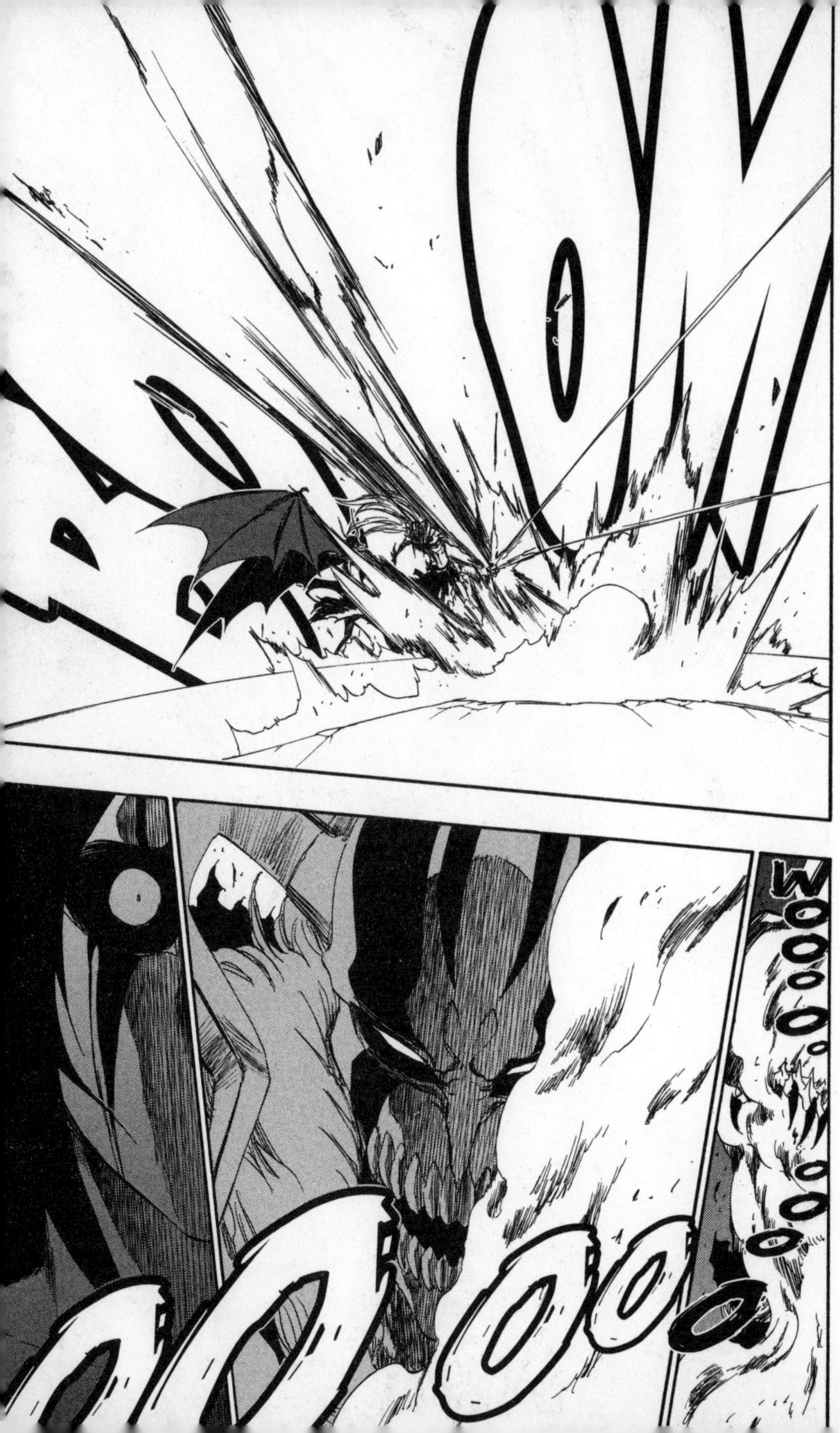

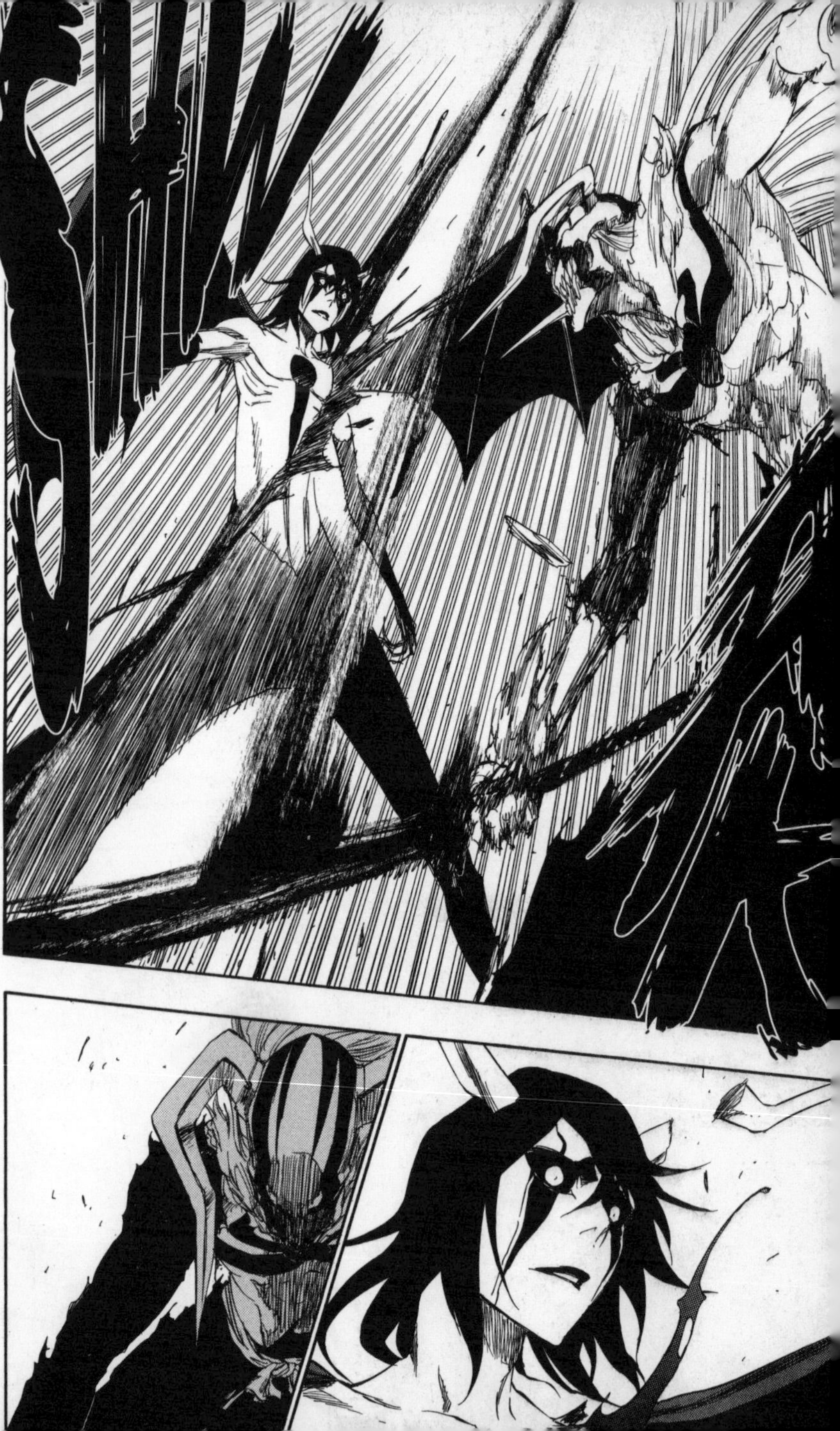

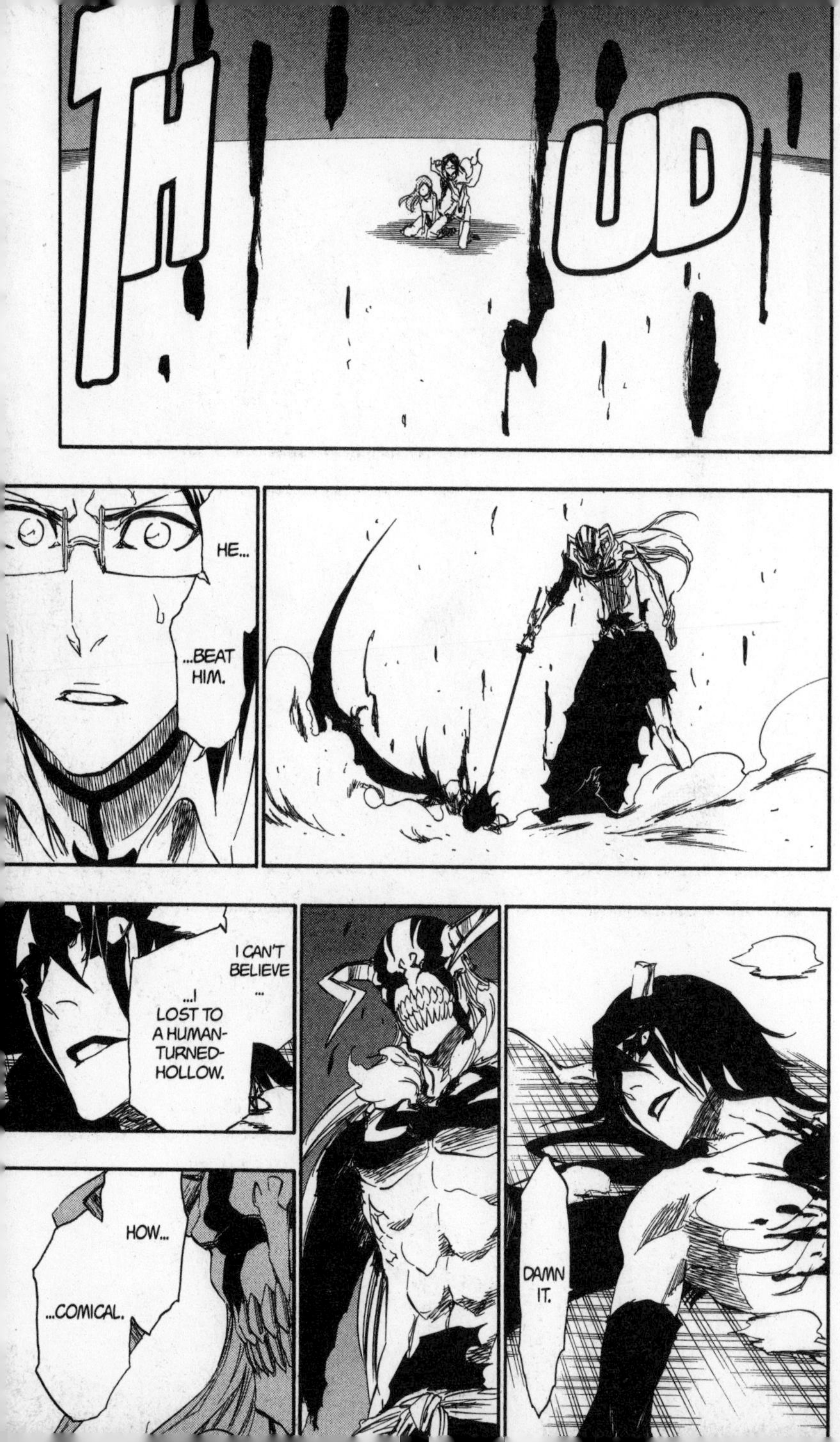
THUD
HE...
...BEAT HIM.
DAMN IT.
I CAN'T BELIEVE...
...I LOST TO A HUMAN-TURNED-HOLLOW.
HOW...
...COMICAL.

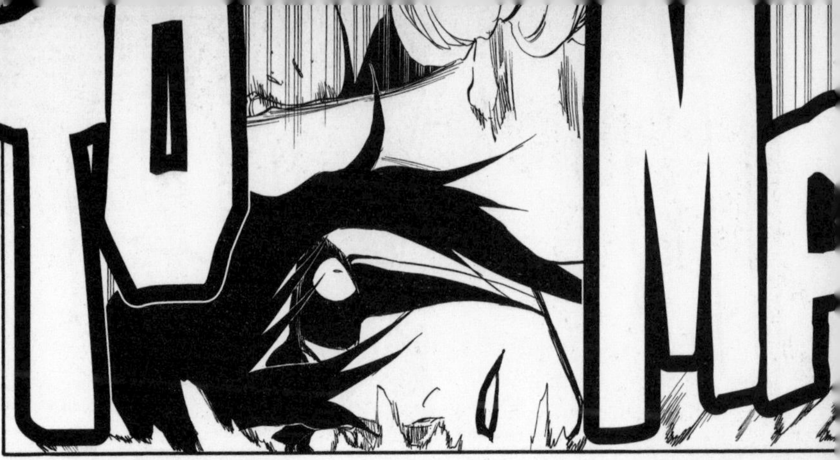
TA
M
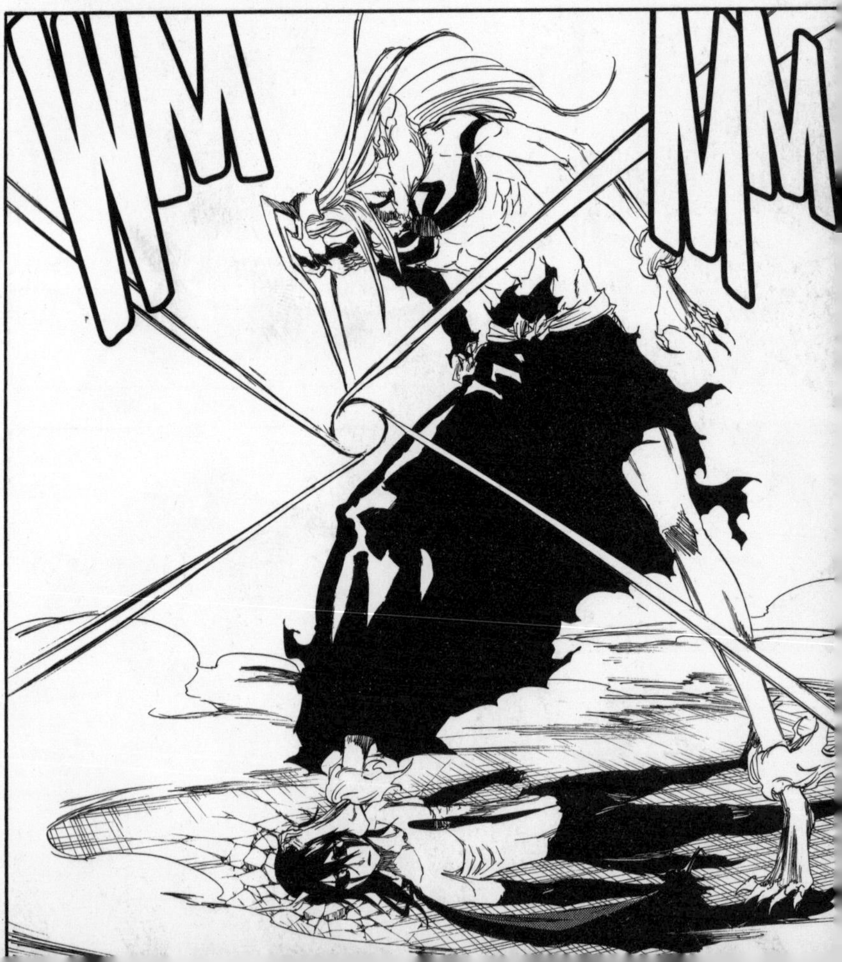
WM
MM

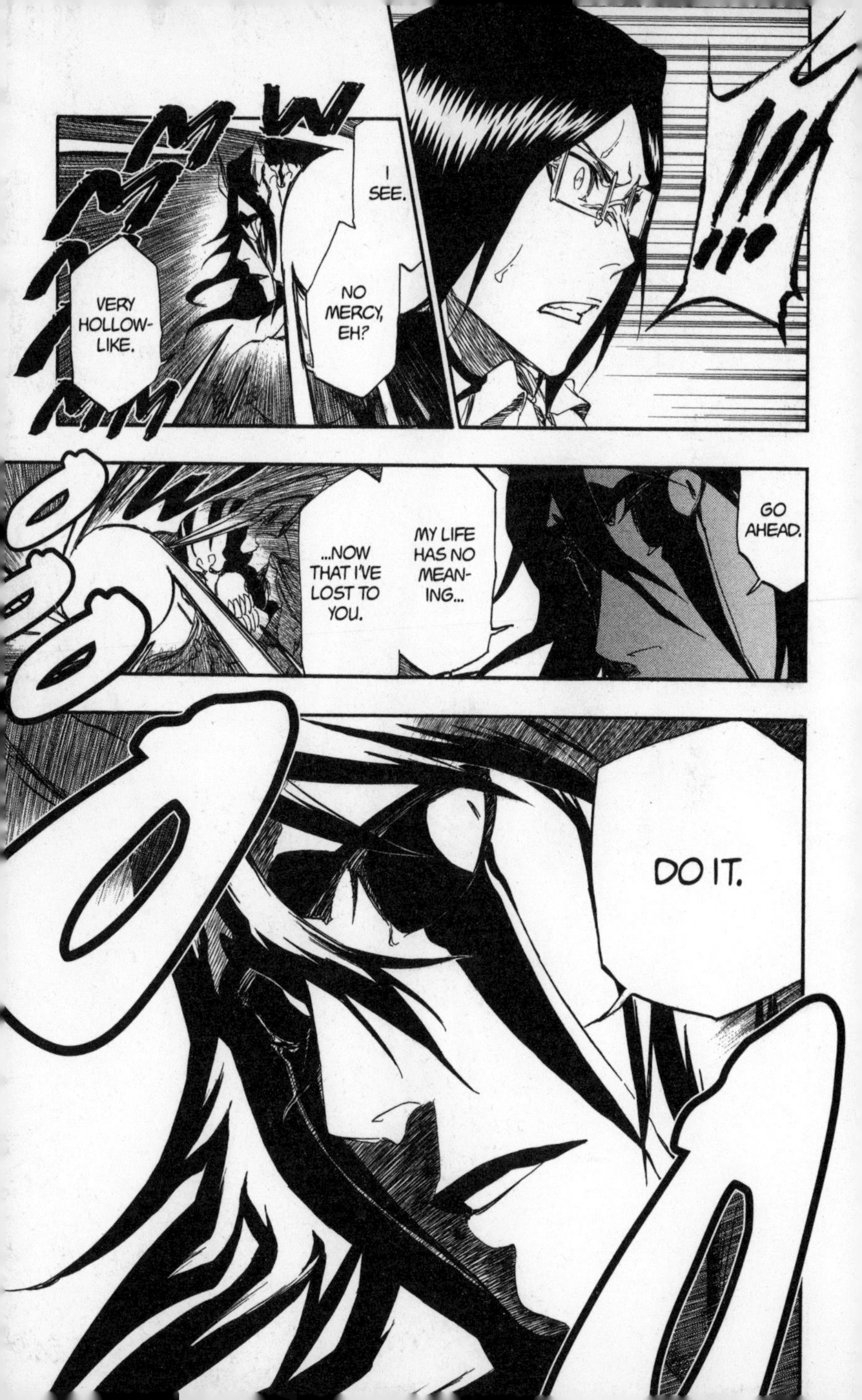
!!!
I SEE.
NO MERCY, EH?
VERY HOLLOW-LIKE.
GO AHEAD.
MY LIFE HAS NO MEANING...
...NOW THAT I'VE LOST TO YOU.
DO IT.

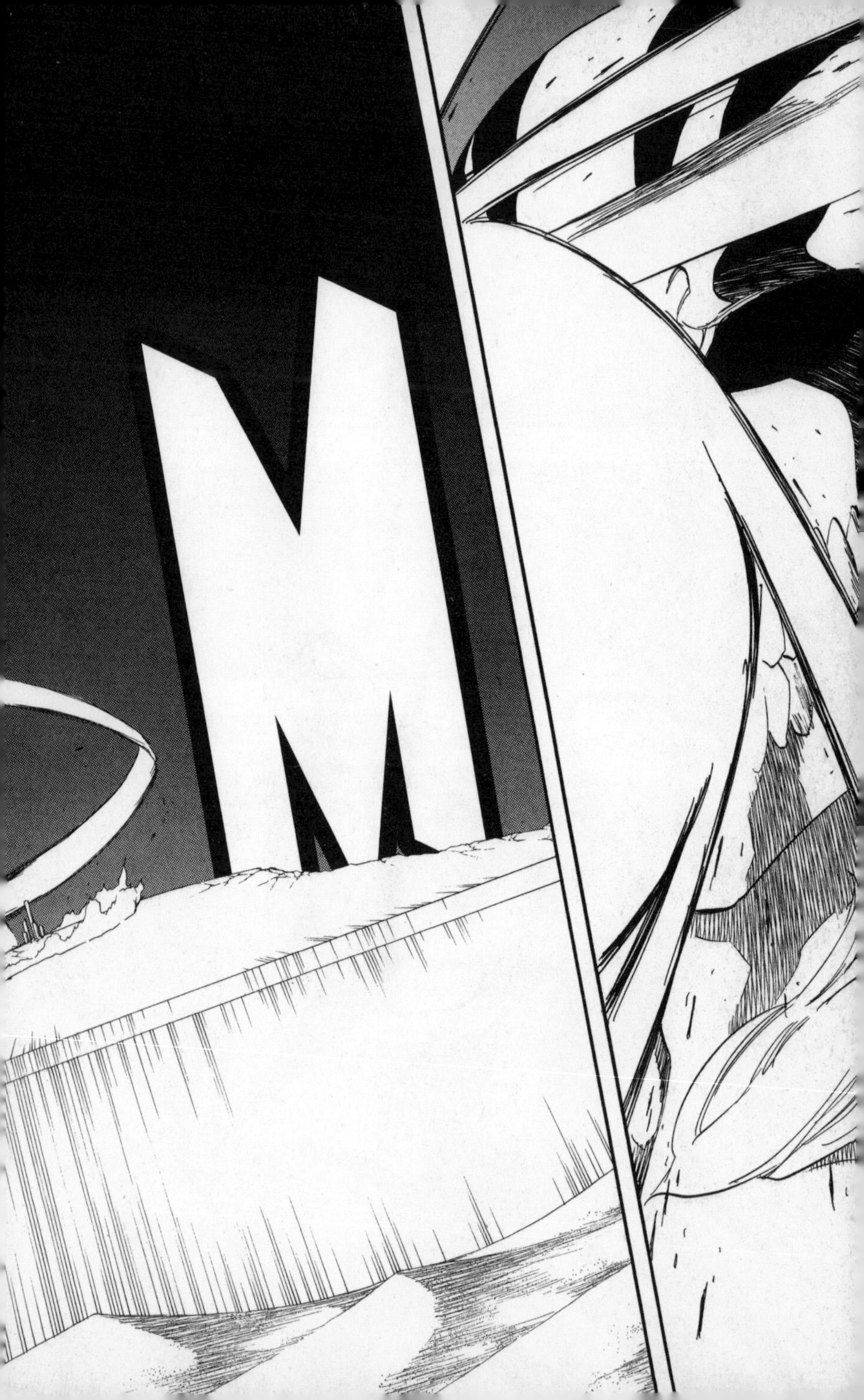
M

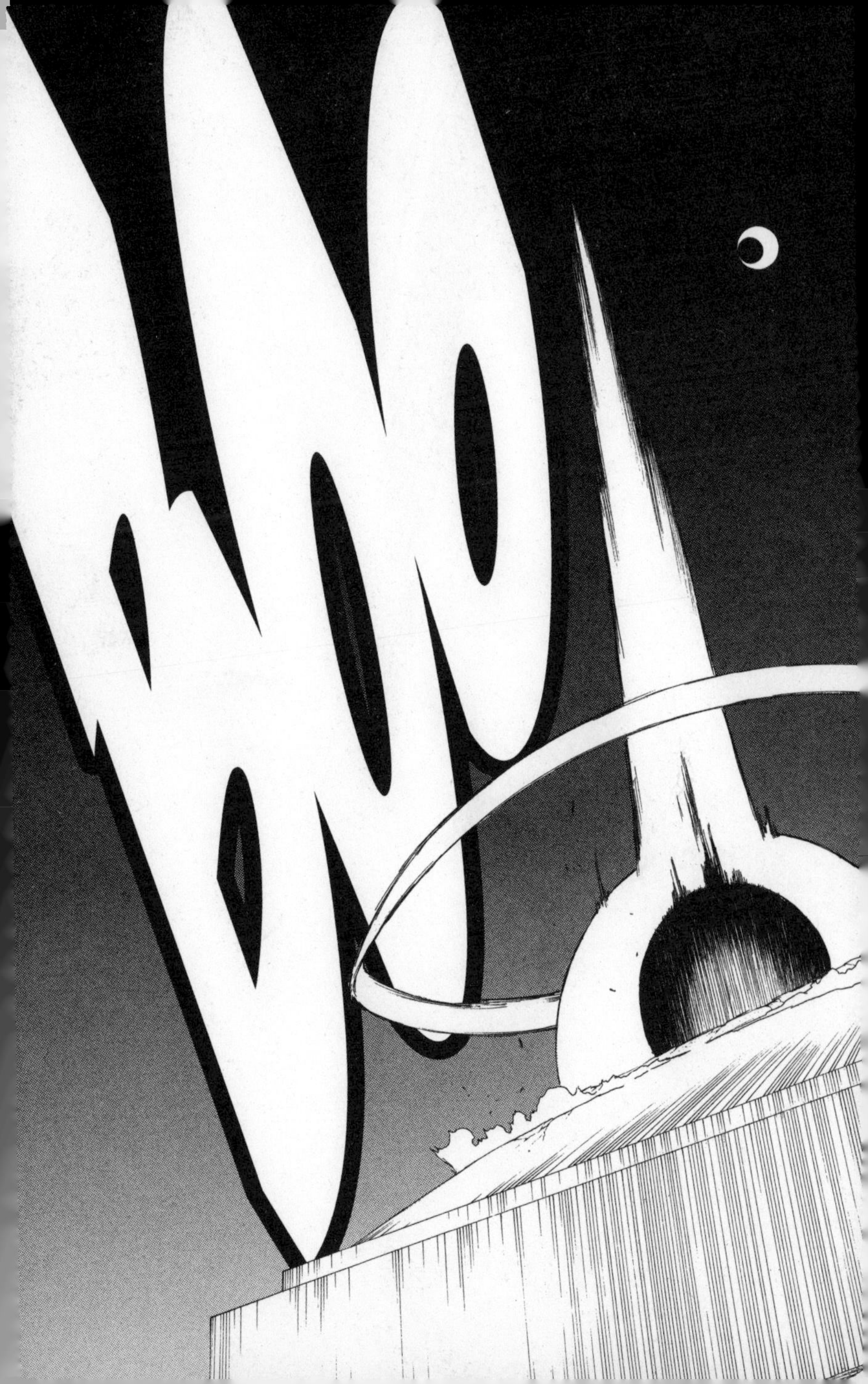

352. The Lust 6

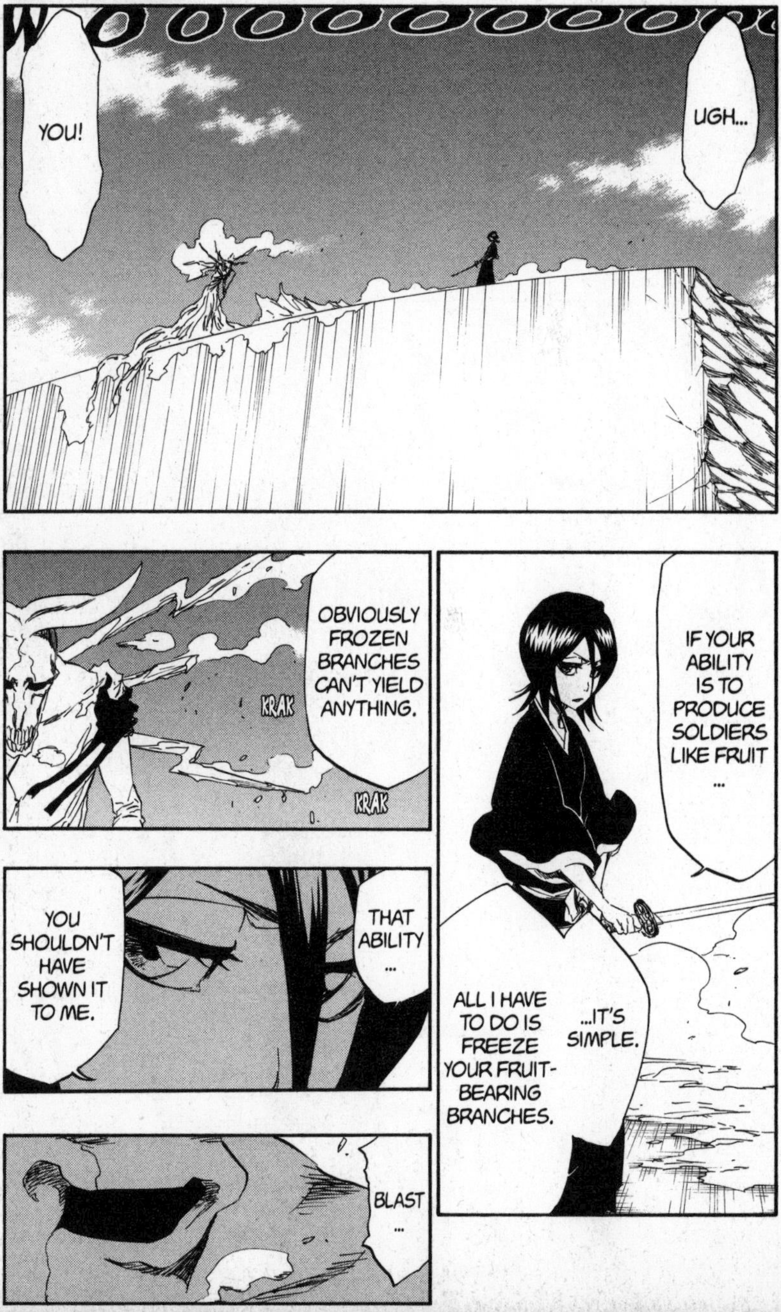
WOOOOOOOOOOOOO
UGH...
YOU!
IF YOUR ABILITY IS TO PRODUCE SOLDIERS LIKE FRUIT...
...IT'S SIMPLE.
ALL I HAVE TO DO IS FREEZE YOUR FRUIT-BEARING BRANCHES.
OBVIOUSLY FROZEN BRANCHES CAN'T YIELD ANYTHING.
KRAK
KRAK
THAT ABILITY...
YOU SHOULDN'T HAVE SHOWN IT TO ME.
BLAST...

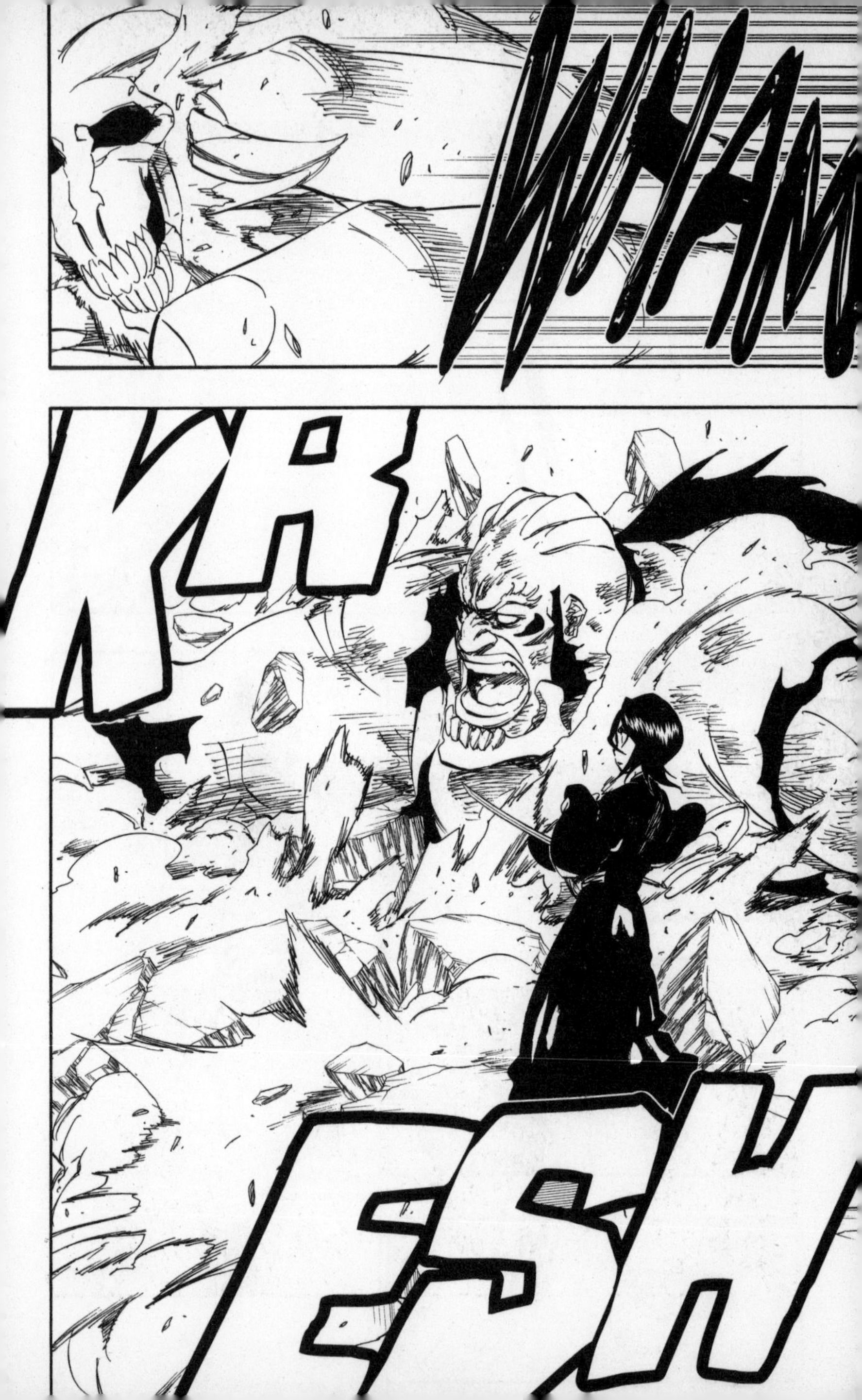
WHAM
KR
FSH

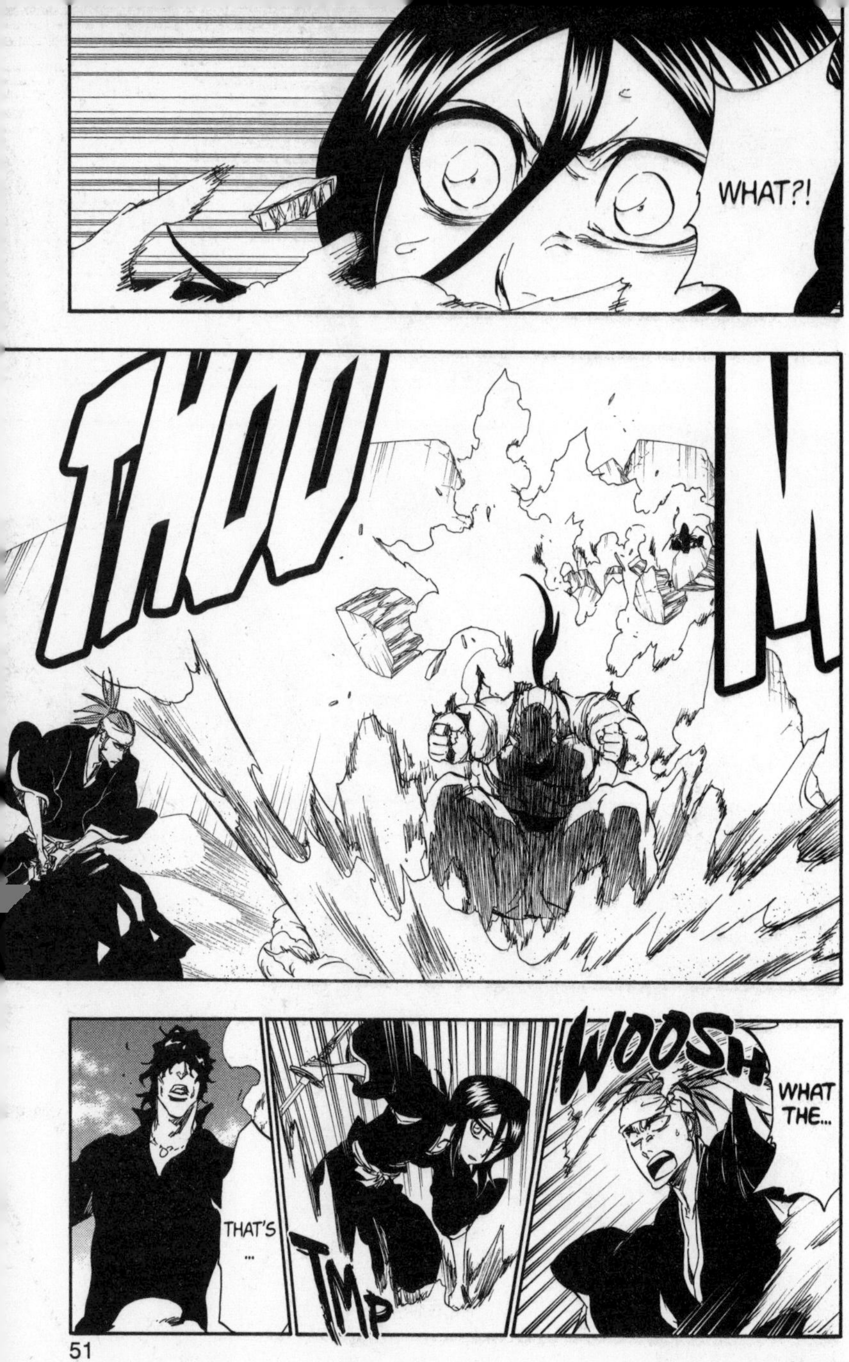
WHAT?!
THOOM
WOOSH
WHAT THE...
TMP
THAT'S ...

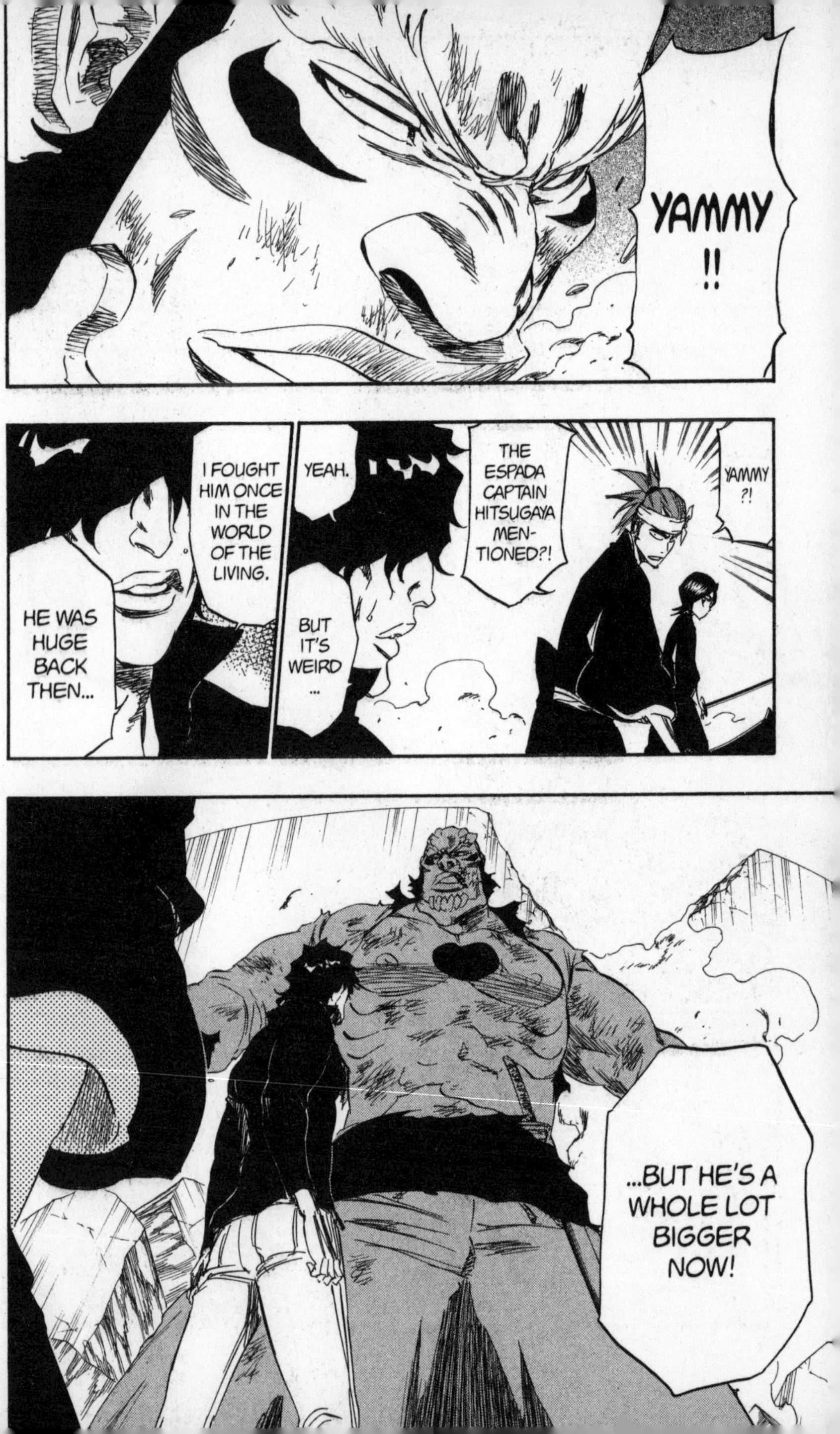
YAMMY !!
YAMMY ?!
THE ESPADA CAPTAIN HITSUGAYA MEN-TIONED?!
YEAH.
BUT IT'S WEIRD ...
I FOUGHT HIM ONCE IN THE WORLD OF THE LIVING.
HE WAS HUGE BACK THEN...
...BUT HE'S A WHOLE LOT BIGGER NOW!

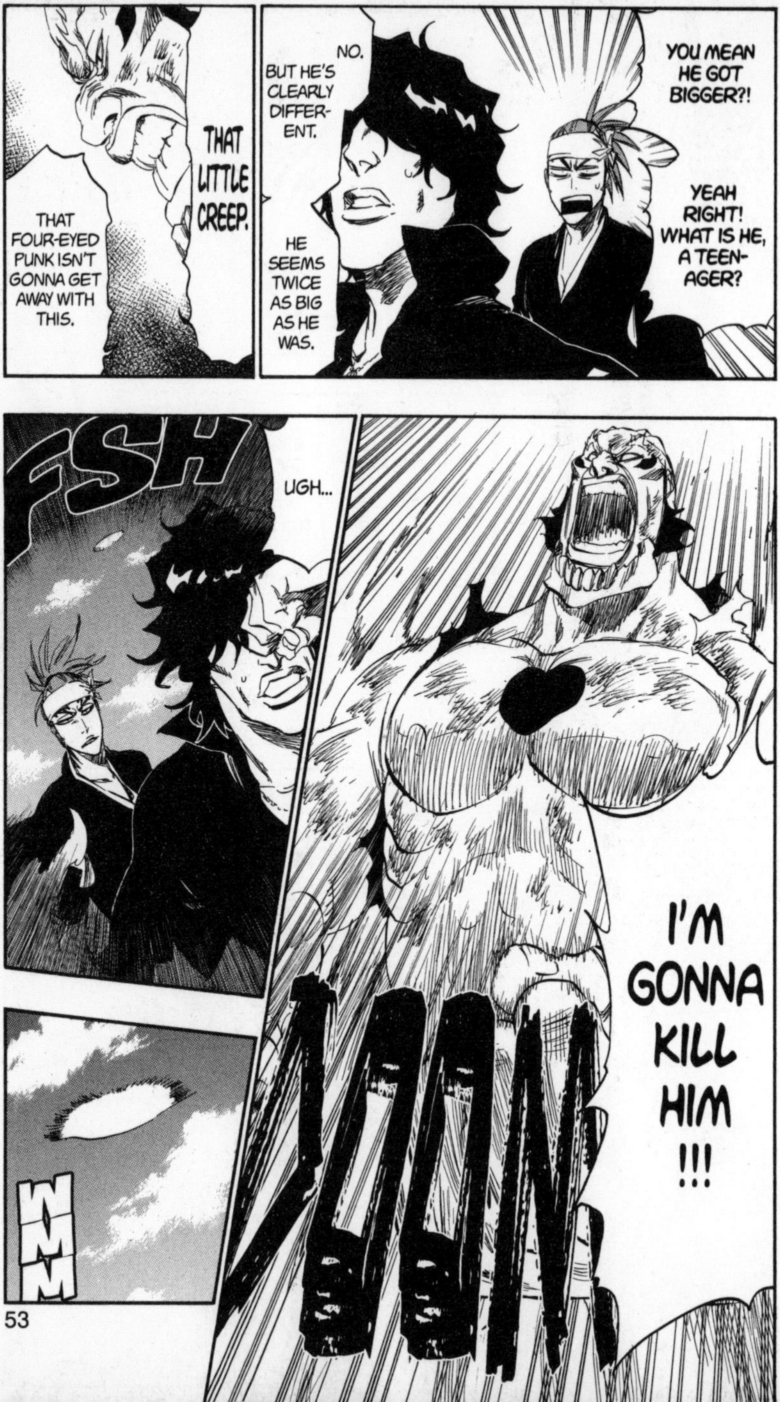
YOU MEAN HE GOT BIGGER?!
NO.
BUT HE'S CLEARLY DIFFERENT.
HE SEEMS TWICE AS BIG AS HE WAS.
YEAH RIGHT! WHAT IS HE, A TEEN-AGER?
THAT LITTLE CREEP.
THAT FOUR-EYED PUNK ISN'T GONNA GET AWAY WITH THIS.
I'M GONNA KILL HIM!!!
FSH
UGH...

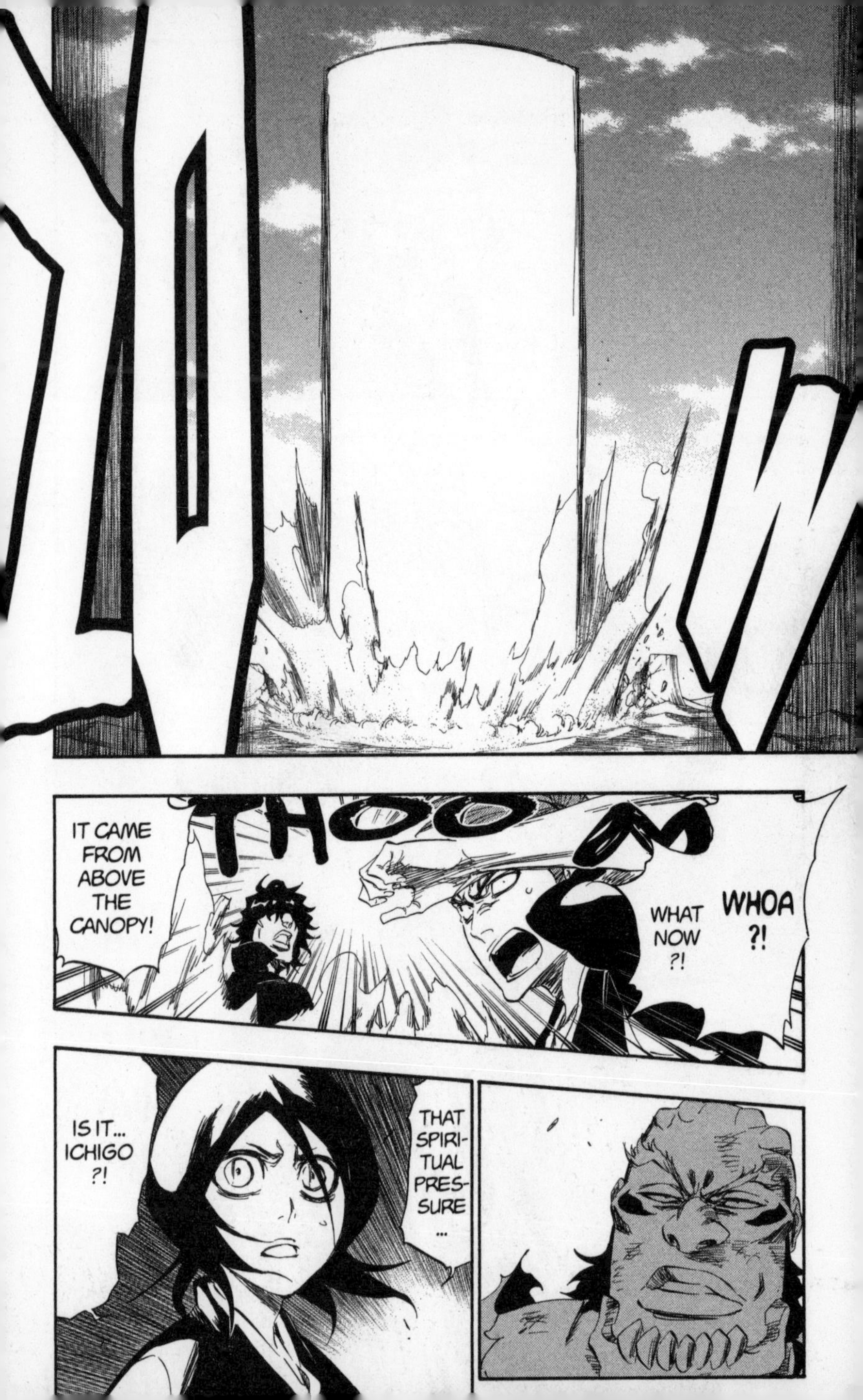
THOOM
WHOA ?!
WHAT NOW ?!
IT CAME FROM ABOVE THE CANOPY!
THAT SPIRI-TUAL PRES-SURE ...
IS IT... ICHIGO ?!

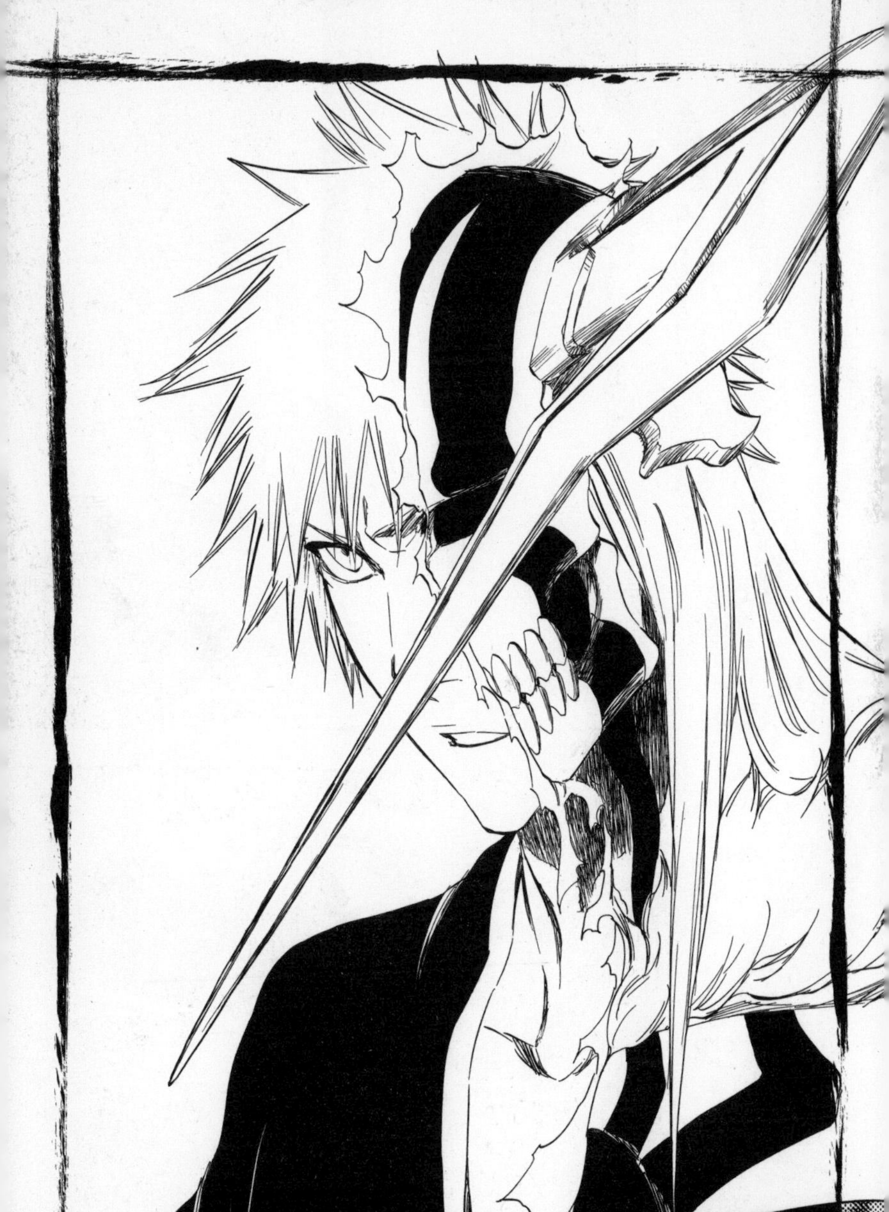

BLEACH 352. The Lust 6

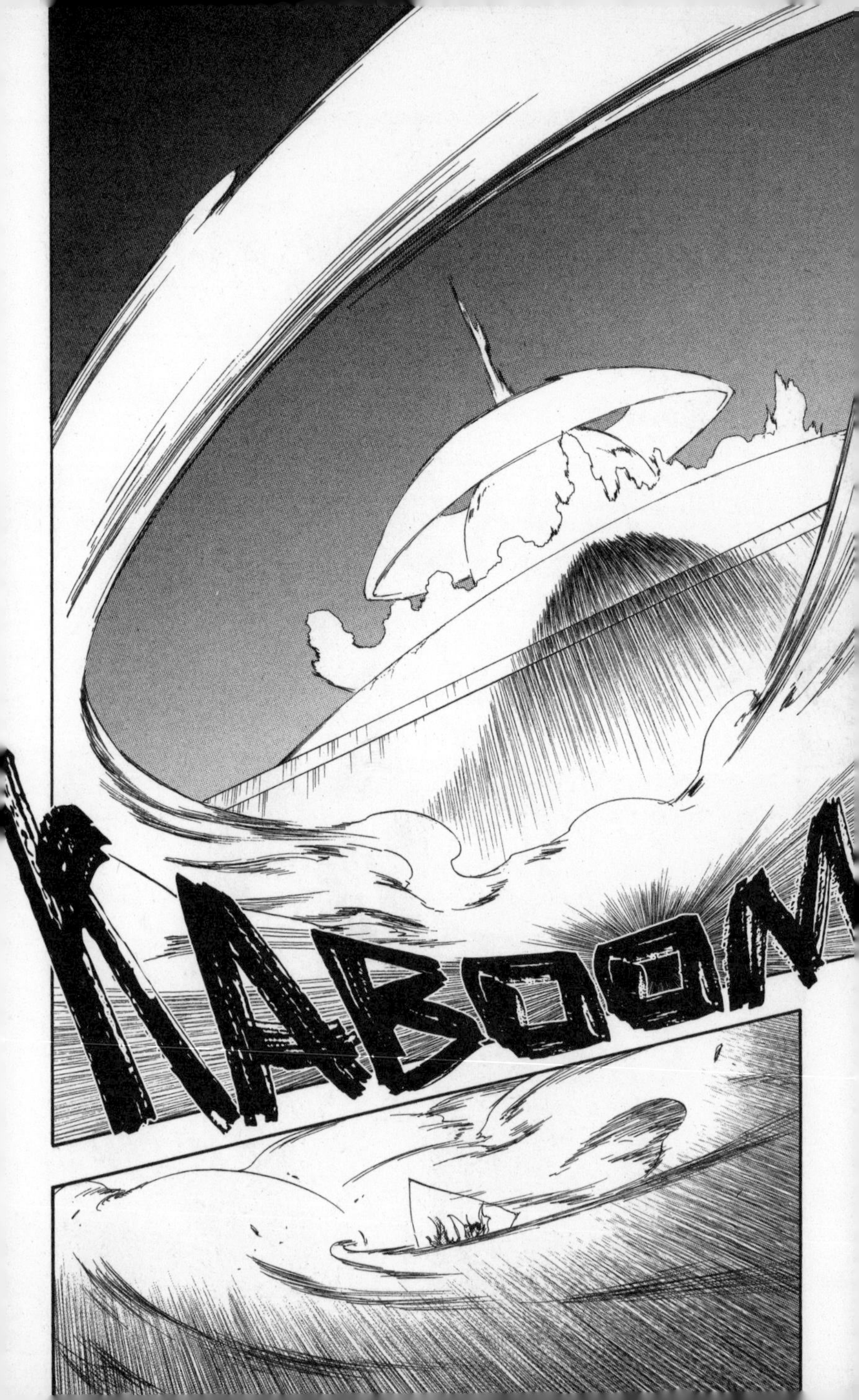
KABOOM

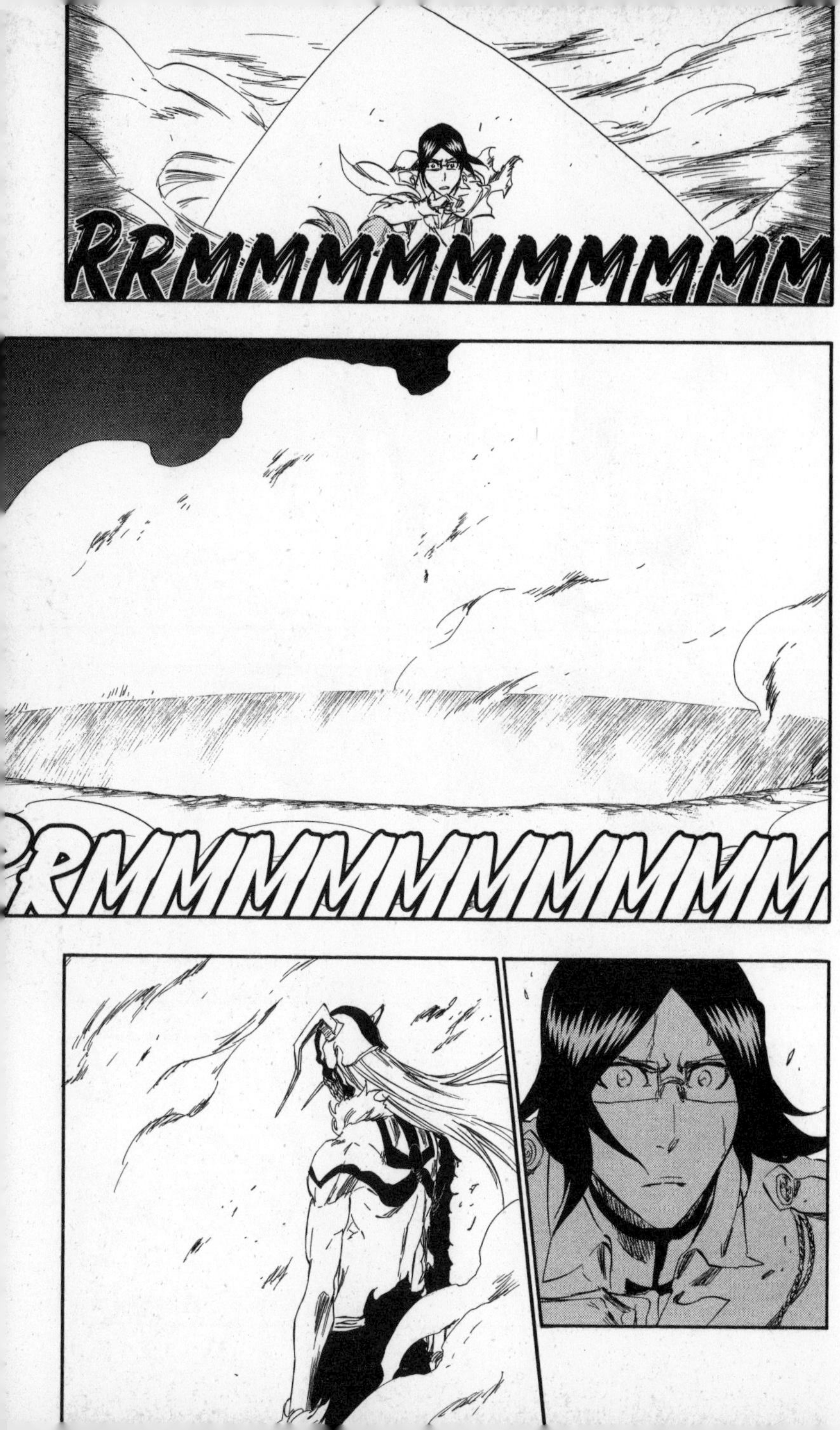
RRMMMMMMMMMMMM
RMMMMMMMMMMMM

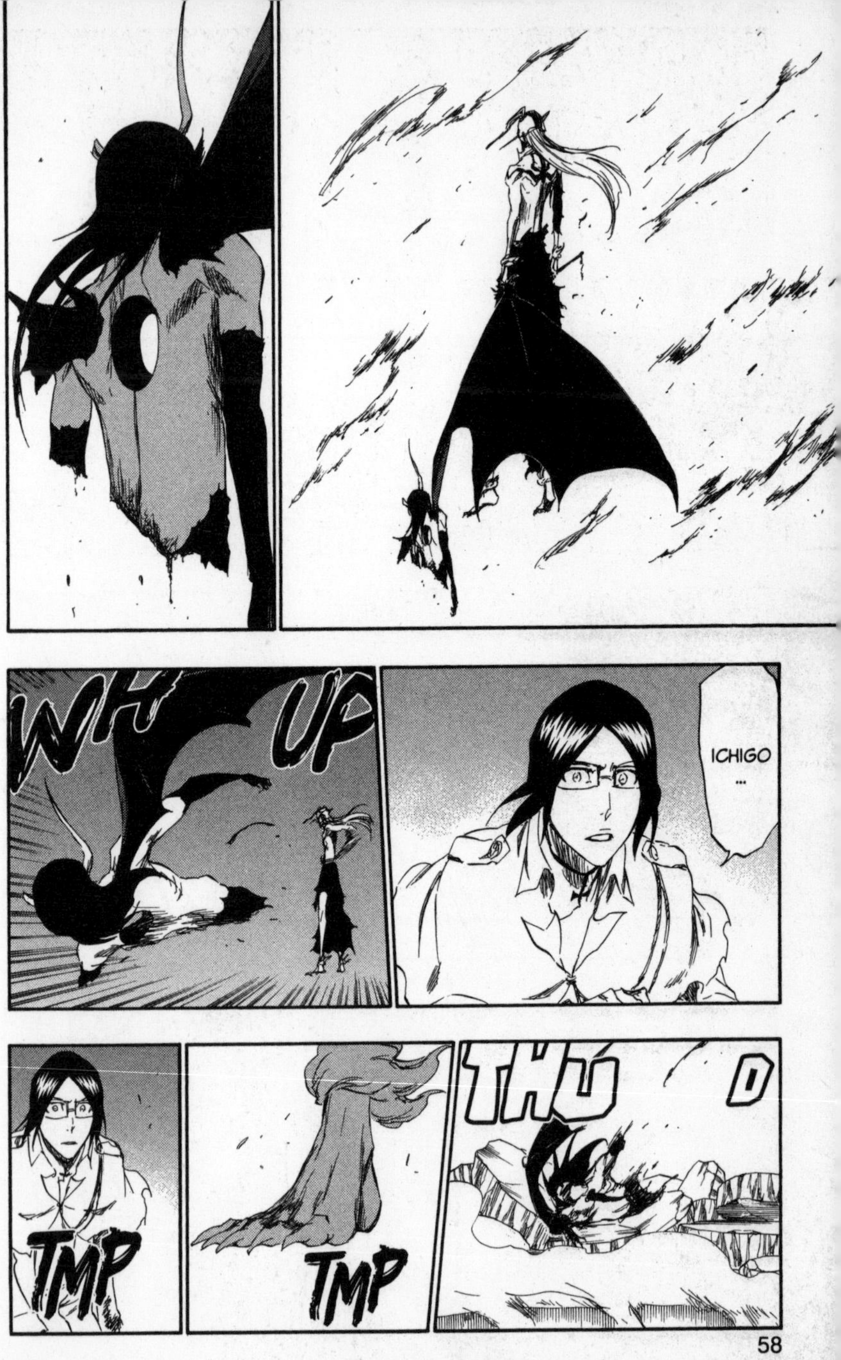
ICHIGO ...
WHUP
THUD
TMP
TMP

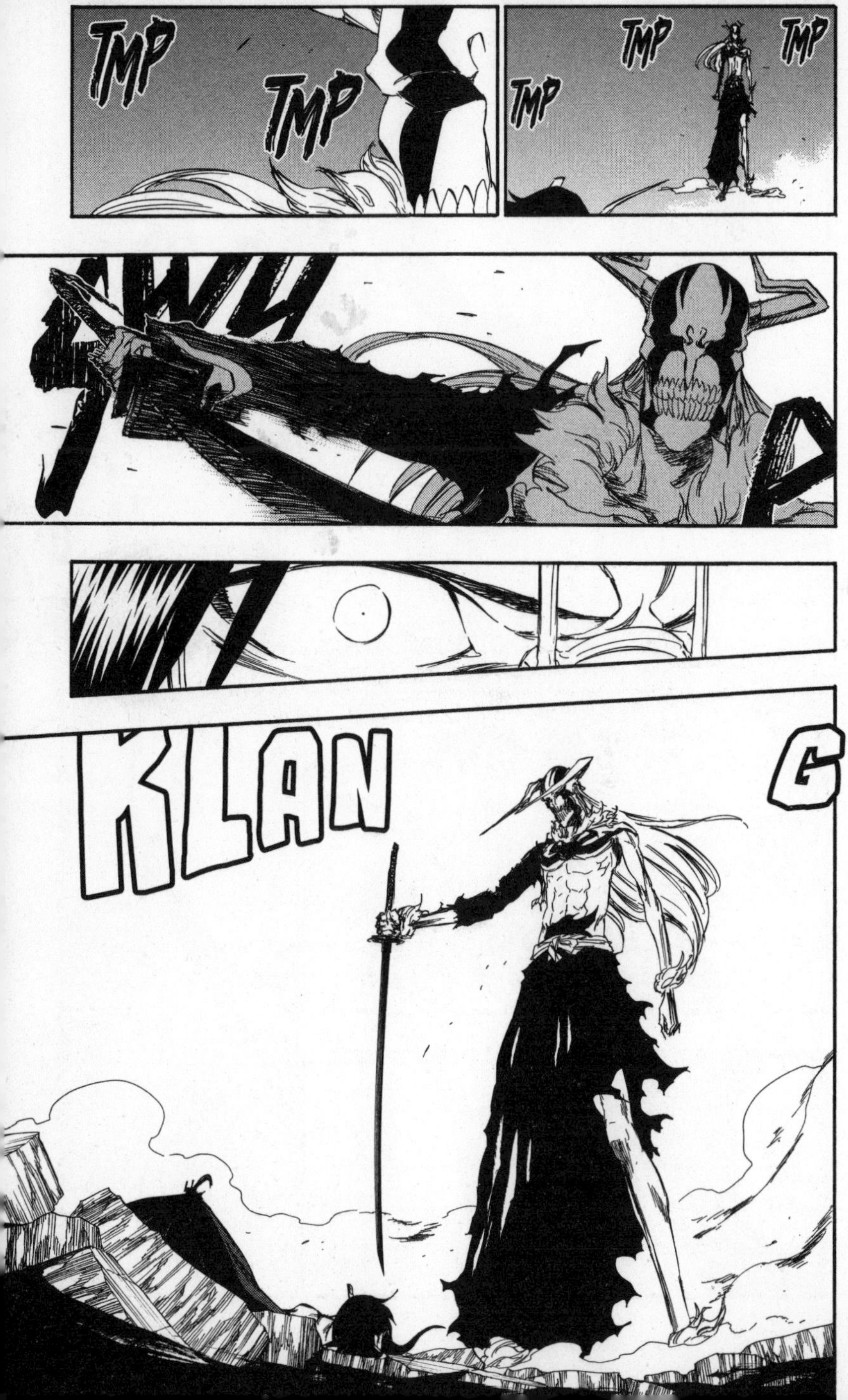
TMP
TMP
TMP
TMP
TMP
KLANG

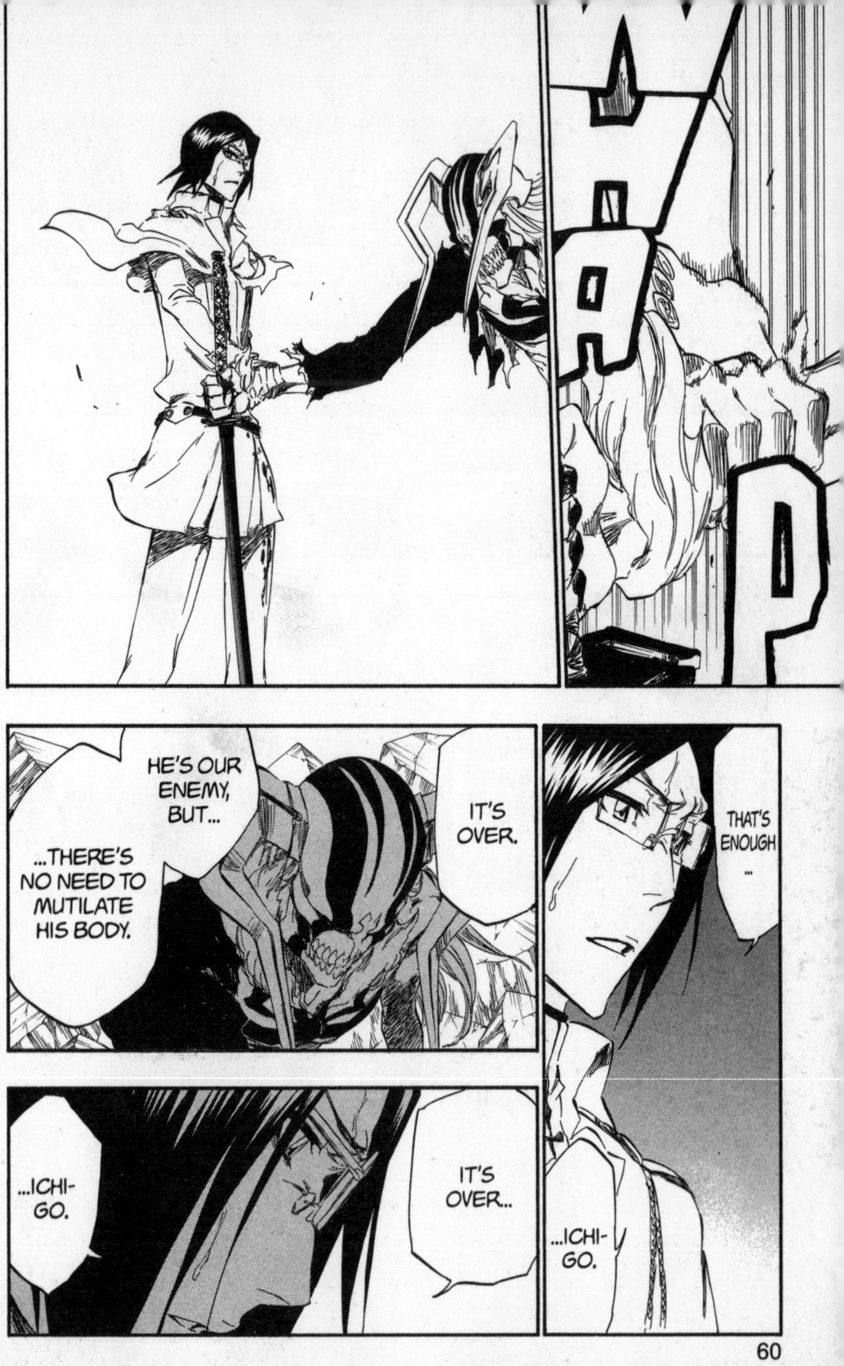
THAT'S ENOUGH ...
...ICHI-GO.
IT'S OVER.
HE'S OUR ENEMY, BUT...
...THERE'S NO NEED TO MUTILATE HIS BODY.
IT'S OVER...
...ICHI-GO.

READ THIS WAY

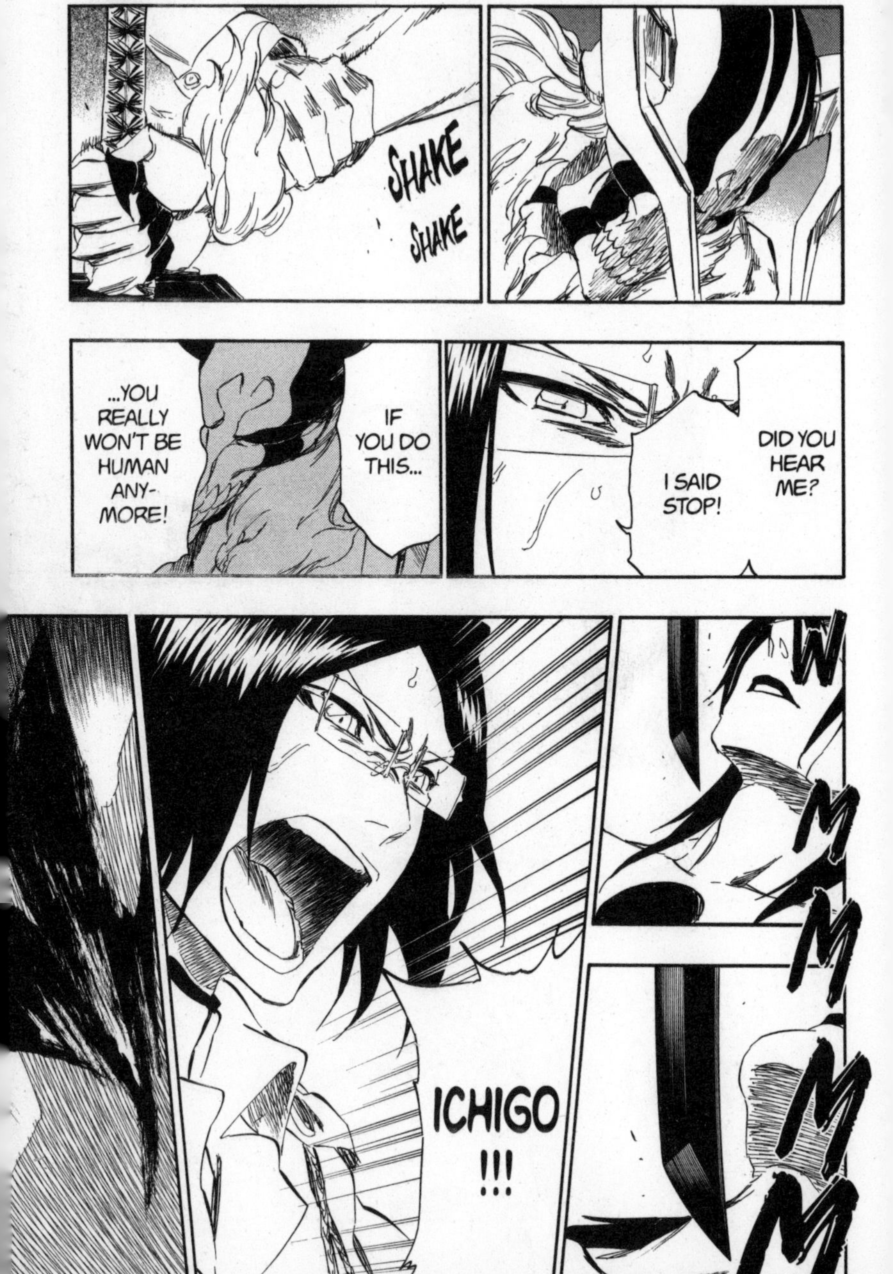

SHAKE
SHAKE
DID YOU HEAR ME?
I SAID STOP!
IF YOU DO THIS...
...YOU REALLY WON'T BE HUMAN ANY-MORE!
WMMMM
ICHIGO !!!

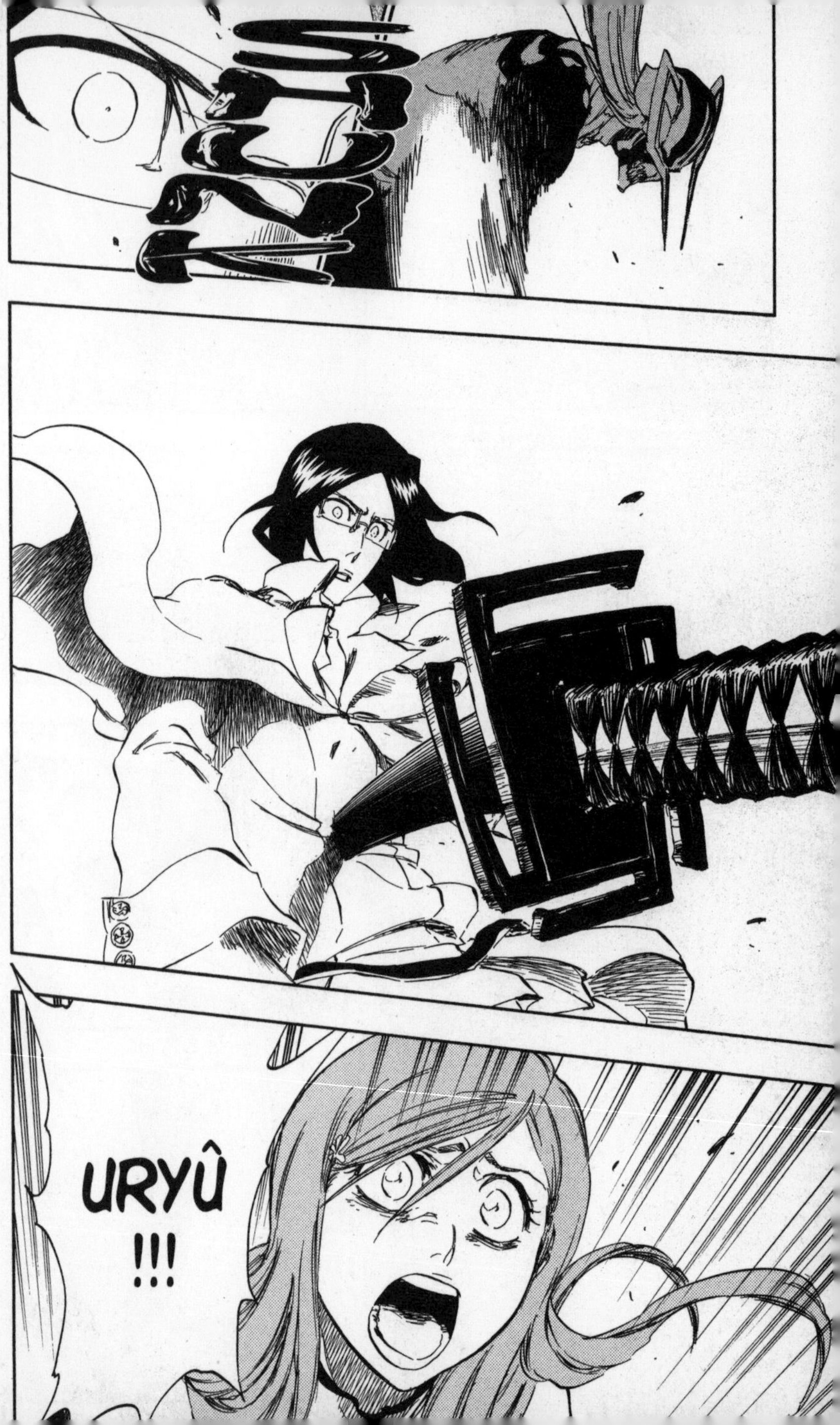
URYÛ
!!!

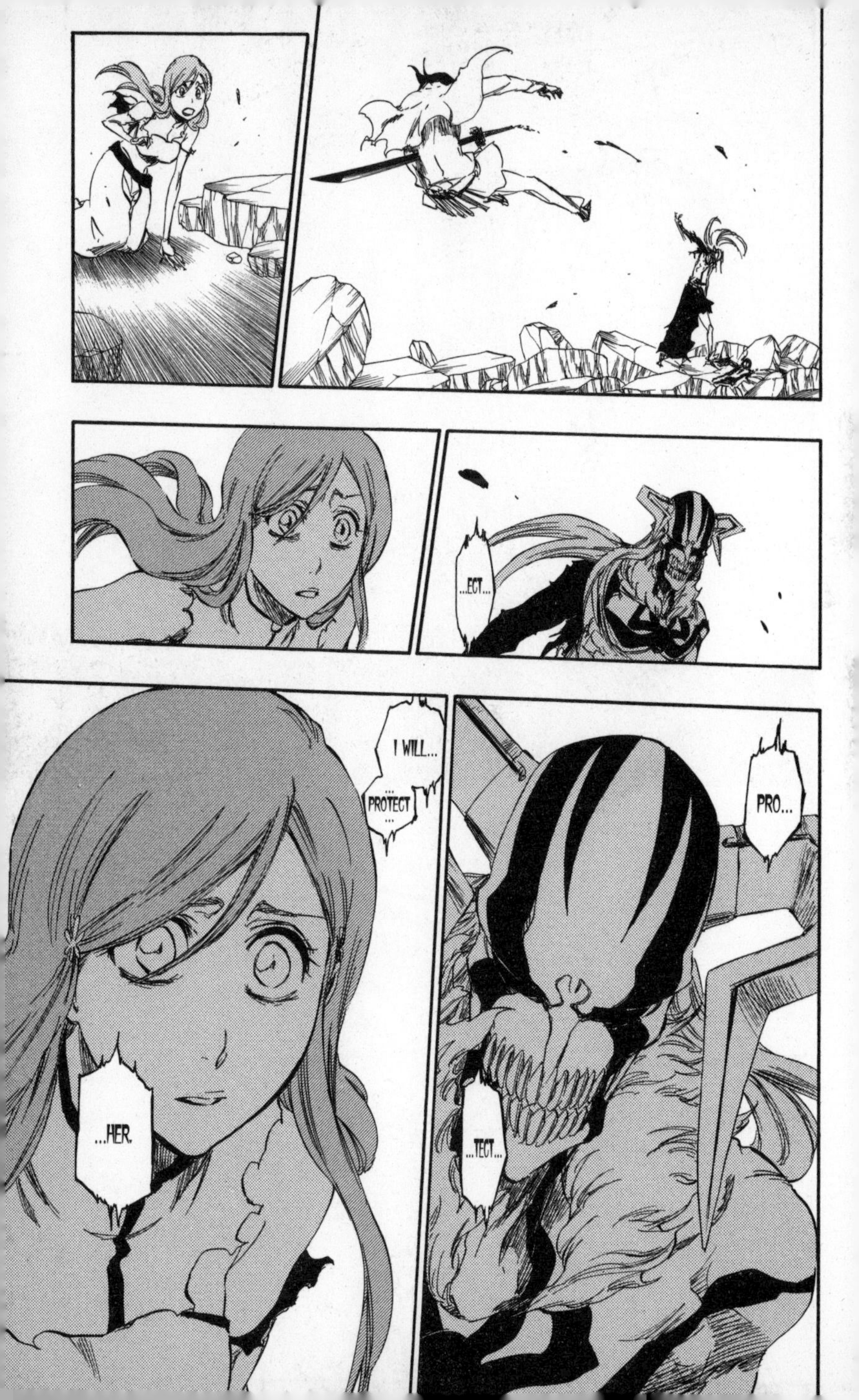
...ECT...
PRO...
...TECT...
I WILL...
...PROTECT...
...HER.

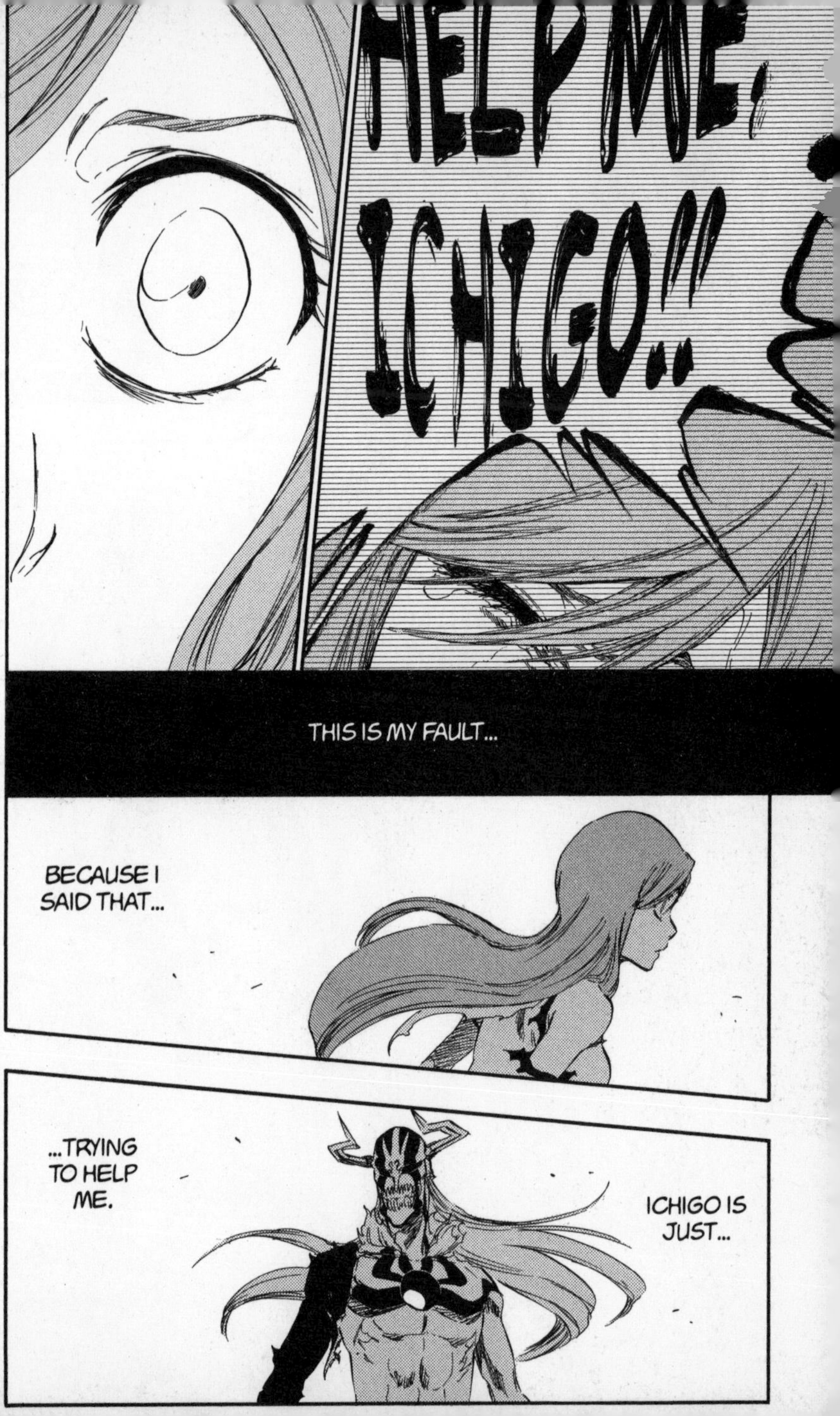
HELP ME, ICHIGO...!!
THIS IS MY FAULT...
BECAUSE I SAID THAT...
ICHIGO IS JUST...
...TRYING TO HELP ME.

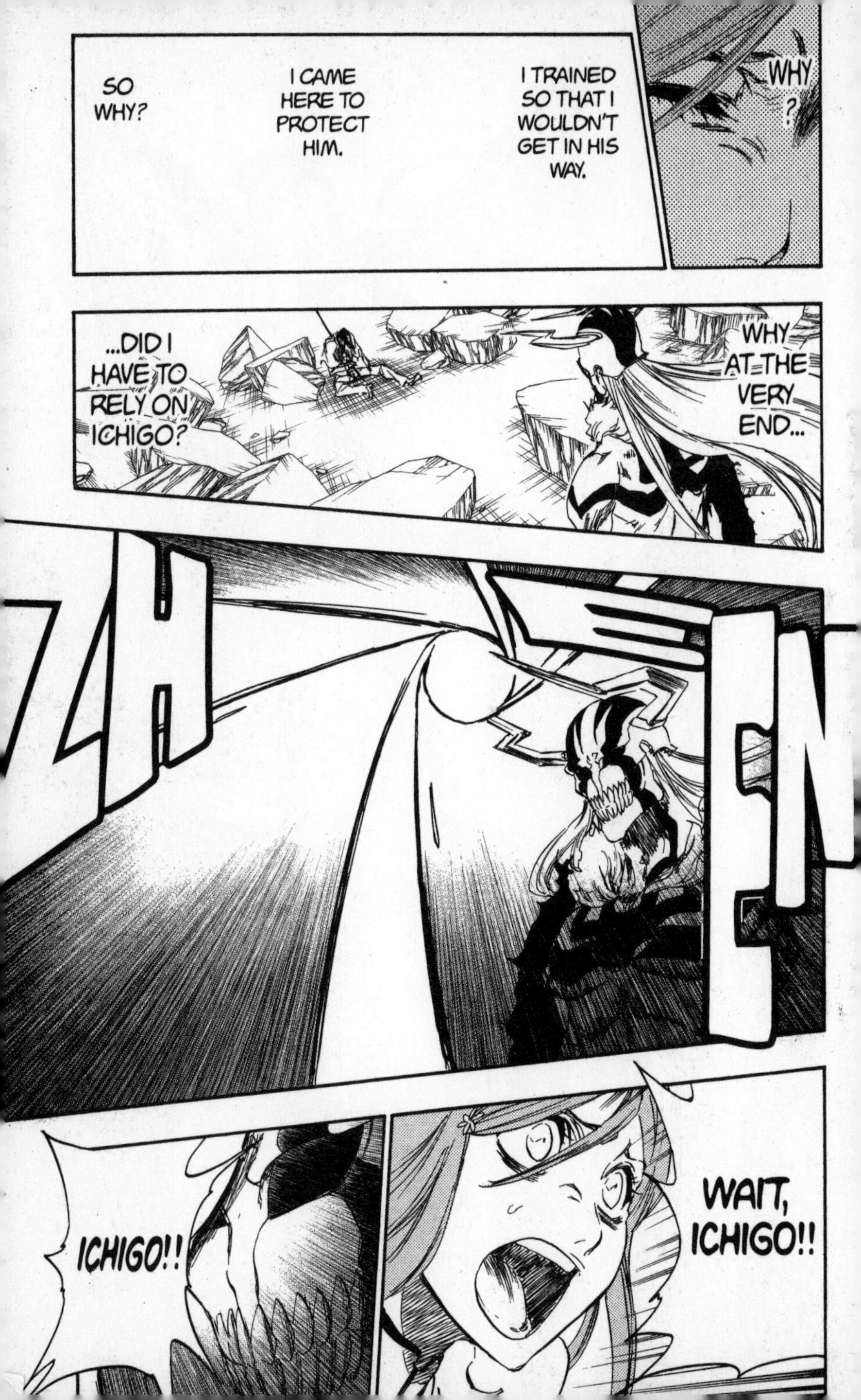
WHY?
I TRAINED SO THAT I WOULDN'T GET IN HIS WAY.
I CAME HERE TO PROTECT HIM.
SO WHY?
WHY AT THE VERY END...
...DID I HAVE TO RELY ON ICHIGO?
ZHEN
WAIT, ICHIGO!!
ICHIGO!!

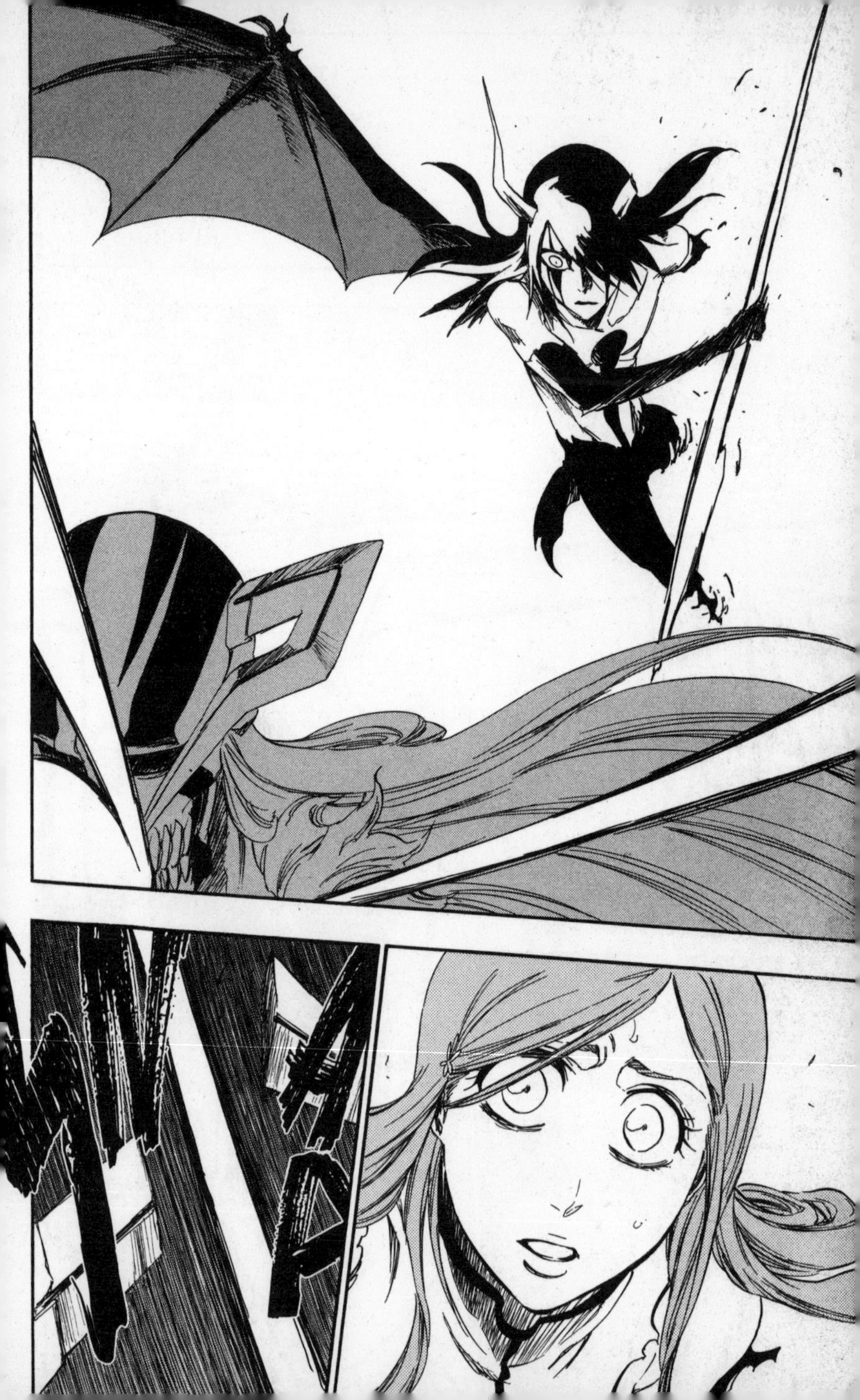

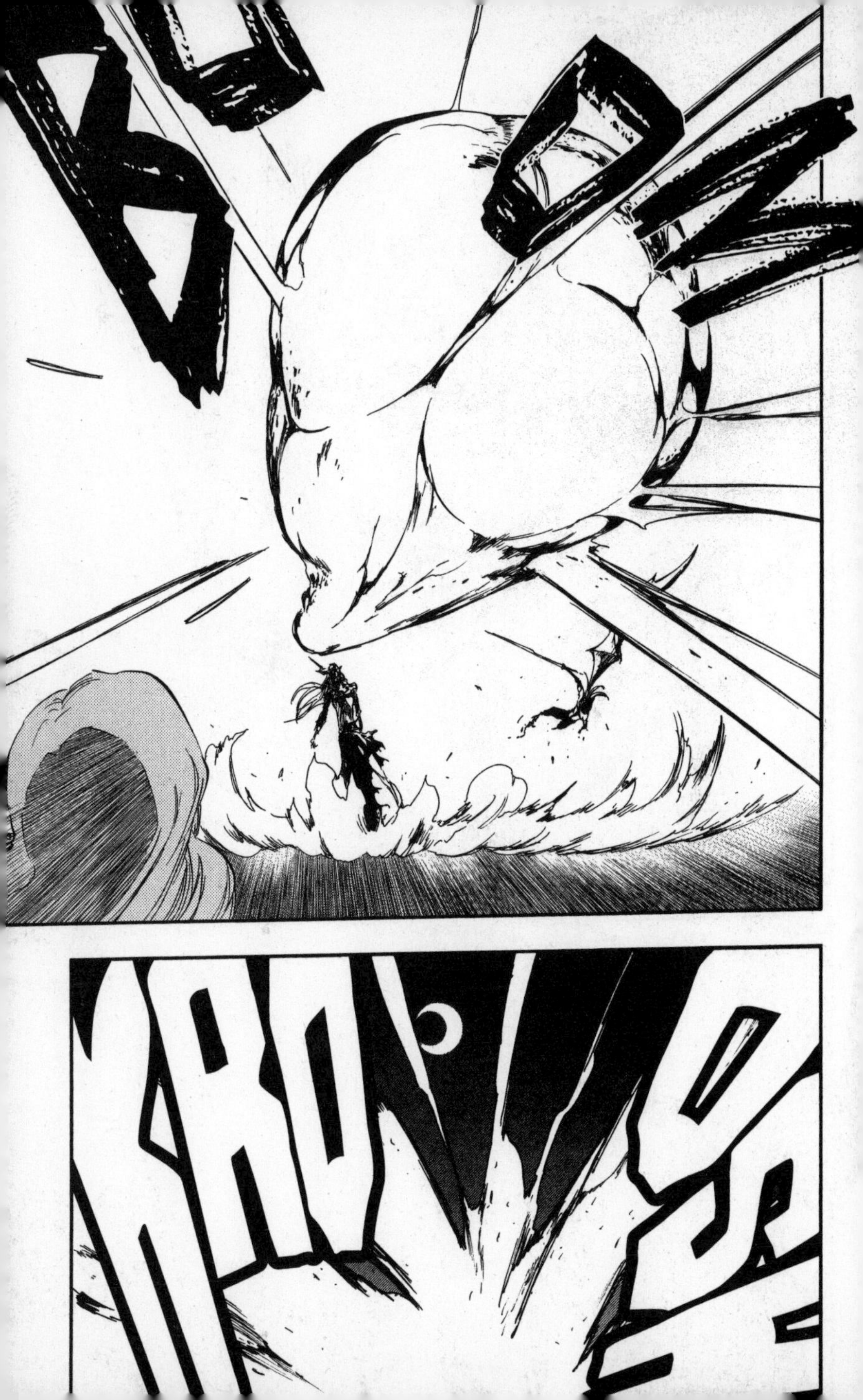
BOOM

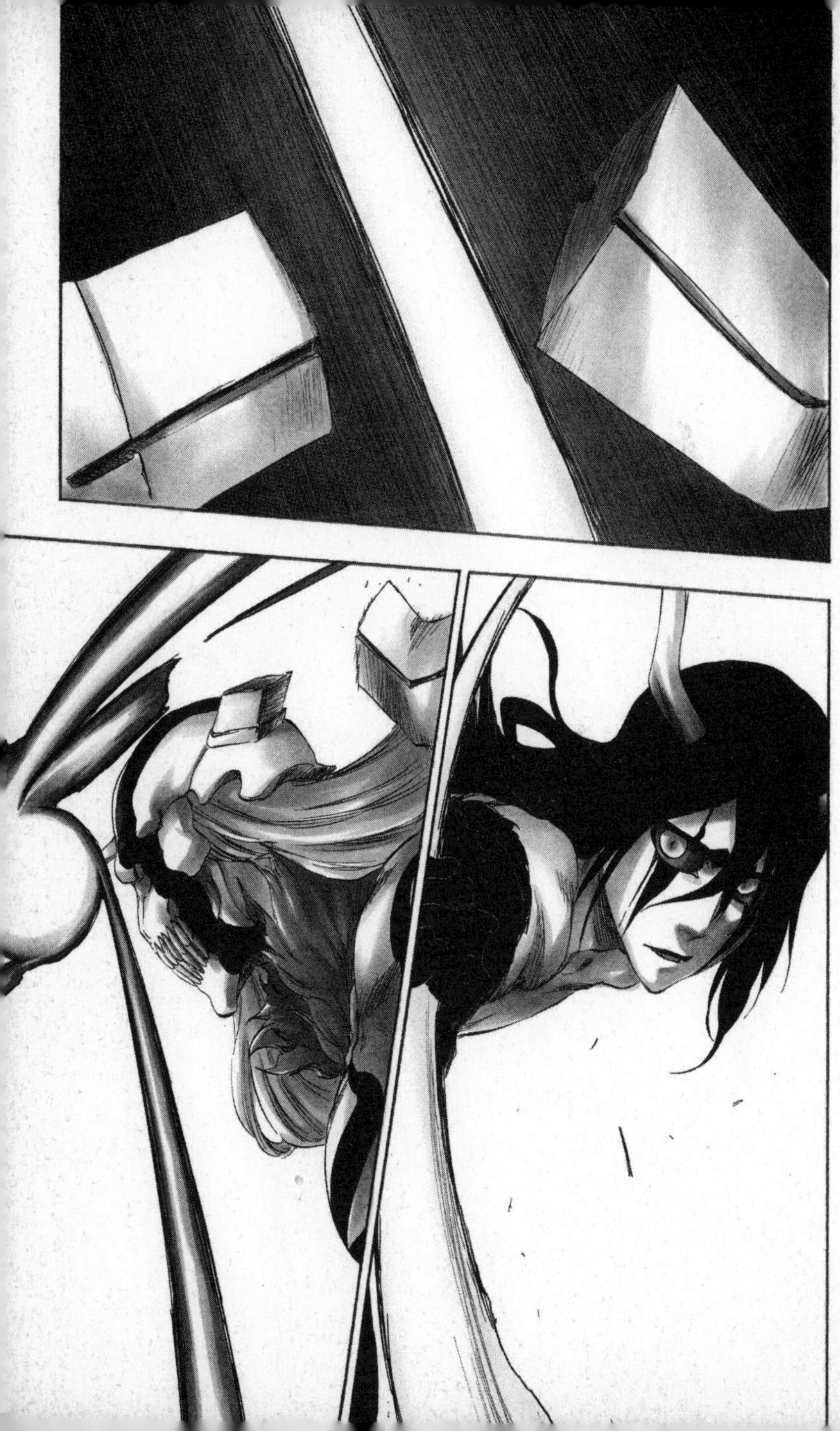

bleach353. The Ash

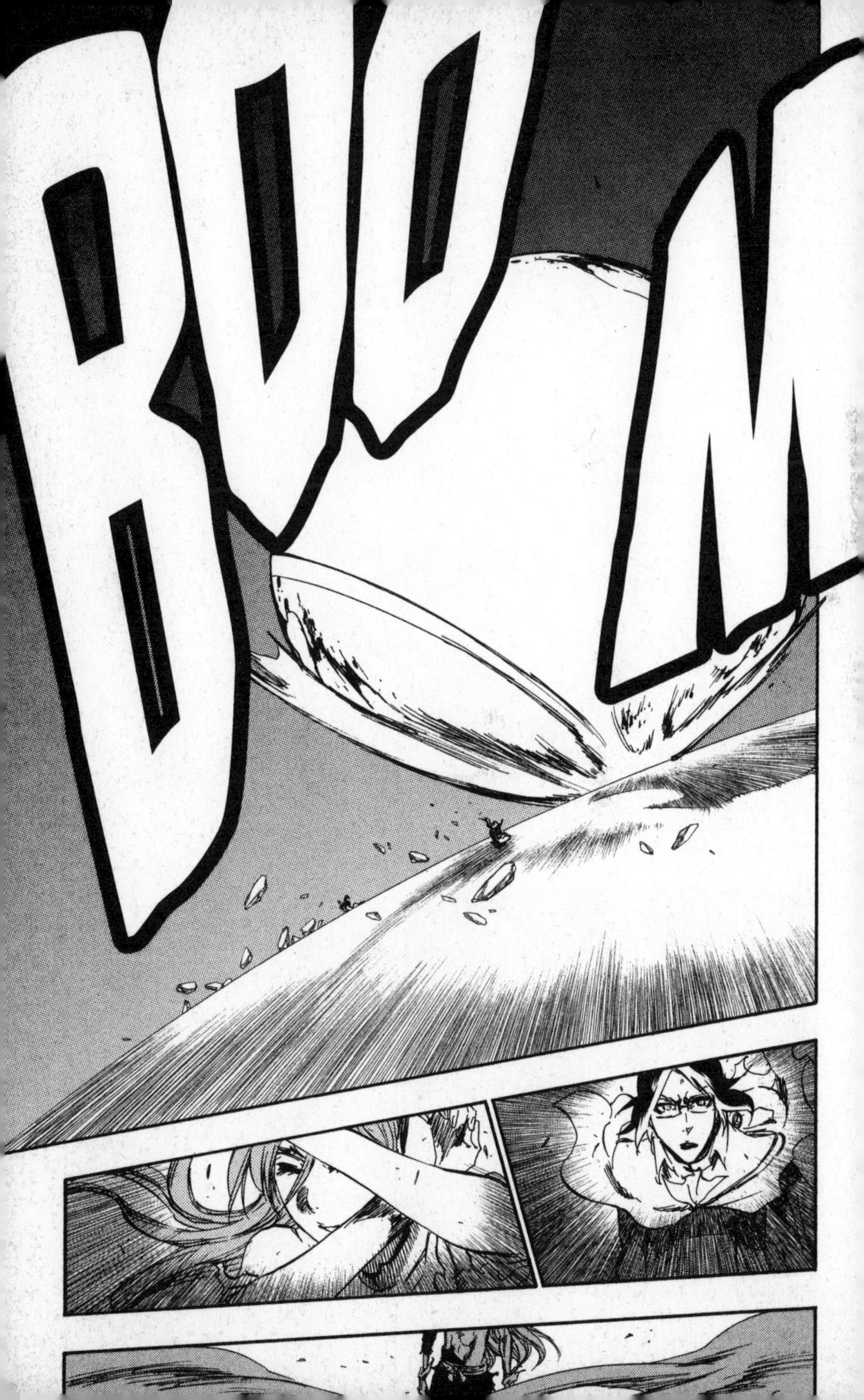
BOOM

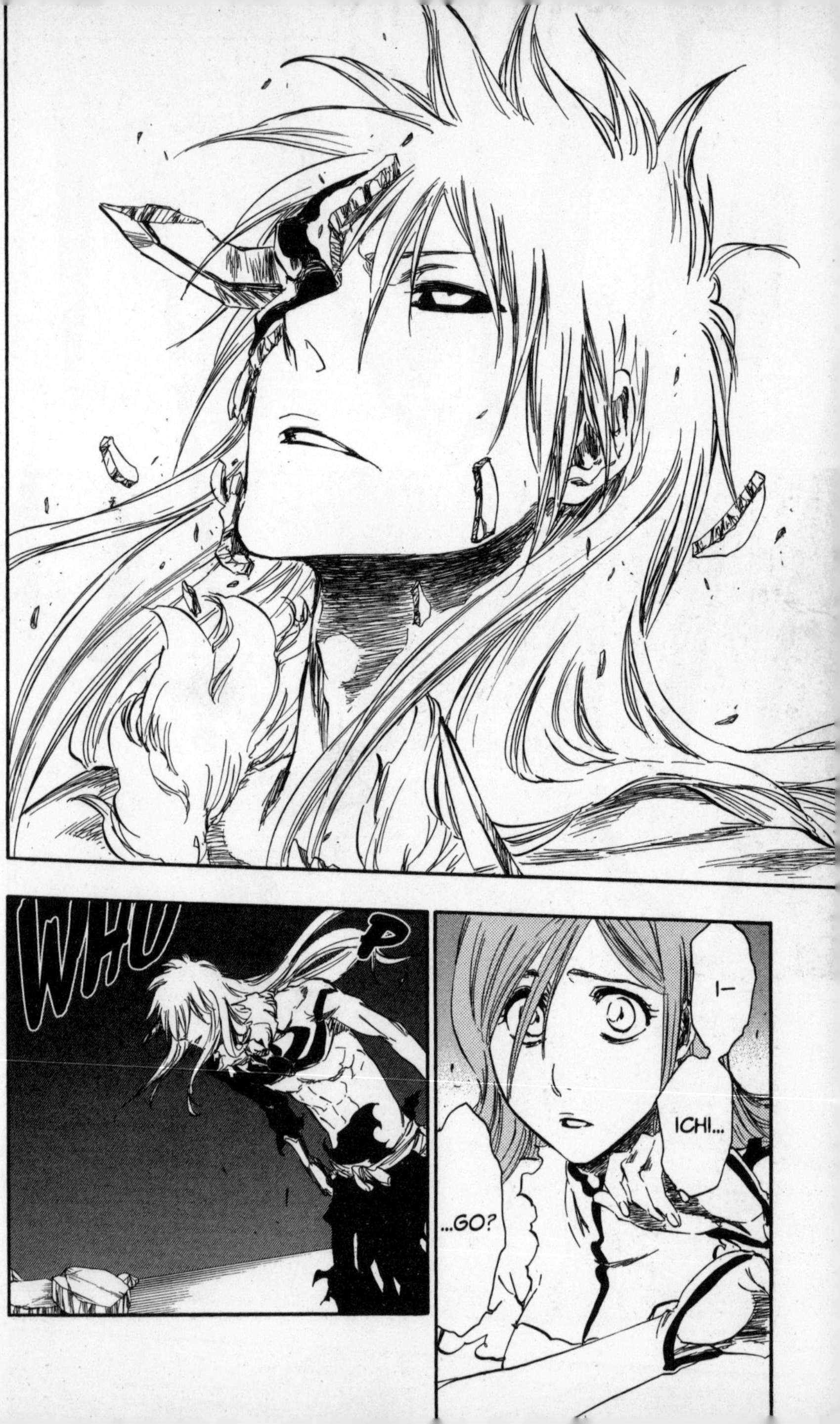
WHUP
I—
ICHI...
...GO?

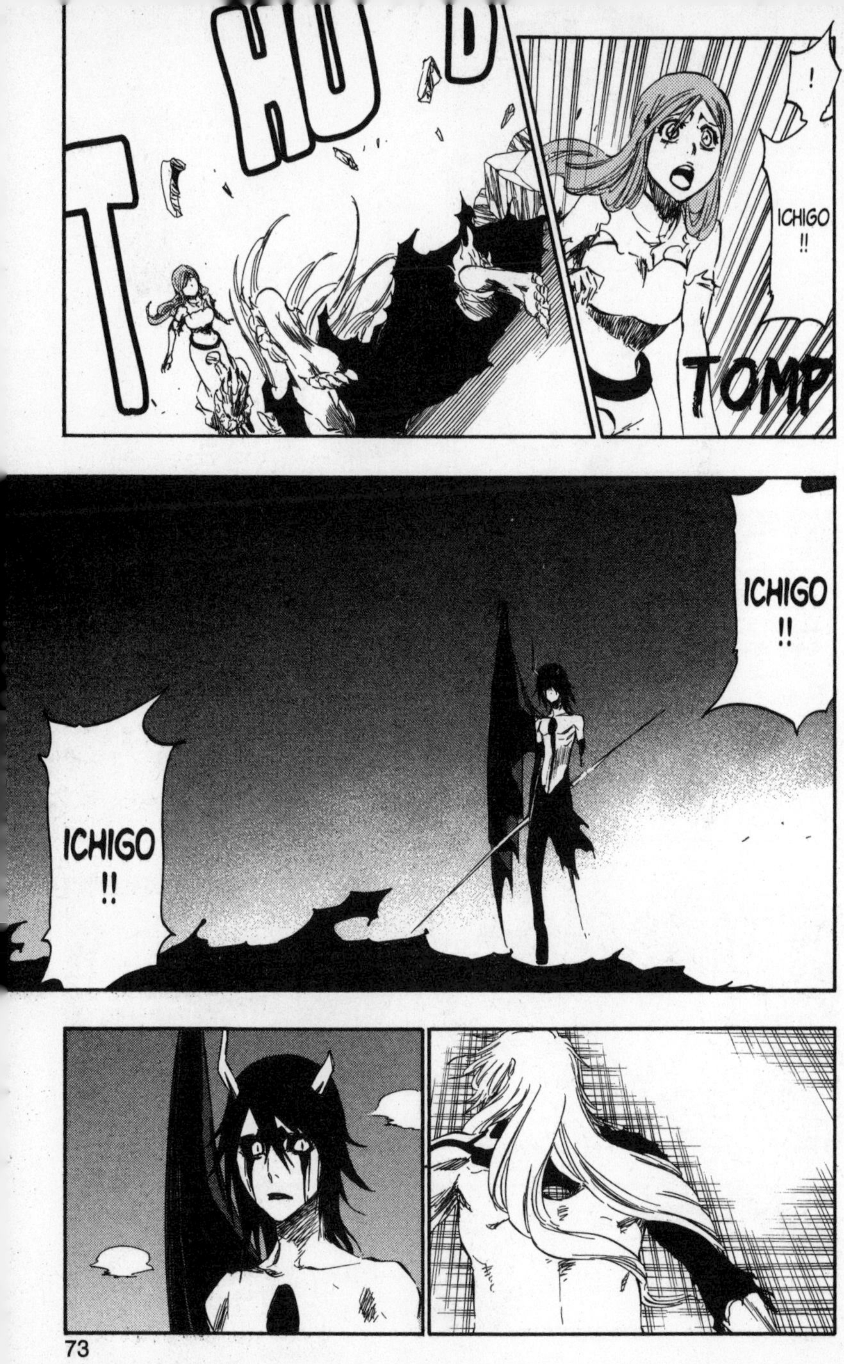
!
ICHIGO !!
TOMP
THUD
ICHIGO !!
ICHIGO !!

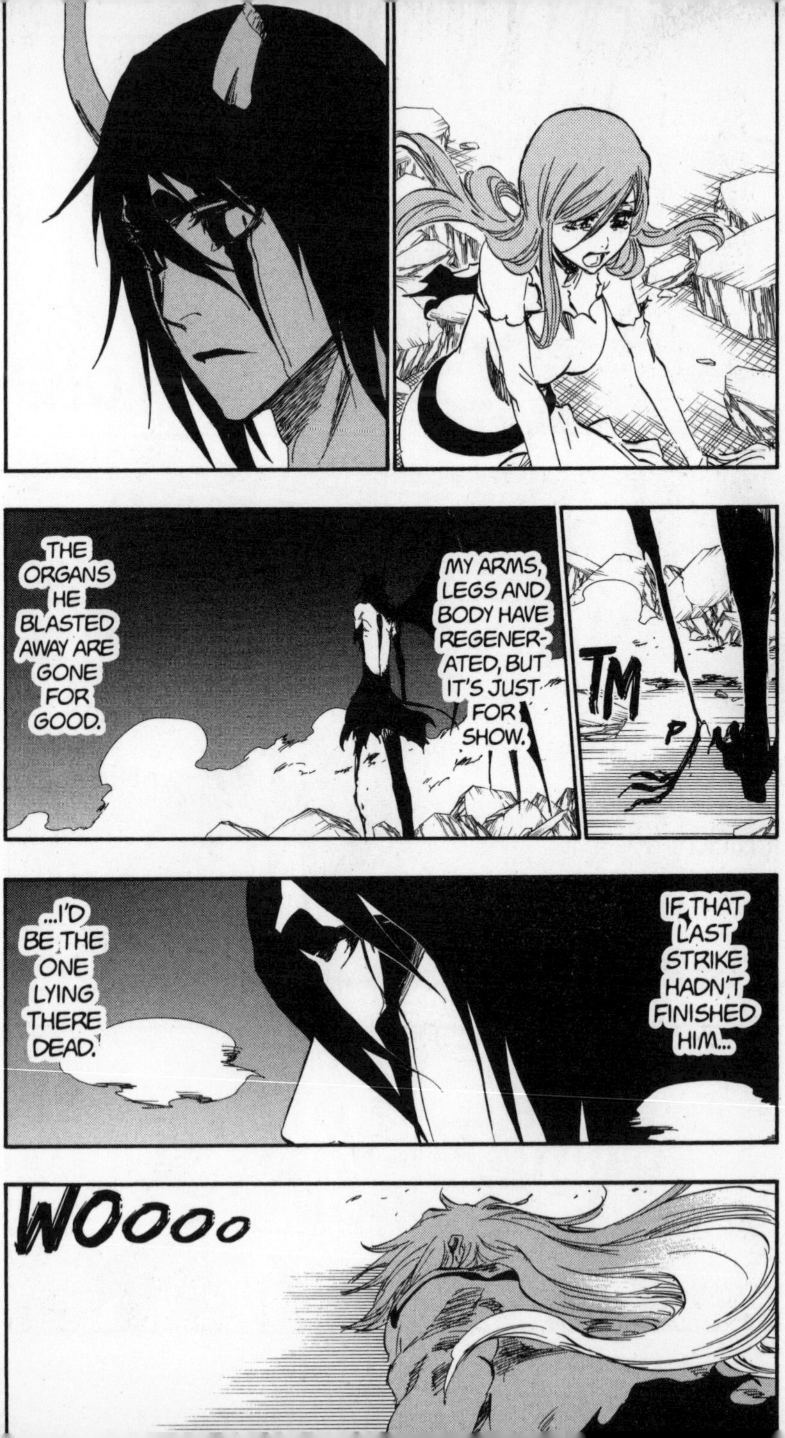
TMP
MY ARMS, LEGS AND BODY HAVE REGENERATED, BUT IT'S JUST FOR SHOW.
THE ORGANS HE BLASTED AWAY ARE GONE FOR GOOD.
IF THAT LAST STRIKE HADN'T FINISHED HIM...
...I'D BE THE ONE LYING THERE DEAD.
WOOOO

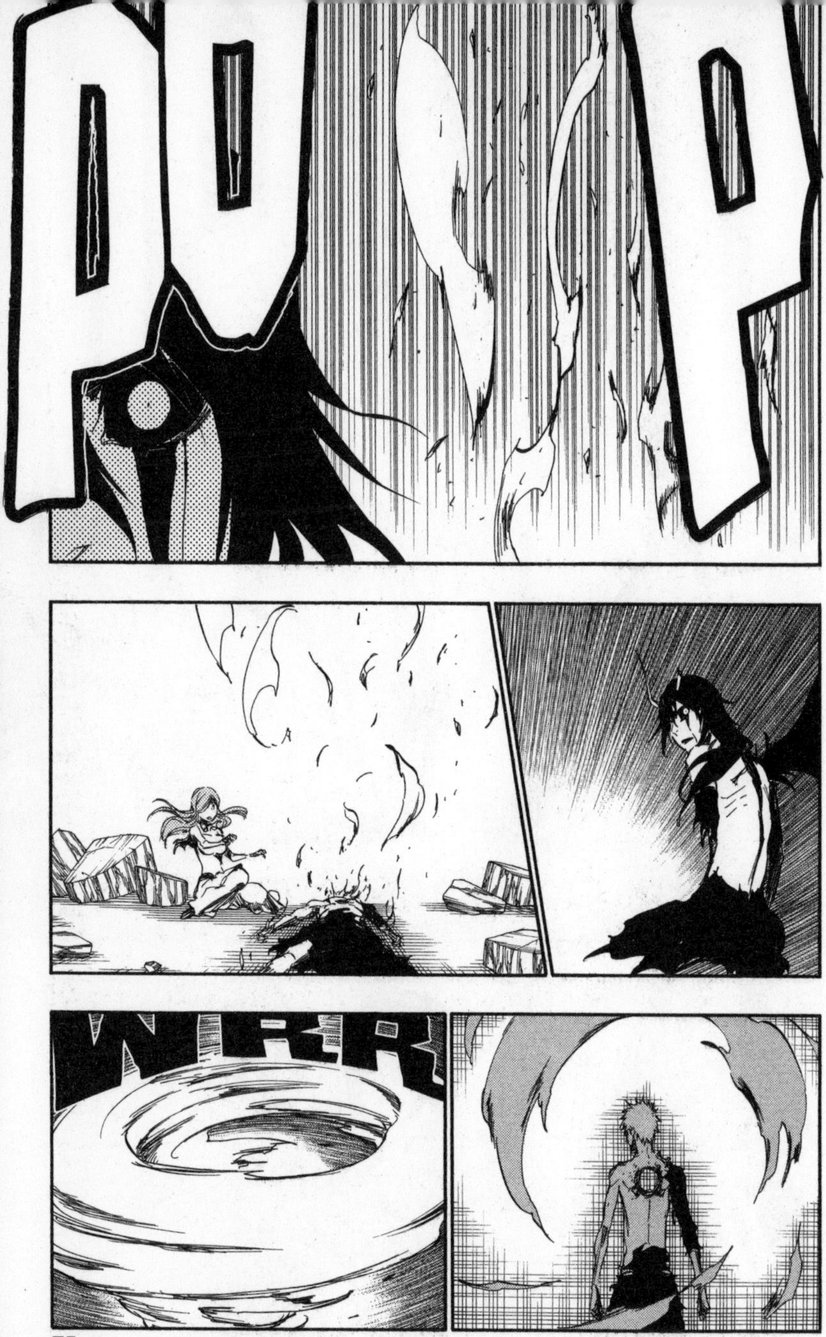
WRR

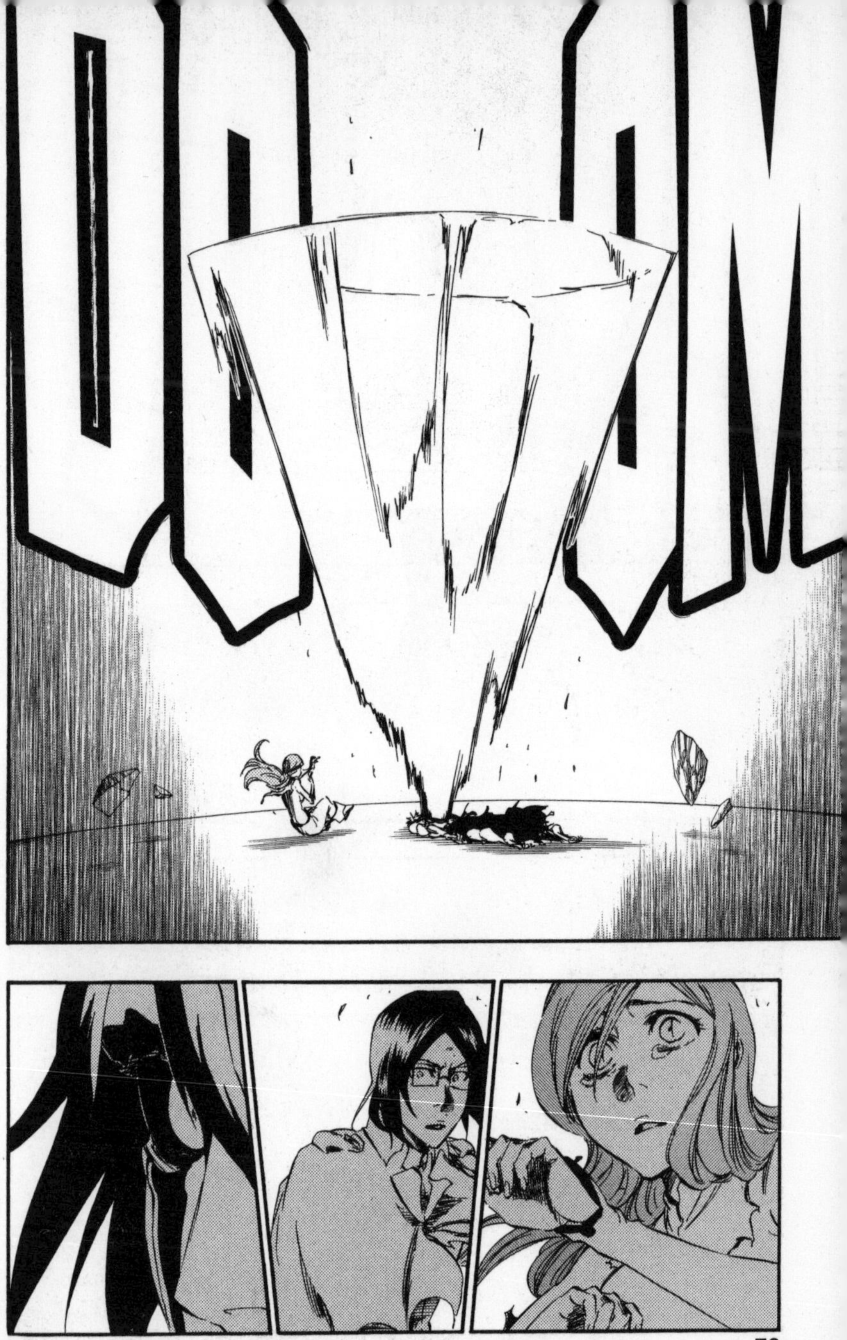

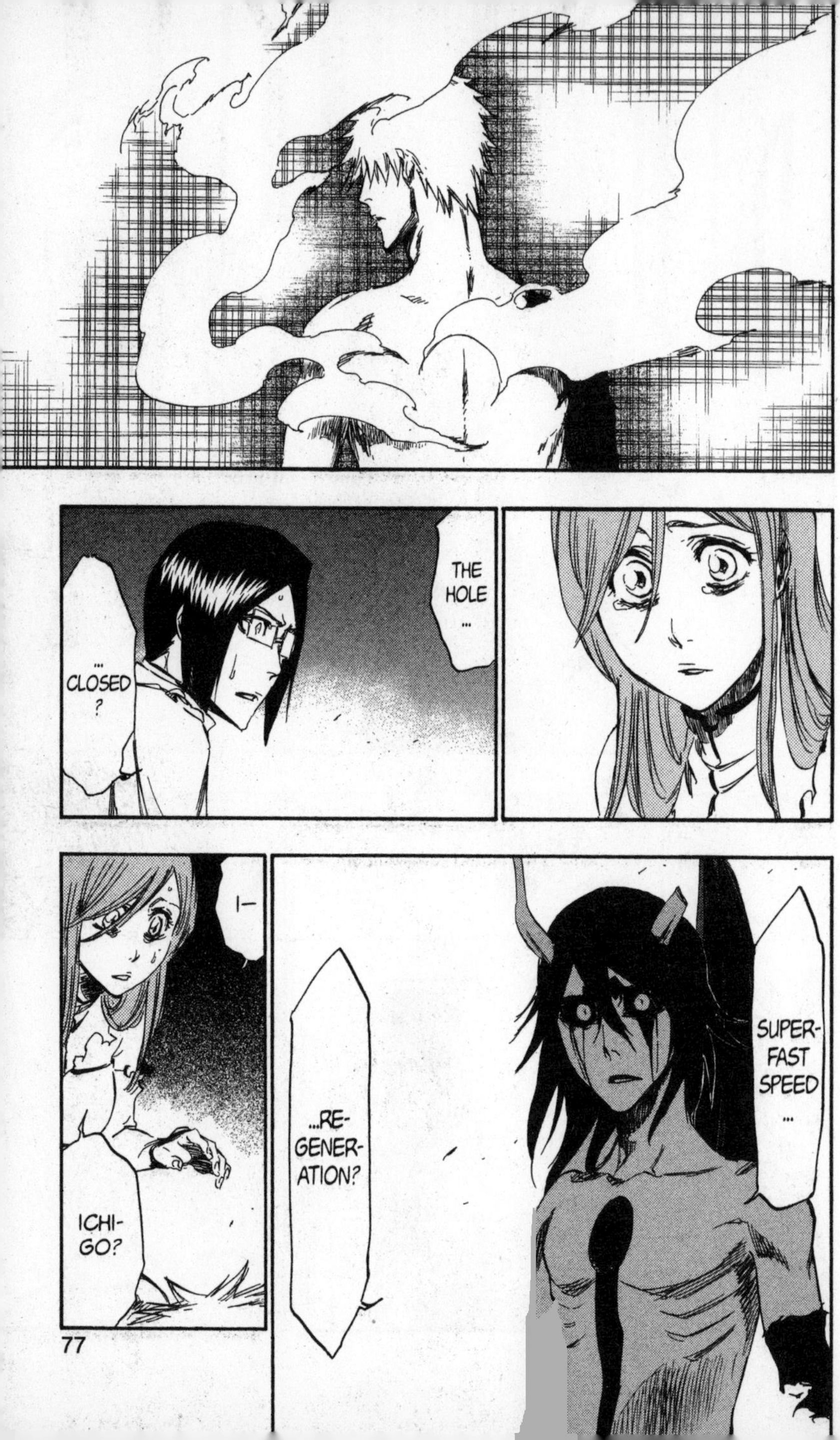
THE HOLE ...
... CLOSED ?
I—
SUPER-FAST SPEED ...
...RE-GENER-ATION?
ICHI-GO?

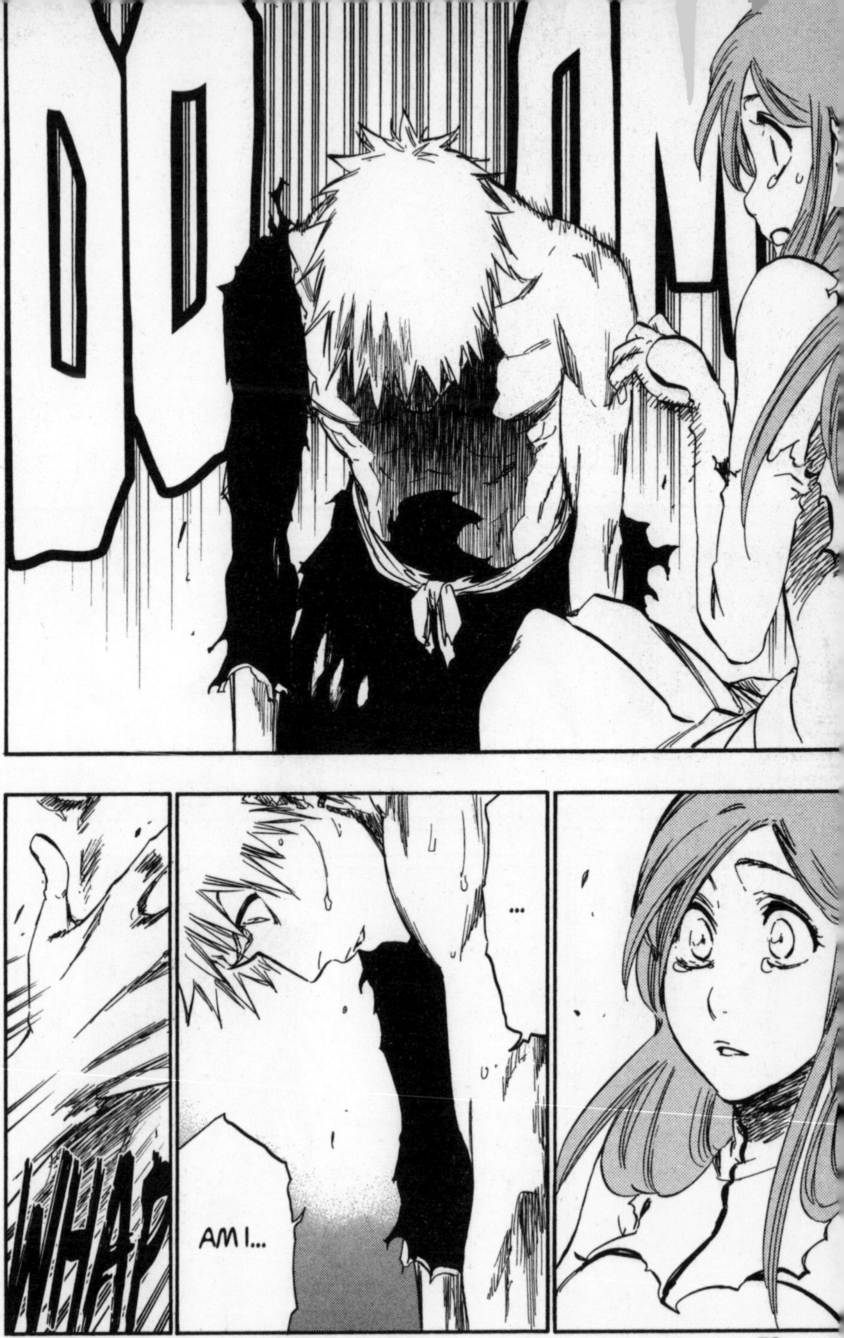
DOOM
...
AM I...
WHAP

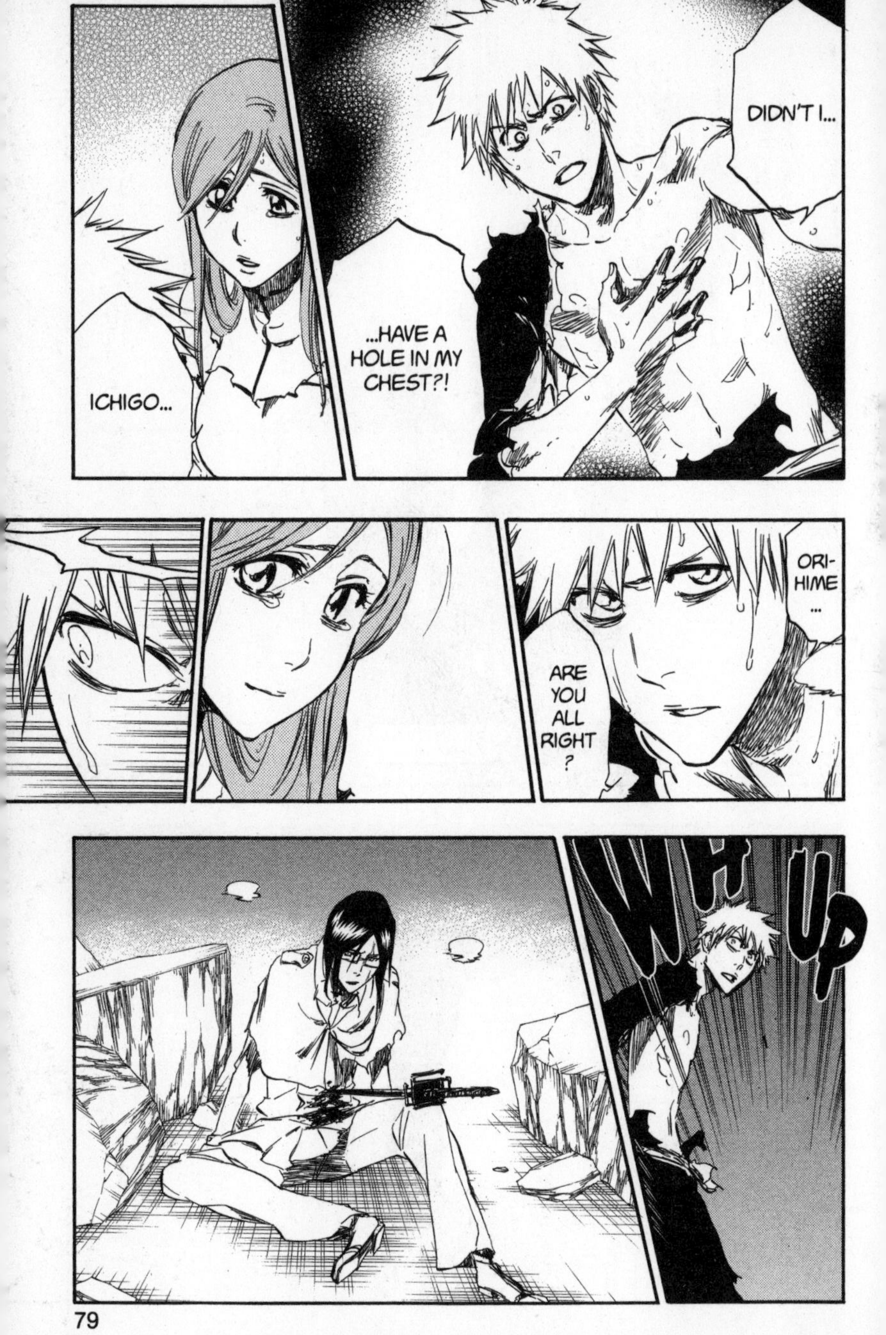
DIDN'T I...
...HAVE A HOLE IN MY CHEST?!
ICHIGO...
ORI-HIME...
ARE YOU ALL RIGHT?
WHUP

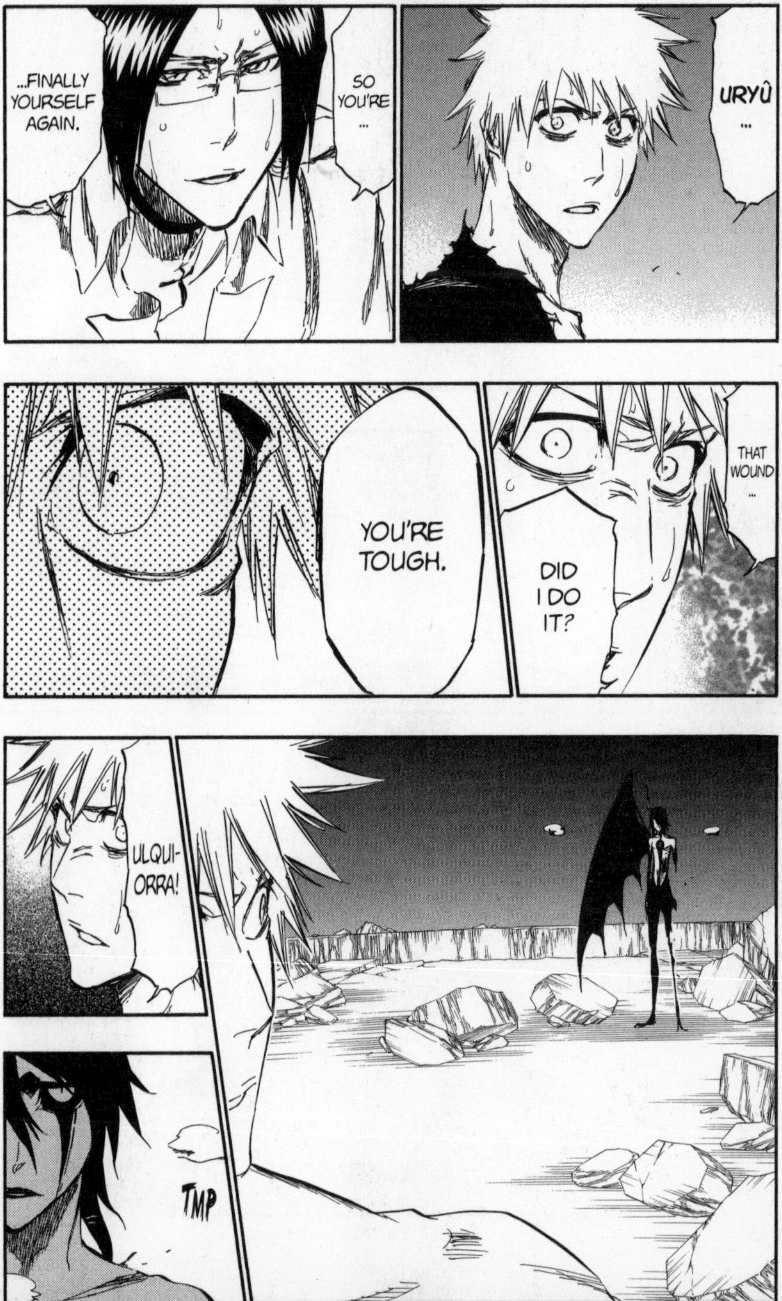
URYÛ ...
SO YOU'RE ...
...FINALLY YOURSELF AGAIN.
THAT WOUND ...
DID I DO IT?
YOU'RE TOUGH.
ULQUI-ORRA!
TMP

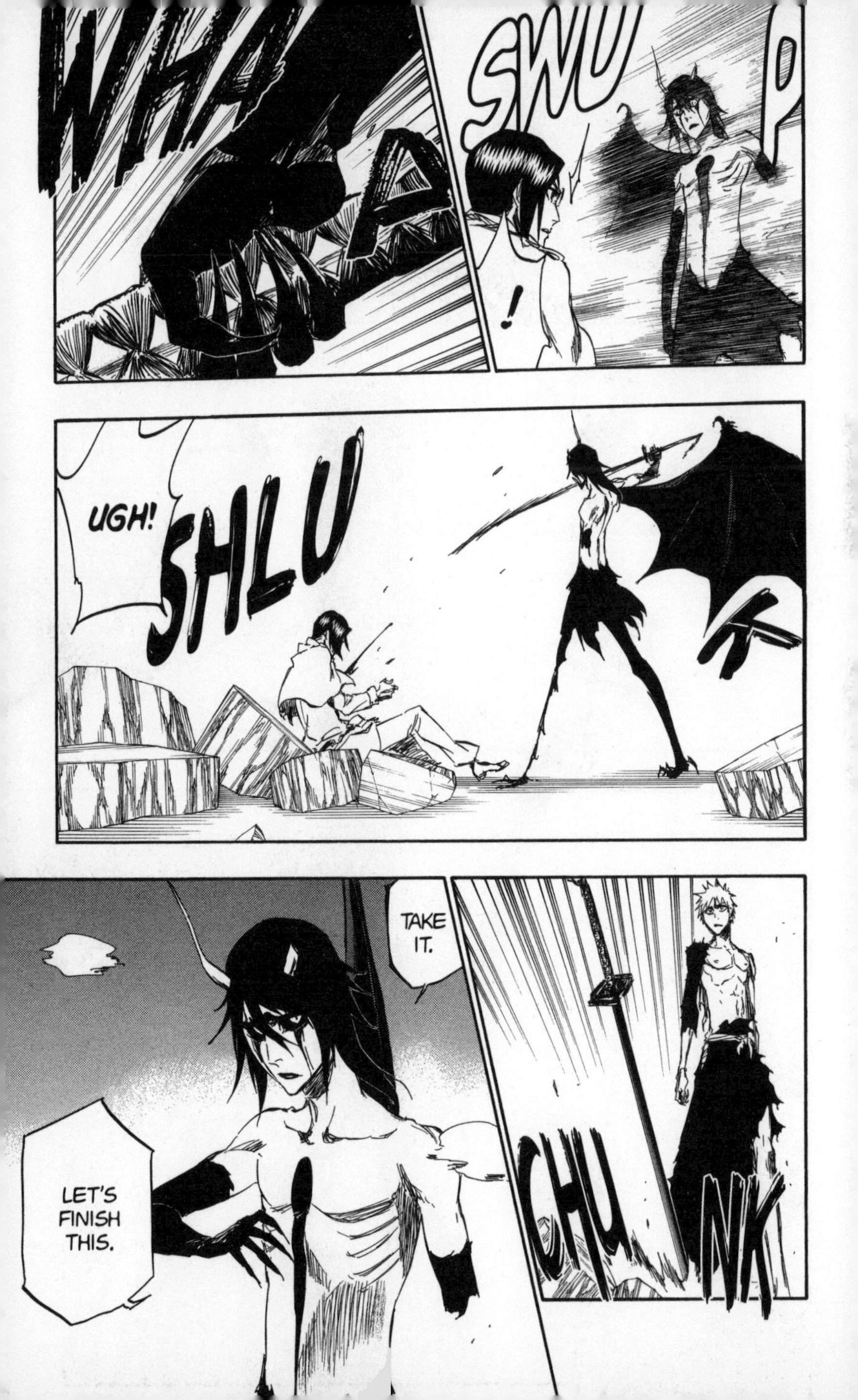
SWU P
!
WHAA
SHLU K
UGH!
TAKE IT.
CHU NK
LET'S FINISH THIS.

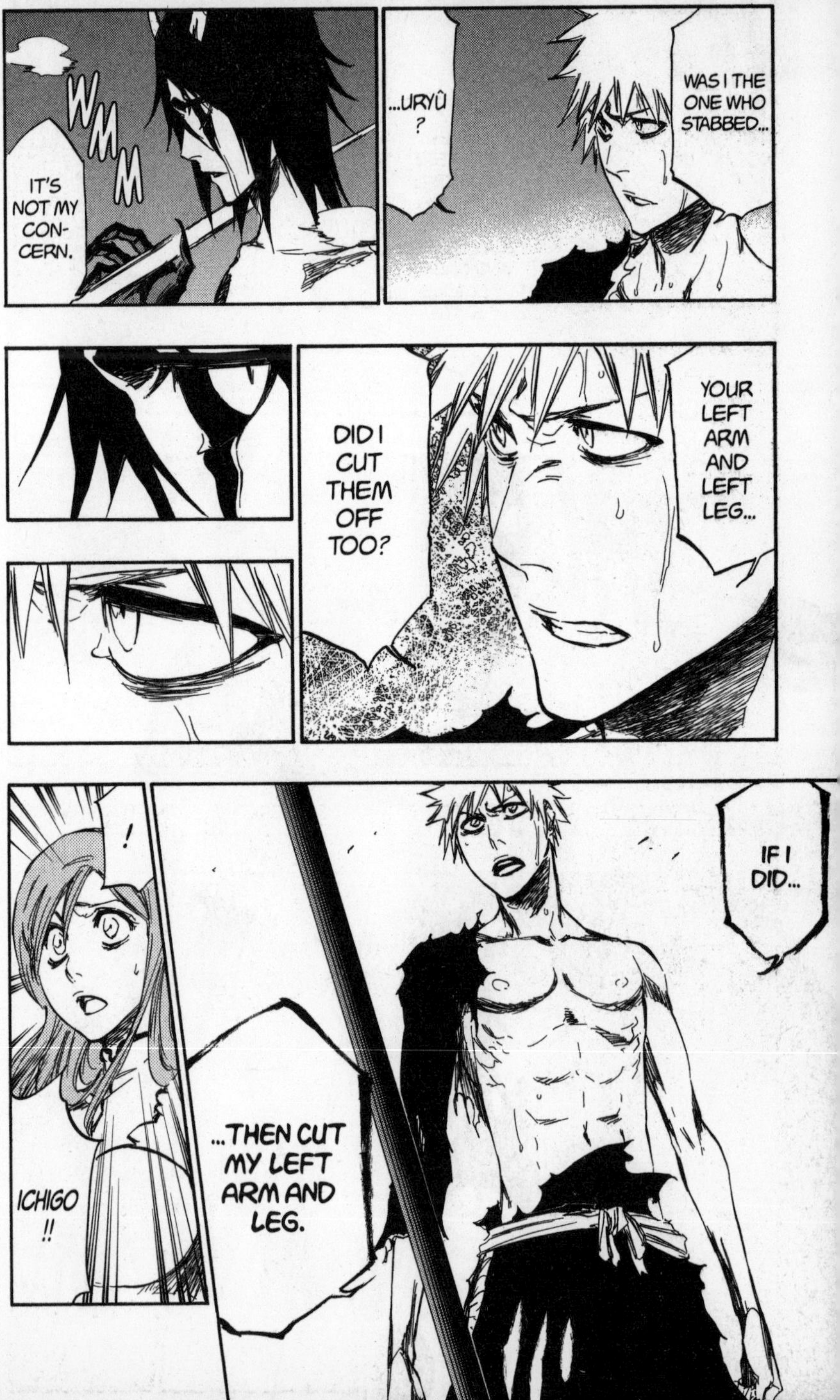
WAS I THE ONE WHO STABBED...
...URYÛ ?
WMMM
IT'S NOT MY CONCERN.
YOUR LEFT ARM AND LEFT LEG...
DID I CUT THEM OFF TOO?
IF I DID...
...THEN CUT MY LEFT ARM AND LEG.
!
ICHIGO !!

READ THIS WAY

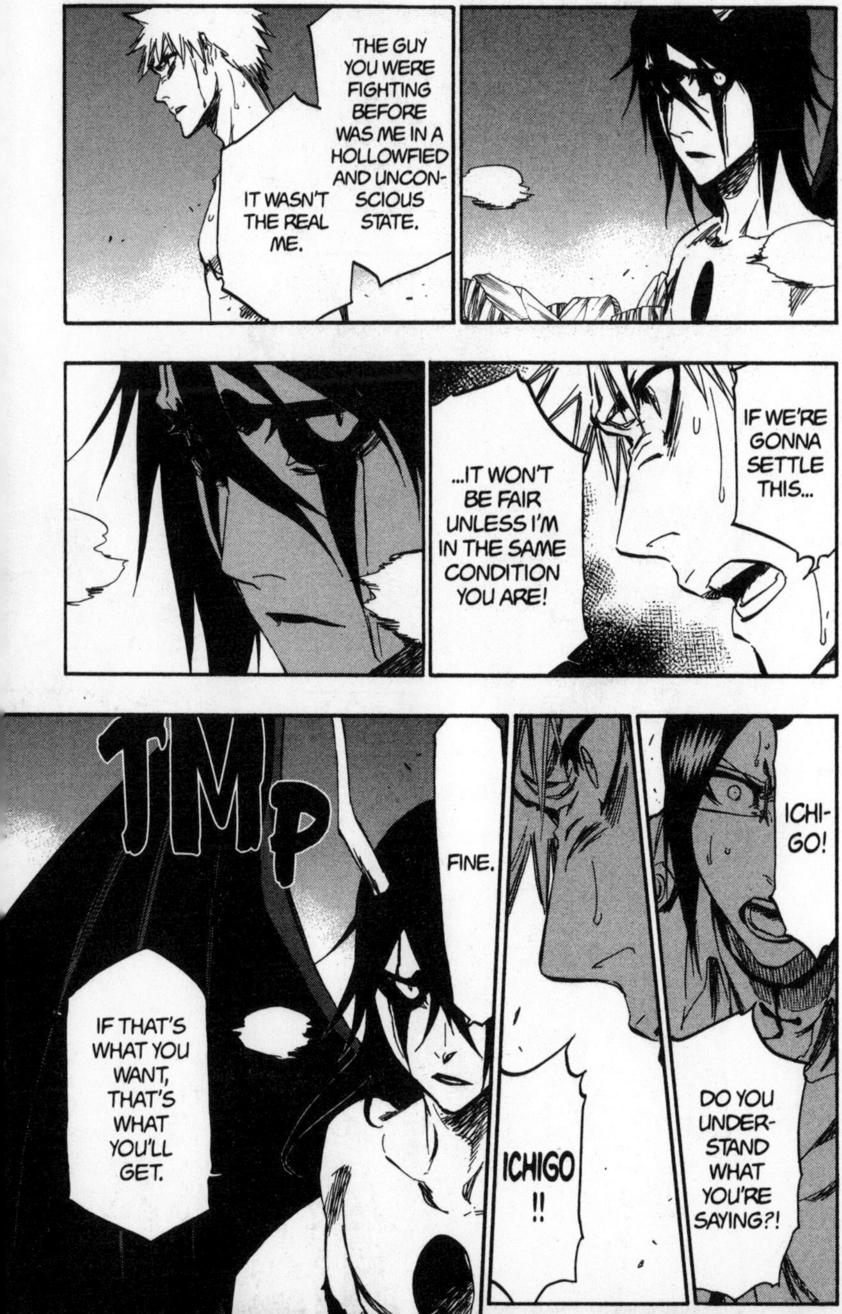
THE GUY YOU WERE FIGHTING BEFORE WAS ME IN A HOLLOWFIED AND UNCONSCIOUS STATE.
IT WASN'T THE REAL ME.
IF WE'RE GONNA SETTLE THIS...
...IT WON'T BE FAIR UNLESS I'M IN THE SAME CONDITION YOU ARE!
ICHIGO!
DO YOU UNDERSTAND WHAT YOU'RE SAYING?!
ICHIGO!!
FINE.
TMP
IF THAT'S WHAT YOU WANT, THAT'S WHAT YOU'LL GET.

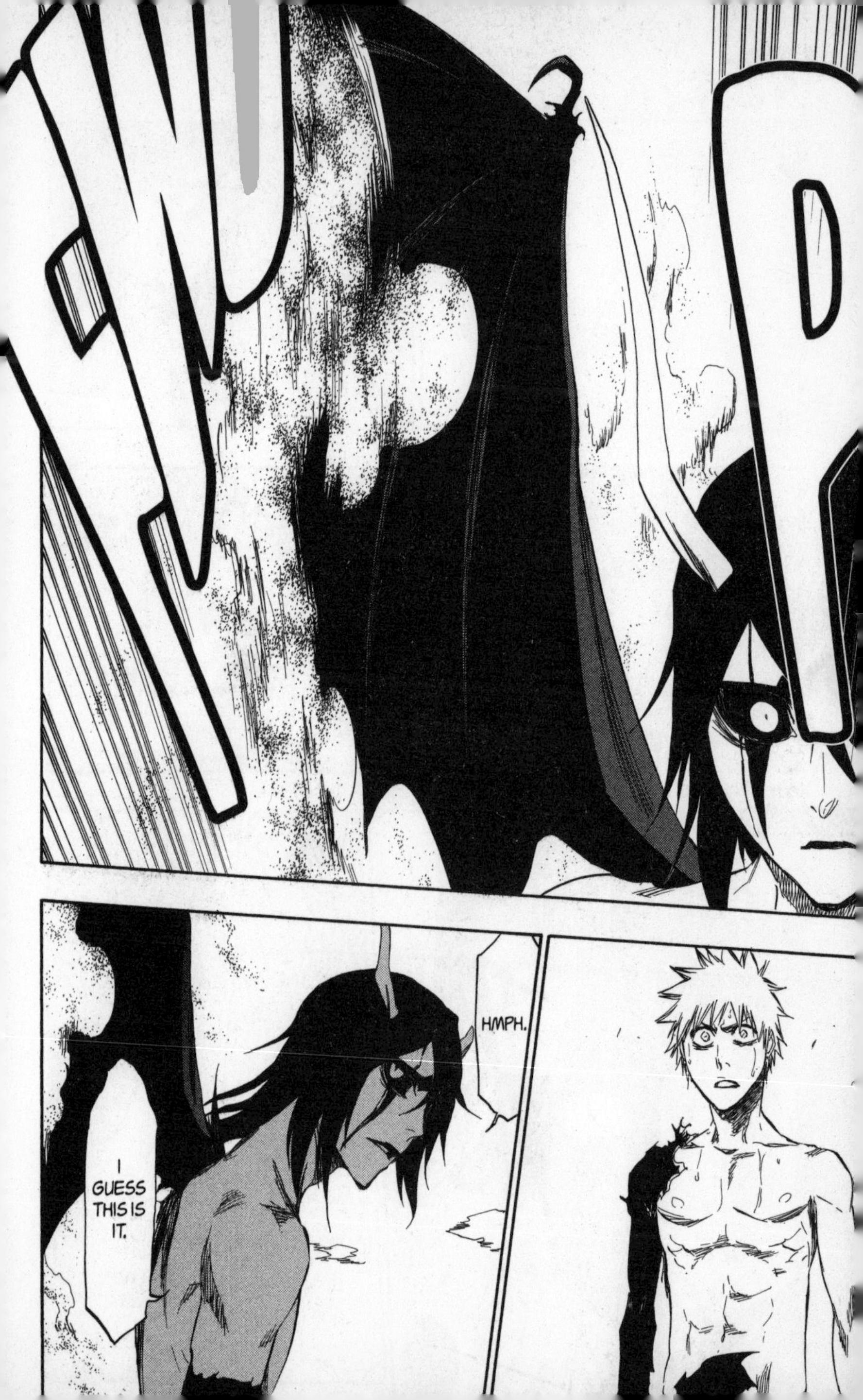
HMPH.
I GUESS THIS IS IT.

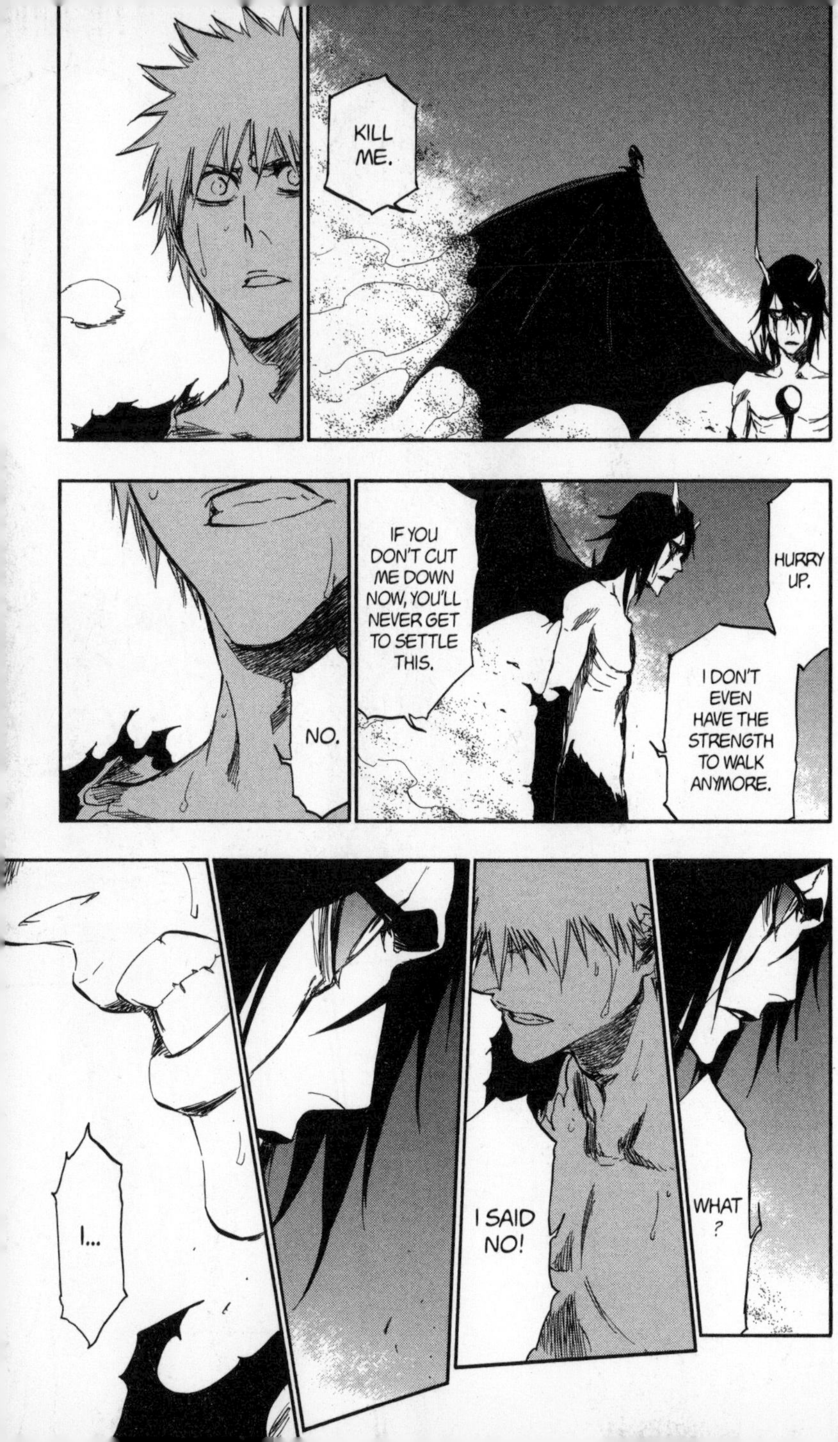
KILL ME.
HURRY UP.
I DON'T EVEN HAVE THE STRENGTH TO WALK ANYMORE.
IF YOU DON'T CUT ME DOWN NOW, YOU'LL NEVER GET TO SETTLE THIS.
NO.
WHAT?
I SAID NO!
I...

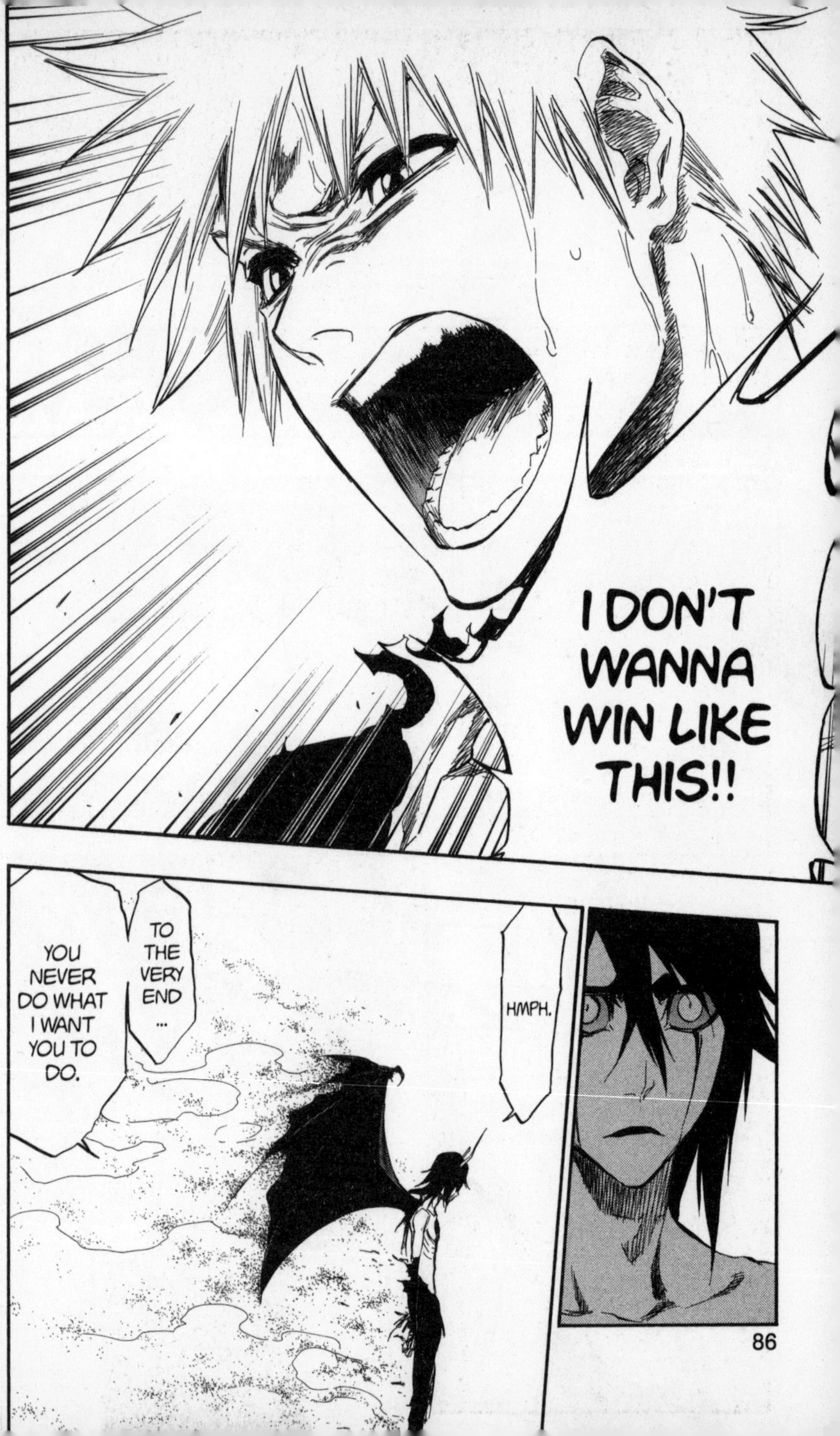
I DON'T WANNA WIN LIKE THIS!!
HMPH.
TO THE VERY END ...
YOU NEVER DO WHAT I WANT YOU TO DO.

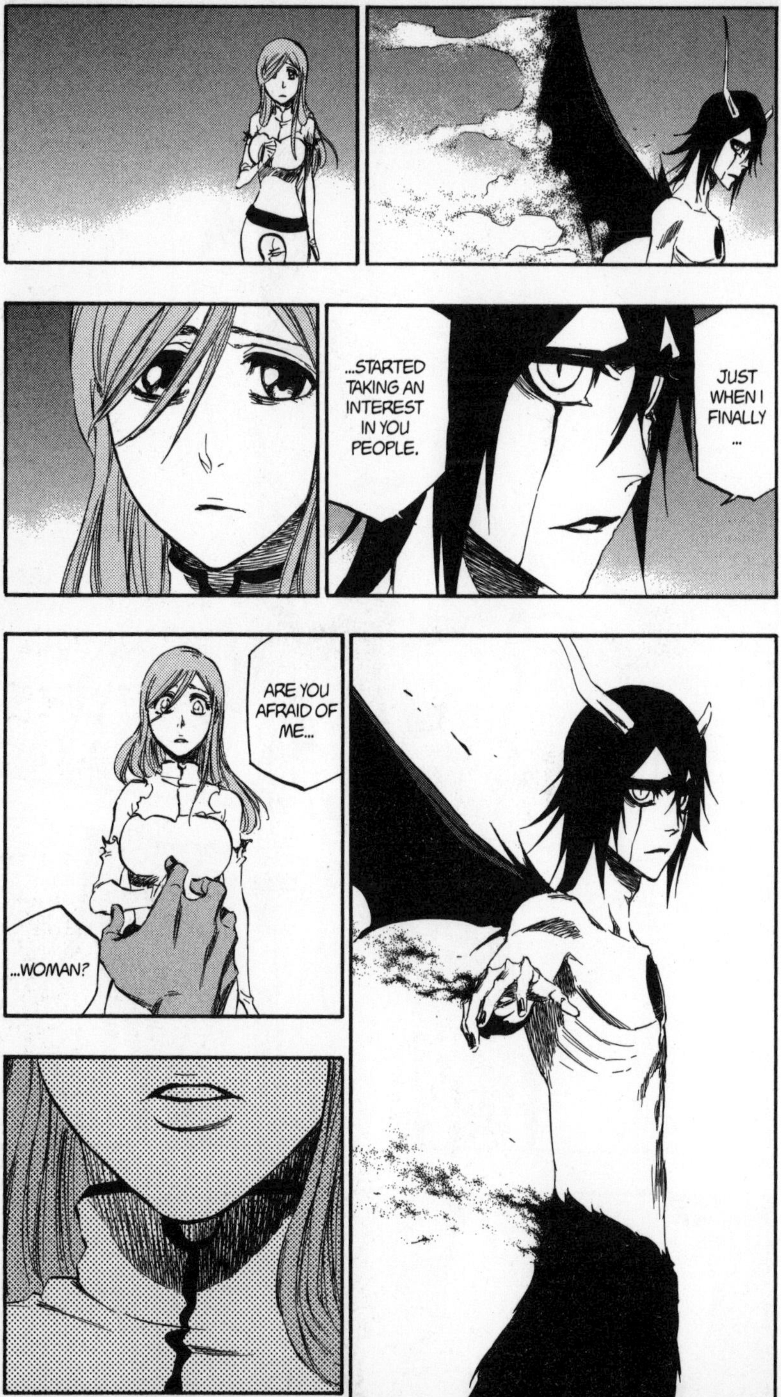
JUST WHEN I FINALLY ...
...STARTED TAKING AN INTEREST IN YOU PEOPLE.
ARE YOU AFRAID OF ME...
...WOMAN?

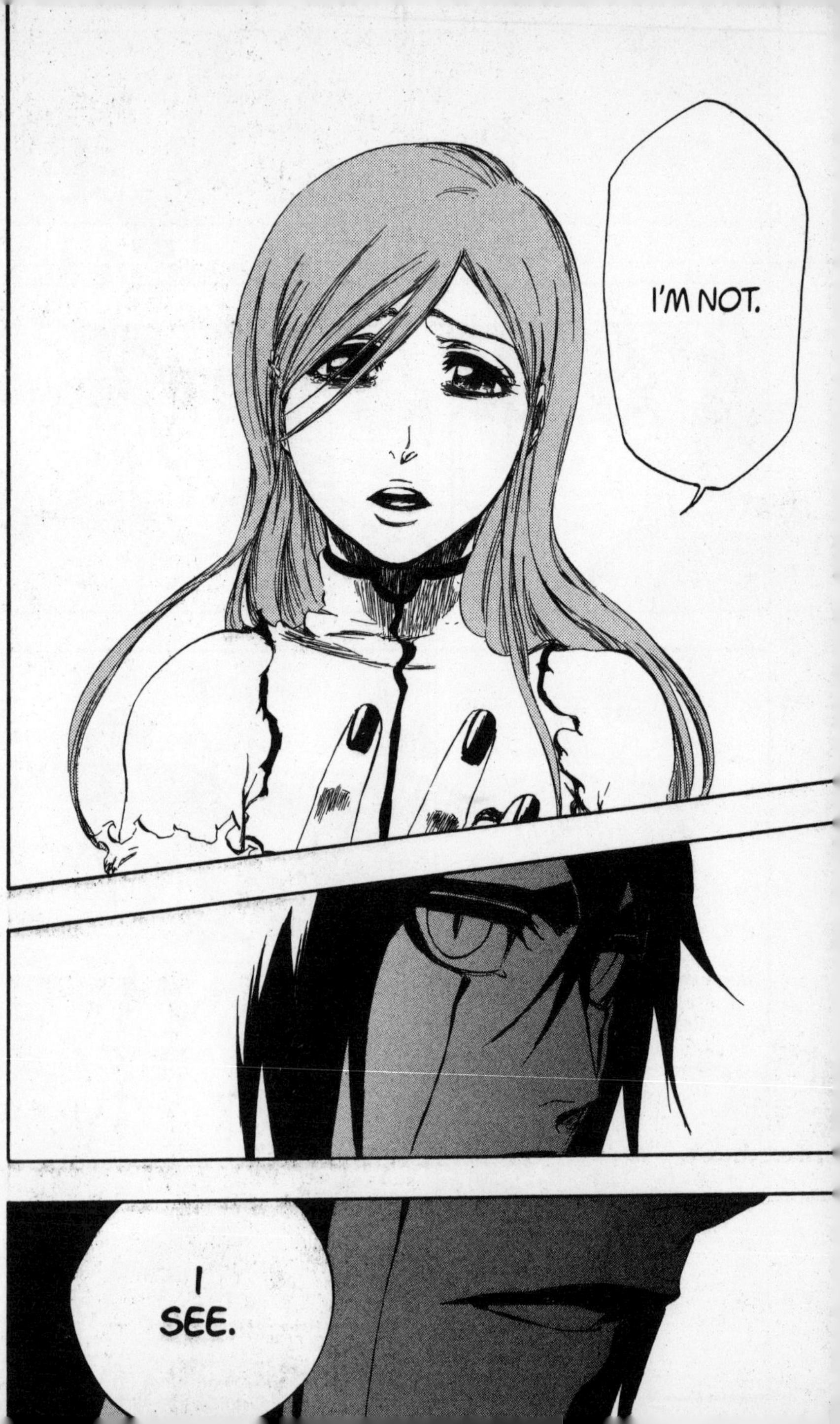
I'M NOT.
I SEE.

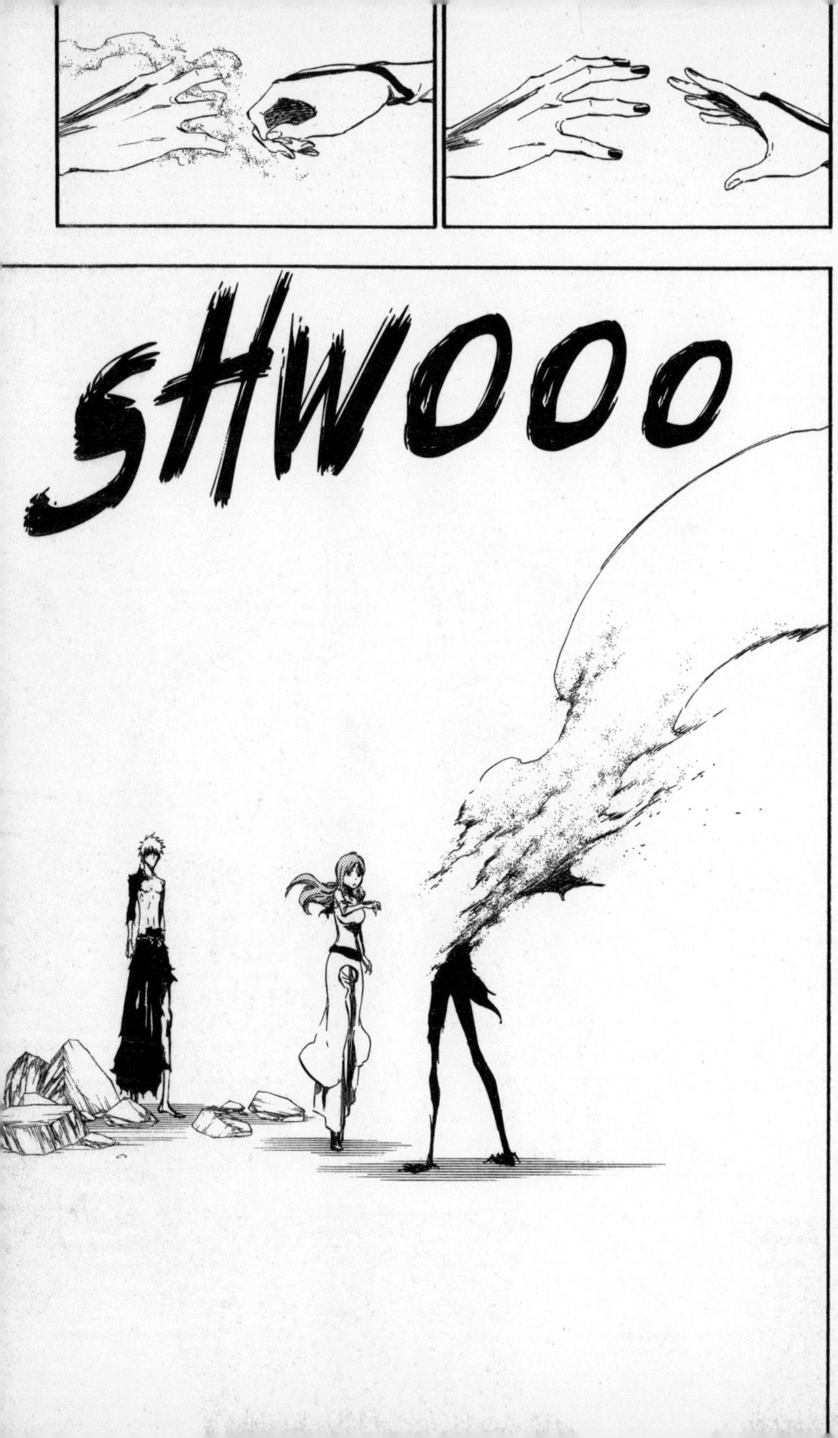
SHWOOO

354. heart

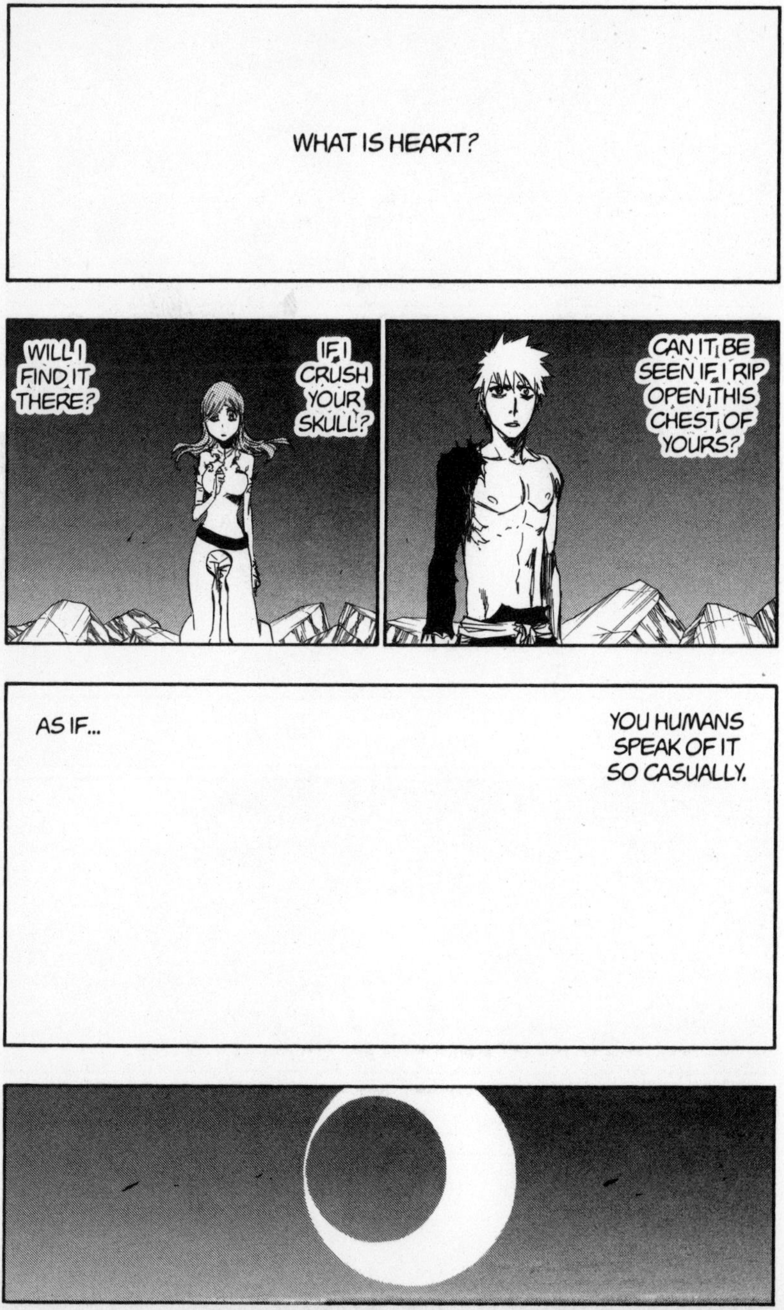
WHAT IS HEART?
CAN IT BE SEEN IF I RIP OPEN THIS CHEST OF YOURS?
IF I CRUSH YOUR SKULL?
WILL I FIND IT THERE?
YOU HUMANS SPEAK OF IT SO CASUALLY.
AS IF...

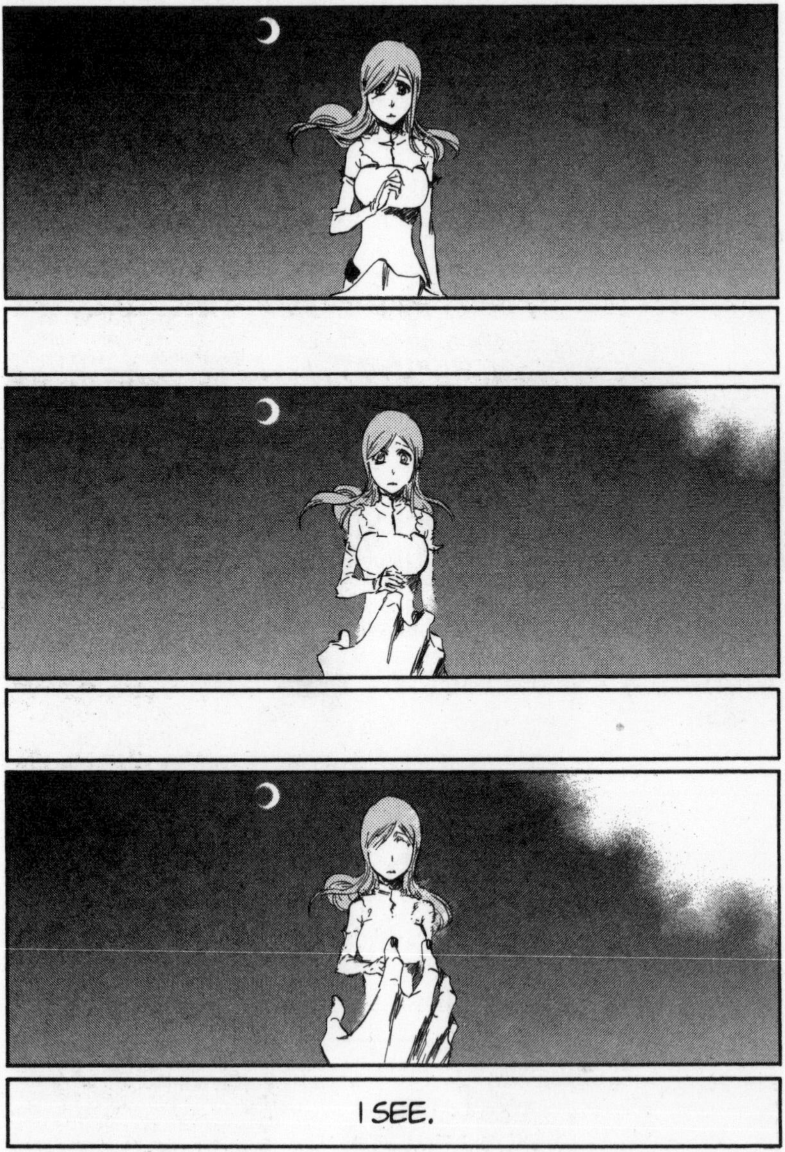
I SEE.

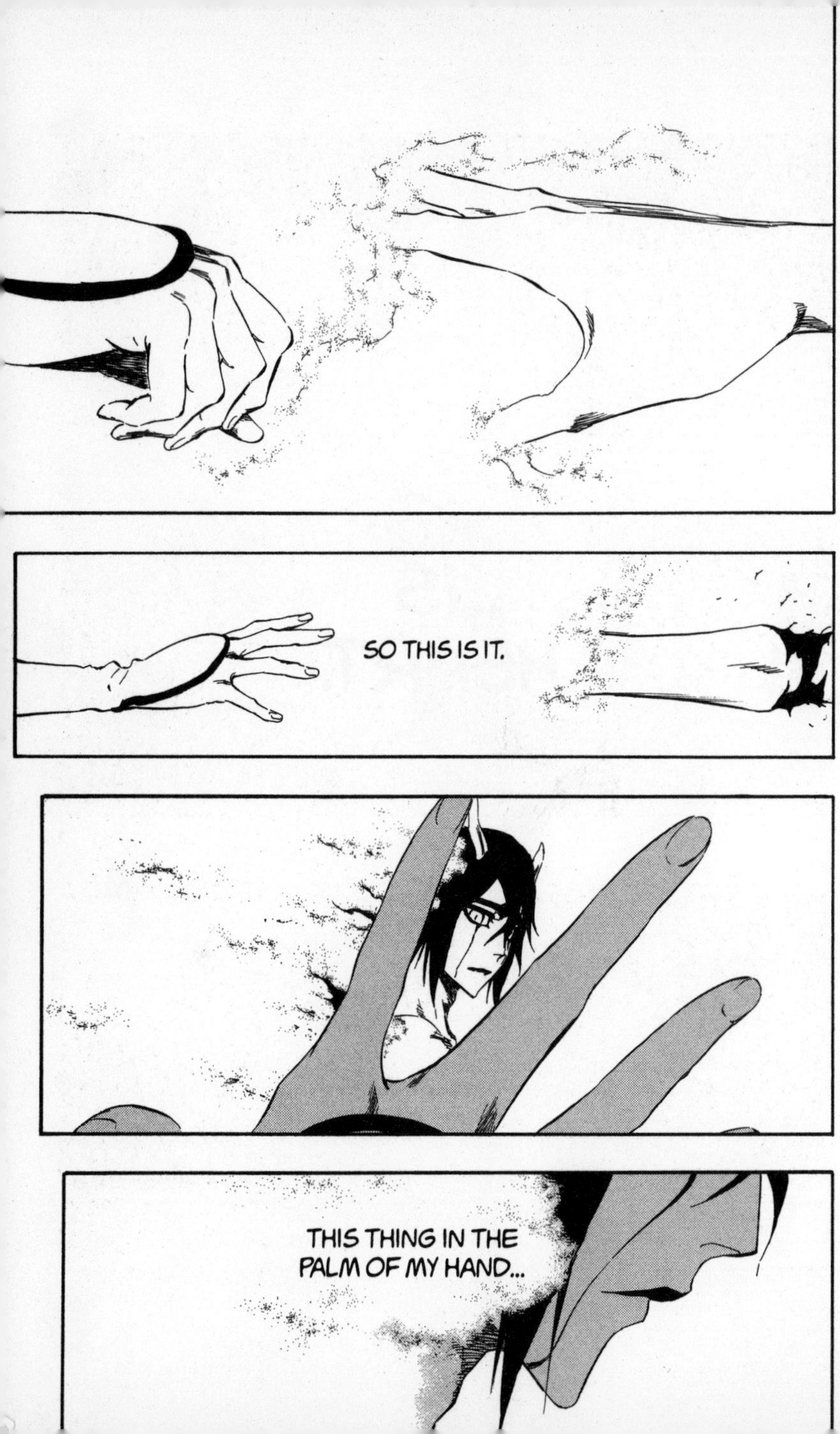
SO THIS IS IT.
THIS THING IN THE PALM OF MY HAND...

...IS
HEART.

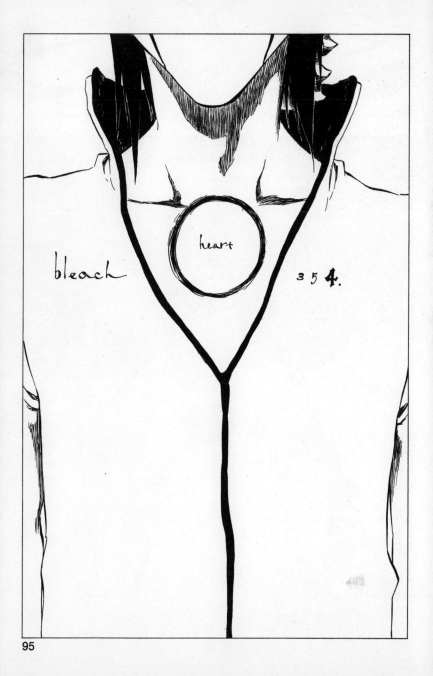

bleach

heart

3 5 4.

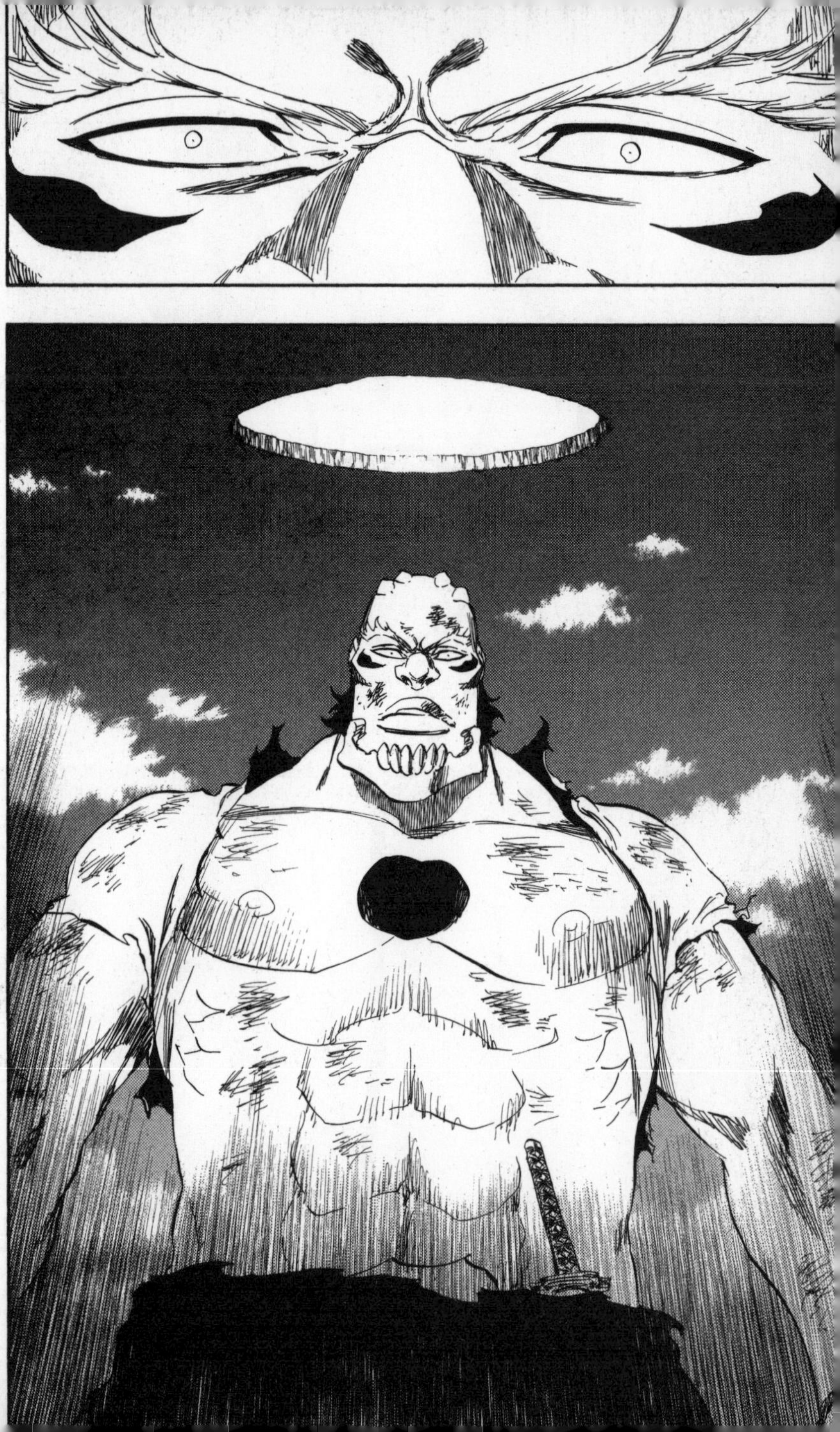

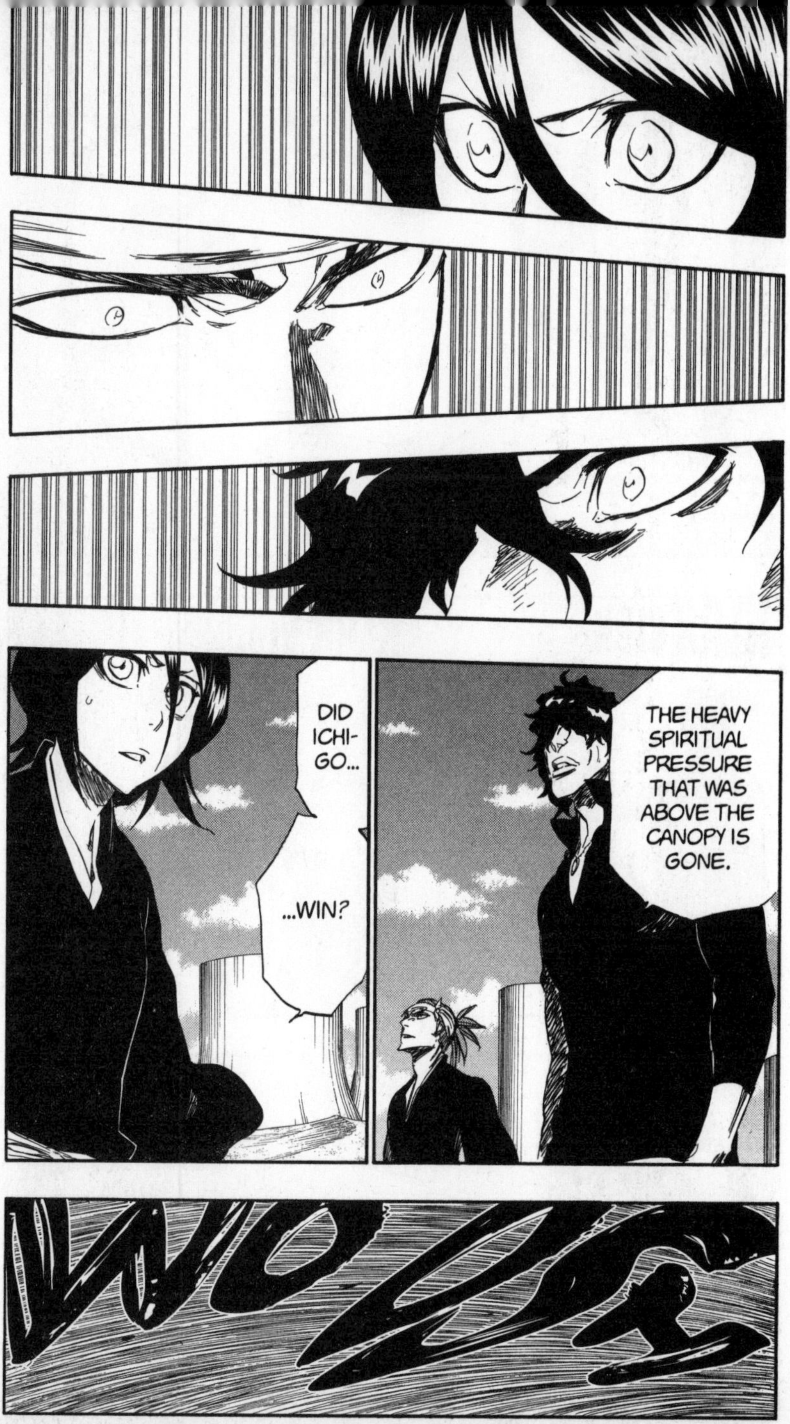
THE HEAVY SPIRITUAL PRESSURE THAT WAS ABOVE THE CANOPY IS GONE.
DID ICHIGO...
...WIN?

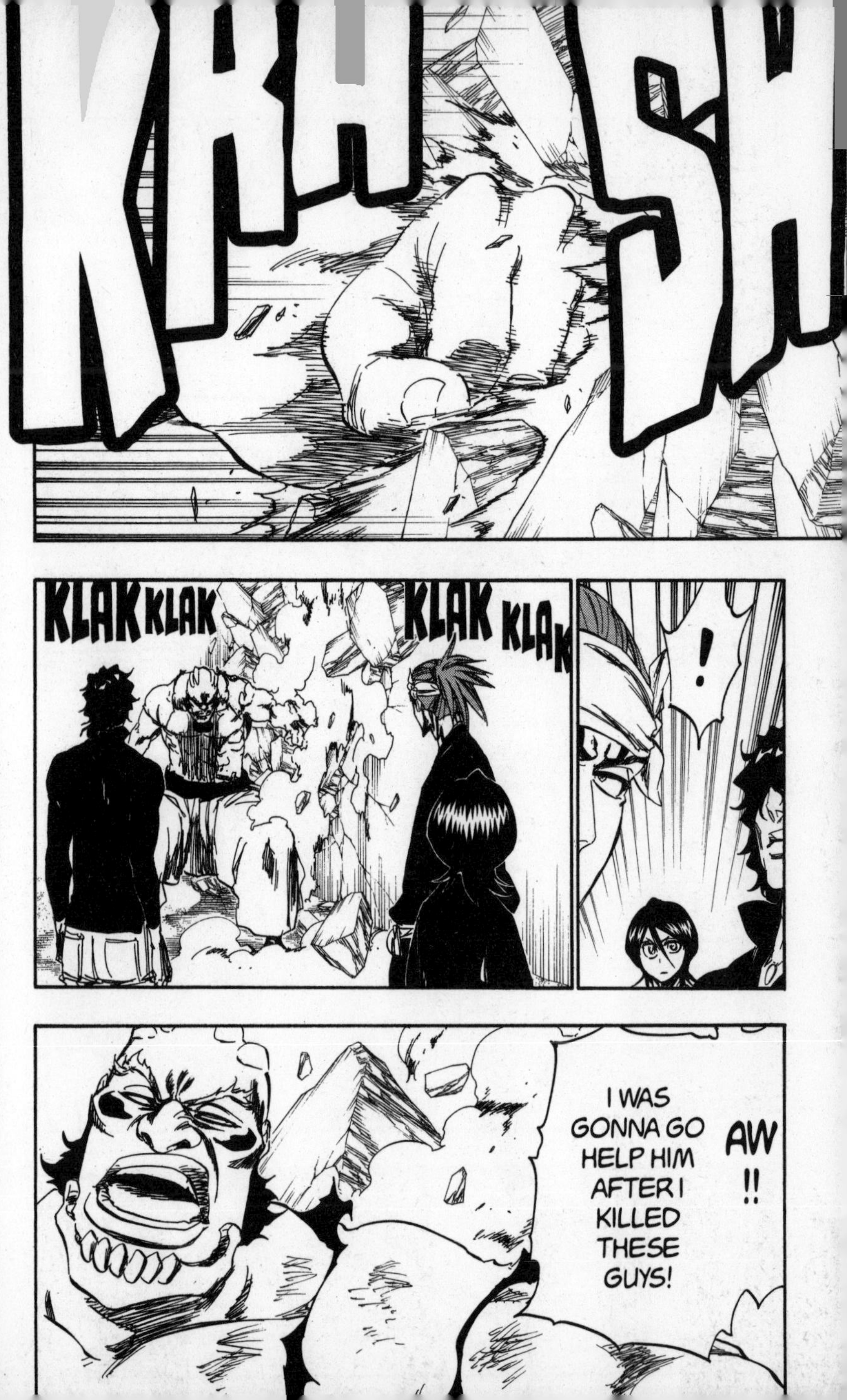
KRASH
!
KLAK KLAK
KLAK KLAK
AW!!
I WAS GONNA GO HELP HIM AFTER I KILLED THESE GUYS!

READ THIS WAY

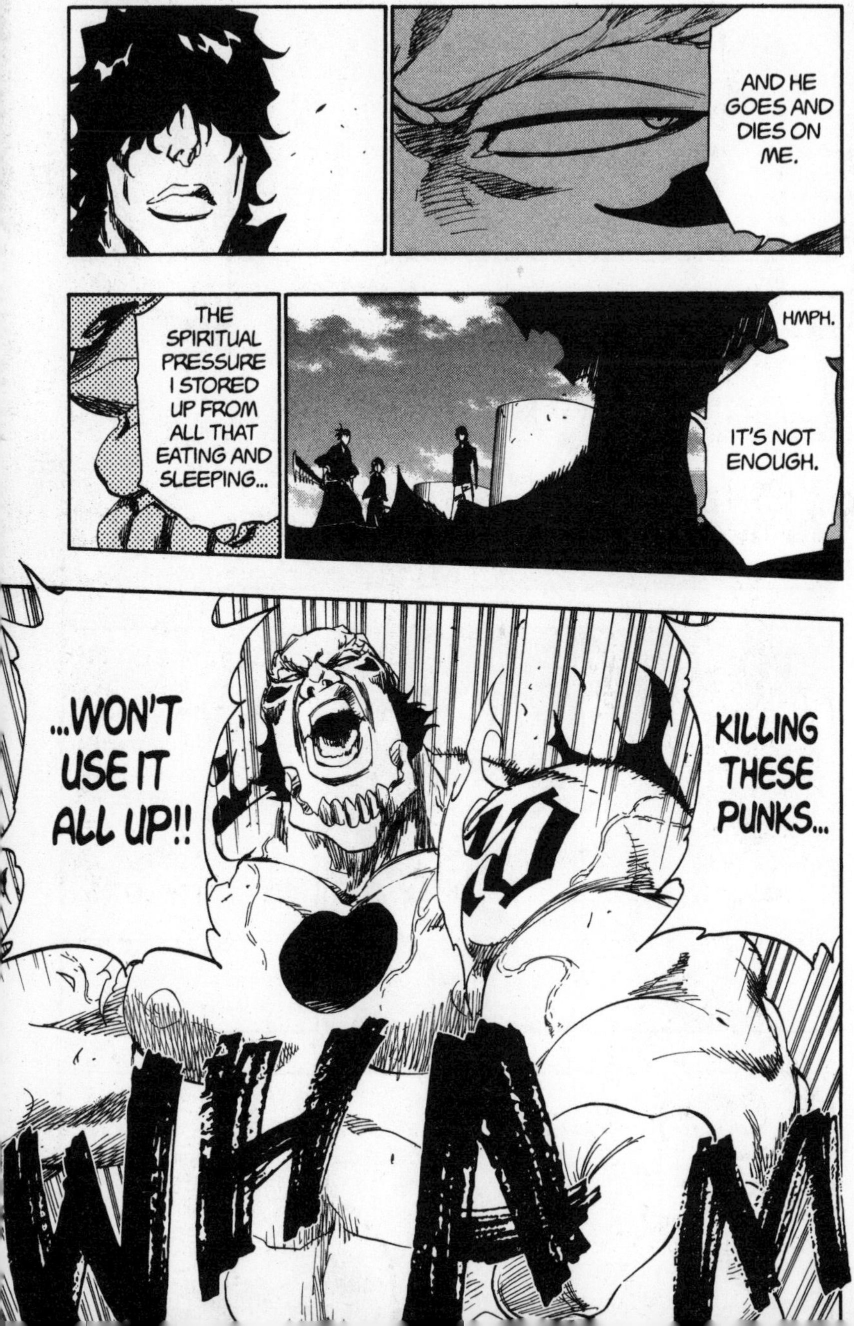
AND HE GOES AND DIES ON ME.
HMPH.
IT'S NOT ENOUGH.
THE SPIRITUAL PRESSURE I STORED UP FROM ALL THAT EATING AND SLEEPING...
KILLING THESE PUNKS...
...WON'T USE IT ALL UP!!
WHAM

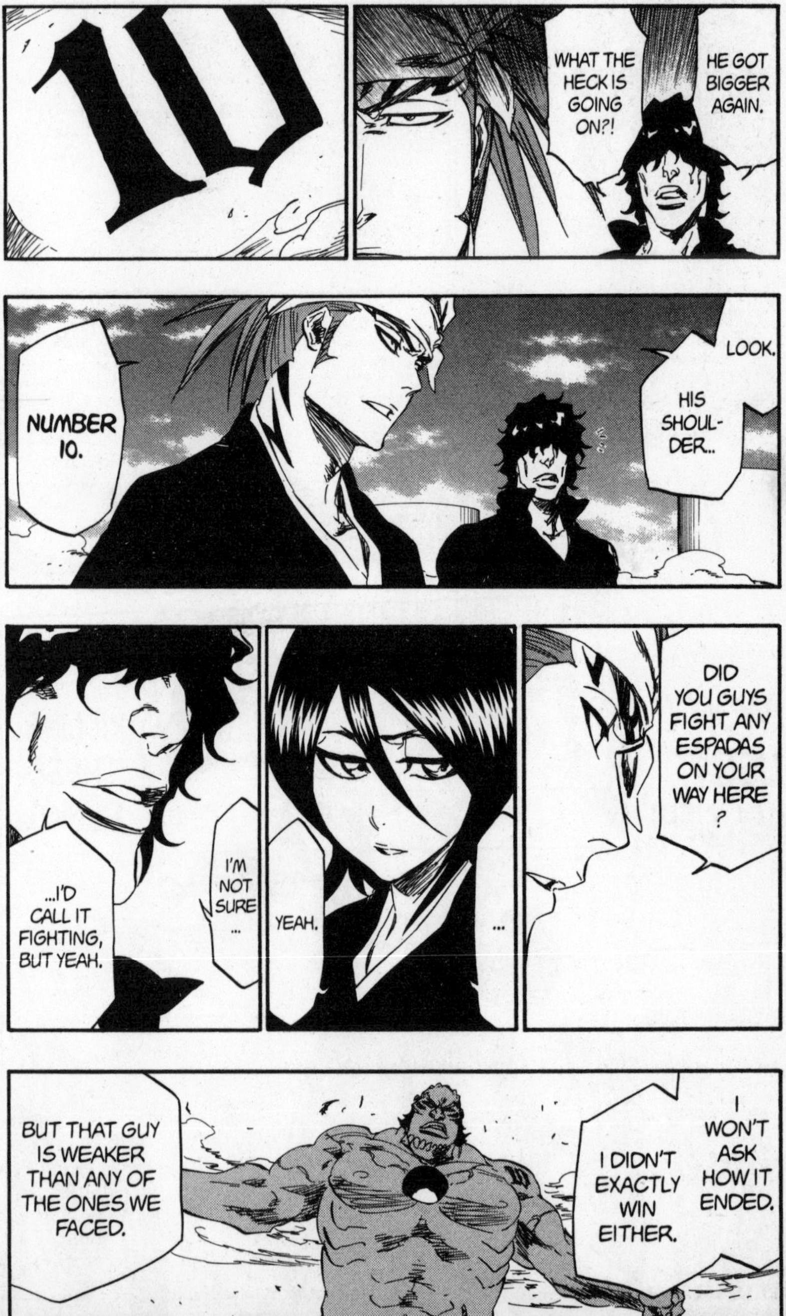
HE GOT BIGGER AGAIN.
WHAT THE HECK IS GOING ON?!
LOOK.
HIS SHOULDER..
NUMBER 10.
DID YOU GUYS FIGHT ANY ESPADAS ON YOUR WAY HERE?
...
YEAH.
I'M NOT SURE...
...I'D CALL IT FIGHTING, BUT YEAH.
I WON'T ASK HOW IT ENDED.
I DIDN'T EXACTLY WIN EITHER.
BUT THAT GUY IS WEAKER THAN ANY OF THE ONES WE FACED.

READ THIS WAY

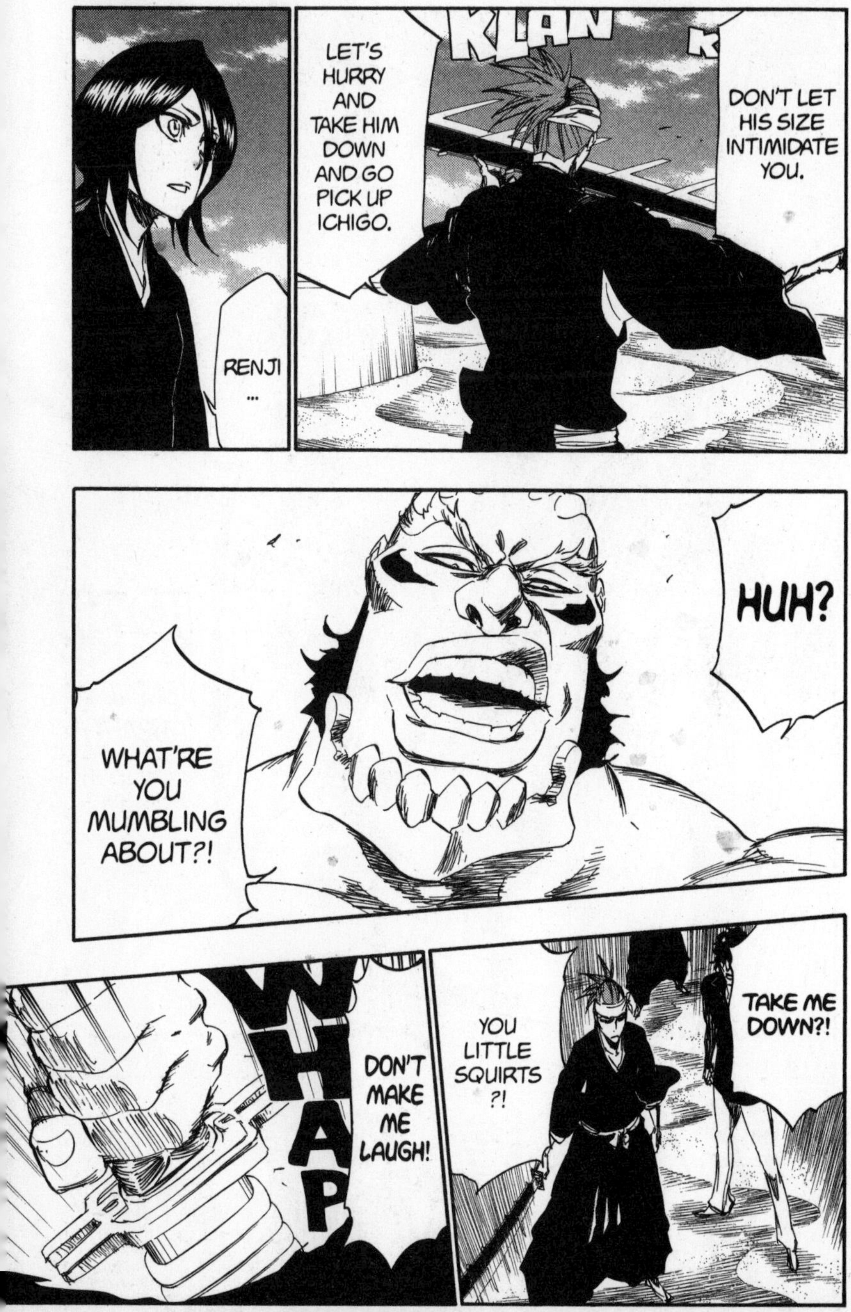
KLAN
K
DON'T LET HIS SIZE INTIMIDATE YOU.
LET'S HURRY AND TAKE HIM DOWN AND GO PICK UP ICHIGO.
RENJI ...
HUH?
WHAT'RE YOU MUMBLING ABOUT?!
TAKE ME DOWN?!
YOU LITTLE SQUIRTS ?!
DON'T MAKE ME LAUGH!
WHAP

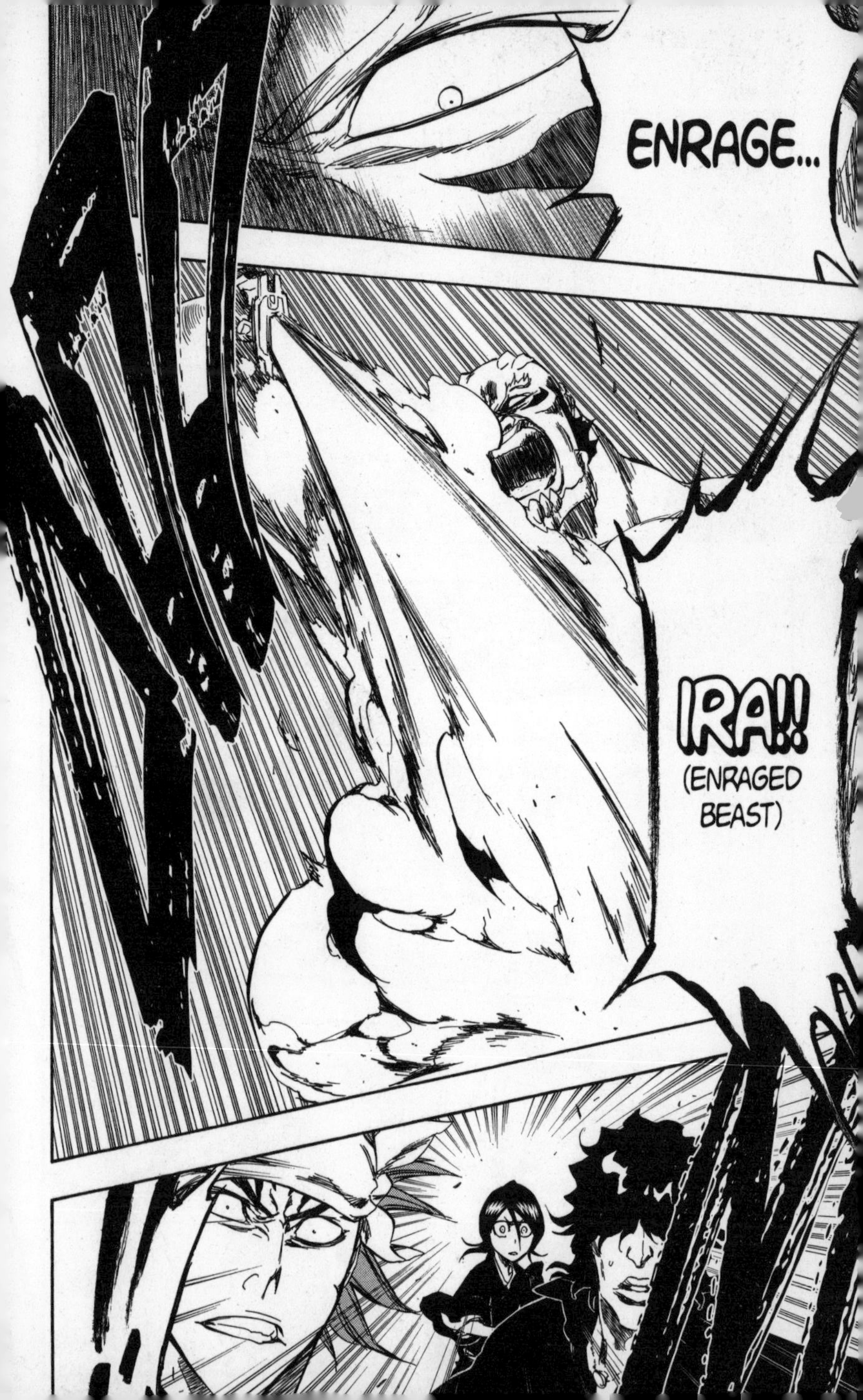
ENRAGE...
IRA!!
(ENRAGED BEAST)

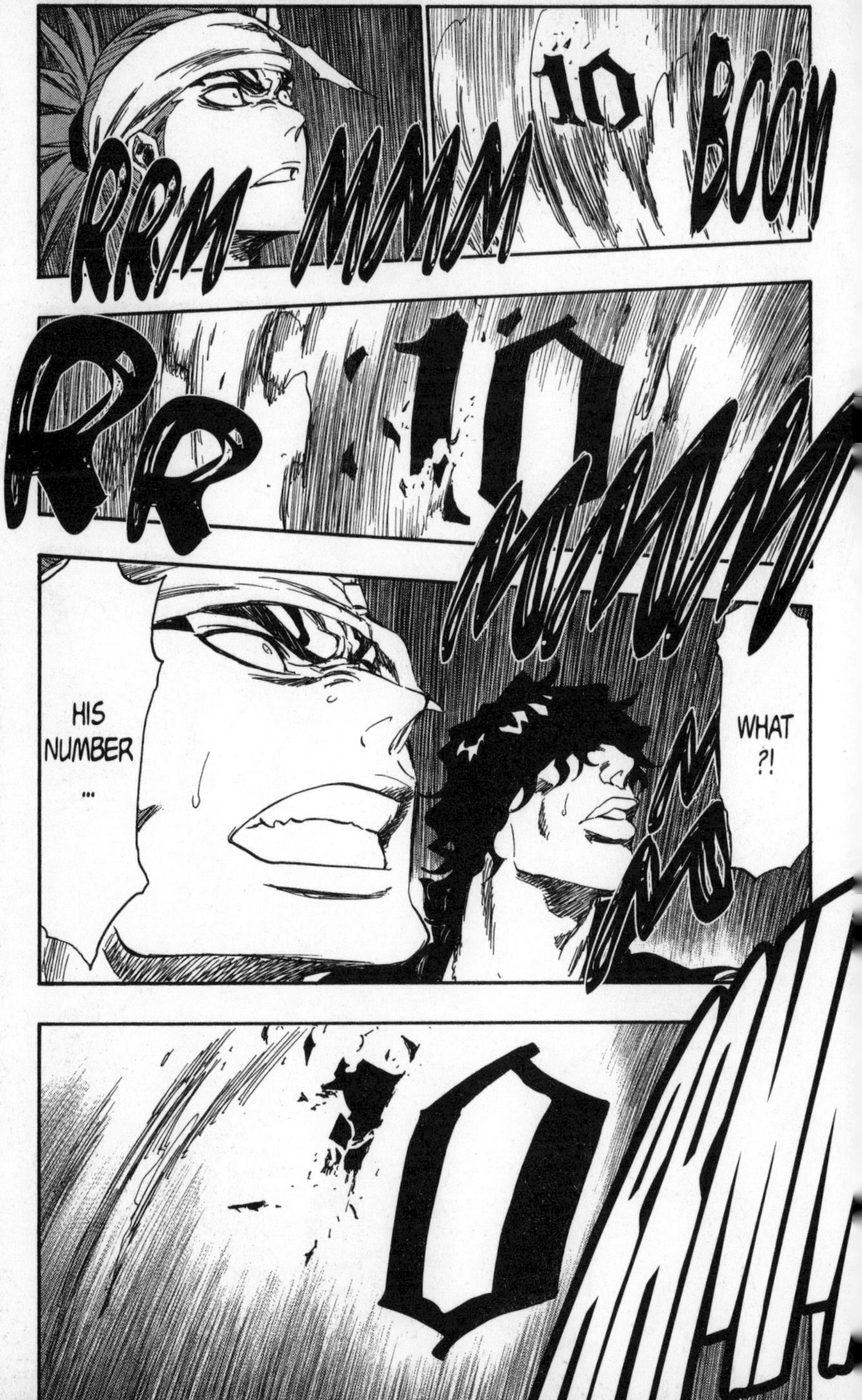
10
BOOM
RRM MMM
RR
10
WHAT ?!
HIS NUMBER ...
0

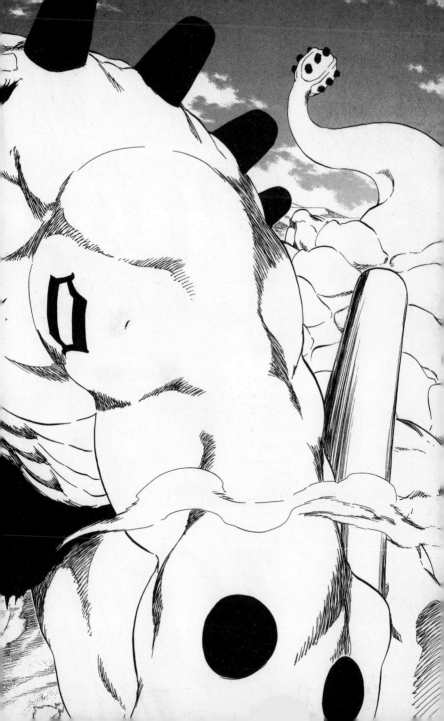

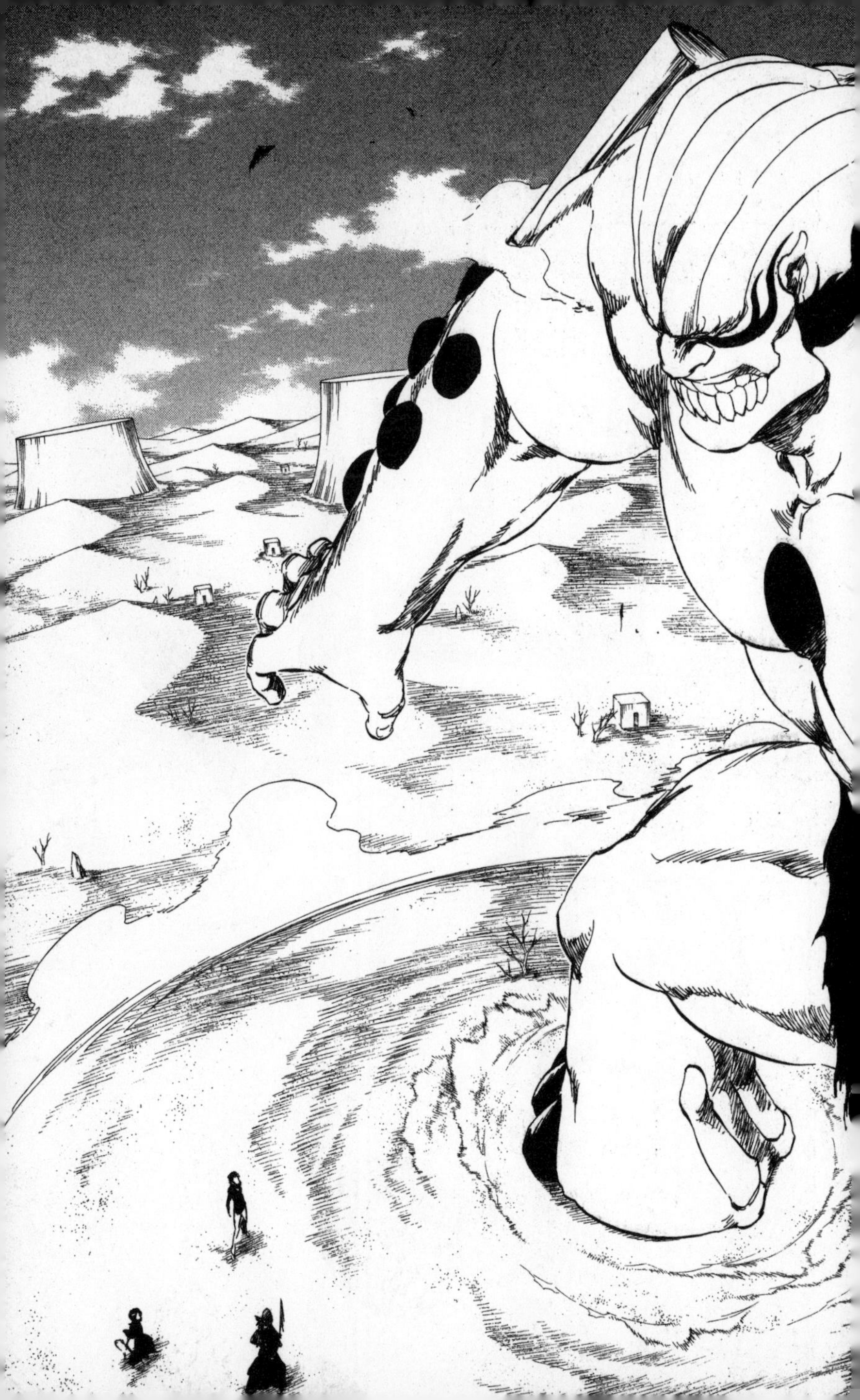

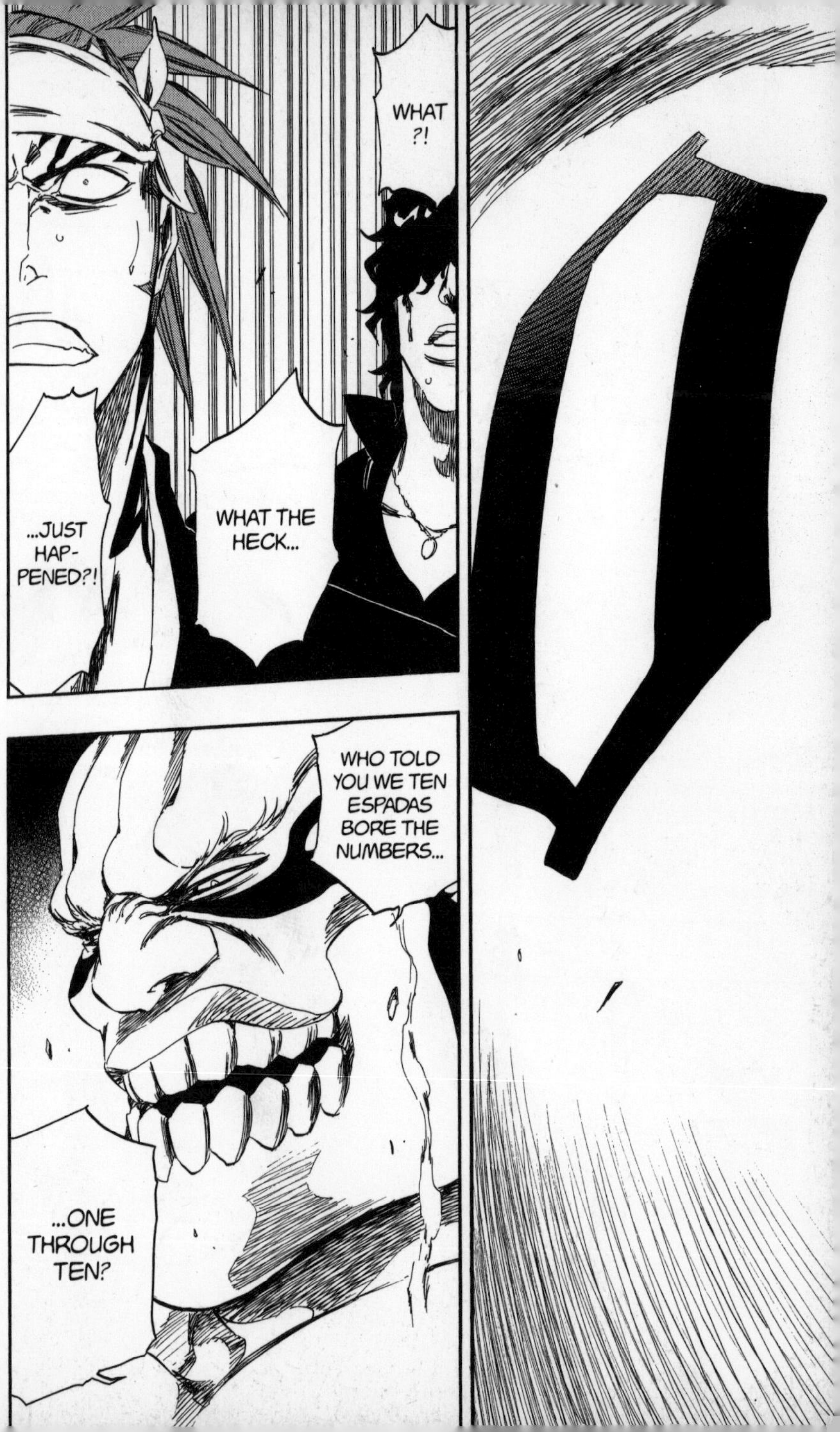
WHAT ?!
WHAT THE HECK...
...JUST HAP- PENED?!
WHO TOLD YOU WE TEN ESPADAS BORE THE NUMBERS...
...ONE THROUGH TEN?

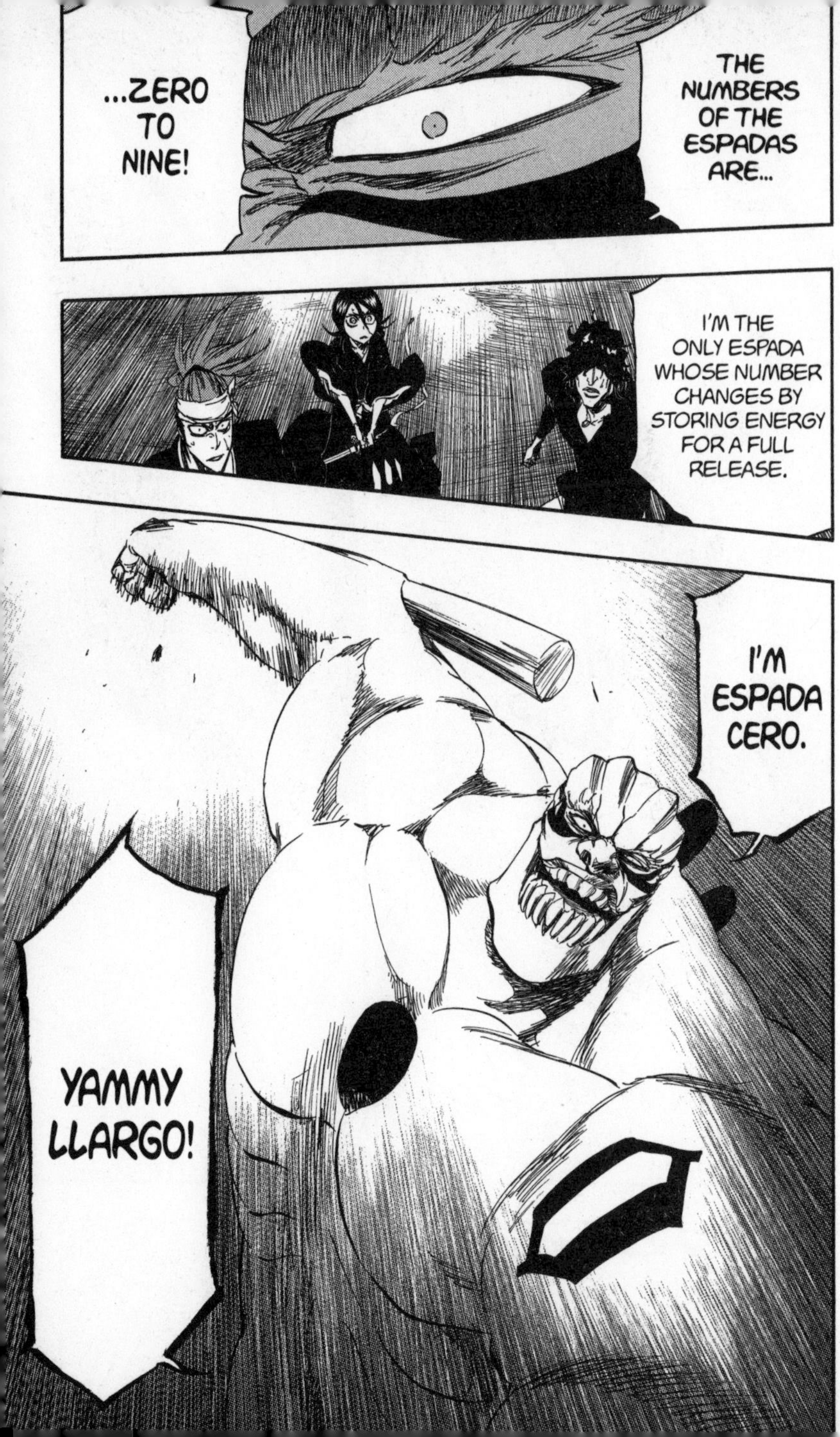
THE NUMBERS OF THE ESPADAS ARE...
...ZERO TO NINE!
I'M THE ONLY ESPADA WHOSE NUMBER CHANGES BY STORING ENERGY FOR A FULL RELEASE.
I'M ESPADA CERO.
YAMMY LLARGO!

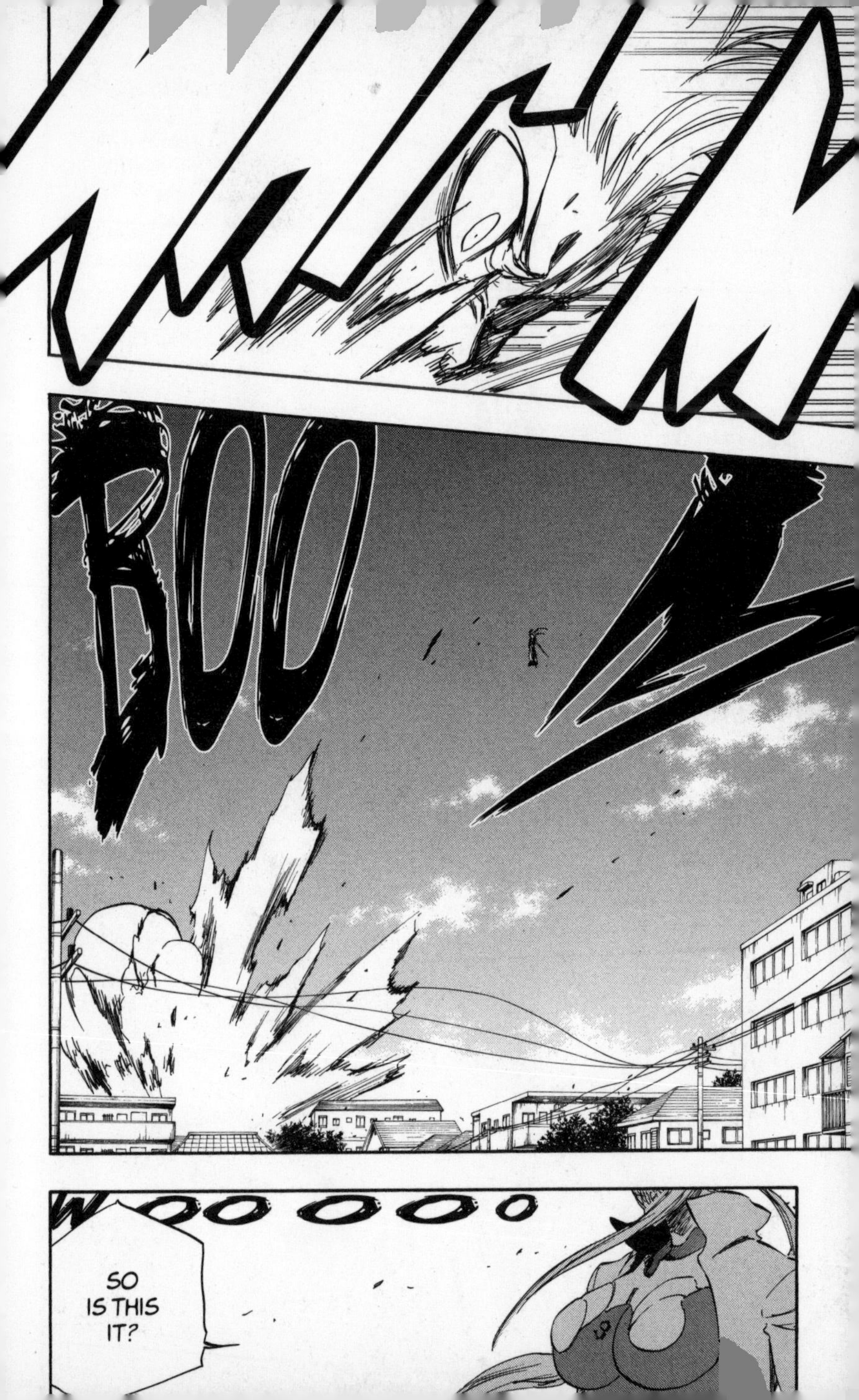

BOOOM
WOOOOOOO
SO IS THIS IT?

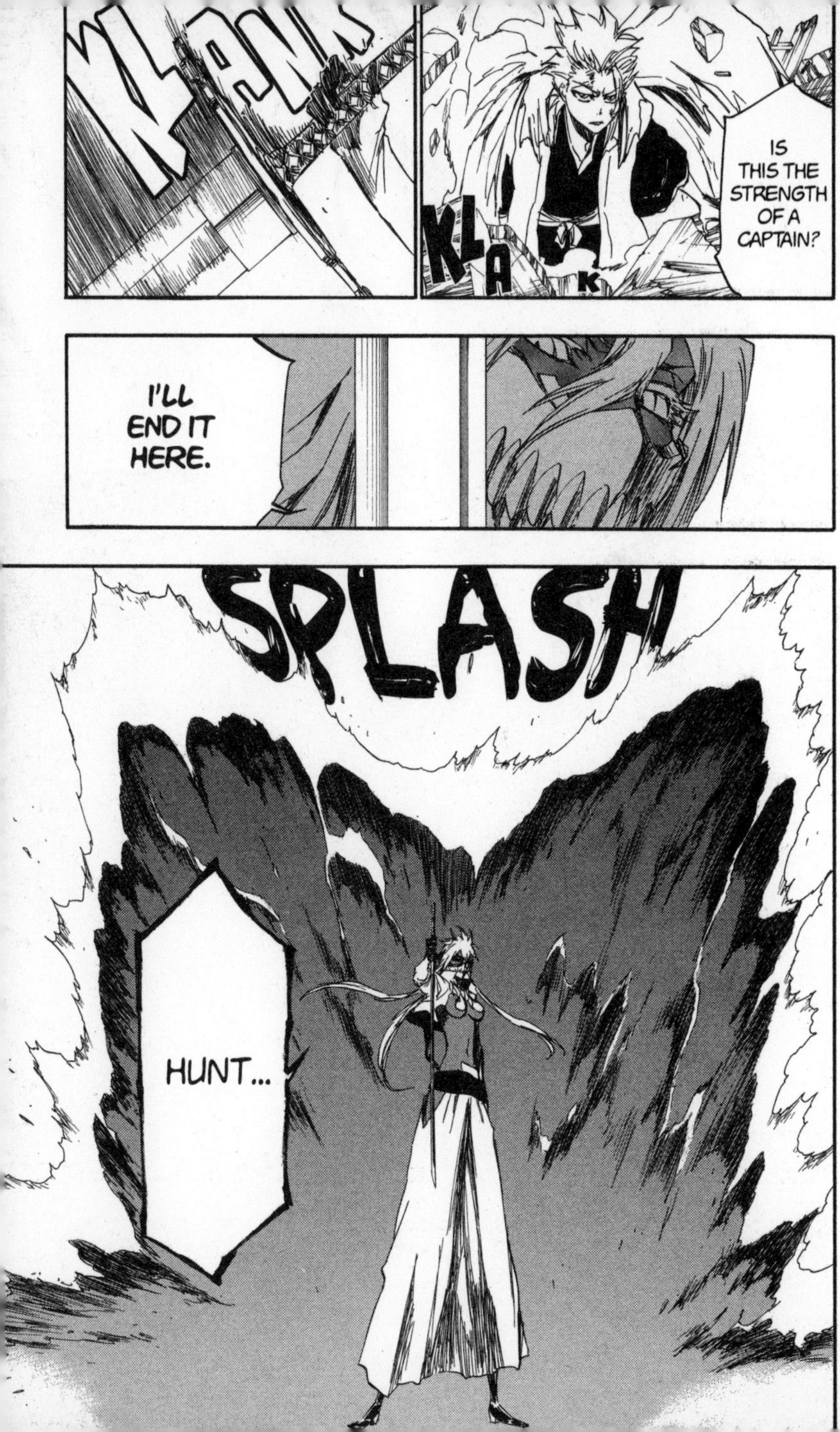
IS THIS THE STRENGTH OF A CAPTAIN?
KLAK
I'LL END IT HERE.
SPLASH
HUNT...

See.

here

it

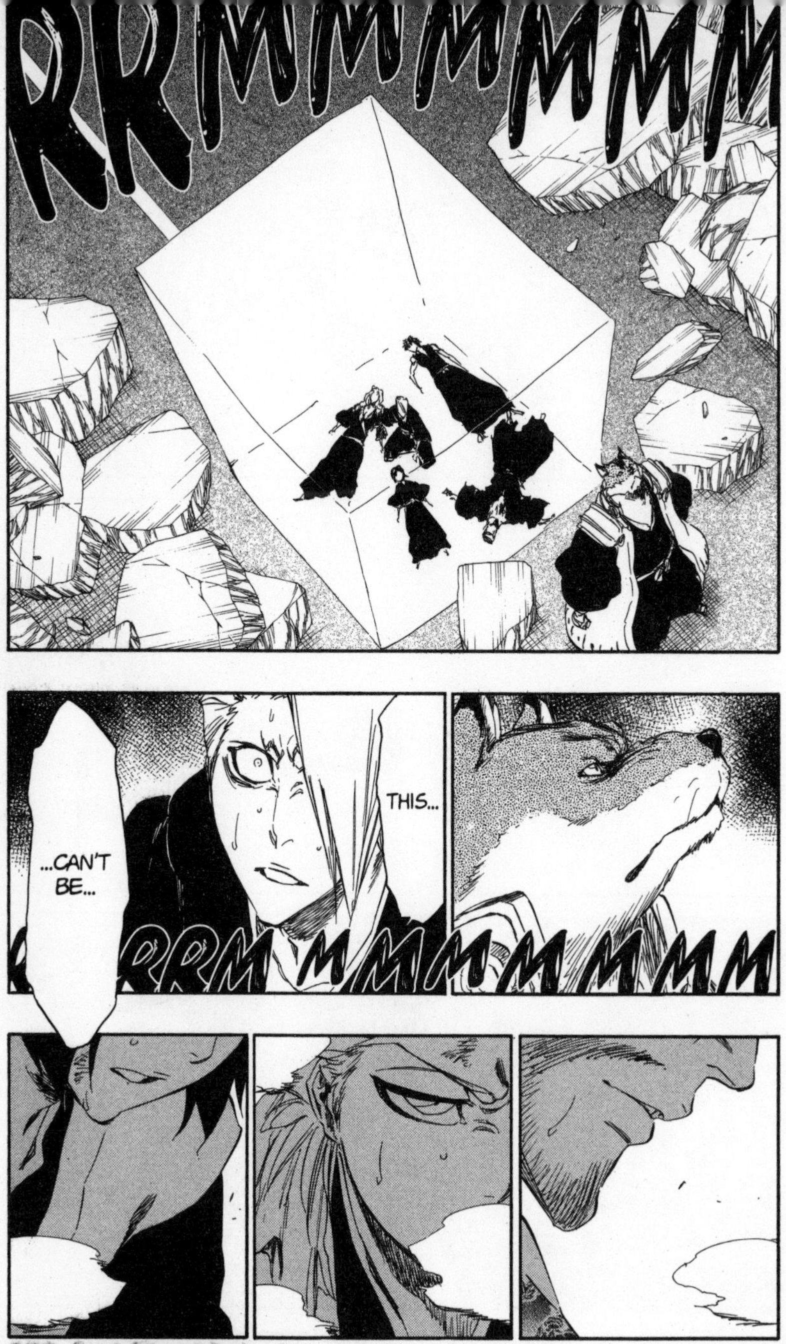
RRMMMMMMM
THIS...
...CAN'T BE...
RRMMMMMMMMMMMM

355. Azul-Blood Splash

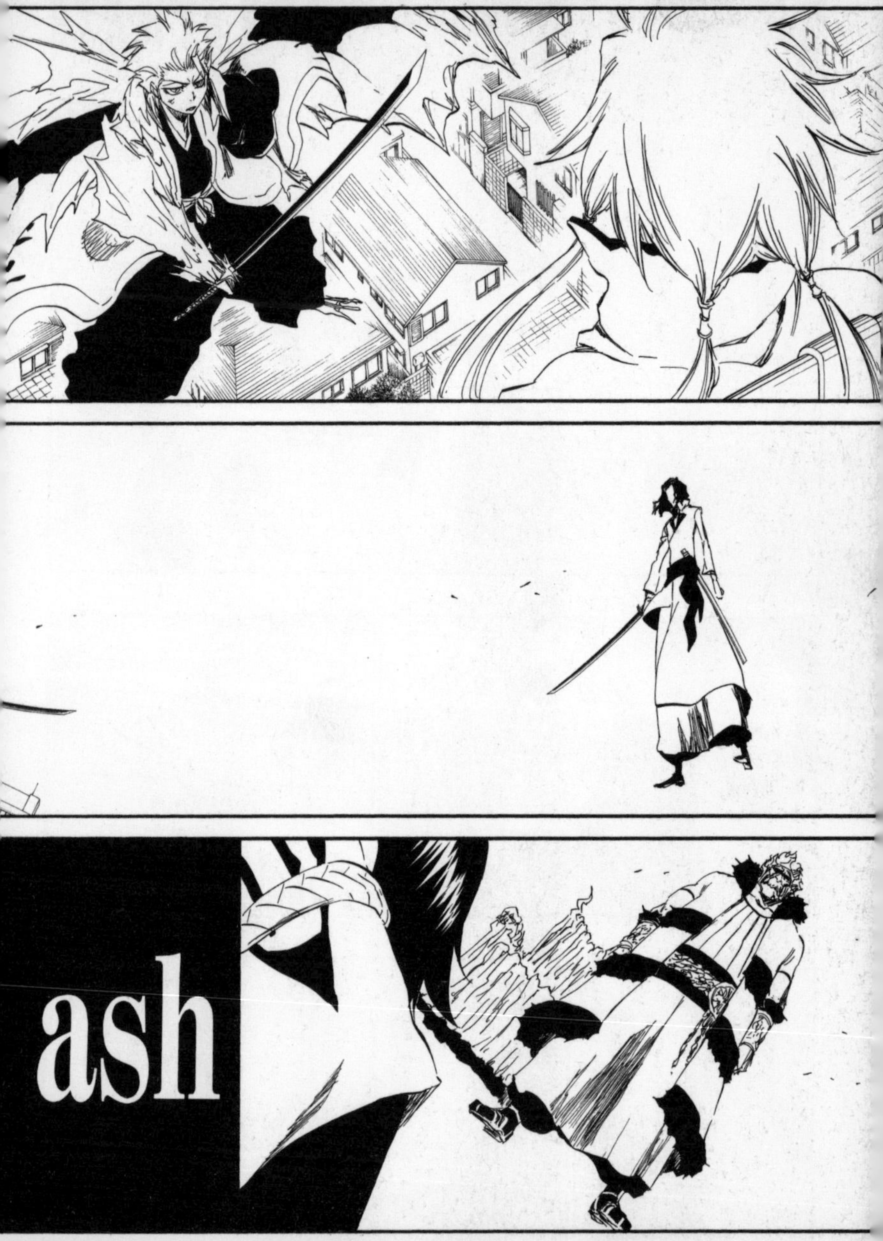
ash

BLEACH

355.

Azul-Blood Spl

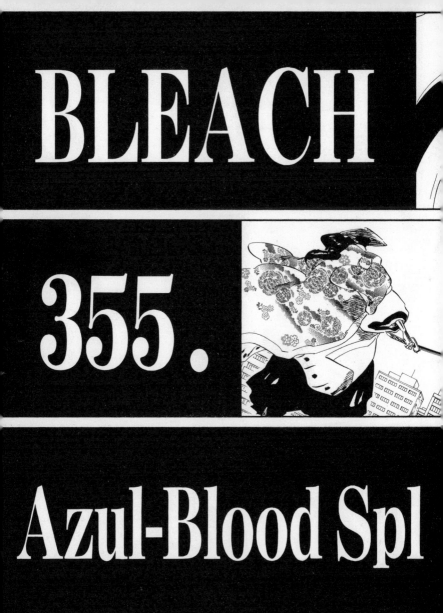

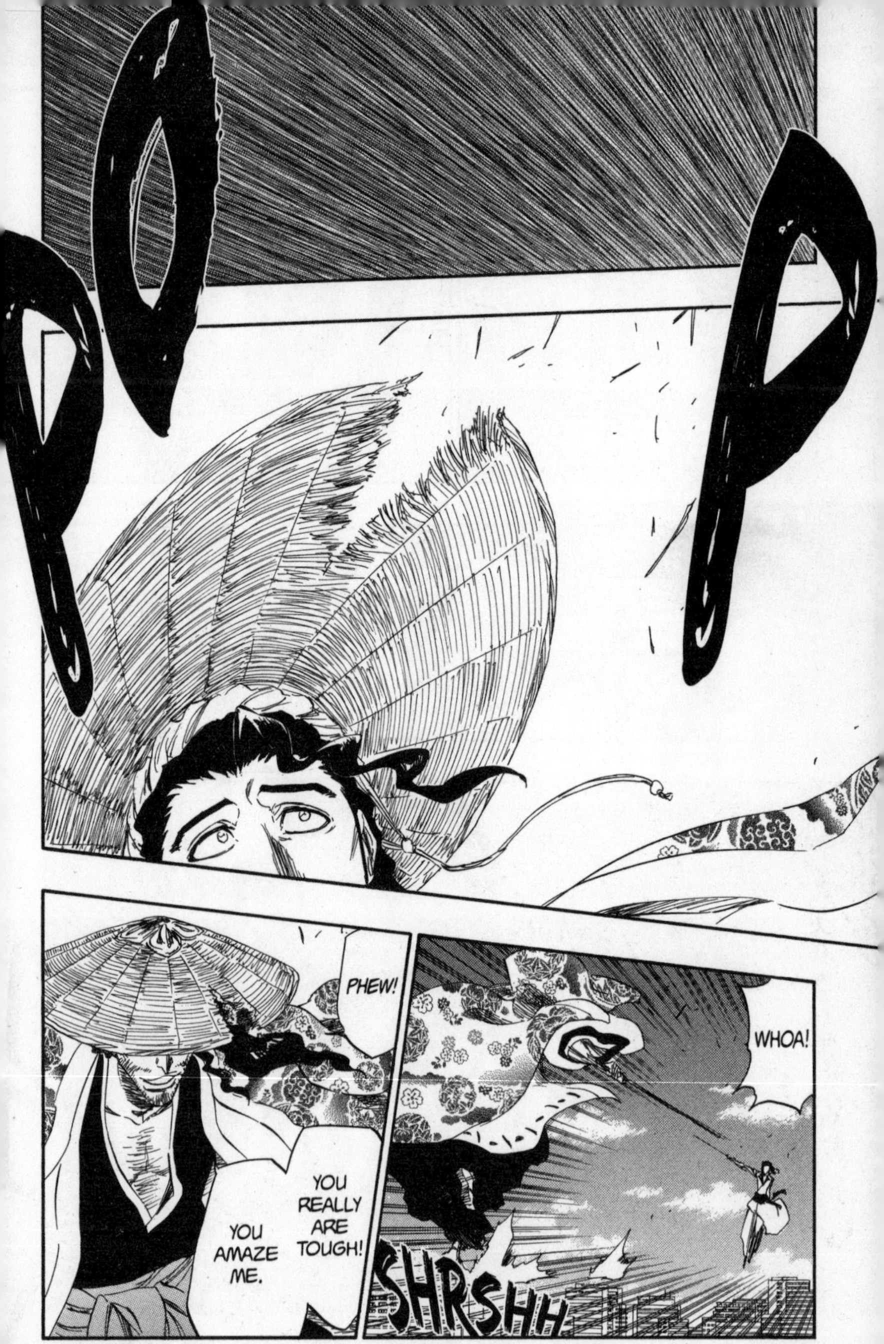
POP
WHOA!
SHRSHH
PHEW!
YOU REALLY ARE TOUGH!
YOU AMAZE ME.

READ THIS WAY

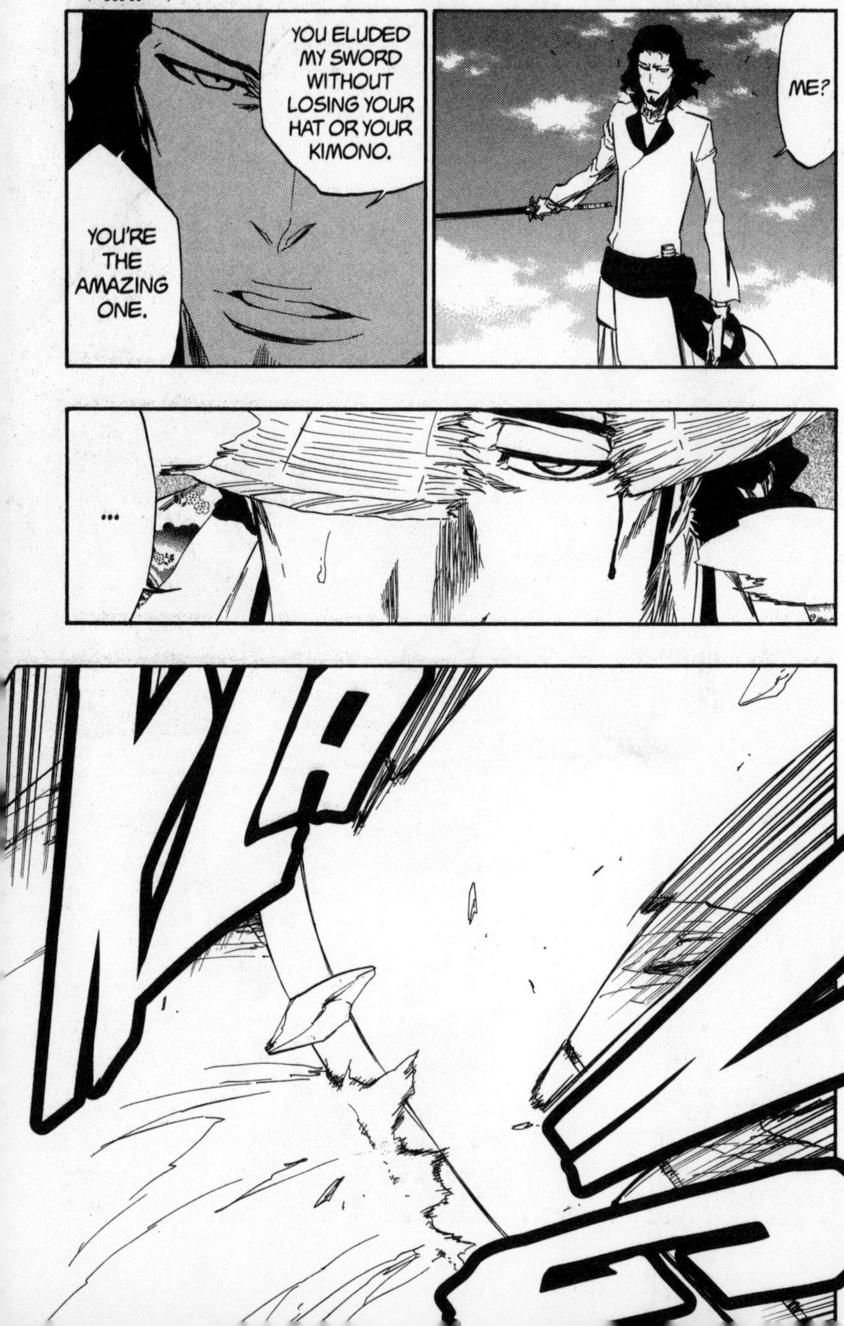
ME?
YOU ELUDED MY SWORD WITHOUT LOSING YOUR HAT OR YOUR KIMONO.
YOU'RE THE AMAZING ONE.
...

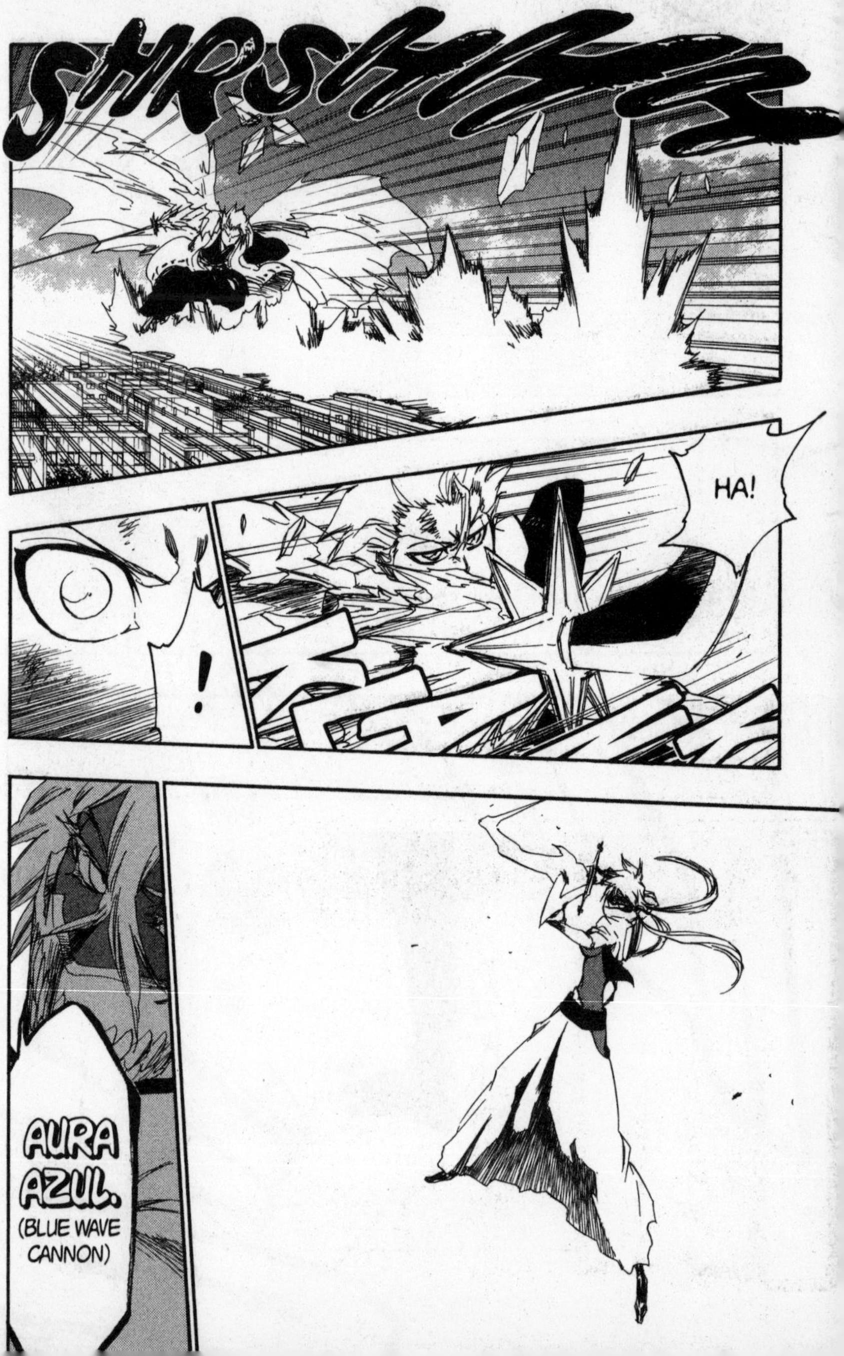
HA!
!
AURA AZUL.
(BLUE WAVE CANNON)

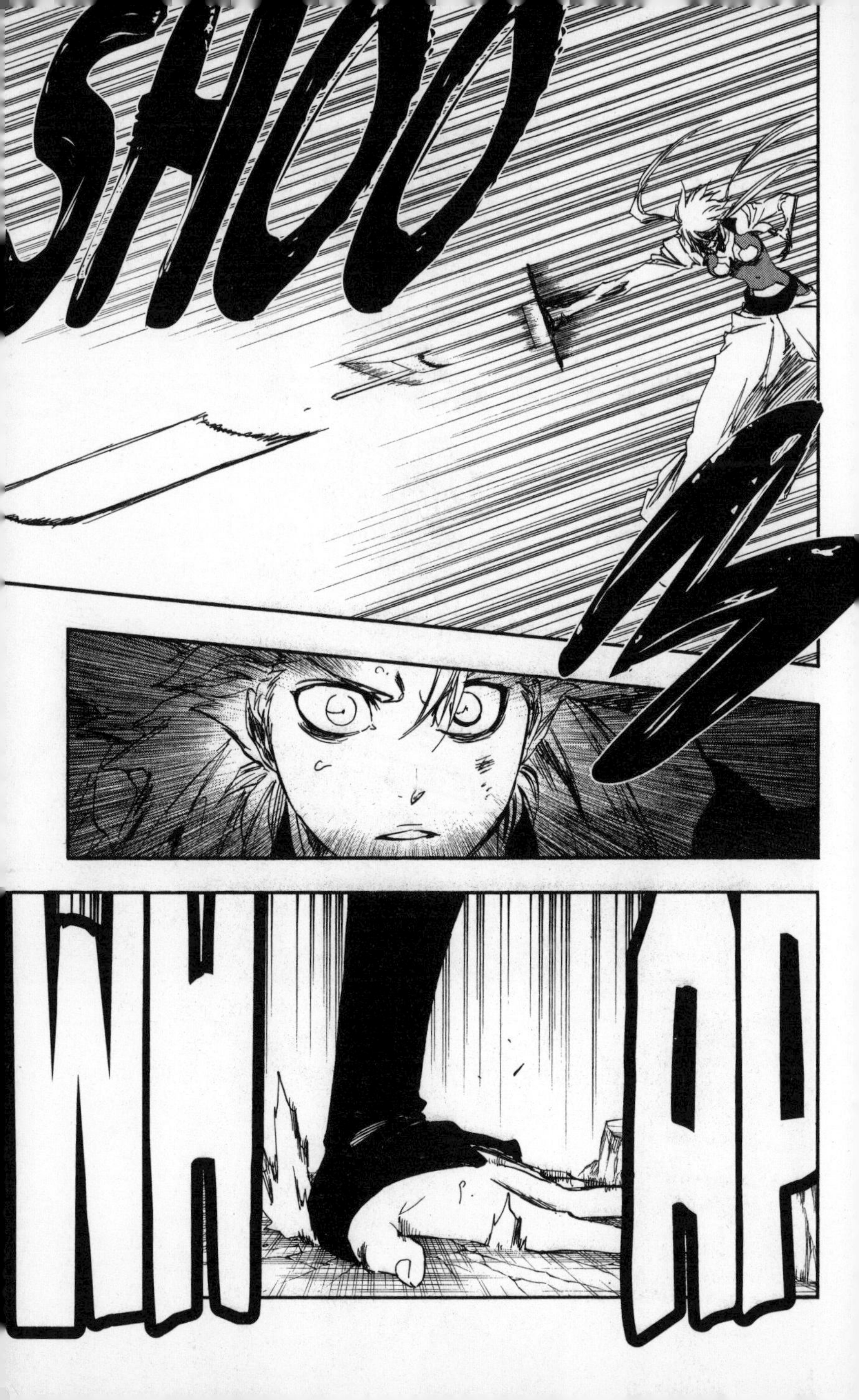
SHOO
SS
WHAP

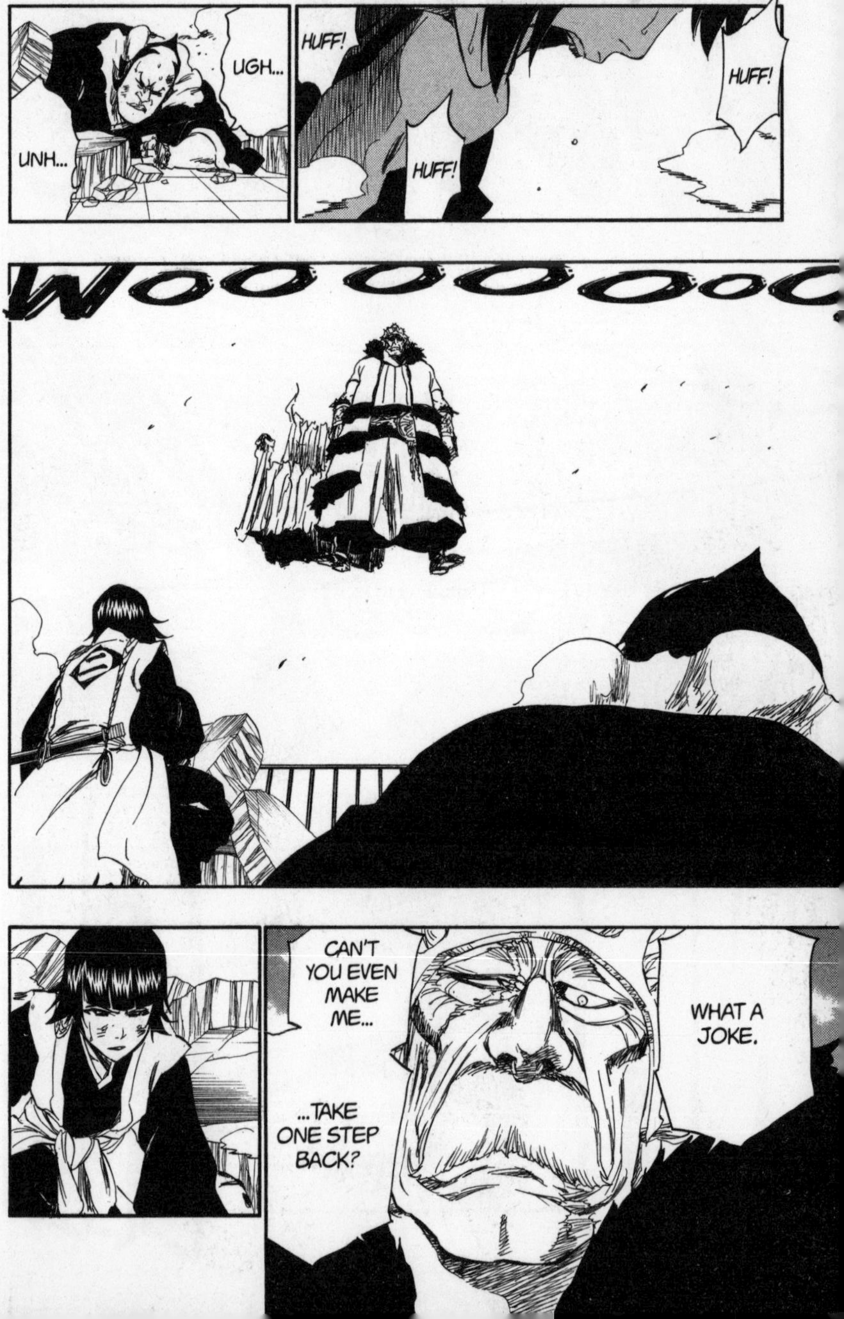
HUFF!
HUFF!
HUFF!
UGH...
UNH...
WOOOOOOO
CAN'T YOU EVEN MAKE ME...
...TAKE ONE STEP BACK?
WHAT A JOKE.

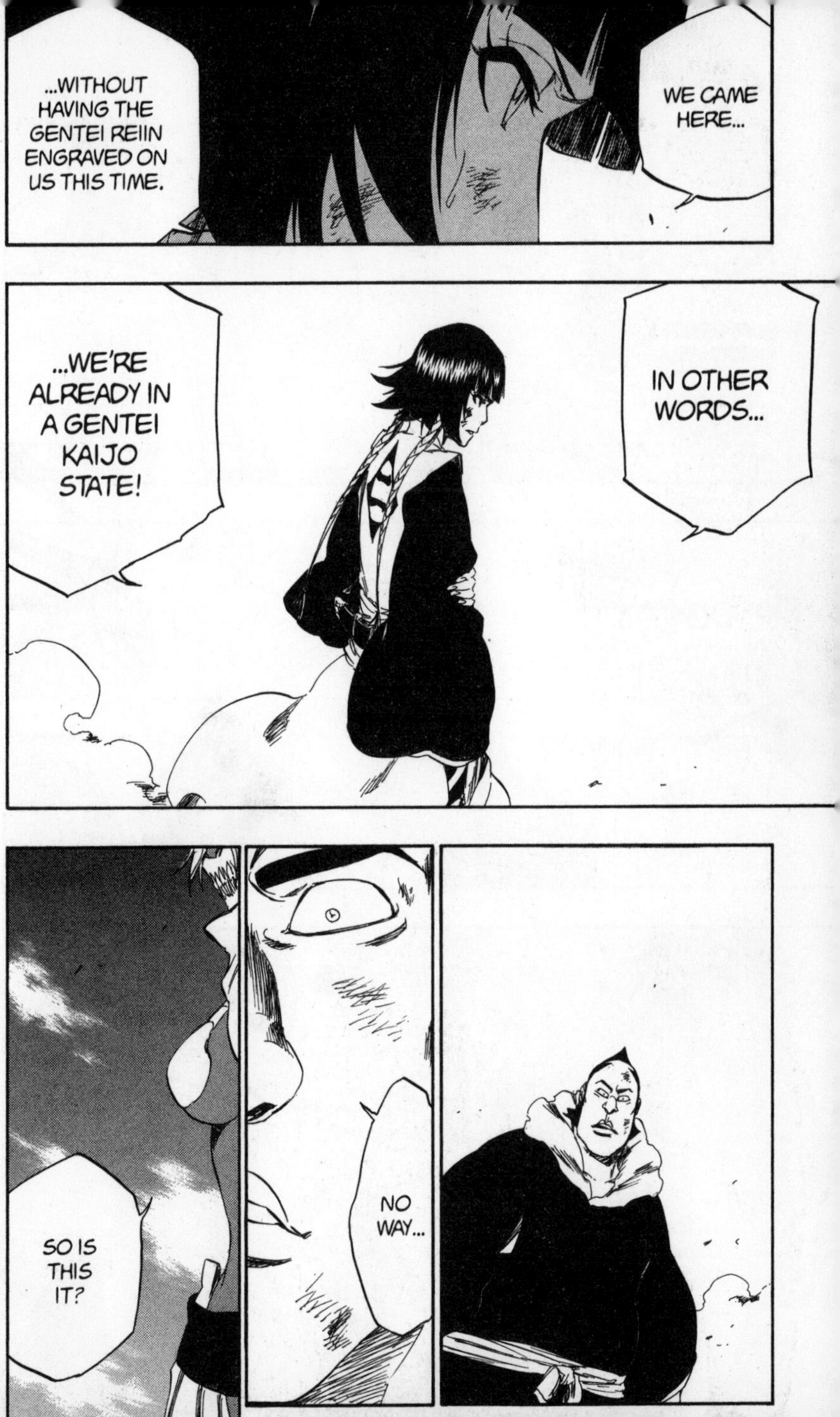
WE CAME HERE...
...WITHOUT HAVING THE GENTEI REIIN ENGRAVED ON US THIS TIME.
IN OTHER WORDS...
...WE'RE ALREADY IN A GENTEI KAIJO STATE!
NO WAY...
SO IS THIS IT?

READ THIS WAY

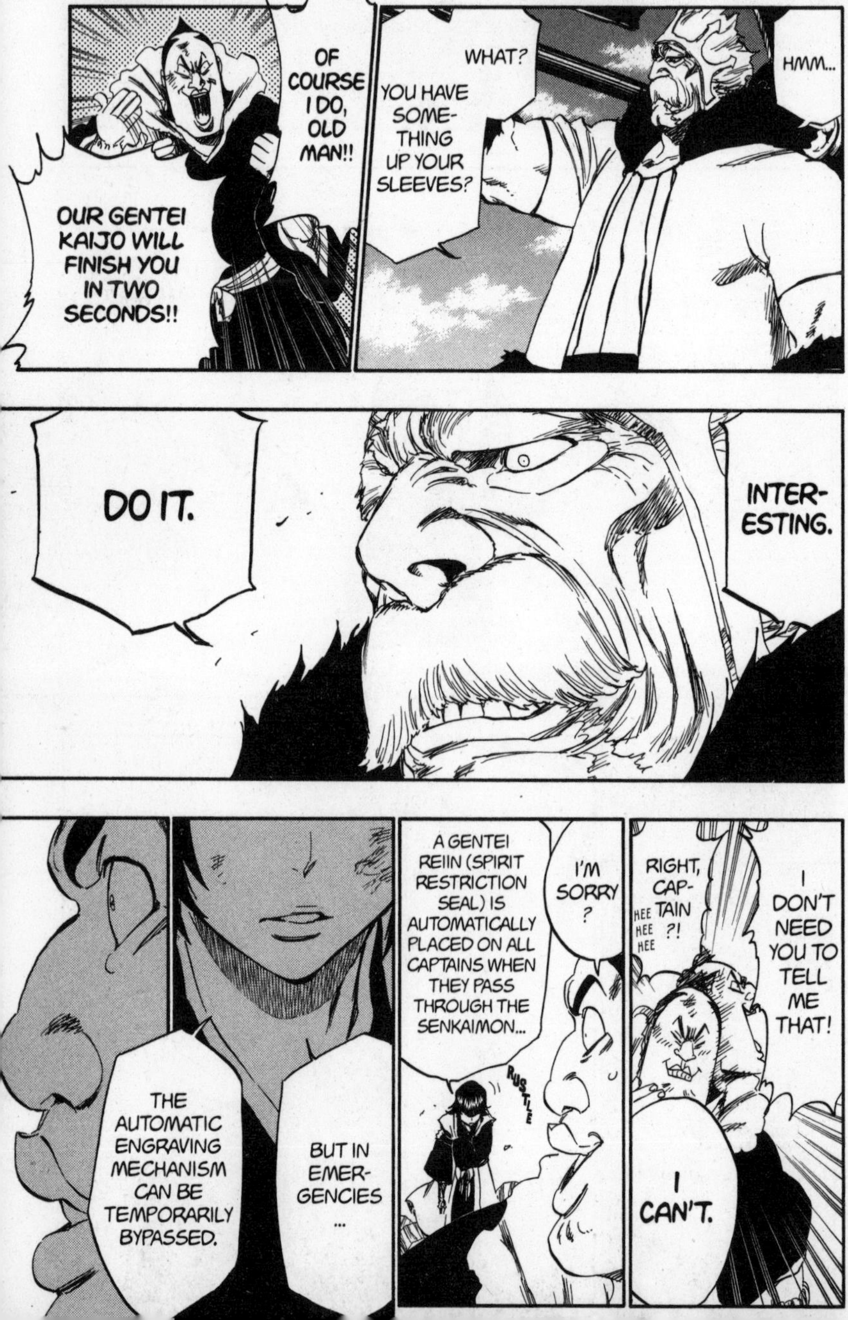
HMM...
WHAT?
YOU HAVE SOME-THING UP YOUR SLEEVES?
OF COURSE I DO, OLD MAN!!
OUR GENTEI KAIJO WILL FINISH YOU IN TWO SECONDS!!
INTER-ESTING.
DO IT.
I DON'T NEED YOU TO TELL ME THAT!
RIGHT, CAP-TAIN ?!
HEE HEE HEE
I CAN'T.
I'M SORRY ?
A GENTEI REIIN (SPIRIT RESTRICTION SEAL) IS AUTOMATICALLY PLACED ON ALL CAPTAINS WHEN THEY PASS THROUGH THE SENKAIMON...
RUSTLE
BUT IN EMER-GENCIES ...
THE AUTOMATIC ENGRAVING MECHANISM CAN BE TEMPORARILY BYPASSED.

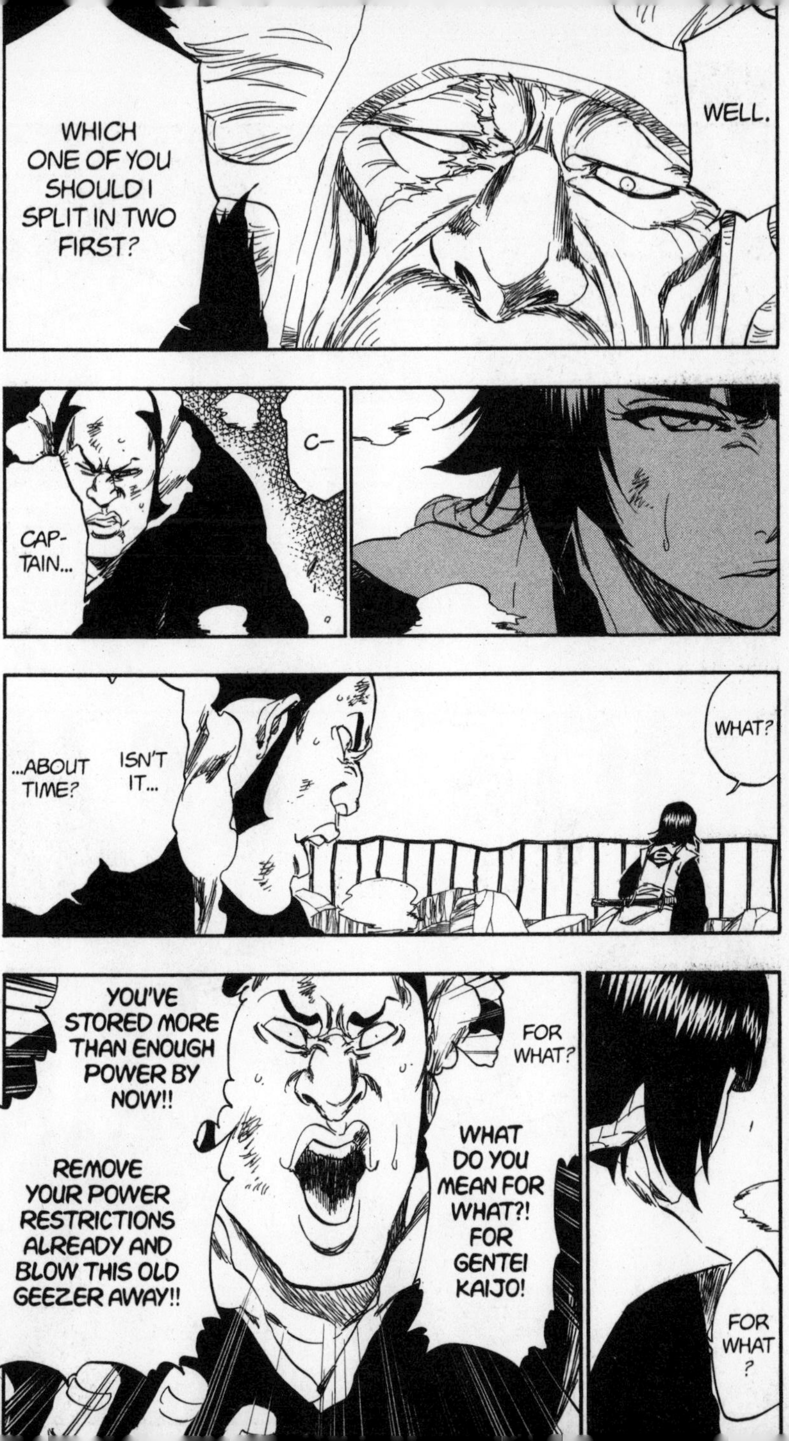
WELL.
WHICH ONE OF YOU SHOULD I SPLIT IN TWO FIRST?
C-
CAP-TAIN...
WHAT?
ISN'T IT...
...ABOUT TIME?
FOR WHAT?
FOR WHAT?
WHAT DO YOU MEAN FOR WHAT?! FOR GENTEI KAIJO!
YOU'VE STORED MORE THAN ENOUGH POWER BY NOW!!
REMOVE YOUR POWER RESTRICTIONS ALREADY AND BLOW THIS OLD GEEZER AWAY!!

READ THIS WAY

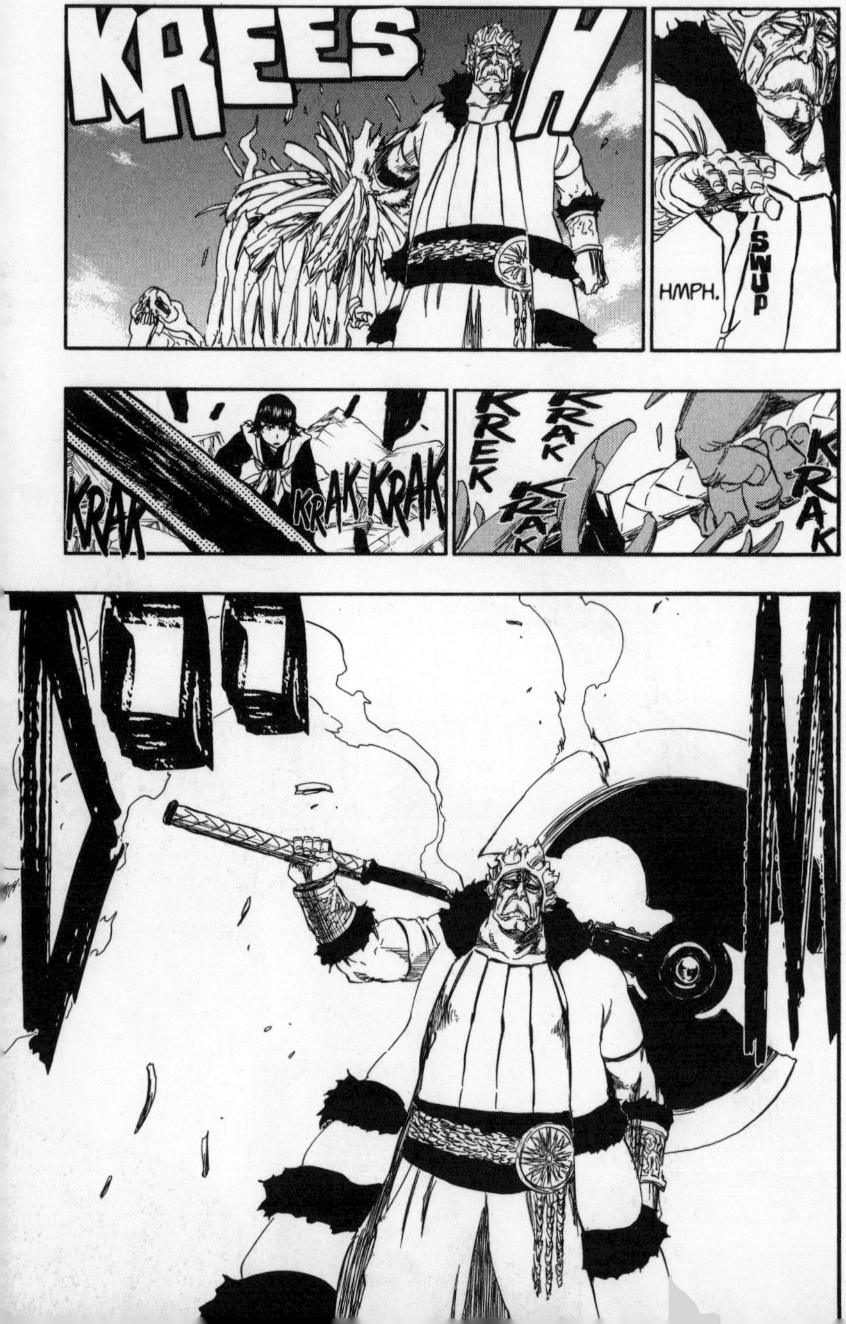
HMPH.
SWUP
KREESH
KRAK
KREK
KRAK
KRAK
KRAK
KRAK
KRAK
KRAK

READ THIS WAY

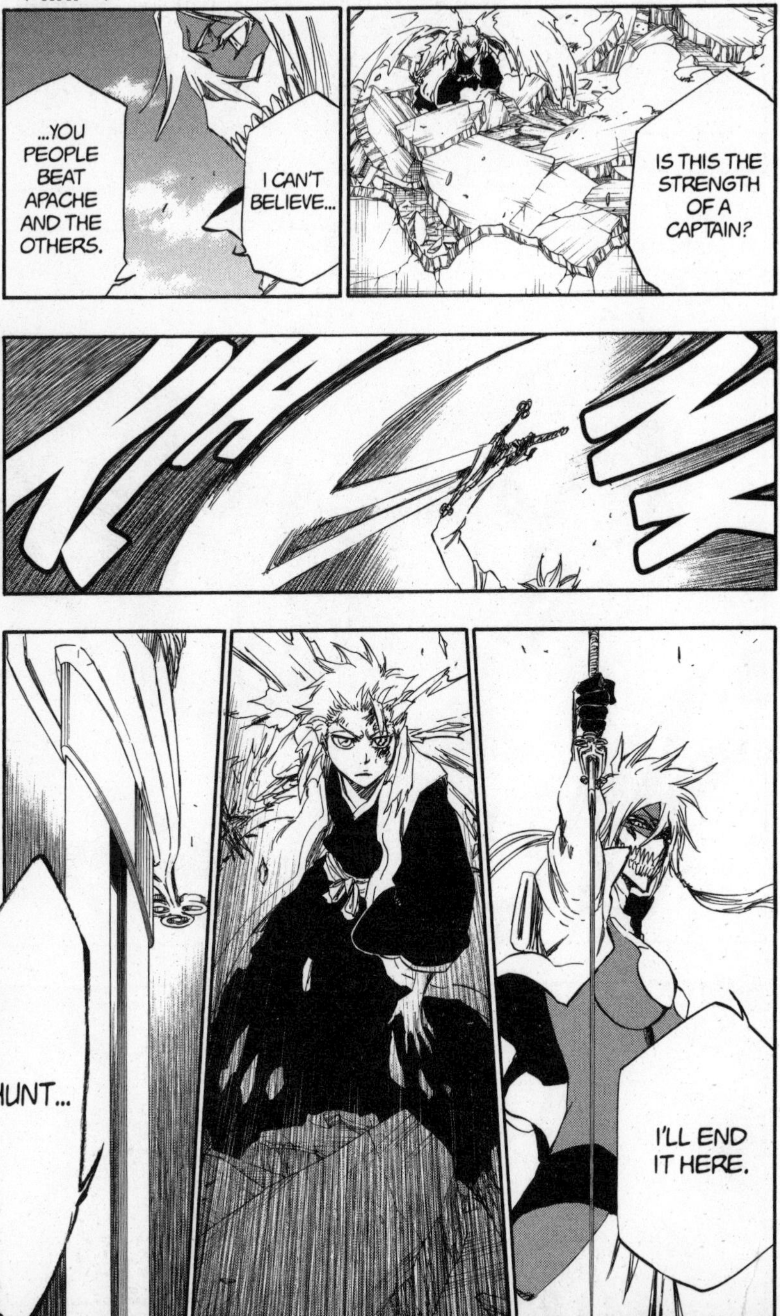
IS THIS THE STRENGTH OF A CAPTAIN?
I CAN'T BELIEVE...
...YOU PEOPLE BEAT APACHE AND THE OTHERS.
I'LL END IT HERE.
HUNT...

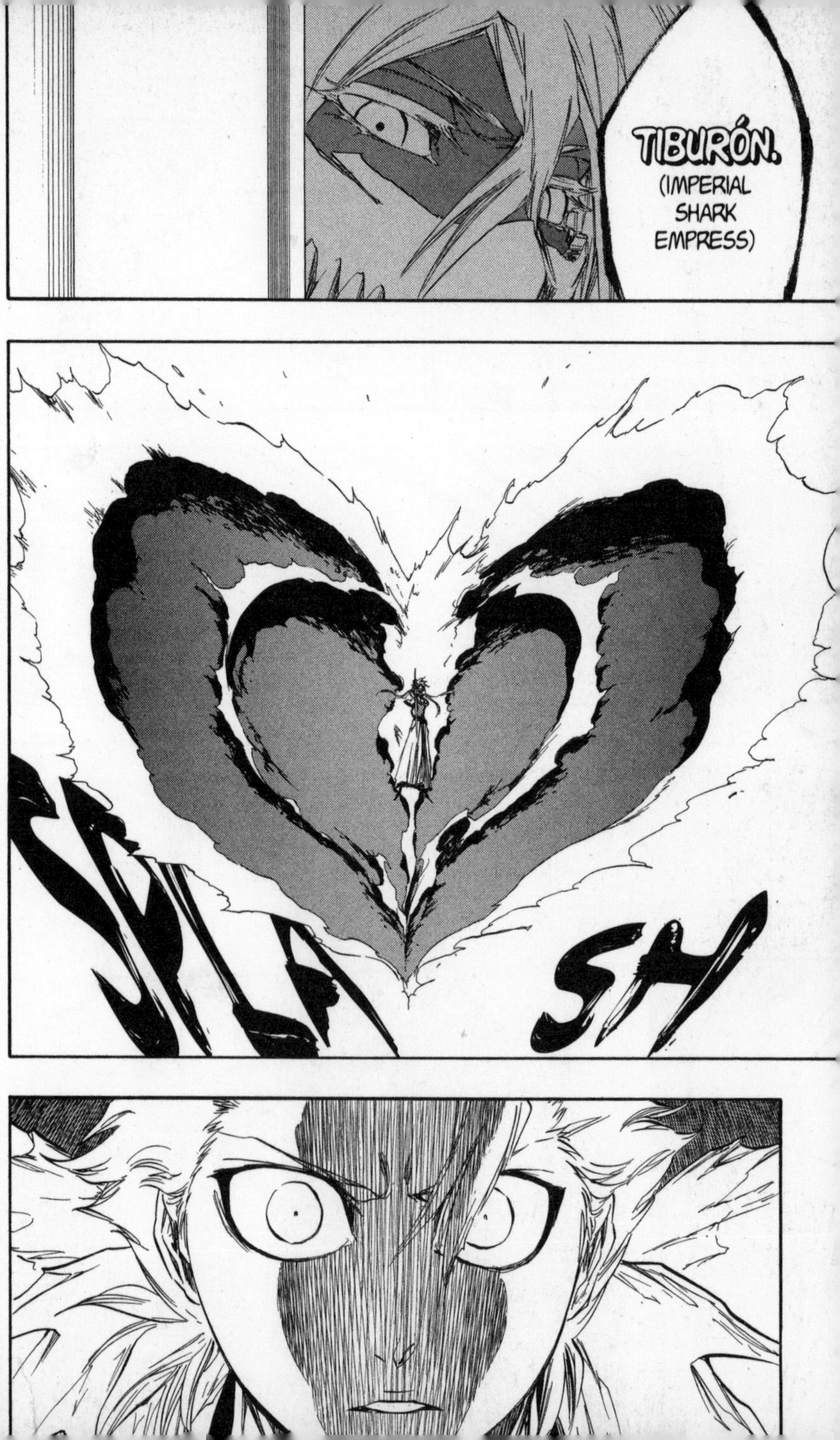
TIBURÓN.
(IMPERIAL SHARK EMPRESS)

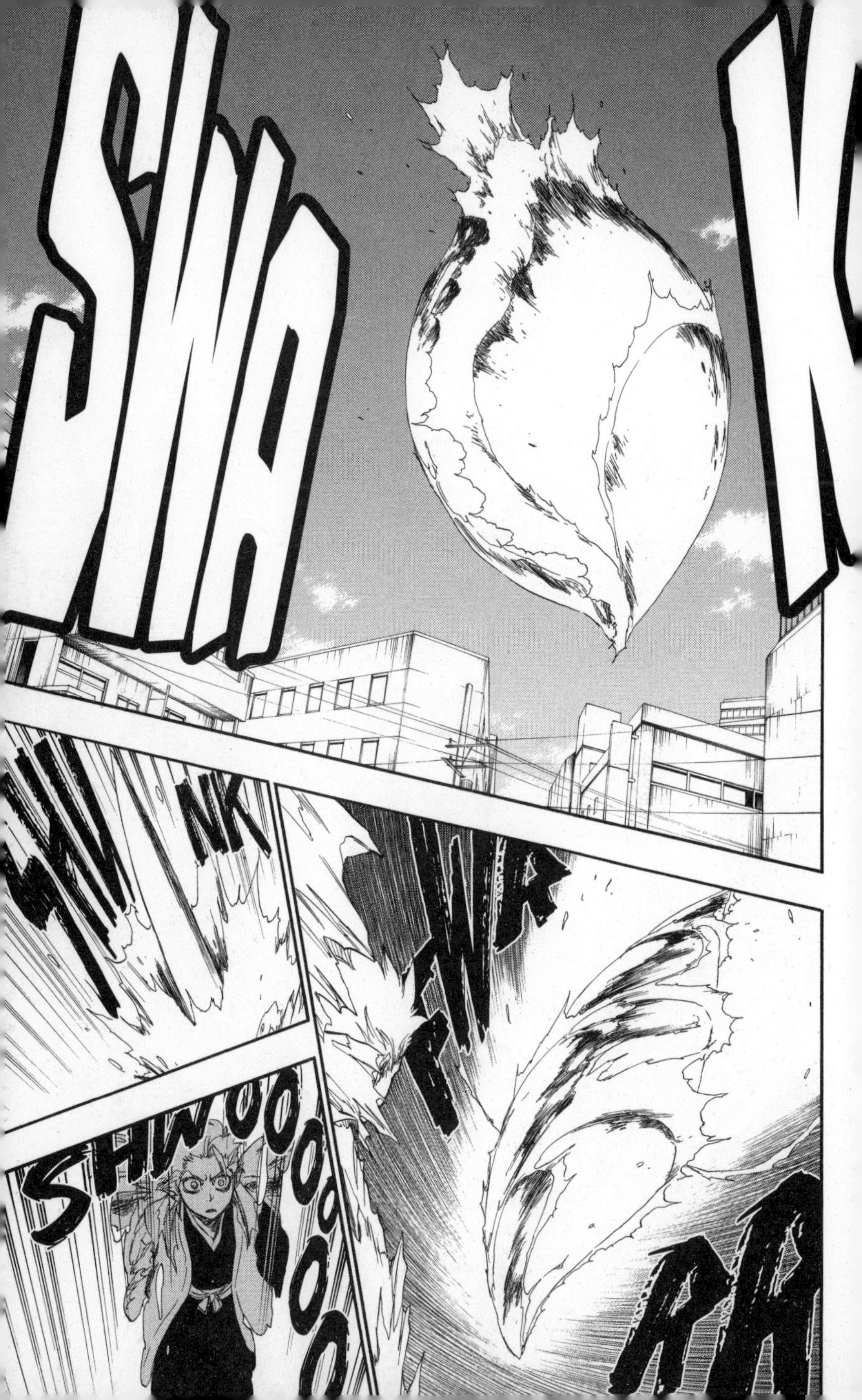
SHWA
SHIINK
SHWOOOOOOO

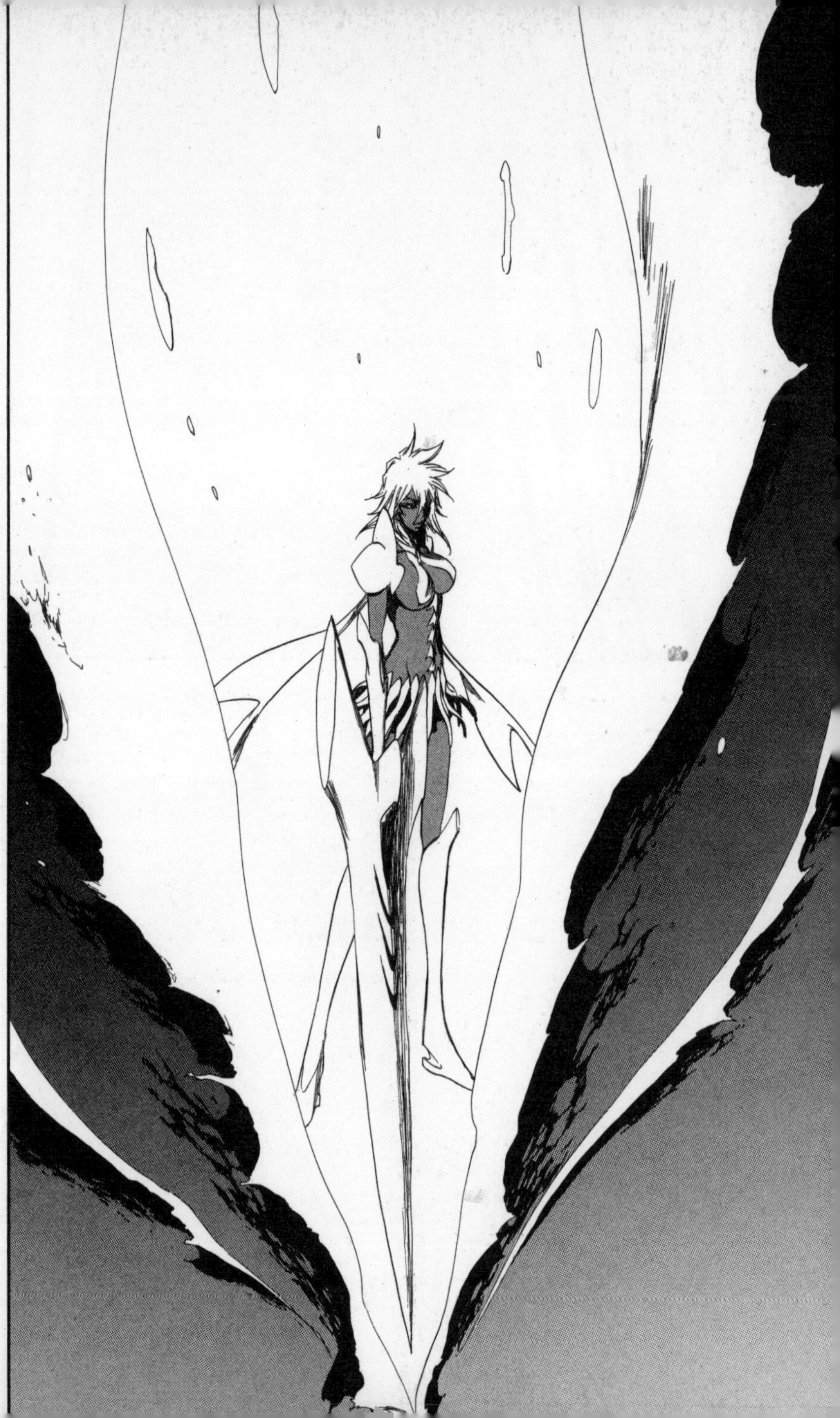

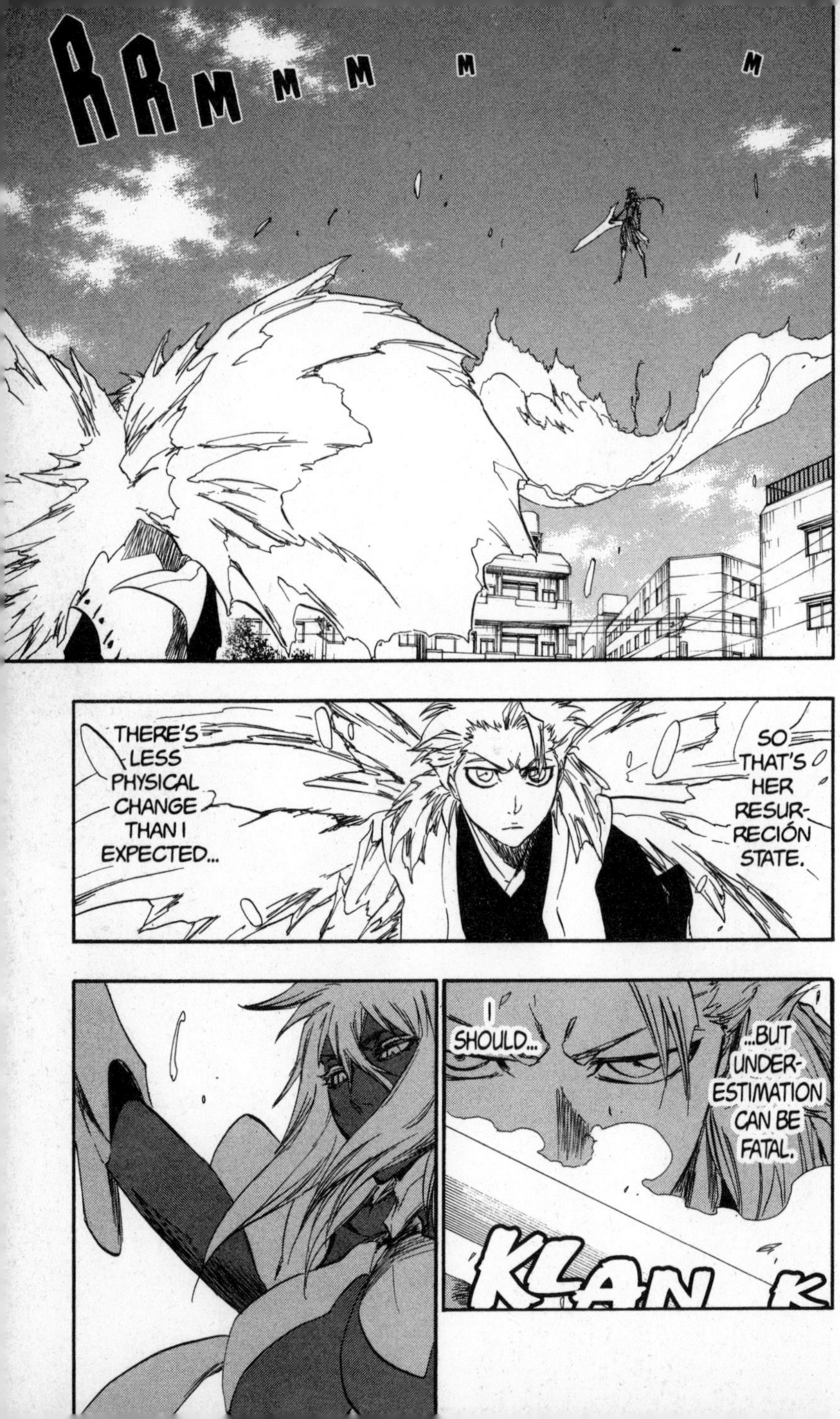
RRMMMMM
SO THAT'S HER RESURRECIÓN STATE.
THERE'S LESS PHYSICAL CHANGE THAN I EXPECTED...
I SHOULD...
...BUT UNDERESTIMATION CAN BE FATAL.
KLANK

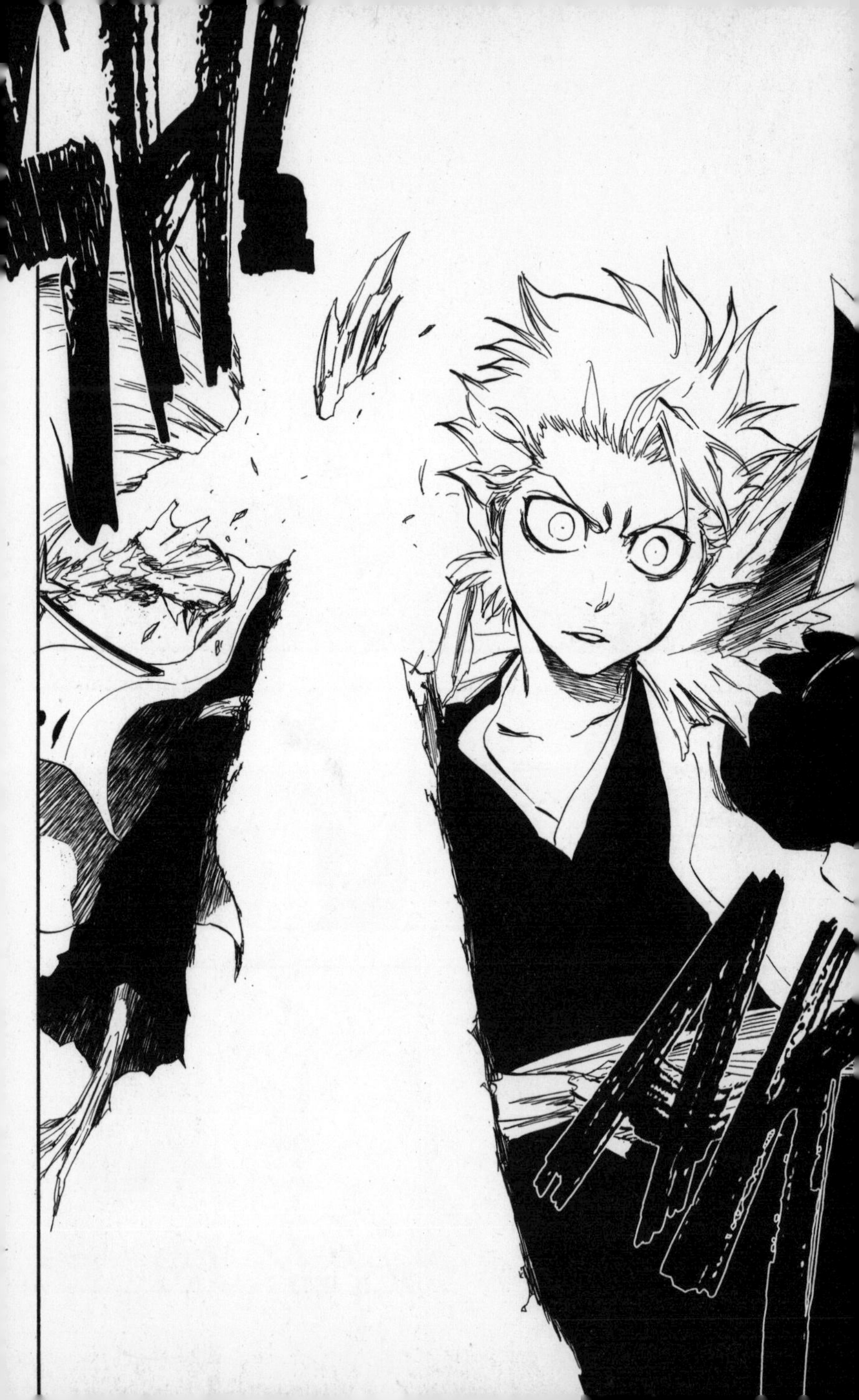

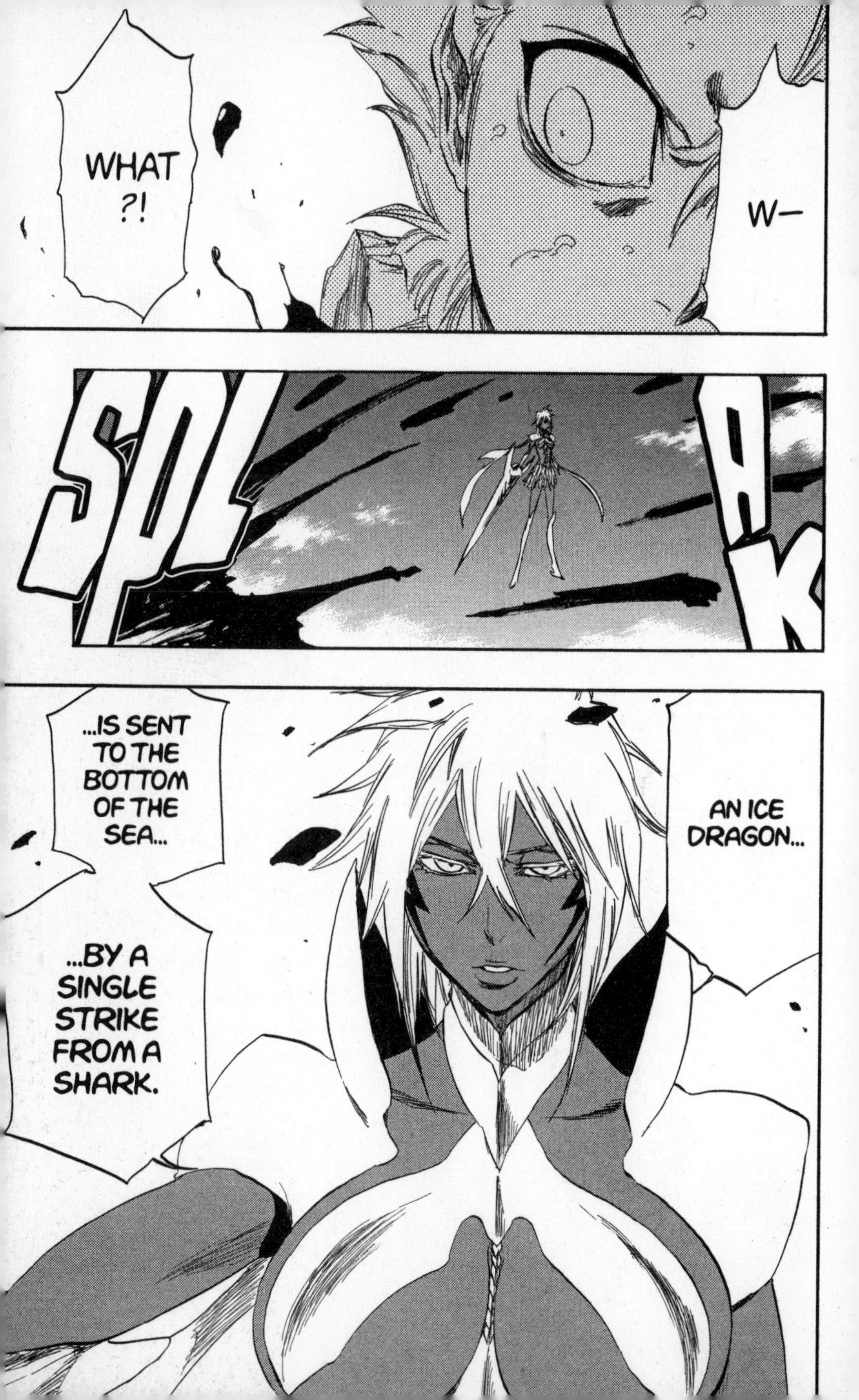
W—
WHAT ?!
SPLAK
AN ICE DRAGON...
...IS SENT TO THE BOTTOM OF THE SEA...
...BY A SINGLE STRIKE FROM A SHARK.

HEY!
IT'S BEEN A LONG TIME!
IT'S ME! BLEACH WORLD'S GREATEST IDOL, KON!!
IT'S BEEN SO LONG I WAS ABOUT TO PASS OUT.
YOU WANNA KNOW HOW LONG IT'S BEEN SINCE
SUPER IDOL KON'S APPEARED IN A STORY?
NOT SINCE VOLUME 25! 25!!
IT'S BEEN THREE YEARS!! WHAT THE HECK?!
THOSE OF YOU WHO ONLY RECENTLY STARTED
READING BLEACH MUST BE THINKING,
"HUH? WHO'S KON? WHAT A COOL NAME."
SO I'LL TELL YOU NEWBIES SOMETHING!
THE REAL HERO OF BLEACH ISN'T ICHIGO,
IT'S ME!!

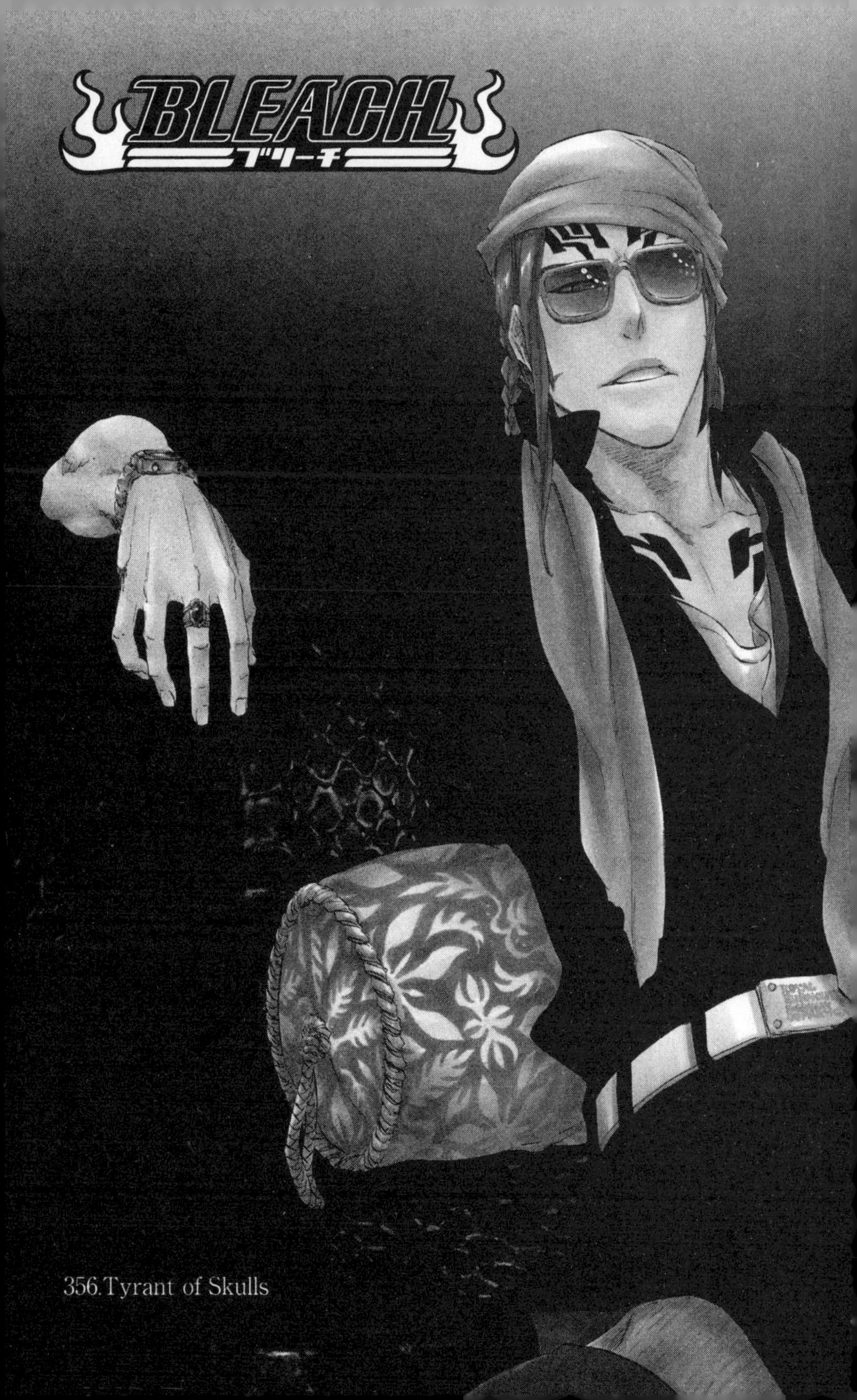
BLEACH
ブリーチ

356.Tyrant of Skulls

BLEACH
ブリーチ

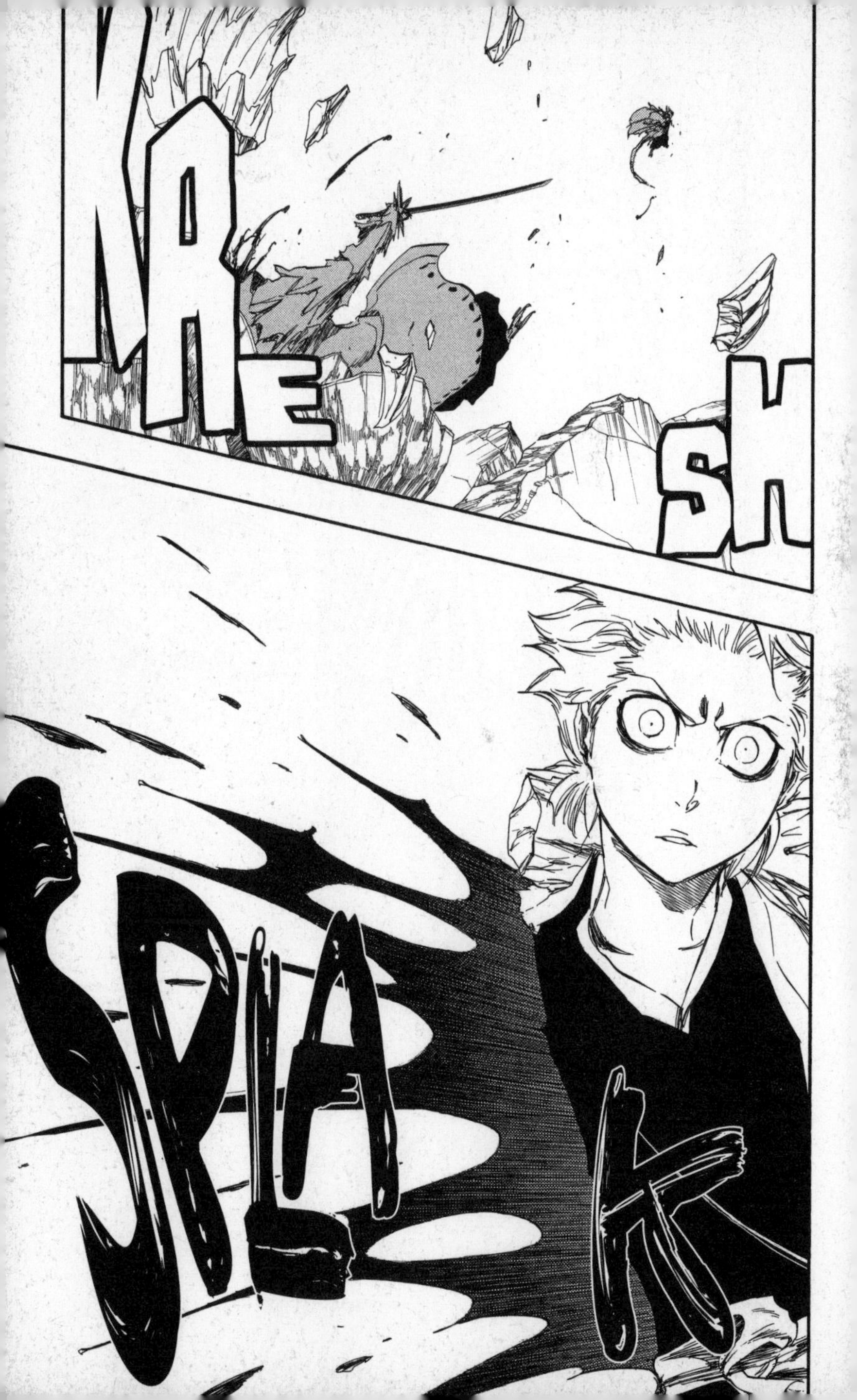
SPLAK

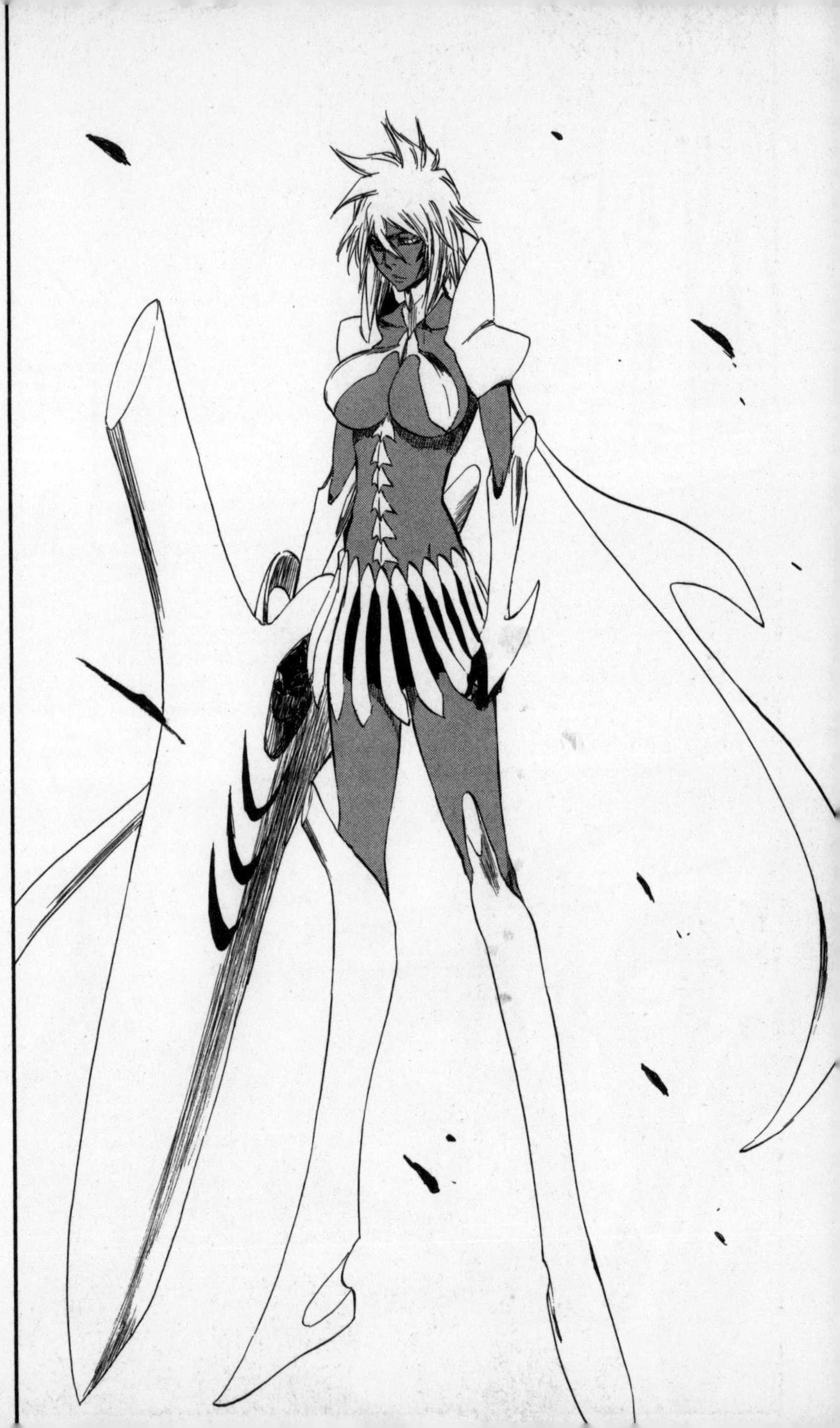

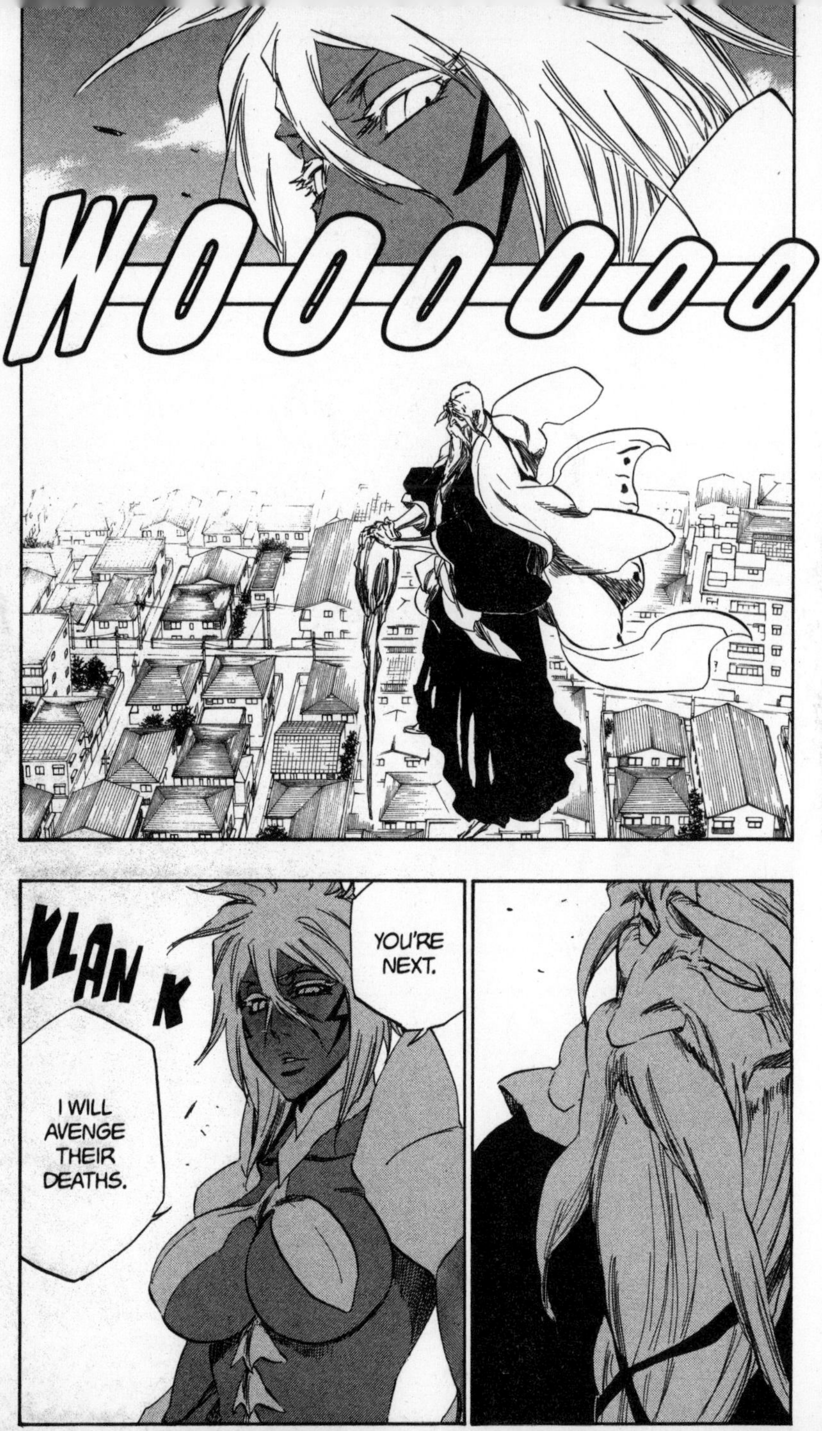

WOOOOOO
YOU'RE NEXT.
KLANK
I WILL AVENGE THEIR DEATHS.

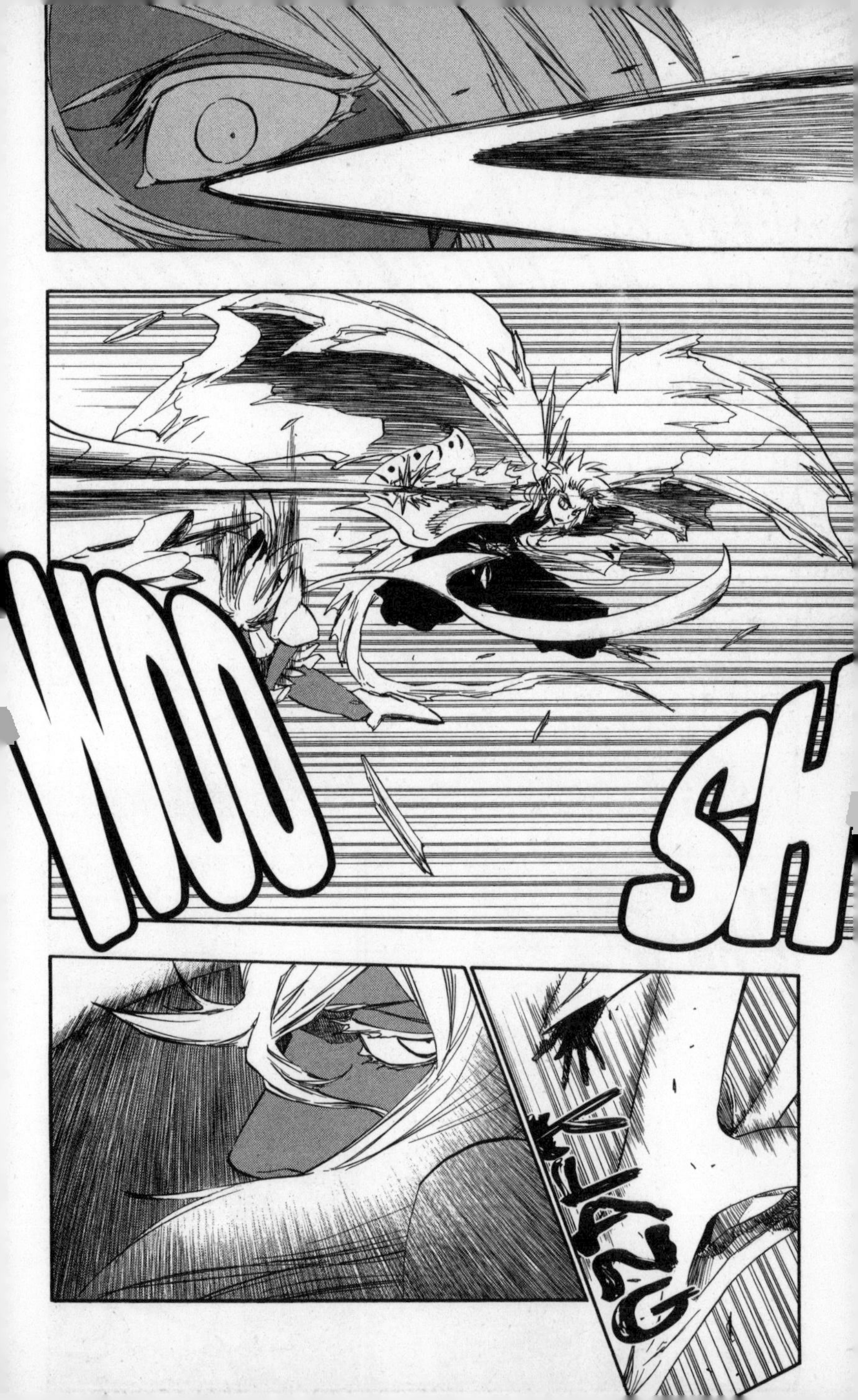
WHOO
SH
KLANG

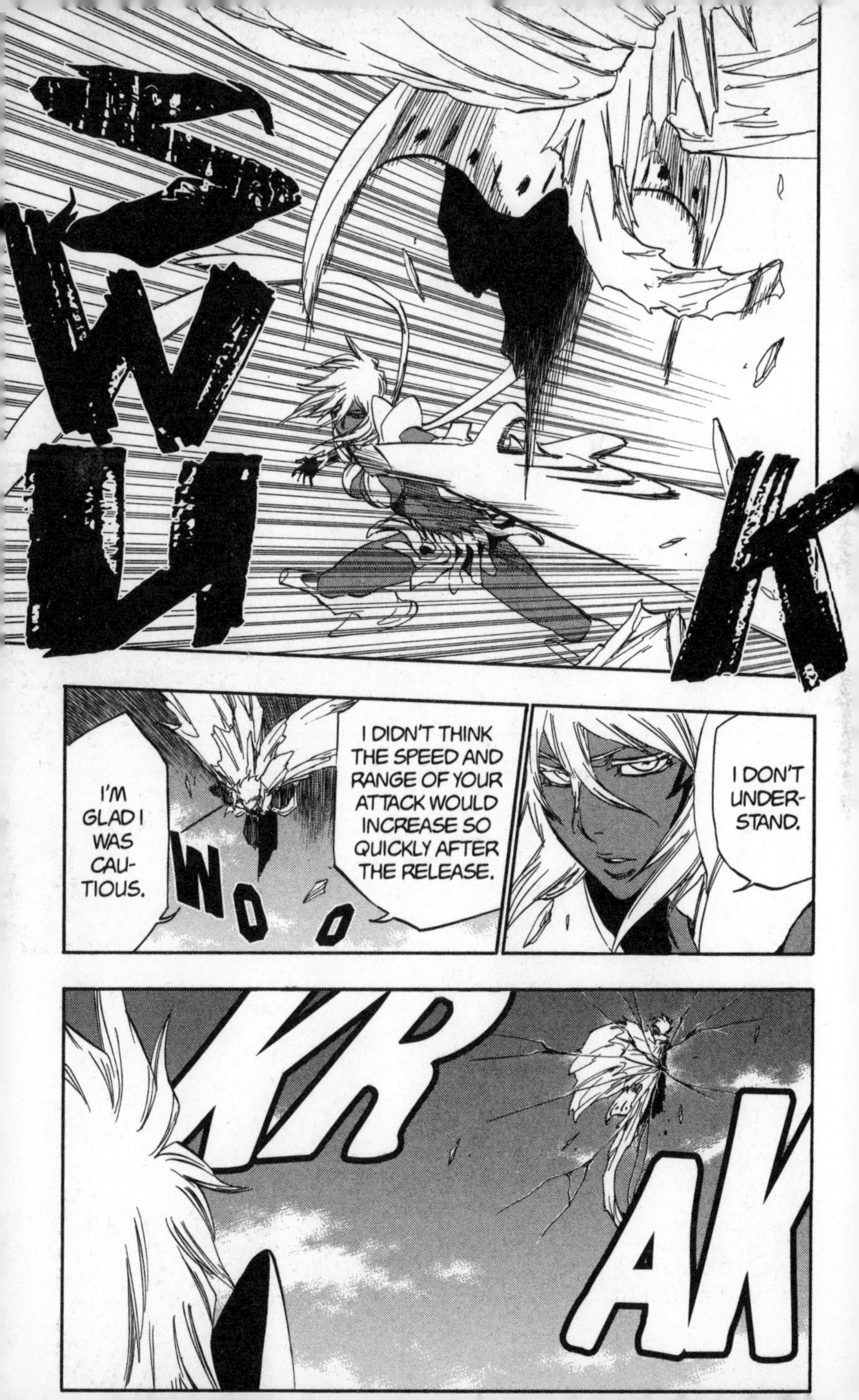
SWUK
I DON'T UNDERSTAND.
I DIDN'T THINK THE SPEED AND RANGE OF YOUR ATTACK WOULD INCREASE SO QUICKLY AFTER THE RELEASE.
I'M GLAD I WAS CAUTIOUS.
WOO
KRAK

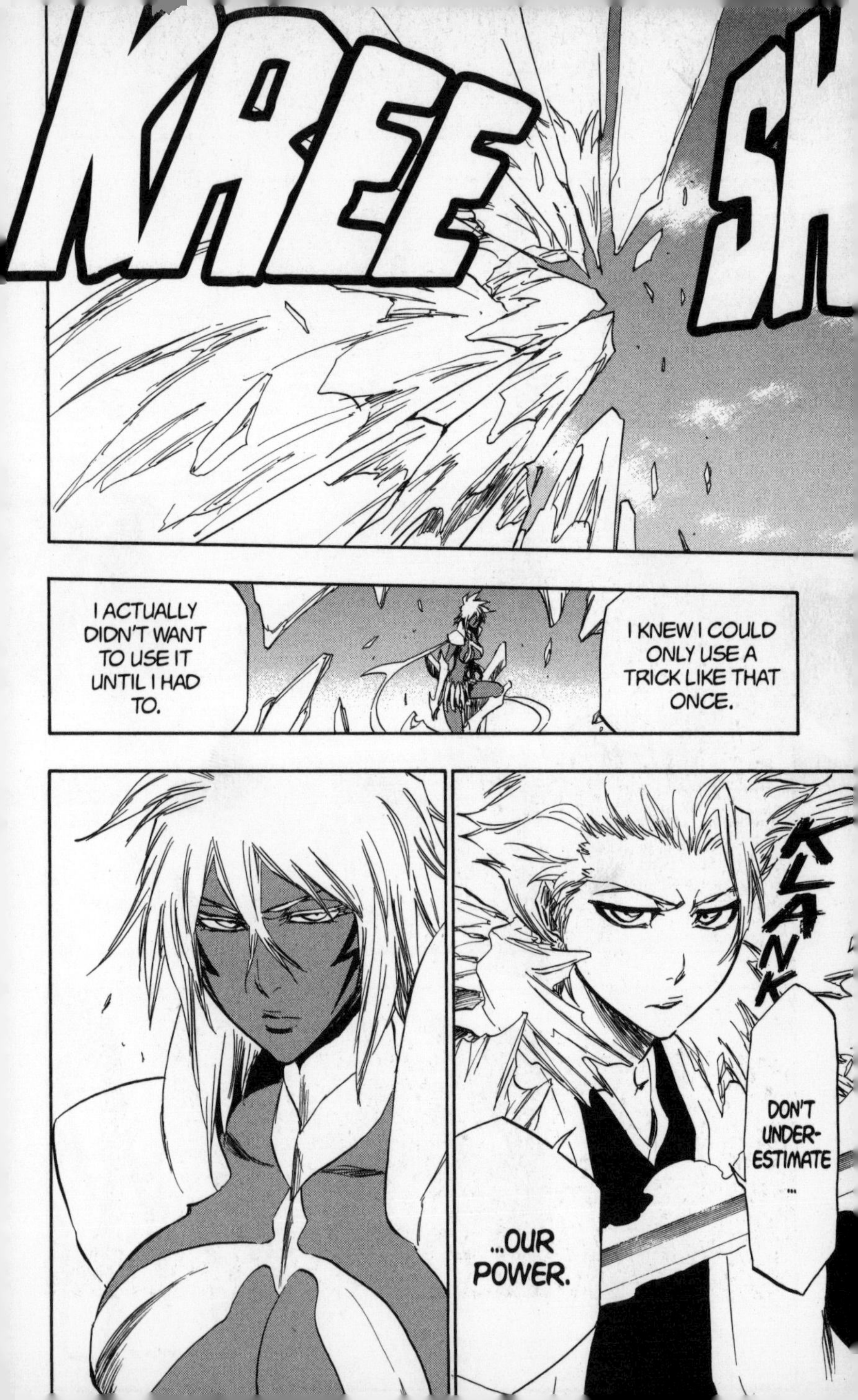

KREE
SH
I KNEW I COULD ONLY USE A TRICK LIKE THAT ONCE.
I ACTUALLY DIDN'T WANT TO USE IT UNTIL I HAD TO.
KLANK
DON'T UNDER-ESTIMATE...
...OUR POWER.

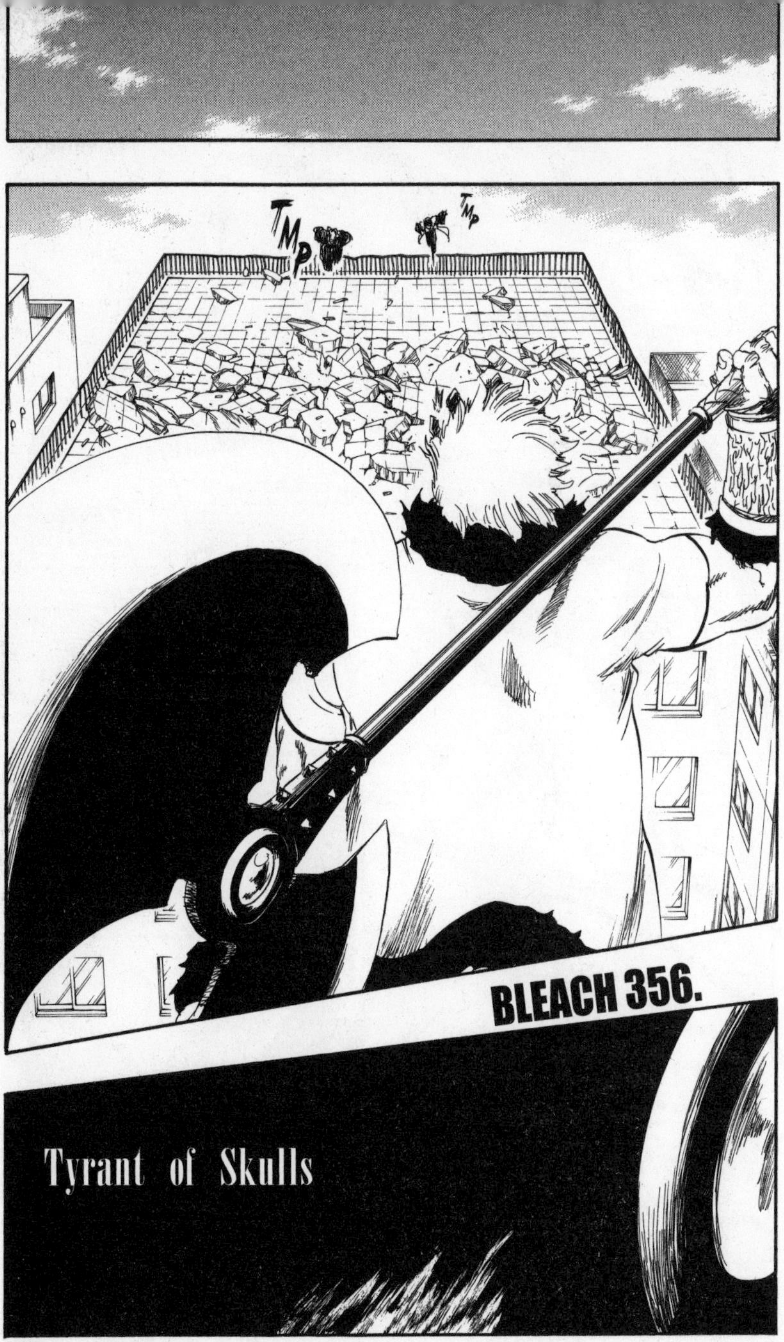
TMP
TMP
BLEACH 356.
Tyrant of Skulls

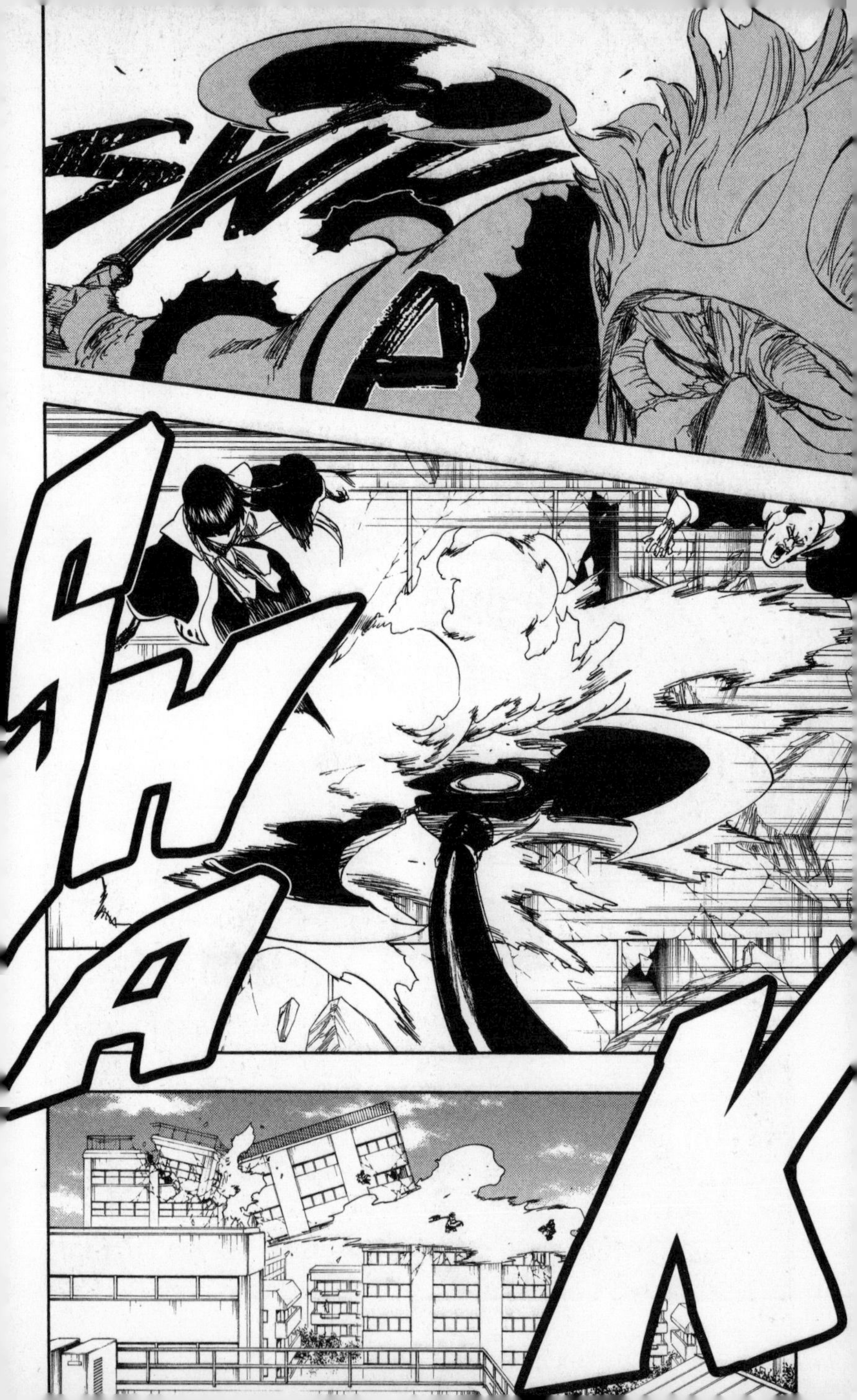

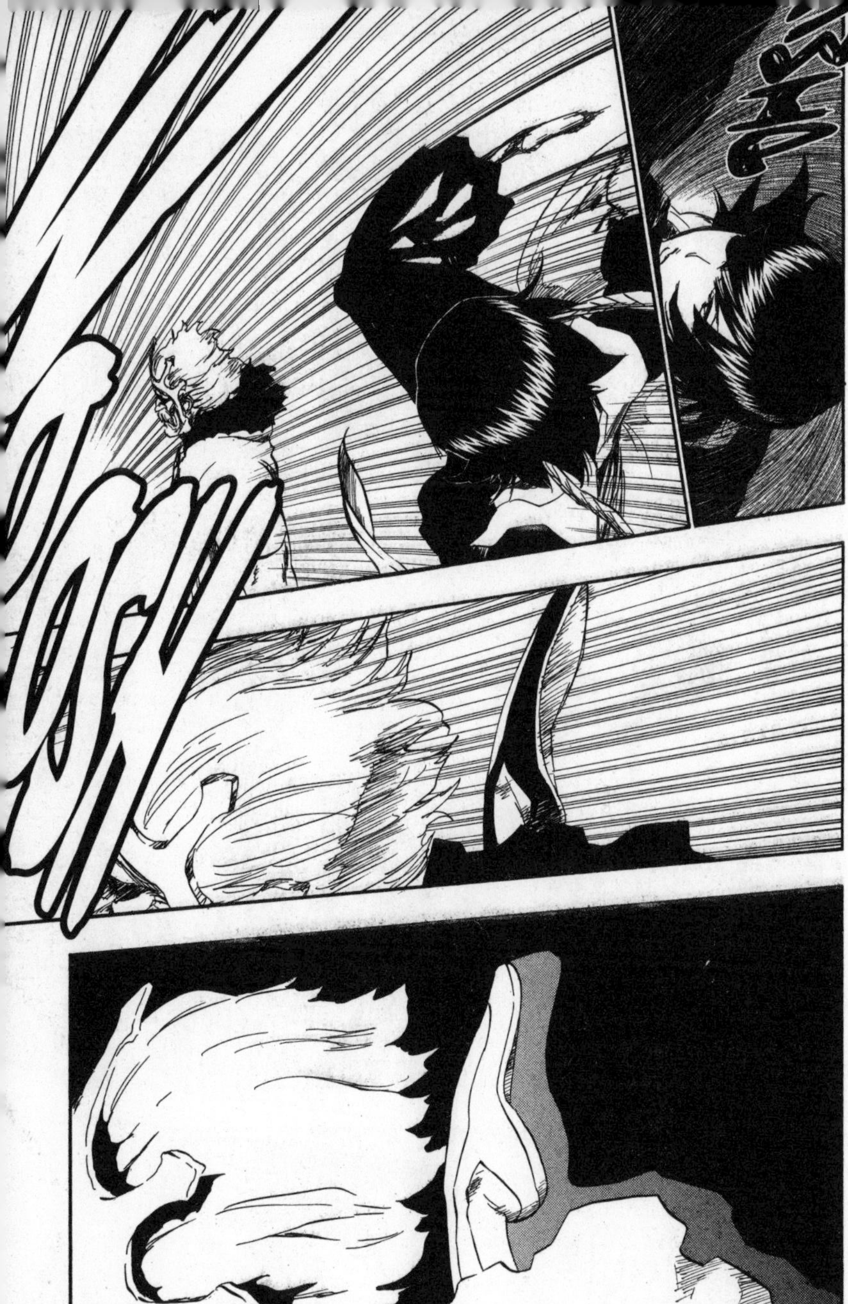

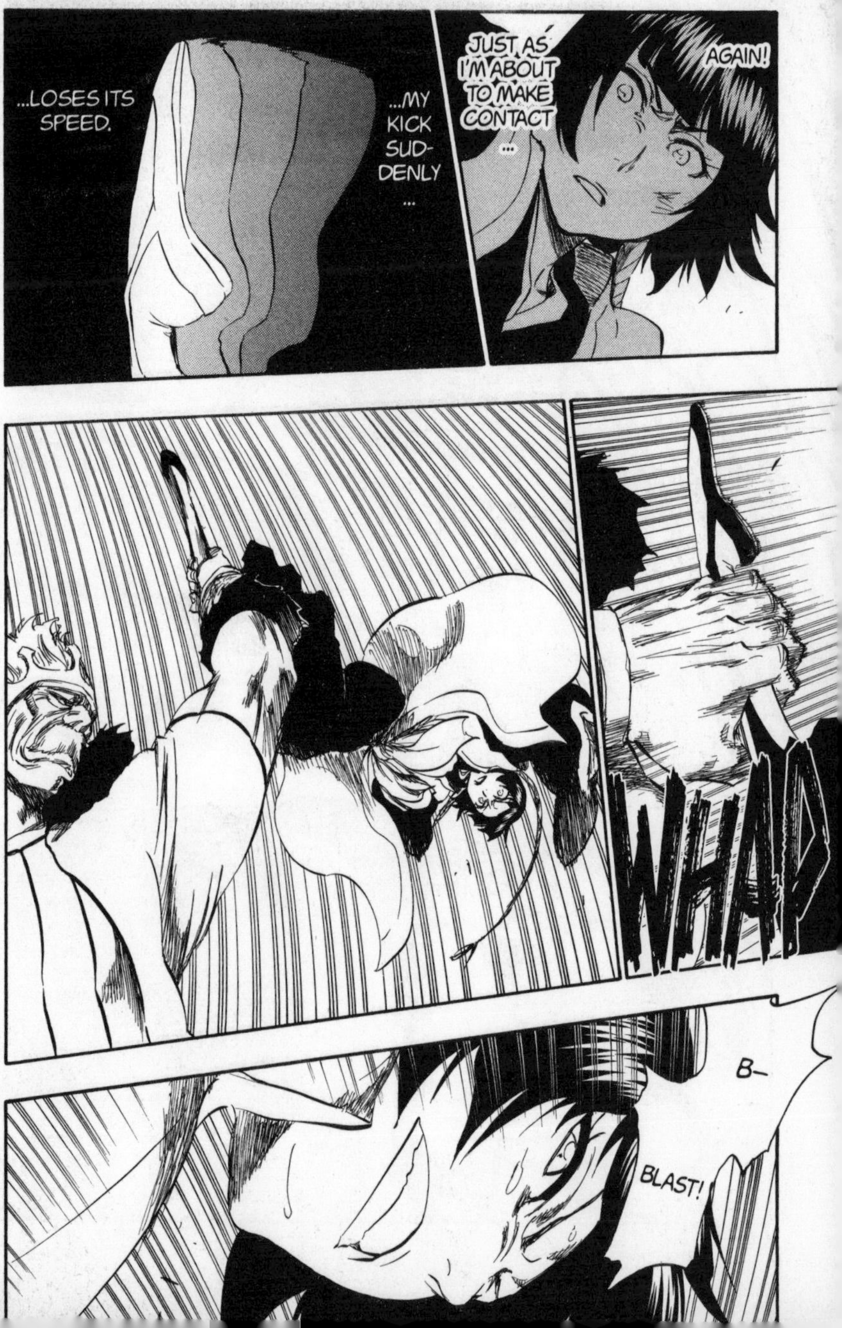
AGAIN!
JUST AS I'M ABOUT TO MAKE CONTACT ...
...MY KICK SUDDENLY ...
...LOSES ITS SPEED.
WHAP
B–
BLAST!

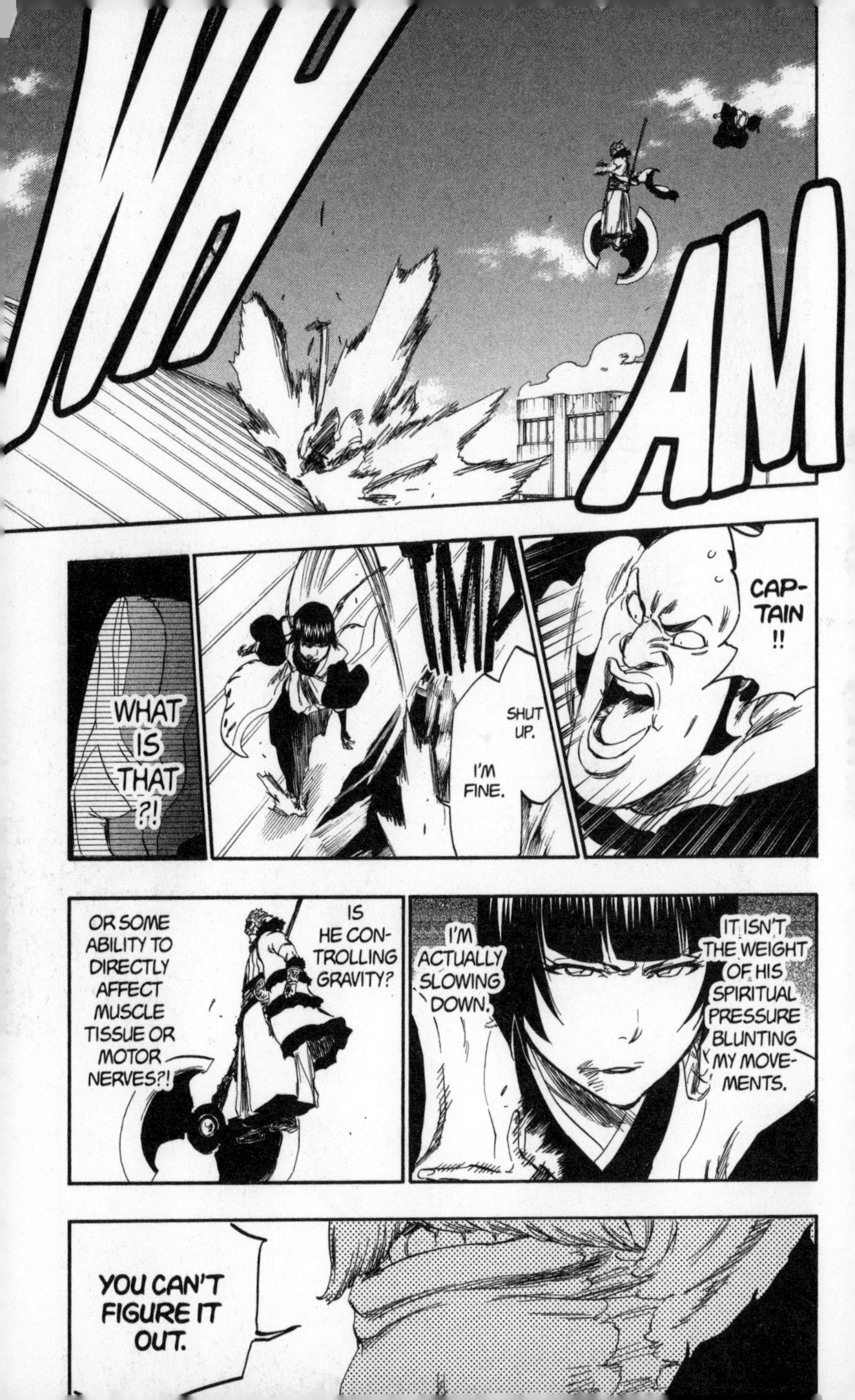
WHAM
CAPTAIN!!
TMP
SHUT UP.
I'M FINE.
WHAT IS THAT?!
IT ISN'T THE WEIGHT OF HIS SPIRITUAL PRESSURE BLUNTING MY MOVEMENTS.
I'M ACTUALLY SLOWING DOWN.
IS HE CONTROLLING GRAVITY?
OR SOME ABILITY TO DIRECTLY AFFECT MUSCLE TISSUE OR MOTOR NERVES?!
YOU CAN'T FIGURE IT OUT.

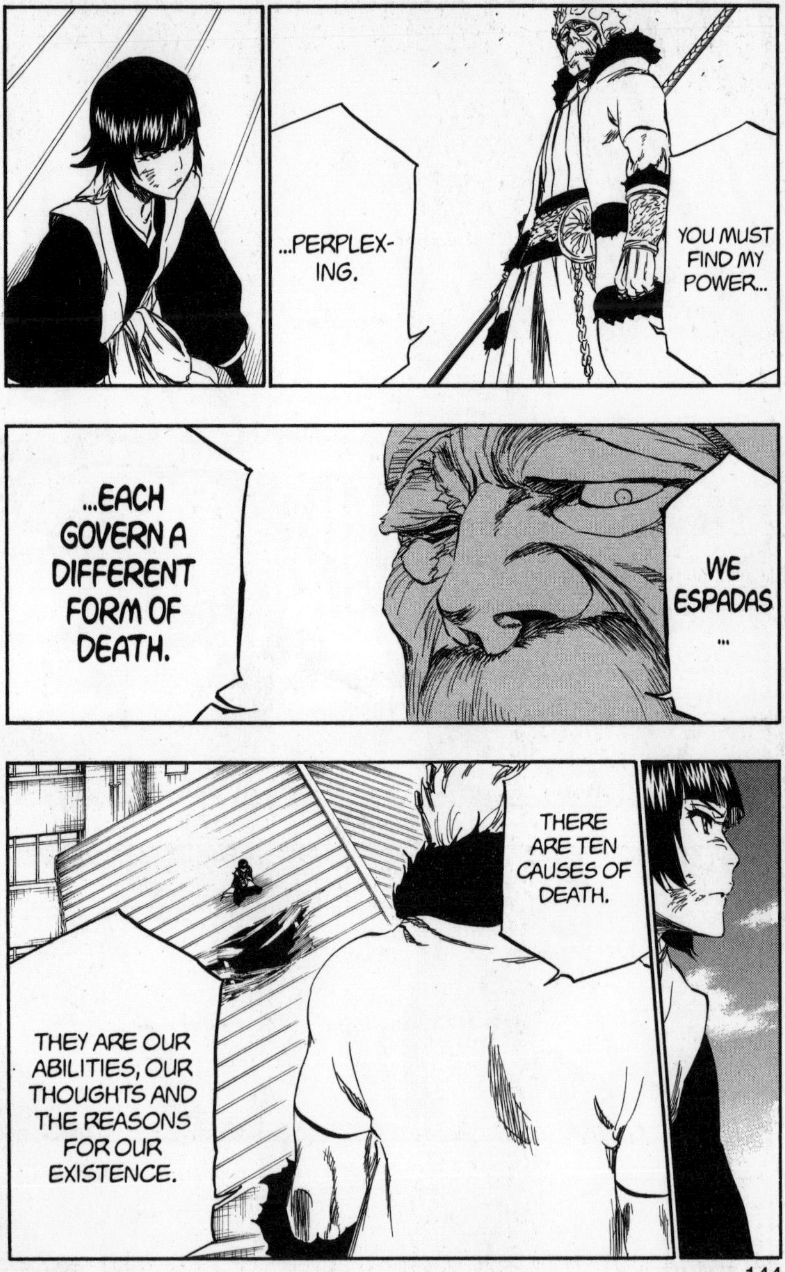
YOU MUST FIND MY POWER...
...PERPLEX-ING.
WE ESPADAS ...
...EACH GOVERN A DIFFERENT FORM OF DEATH.
THERE ARE TEN CAUSES OF DEATH.
THEY ARE OUR ABILITIES, OUR THOUGHTS AND THE REASONS FOR OUR EXISTENCE.

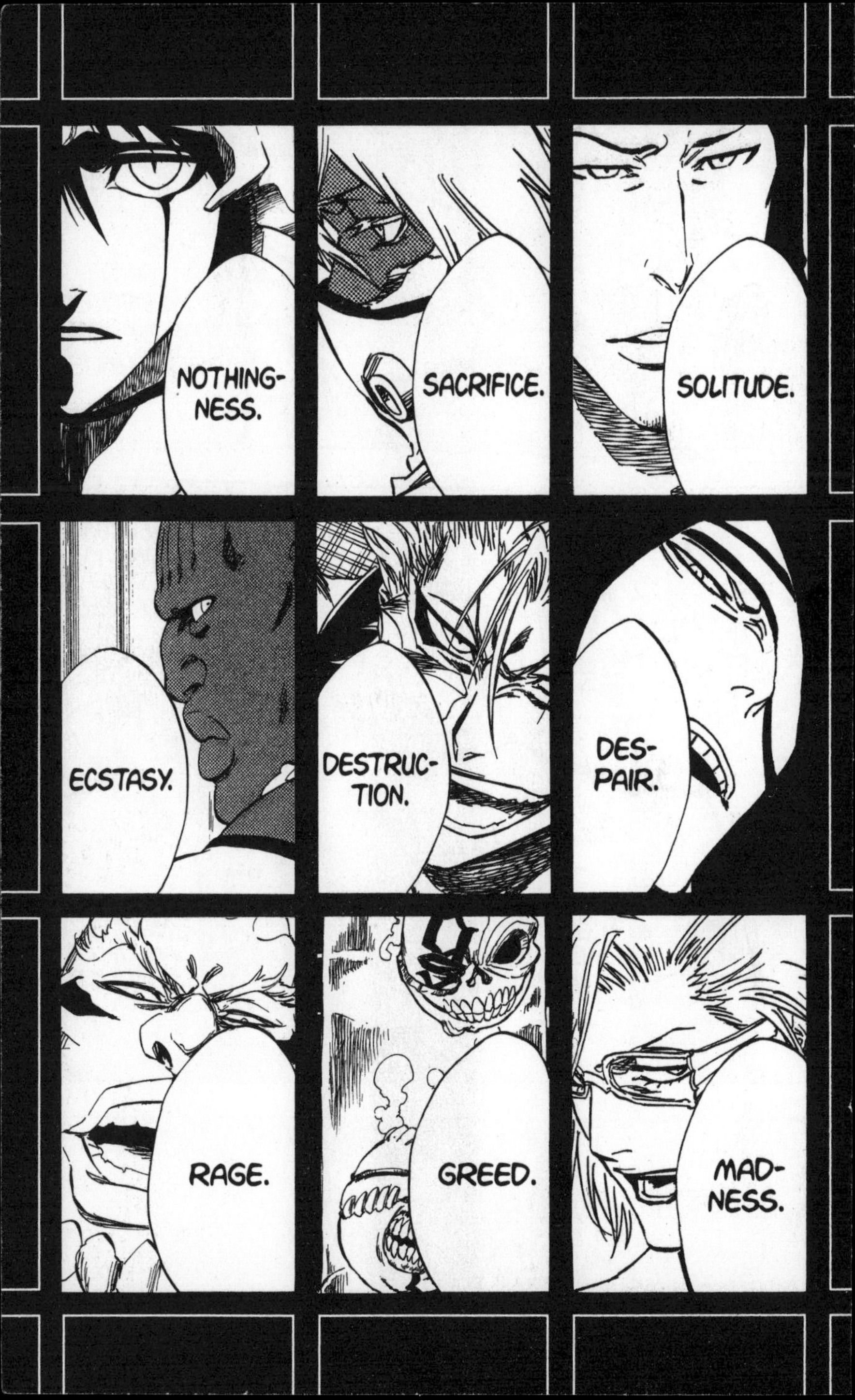
SOLITUDE.
SACRIFICE.
NOTHING-NESS.
DES-PAIR.
DESTRUC-TION.
ECSTASY.
MAD-NESS.
GREED.
RAGE.

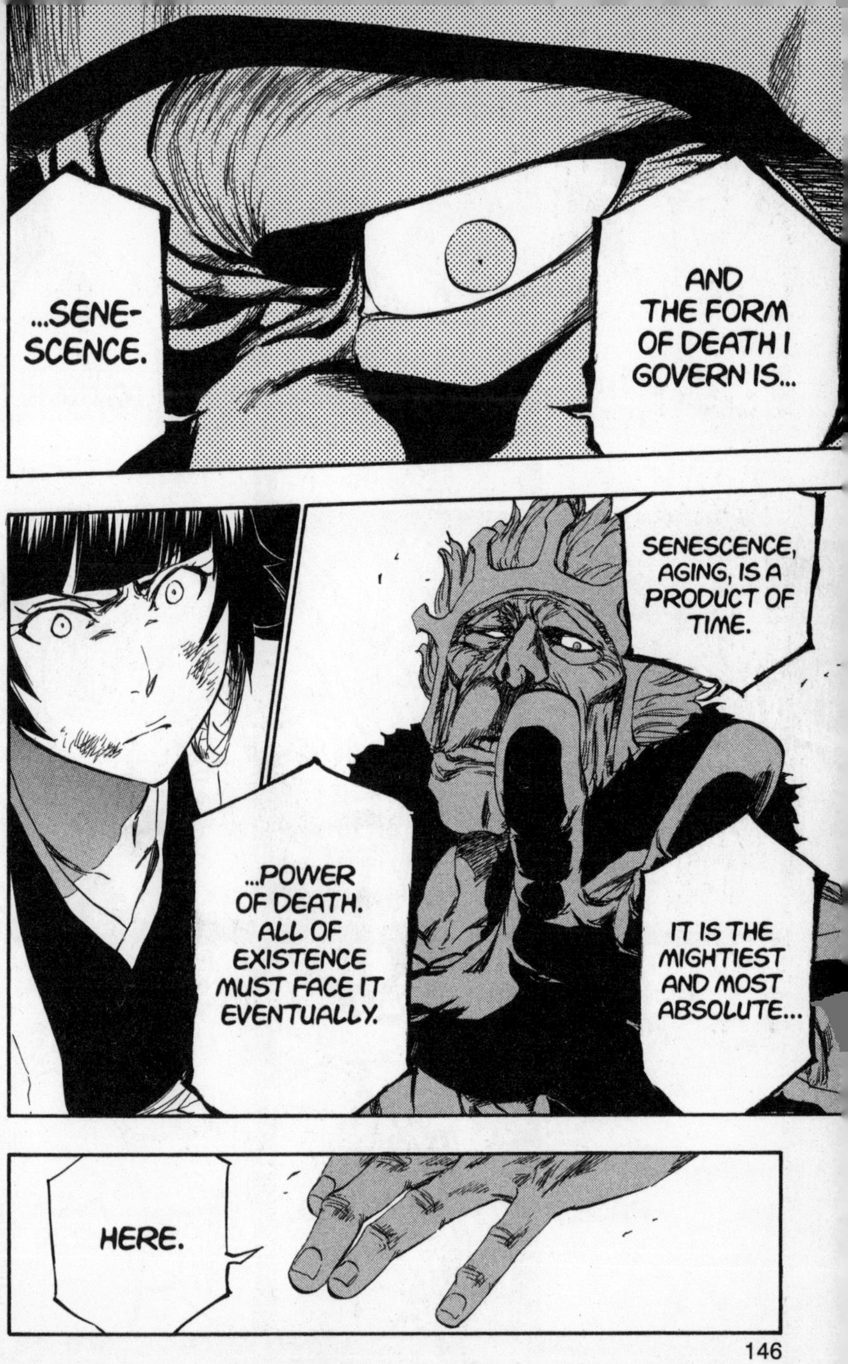
AND THE FORM OF DEATH I GOVERN IS...
...SENE-SCENCE.
SENESCENCE, AGING, IS A PRODUCT OF TIME.
IT IS THE MIGHTIEST AND MOST ABSOLUTE...
...POWER OF DEATH. ALL OF EXISTENCE MUST FACE IT EVENTUALLY.
HERE.

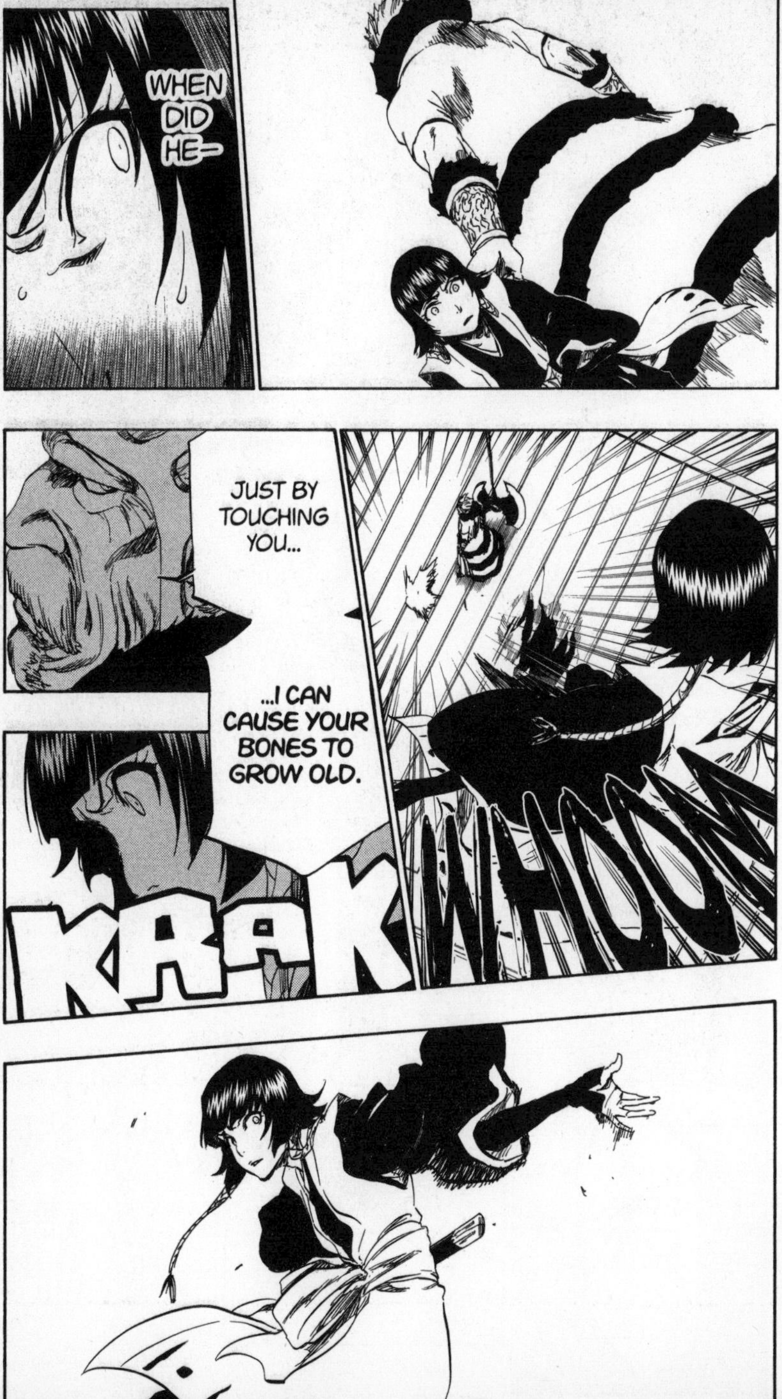
WHEN DID HE–
WHOOM
JUST BY TOUCHING YOU...
...I CAN CAUSE YOUR BONES TO GROW OLD.
KRAK

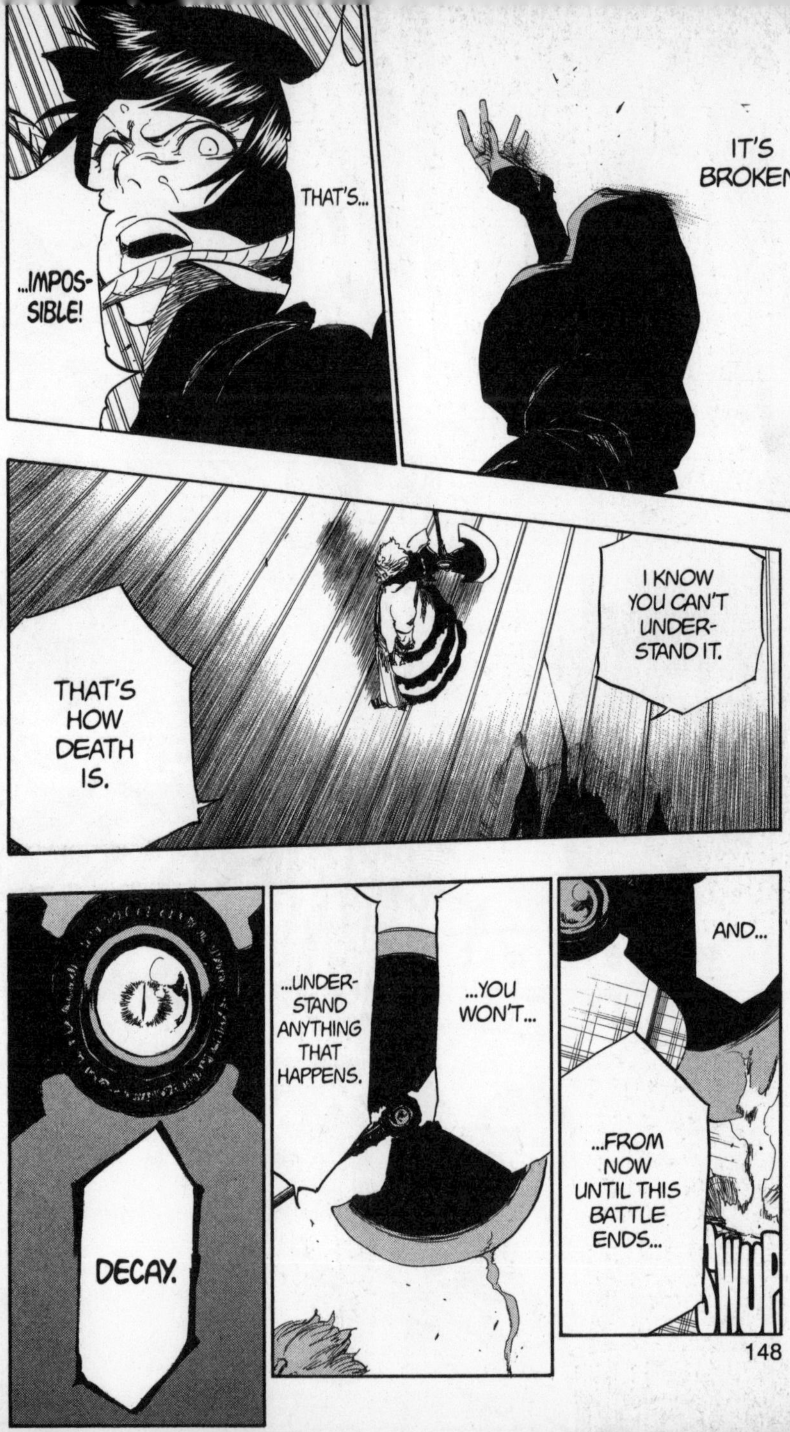
IT'S BROKEN.
THAT'S...
...IMPOSSIBLE!
I KNOW YOU CAN'T UNDERSTAND IT.
THAT'S HOW DEATH IS.
AND...
...FROM NOW UNTIL THIS BATTLE ENDS...
SWOP
...YOU WON'T...
...UNDERSTAND ANYTHING THAT HAPPENS.
DECAY.

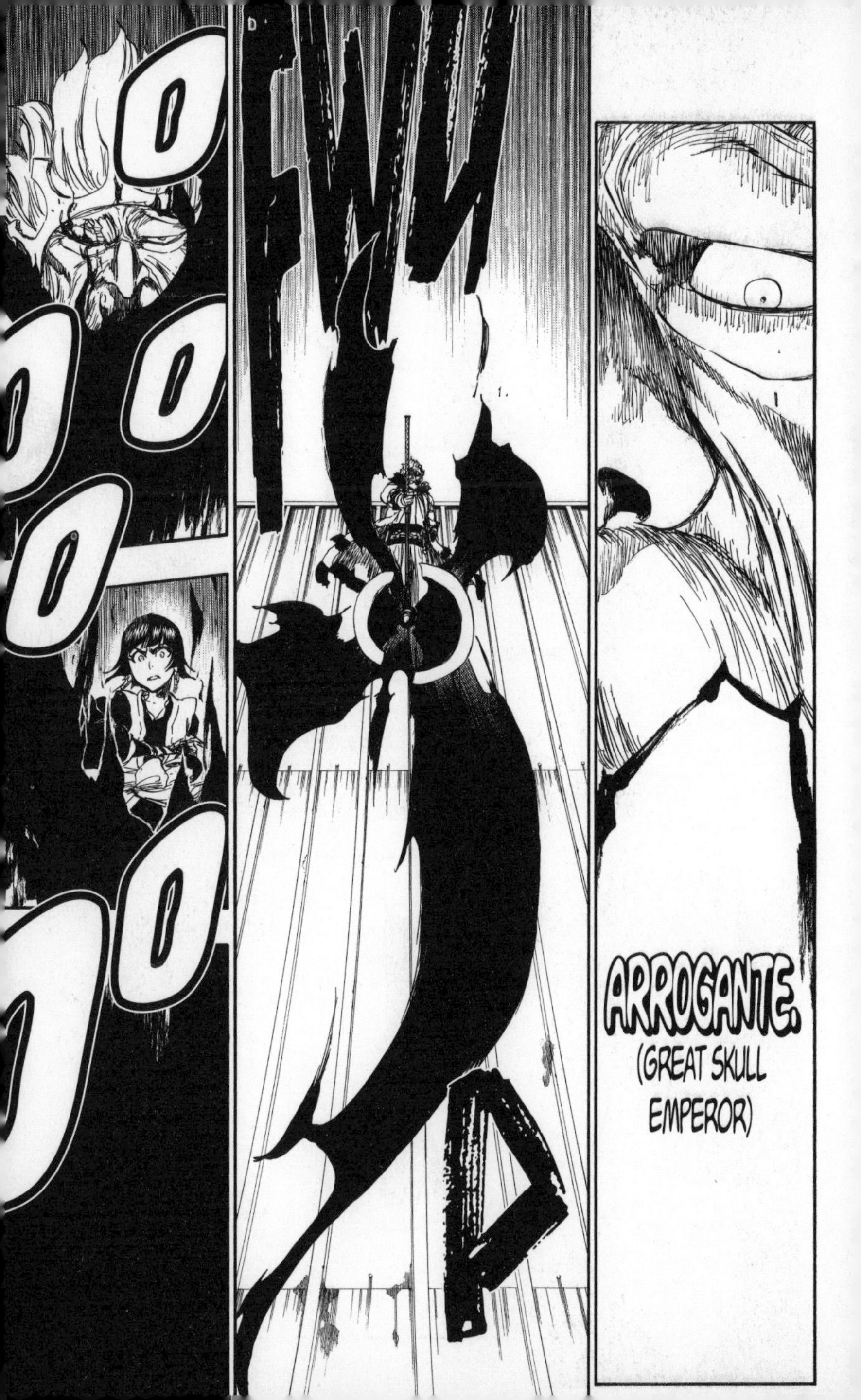
ARROGANTE.
(GREAT SKULL EMPEROR)

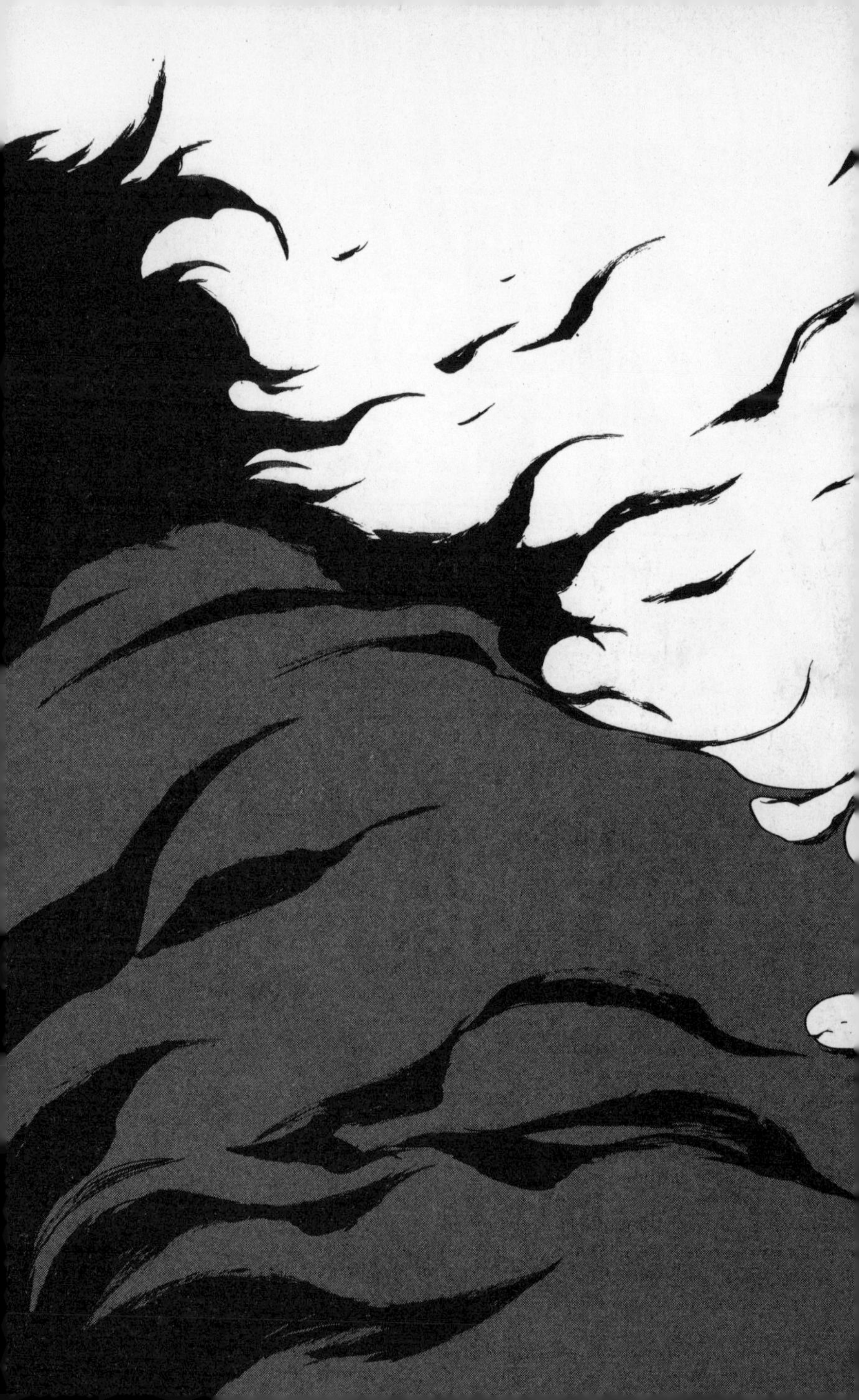

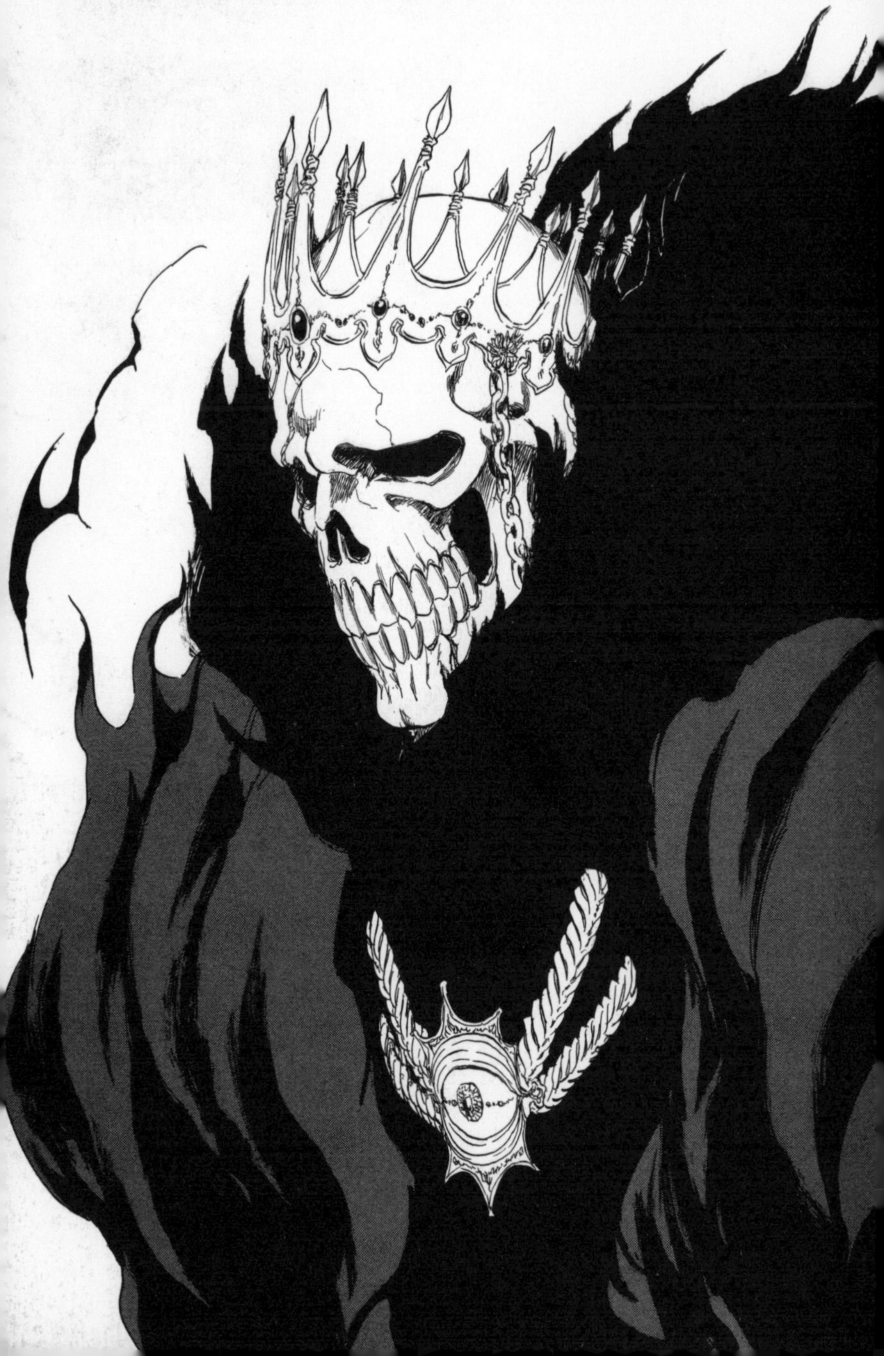

SO IT'S BEEN A LONG TIME SINCE I, THE MAIN CHARACTER AND SUPER IDOL, MADE AN APPEARANCE. LET ME EXPLAIN WHY I'M ON THE GROUND LIKE THIS.
WHILE WALKING AROUND TOWN IN ICHIGO'S BODY, I SUDDENLY GOT SLEEPY AND PASSED OUT.
THE TOWN SEEMED DIFFERENT WHEN I WOKE UP SO I DIDN'T KNOW IF I SHOULD GET UP OR NOT. SO I'M MONITORING THE SITUATION FROM THIS POSITION!
BUT IT SEEMS TO ME THIS TOWN LOOKS LIKE THE RUKONGAI I SAW A LONG TIME AGO.
YACK YACK YACK
HUH? IS SOMEBODY COMING? I HOPE IT'S A HOTTIE WITH HUGE...

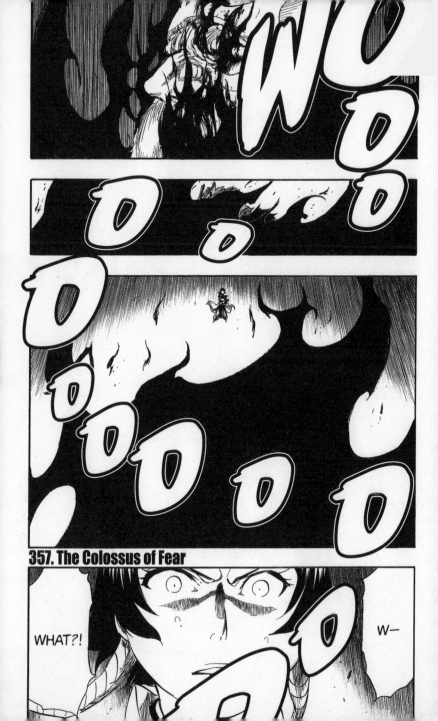

357. The Colossus of Fear

WHAT?!

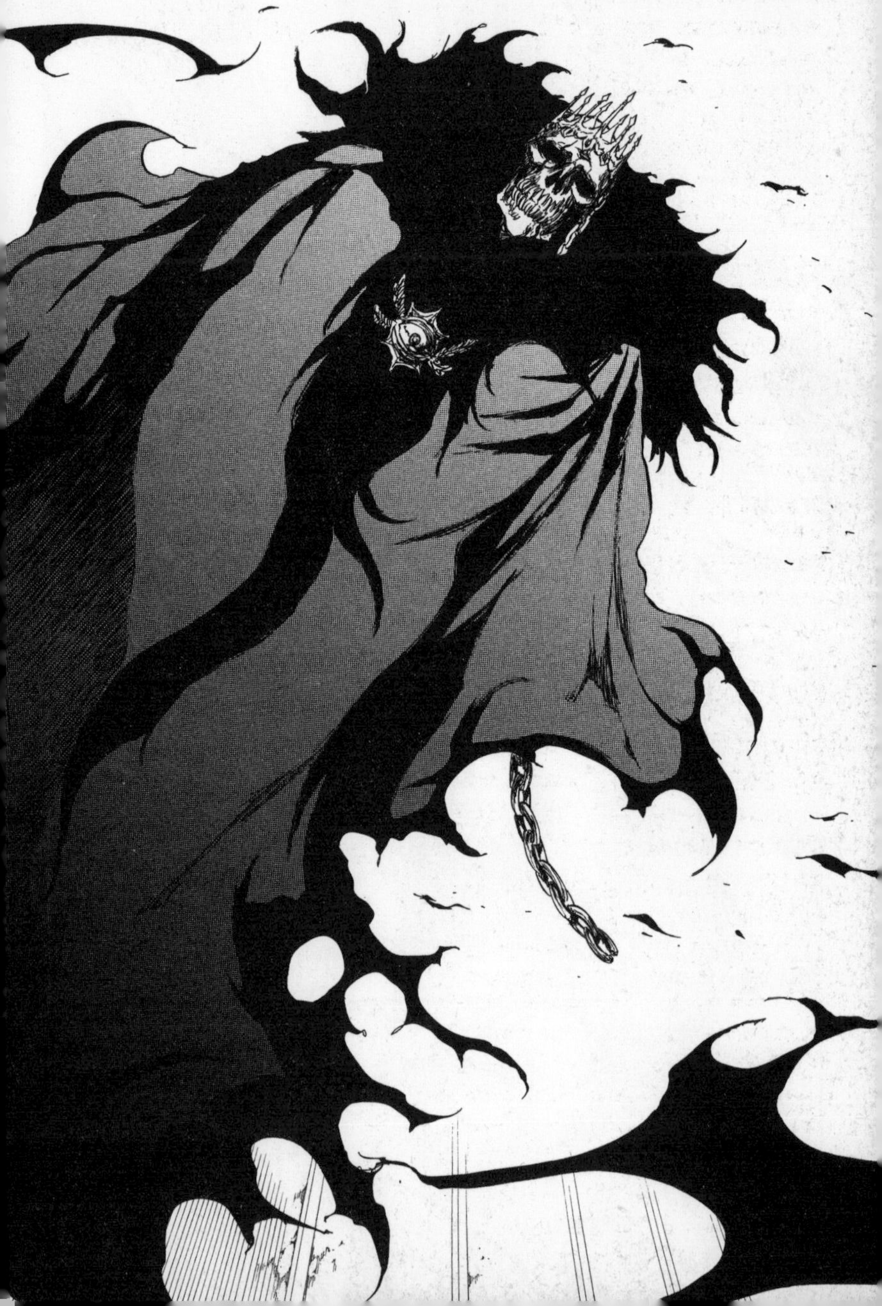

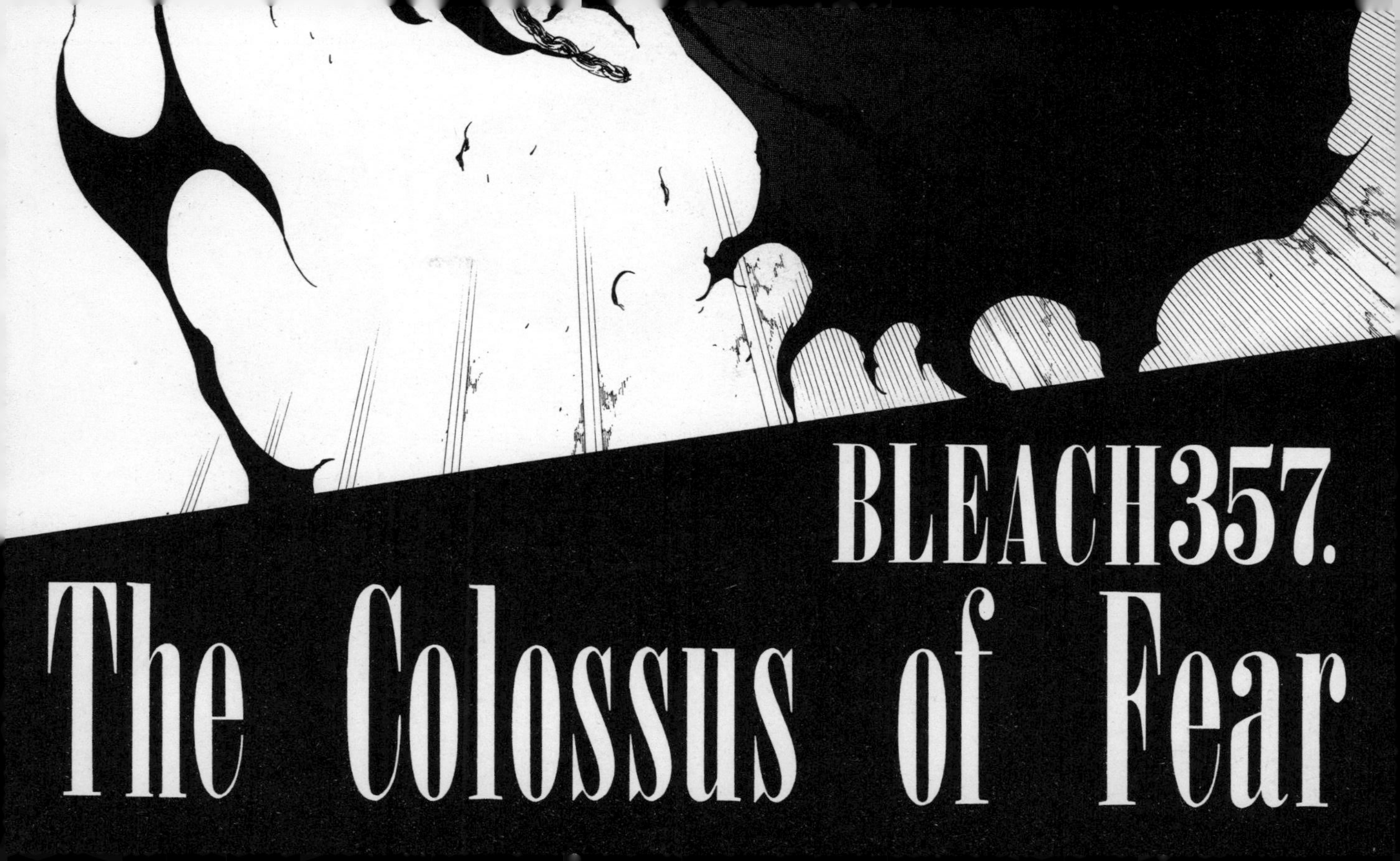

BLEACH357.

The Colossus of Fear

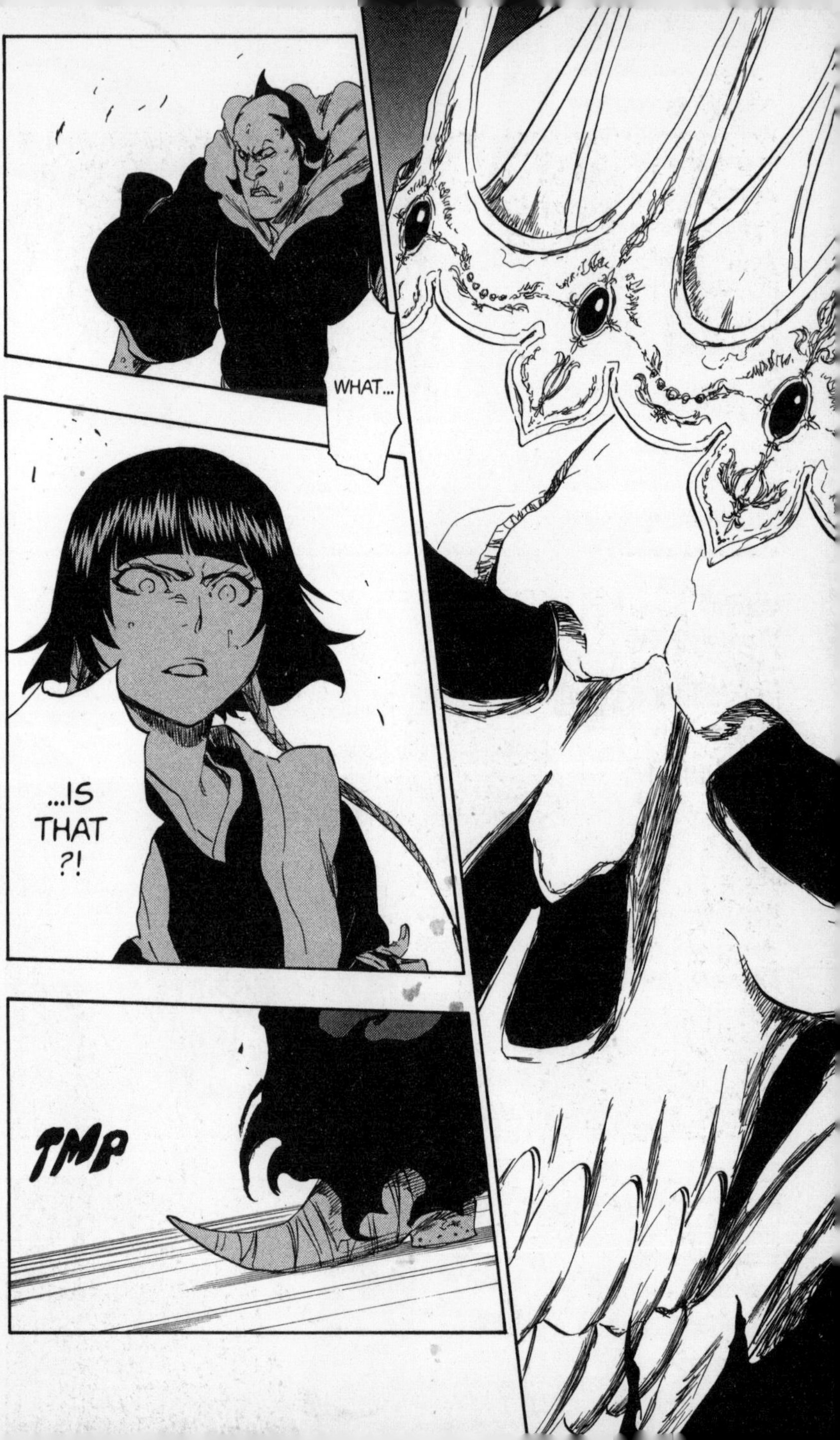
WHAT...
...IS THAT ?!
TMP

READ THIS WAY

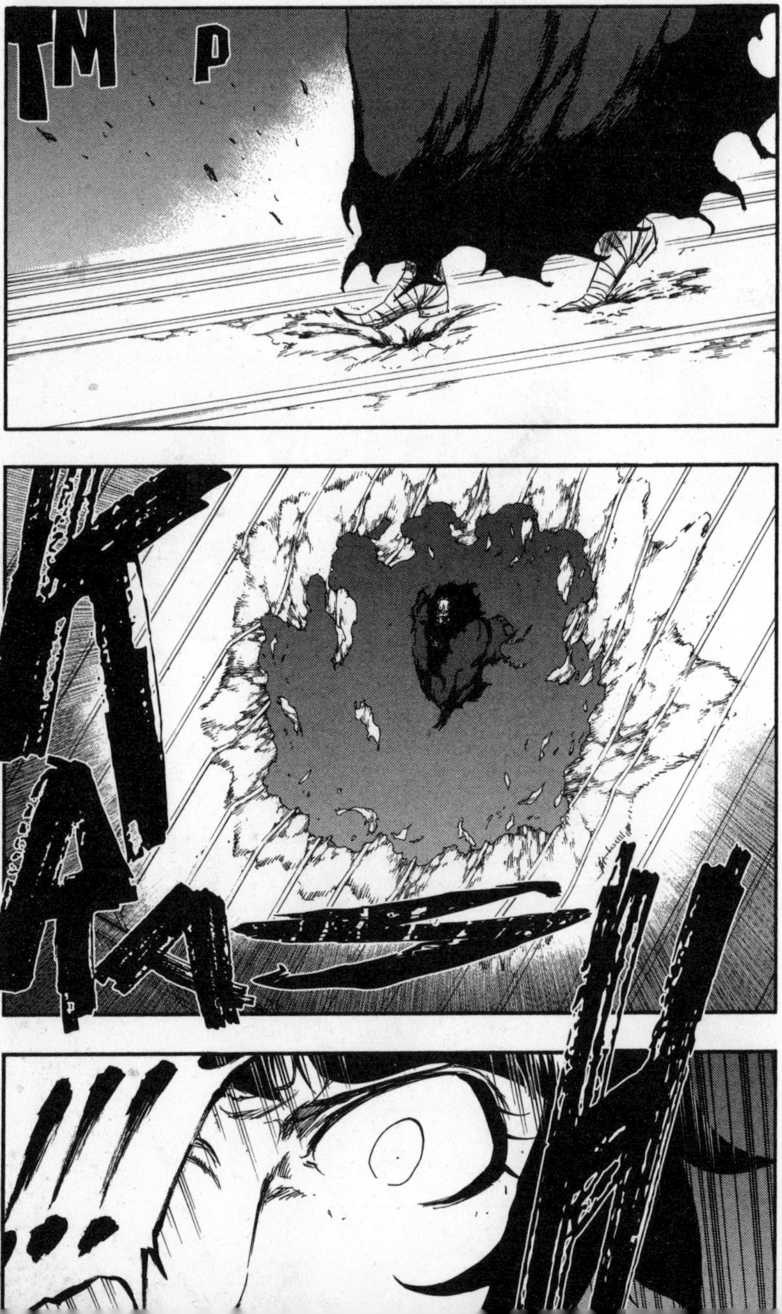
TMP
!!!

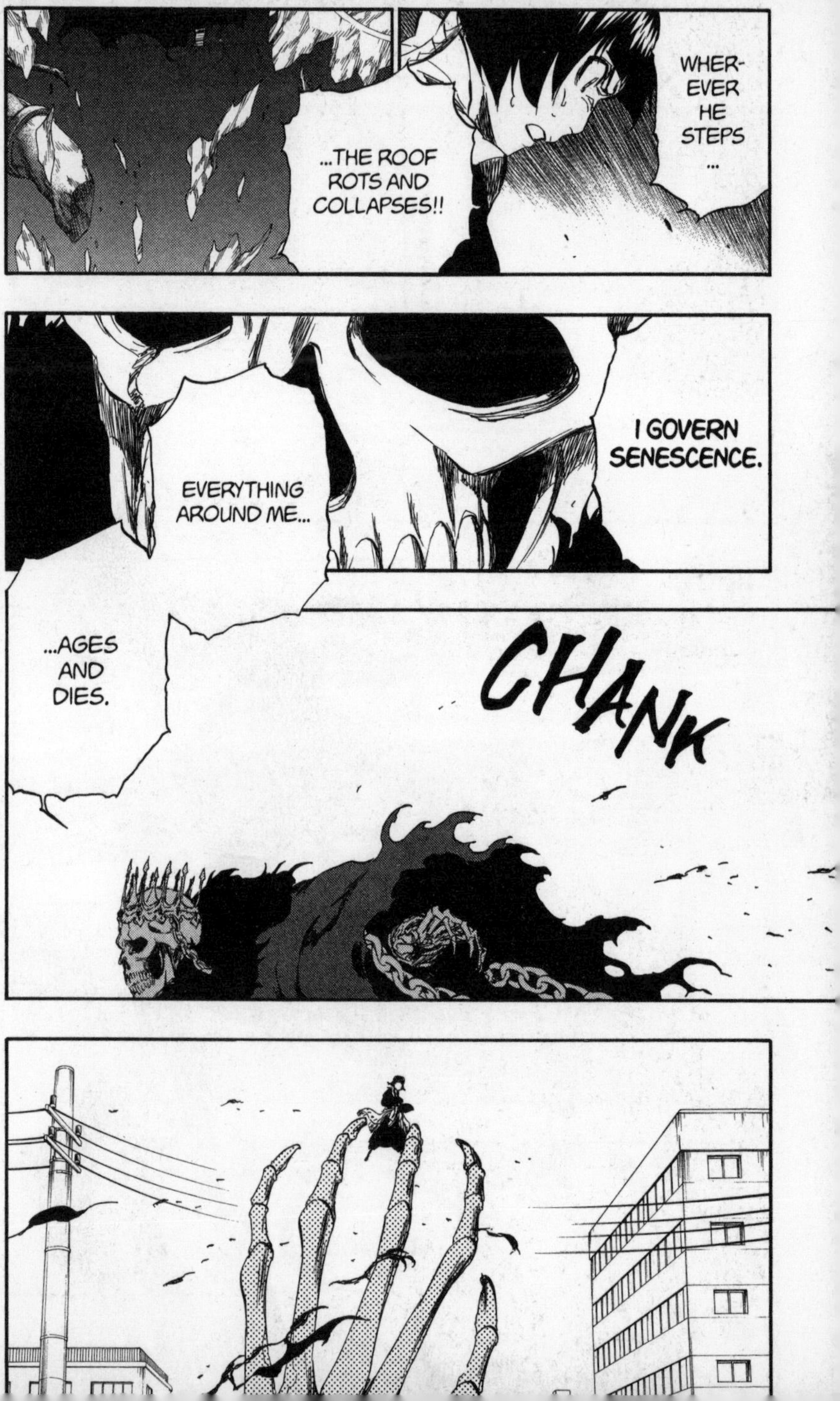
WHER-EVER HE STEPS...
...THE ROOF ROTS AND COLLAPSES!!
I GOVERN SENESCENCE.
EVERYTHING AROUND ME...
...AGES AND DIES.
CHANK

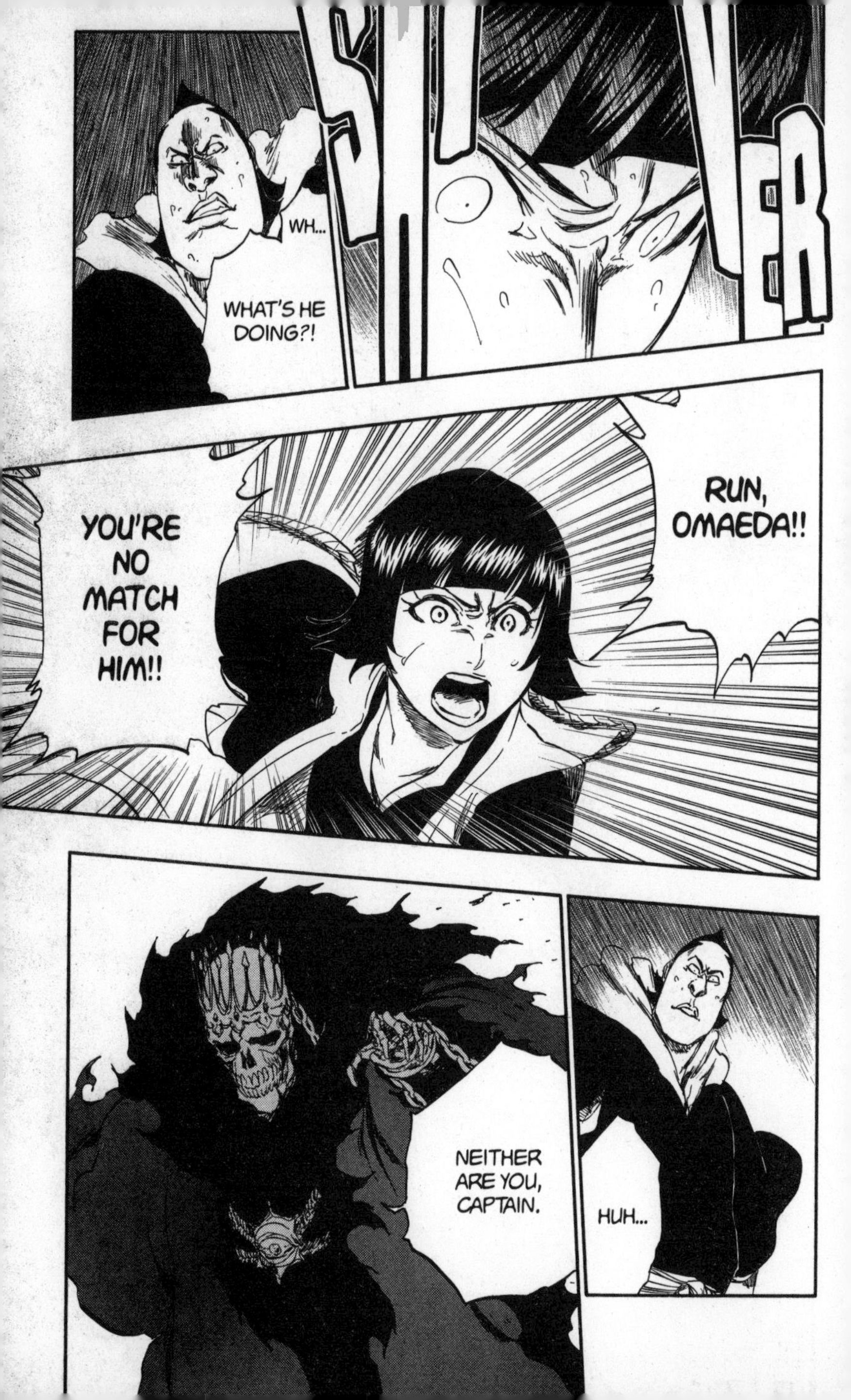
WH...
WHAT'S HE DOING?!
RUN, OMAEDA!!
YOU'RE NO MATCH FOR HIM!!
HUH...
NEITHER ARE YOU, CAPTAIN.

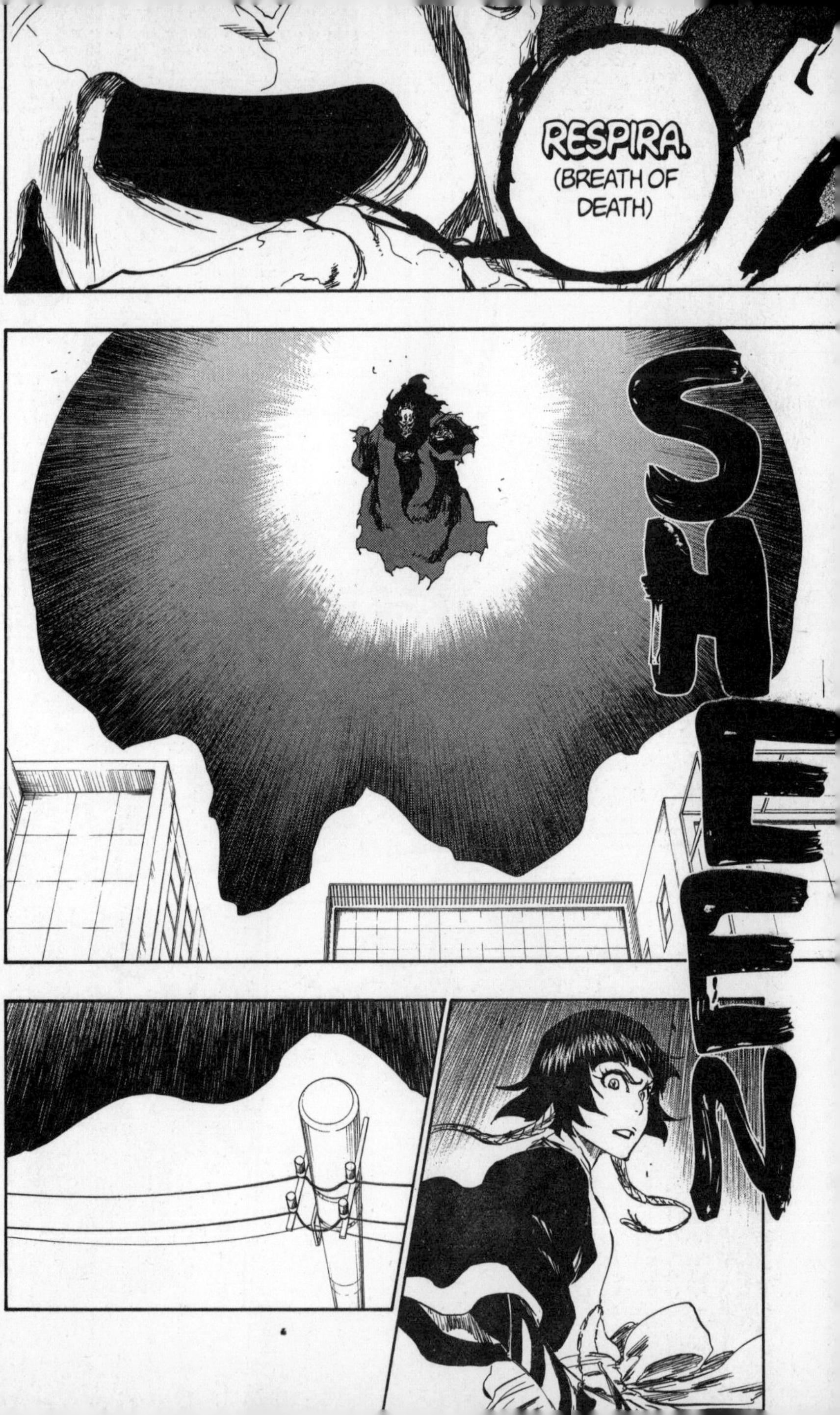
RESPIRA.
(BREATH OF DEATH)
SHEEN

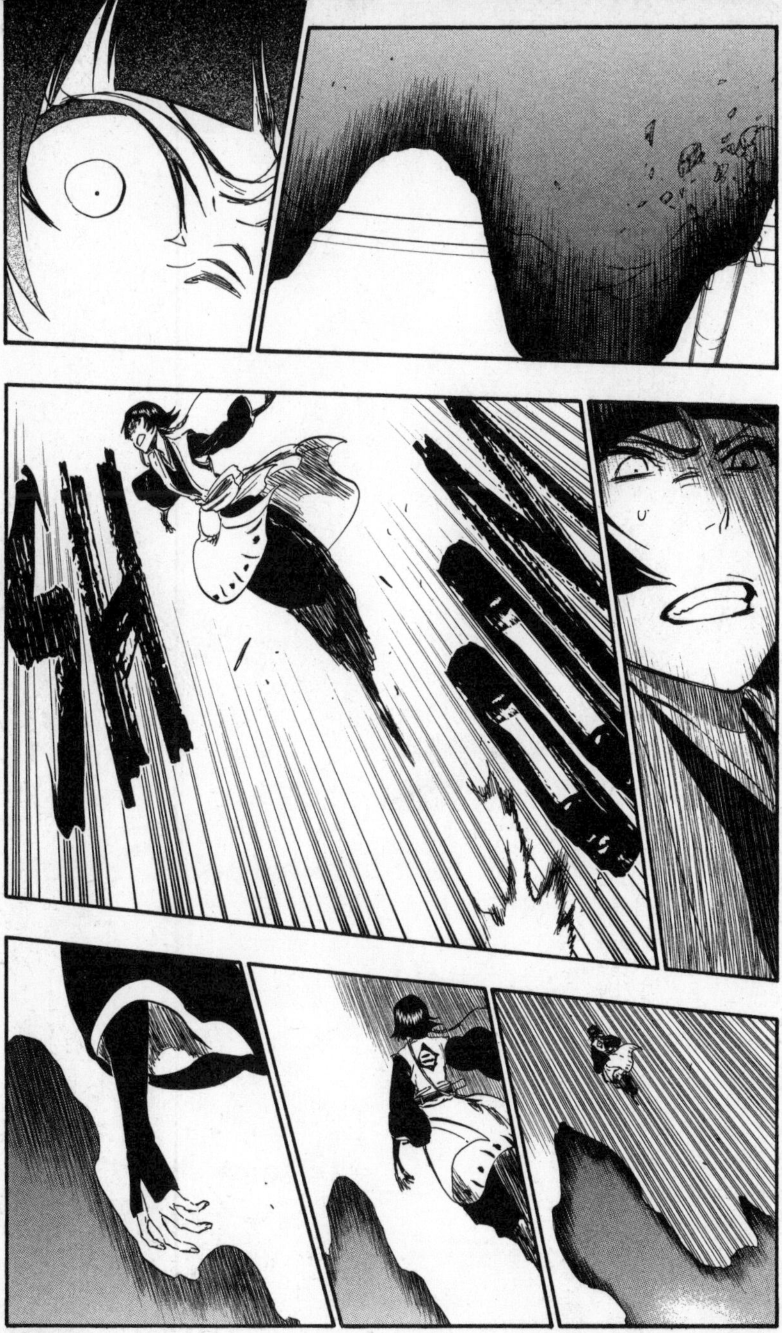

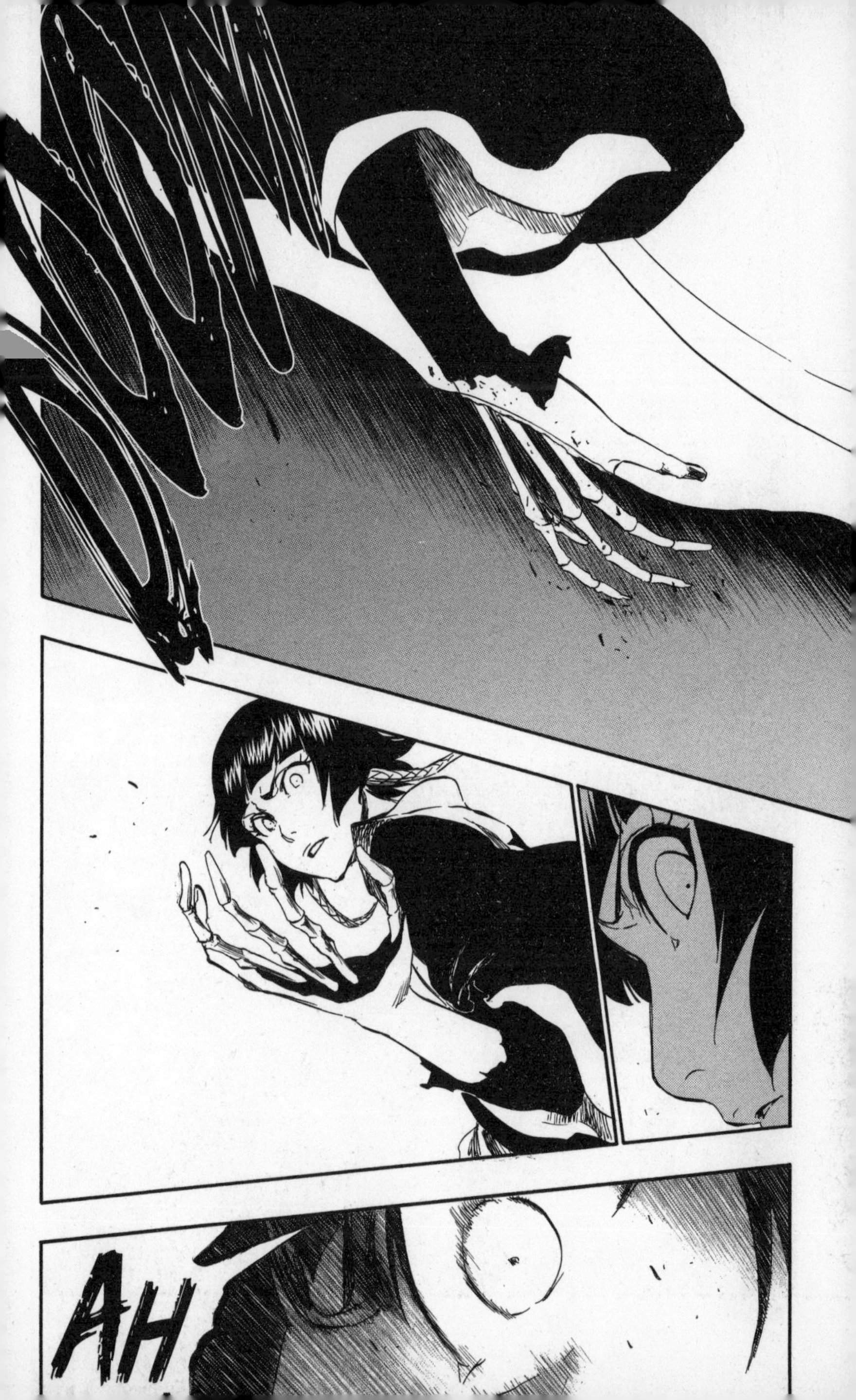
AH

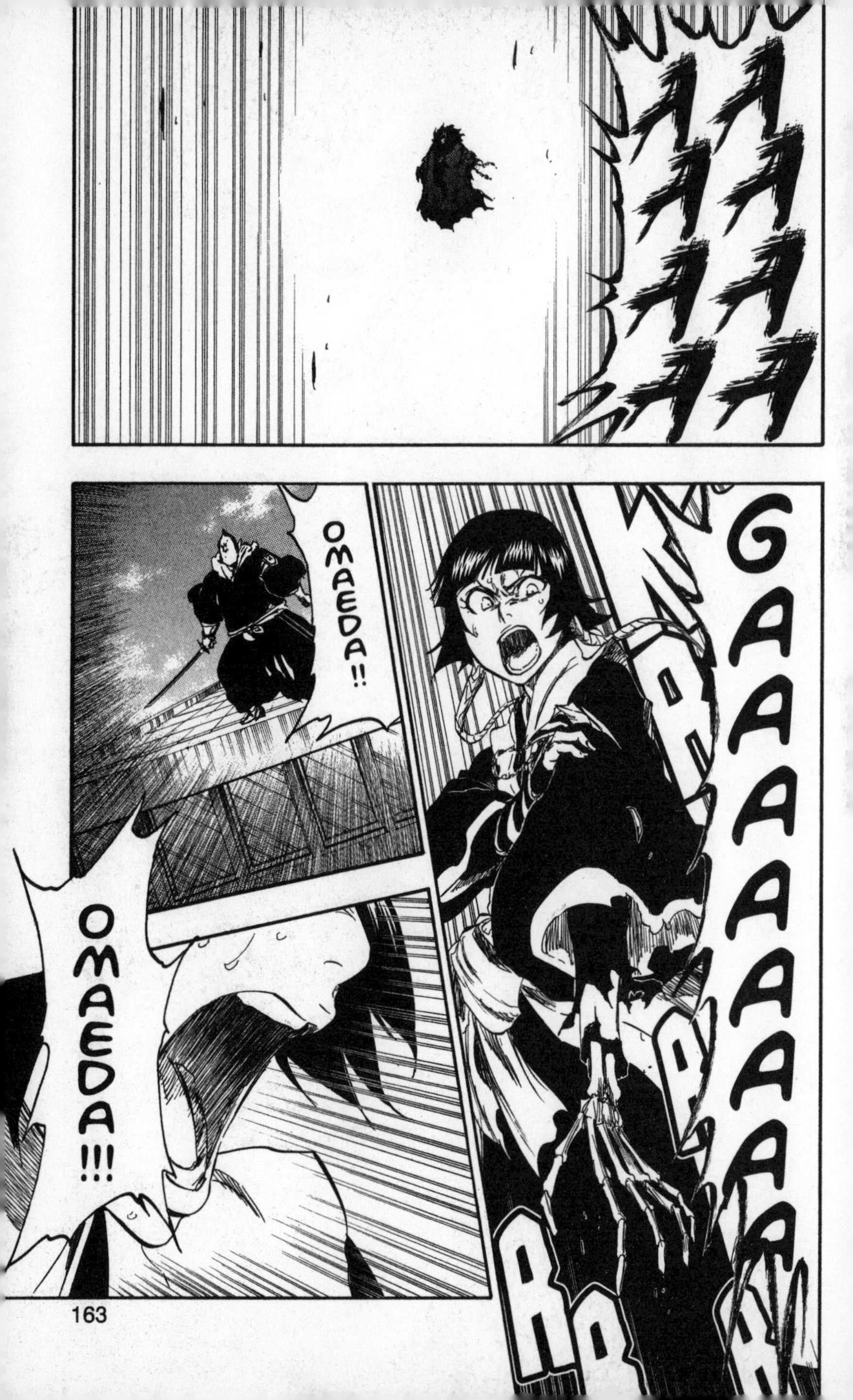
OMAEDA!!
OMAEDA!!!

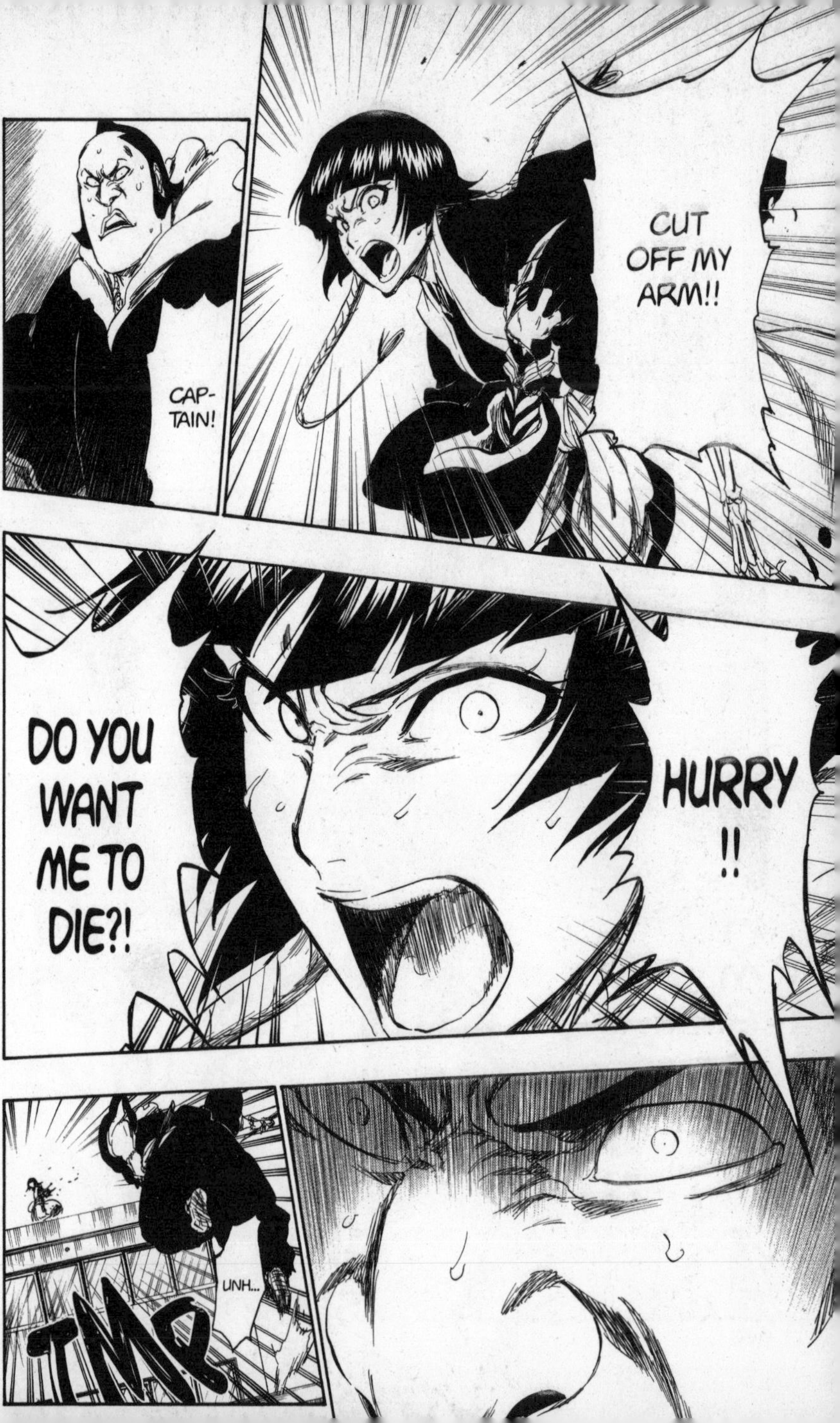
CUT OFF MY ARM!!
CAP-TAIN!
HURRY!!
DO YOU WANT ME TO DIE?!
UNH...
TMP

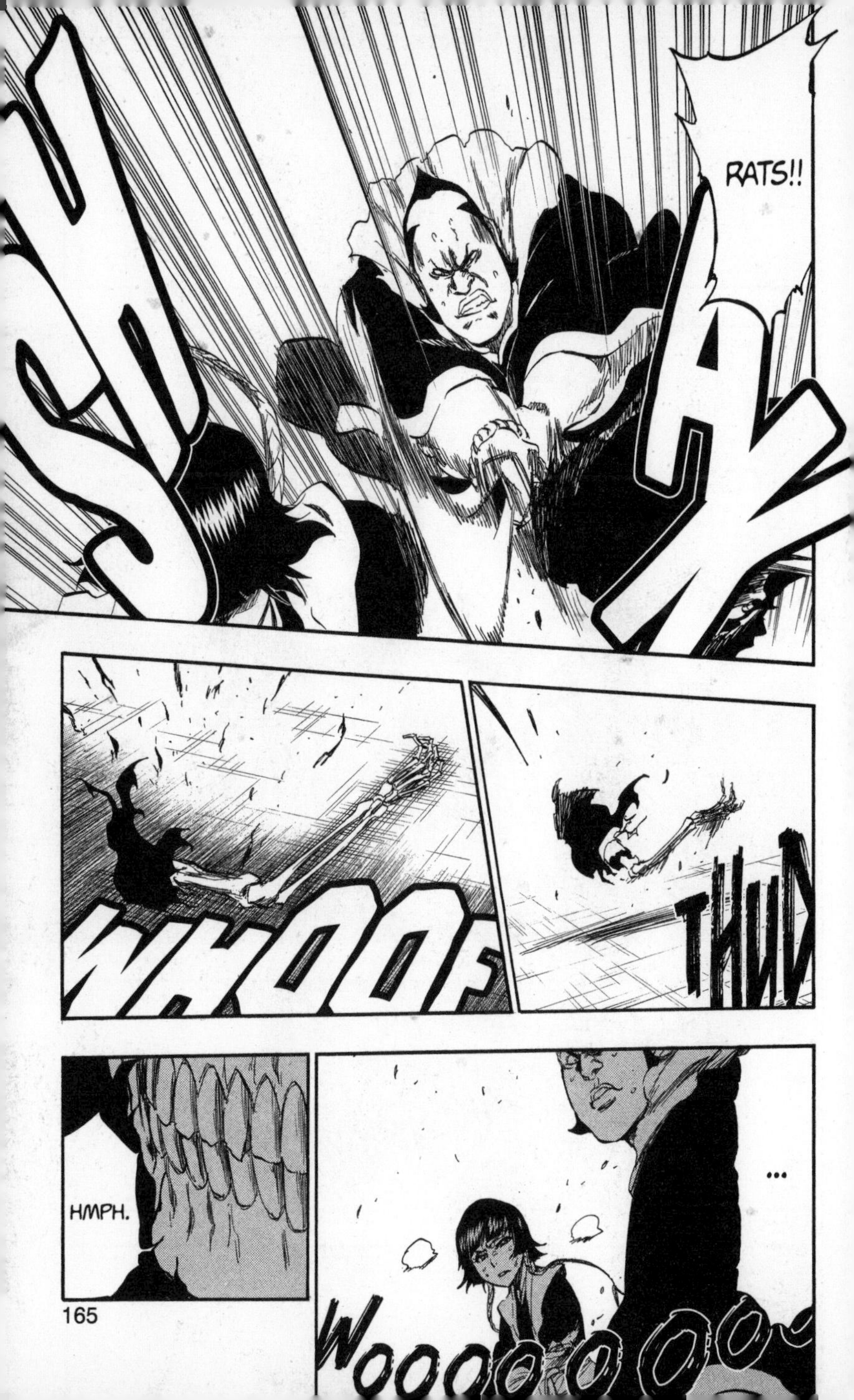

RATS!!
THUD
WHOOF
...
WOOOOOOOO
HMPH.

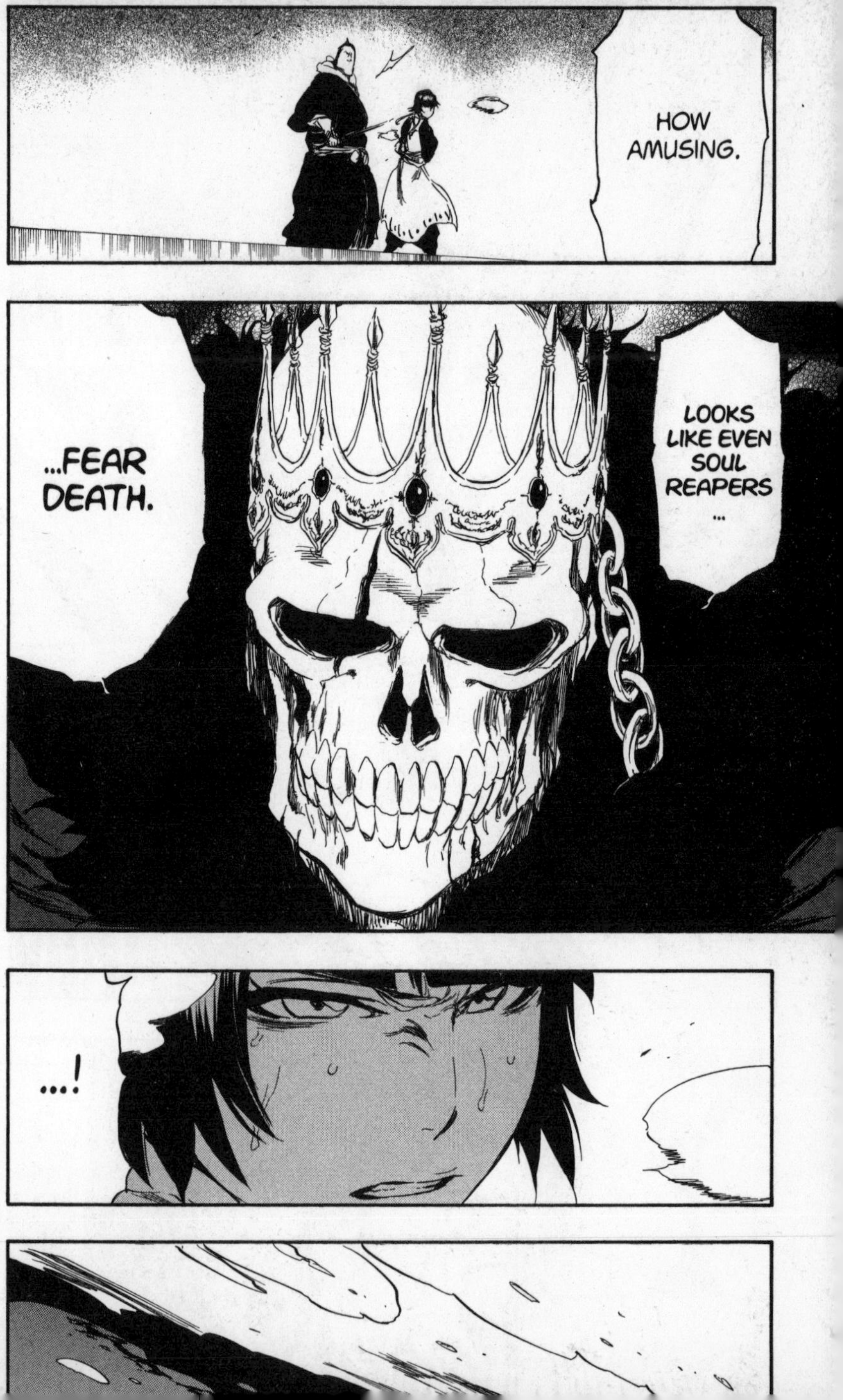
HOW AMUSING.
LOOKS LIKE EVEN SOUL REAPERS ...
...FEAR DEATH.
...!

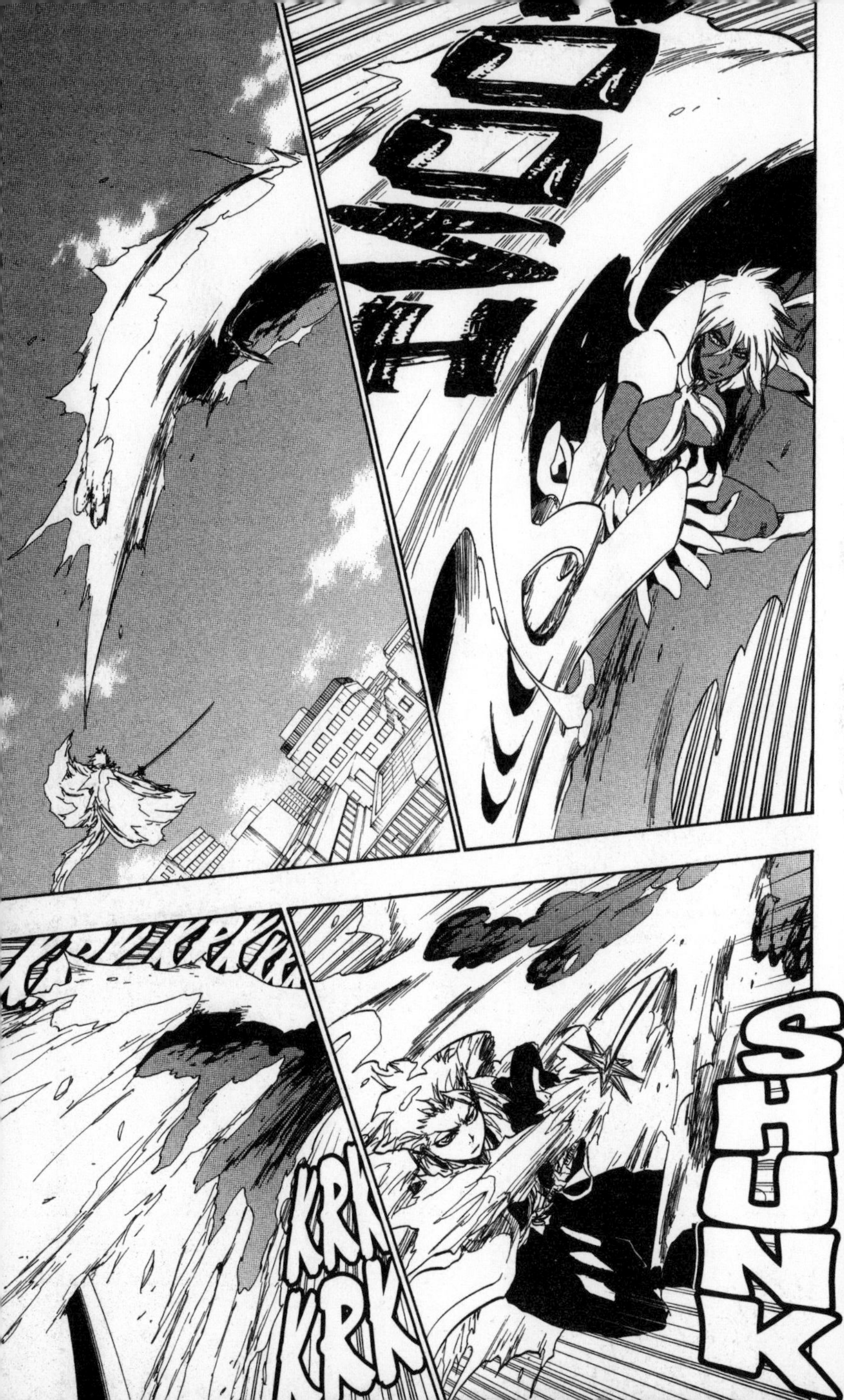
SHUNK
KRK
KRK

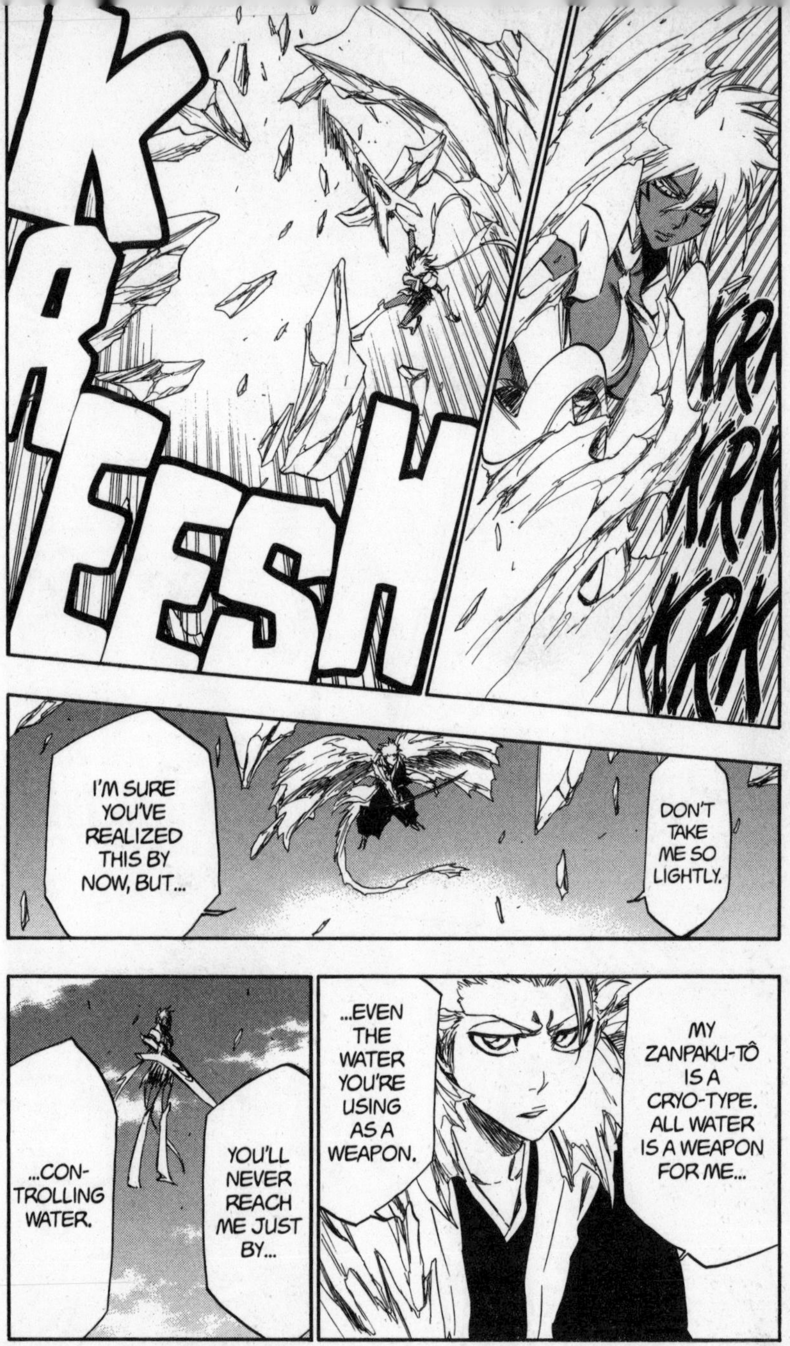
KRK
KRK
KRK
DON'T TAKE ME SO LIGHTLY.
I'M SURE YOU'VE REALIZED THIS BY NOW, BUT...
MY ZANPAKU-TÔ IS A CRYO-TYPE. ALL WATER IS A WEAPON FOR ME...
...EVEN THE WATER YOU'RE USING AS A WEAPON.
YOU'LL NEVER REACH ME JUST BY...
...CON-TROLLING WATER.

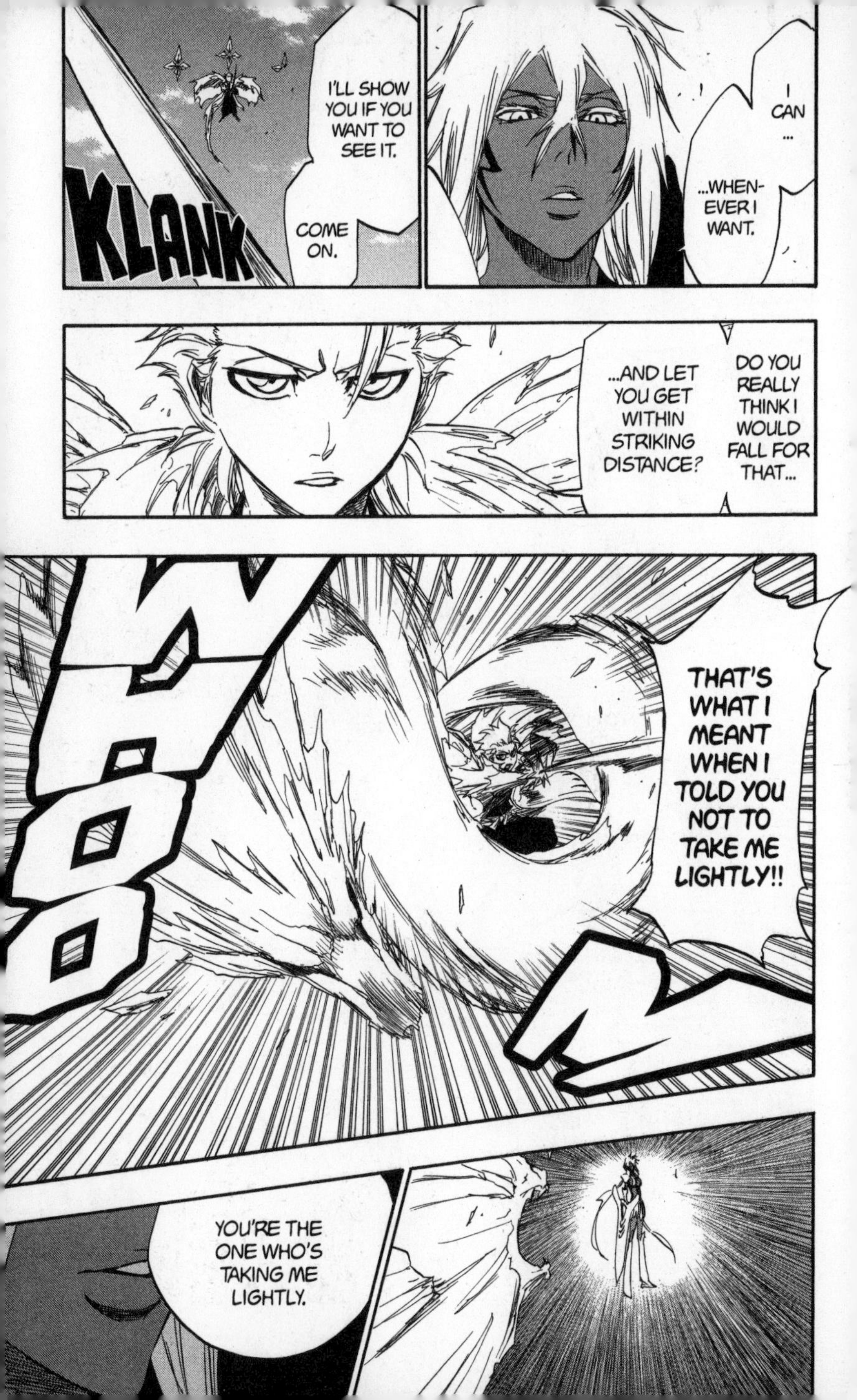
I CAN ...
...WHEN- EVER I WANT.
I'LL SHOW YOU IF YOU WANT TO SEE IT.
COME ON.
KLANK
DO YOU REALLY THINK I WOULD FALL FOR THAT...
...AND LET YOU GET WITHIN STRIKING DISTANCE?
THAT'S WHAT I MEANT WHEN I TOLD YOU NOT TO TAKE ME LIGHTLY!!
YOU'RE THE ONE WHO'S TAKING ME LIGHTLY.

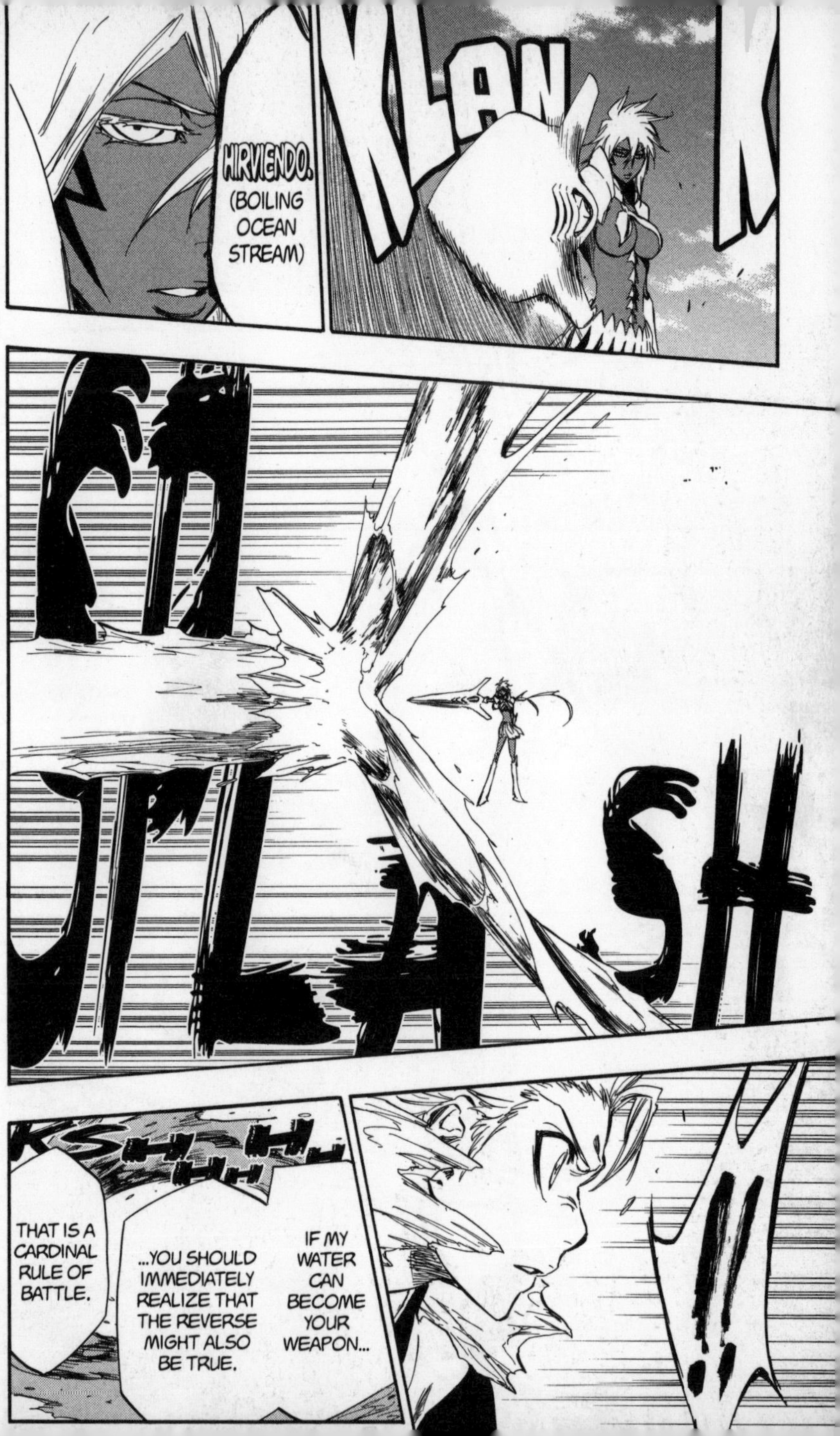
HIRVIENDO.
(BOILING OCEAN STREAM)
!!
IF MY WATER CAN BECOME YOUR WEAPON...
...YOU SHOULD IMMEDIATELY REALIZE THAT THE REVERSE MIGHT ALSO BE TRUE.
THAT IS A CARDINAL RULE OF BATTLE.

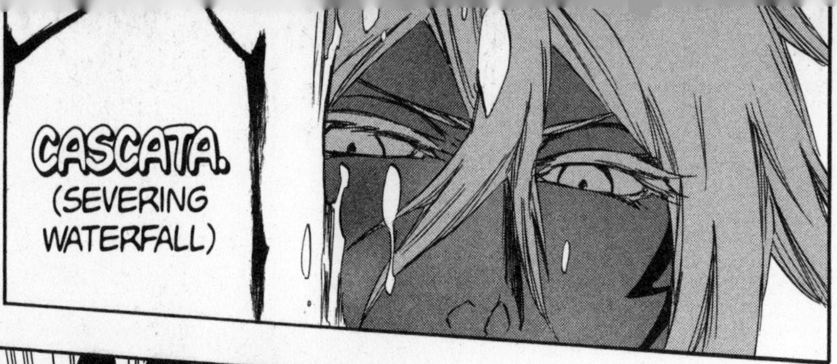
CASCATA.
(SEVERING WATERFALL)
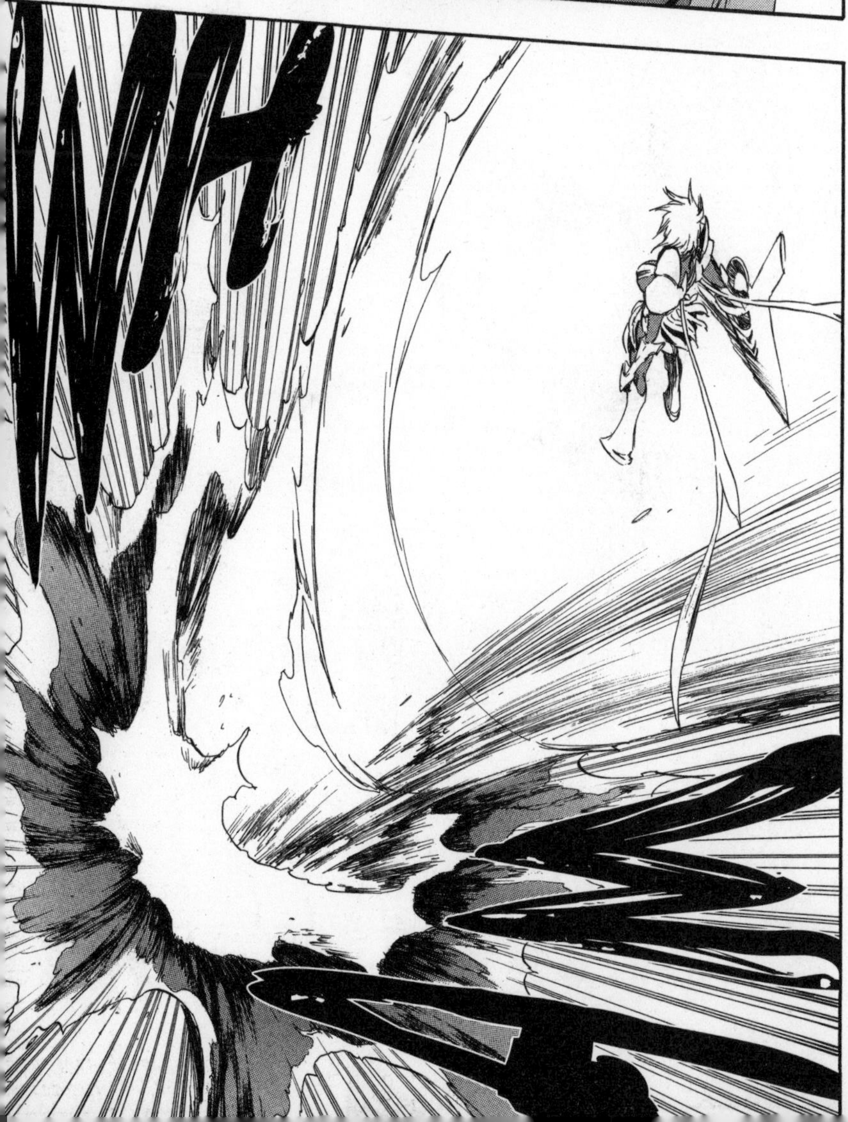

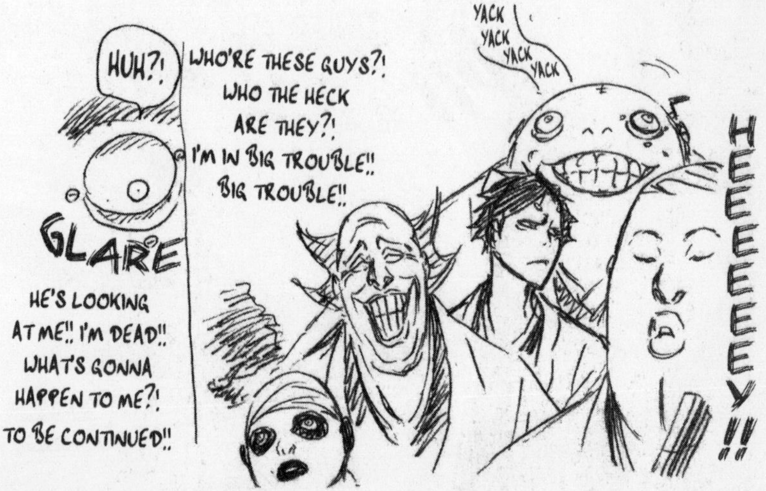
YACK YACK YACK YACK
HEEEEEEEY!!
WHO'RE THESE GUYS?! WHO THE HECK ARE THEY?! I'M IN BIG TROUBLE!! BIG TROUBLE!!
HUH?!
GLARE
HE'S LOOKING AT ME!! I'M DEAD!! WHAT'S GONNA HAPPEN TO ME?! TO BE CONTINUED!!

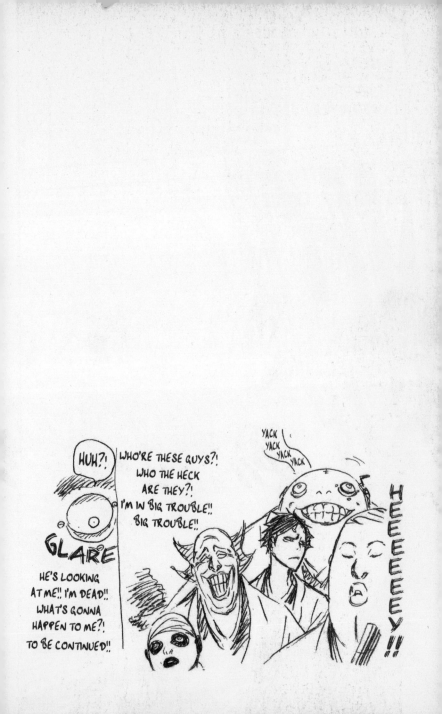

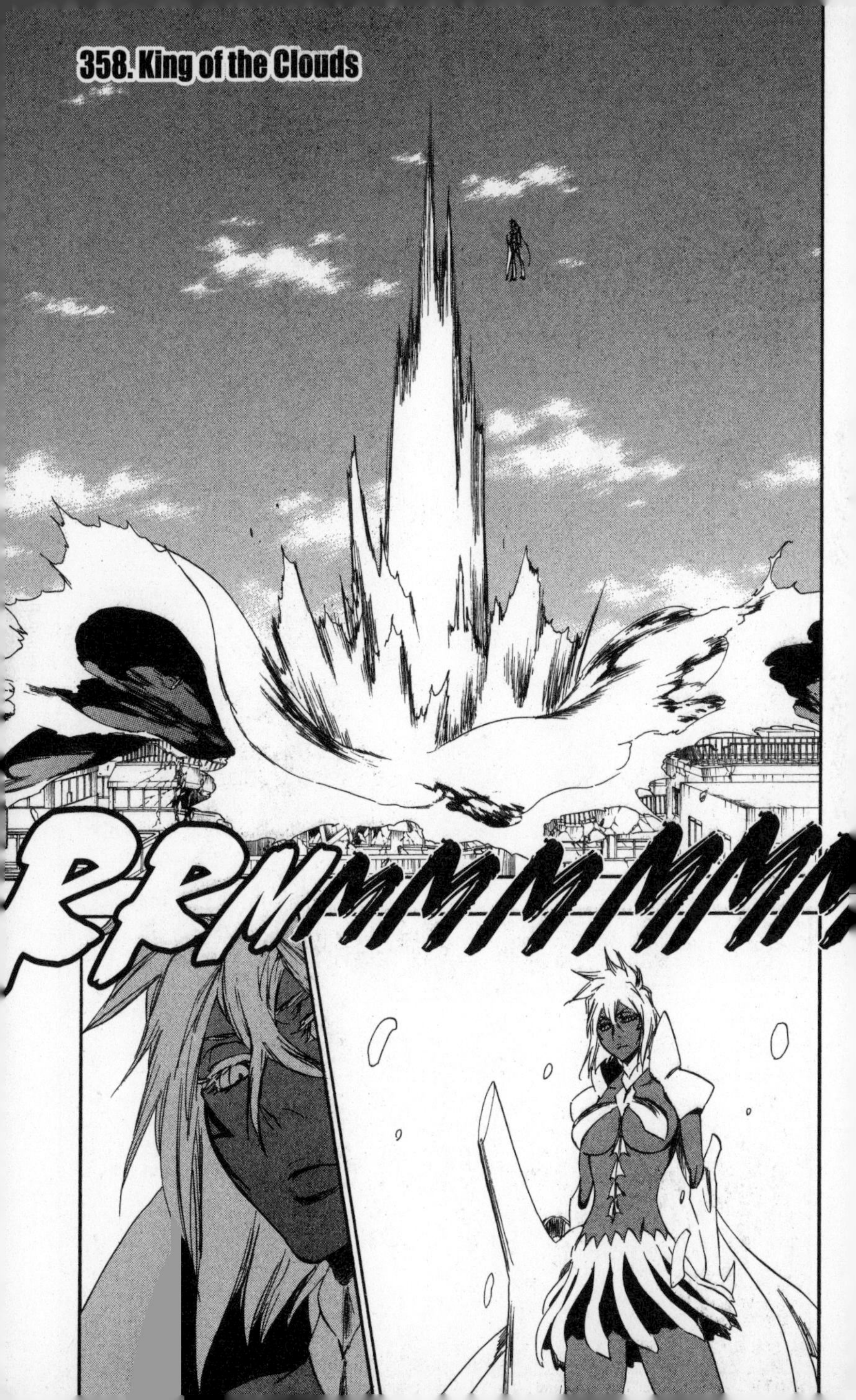
358. King of the Clouds
RRMMMMMMMMM

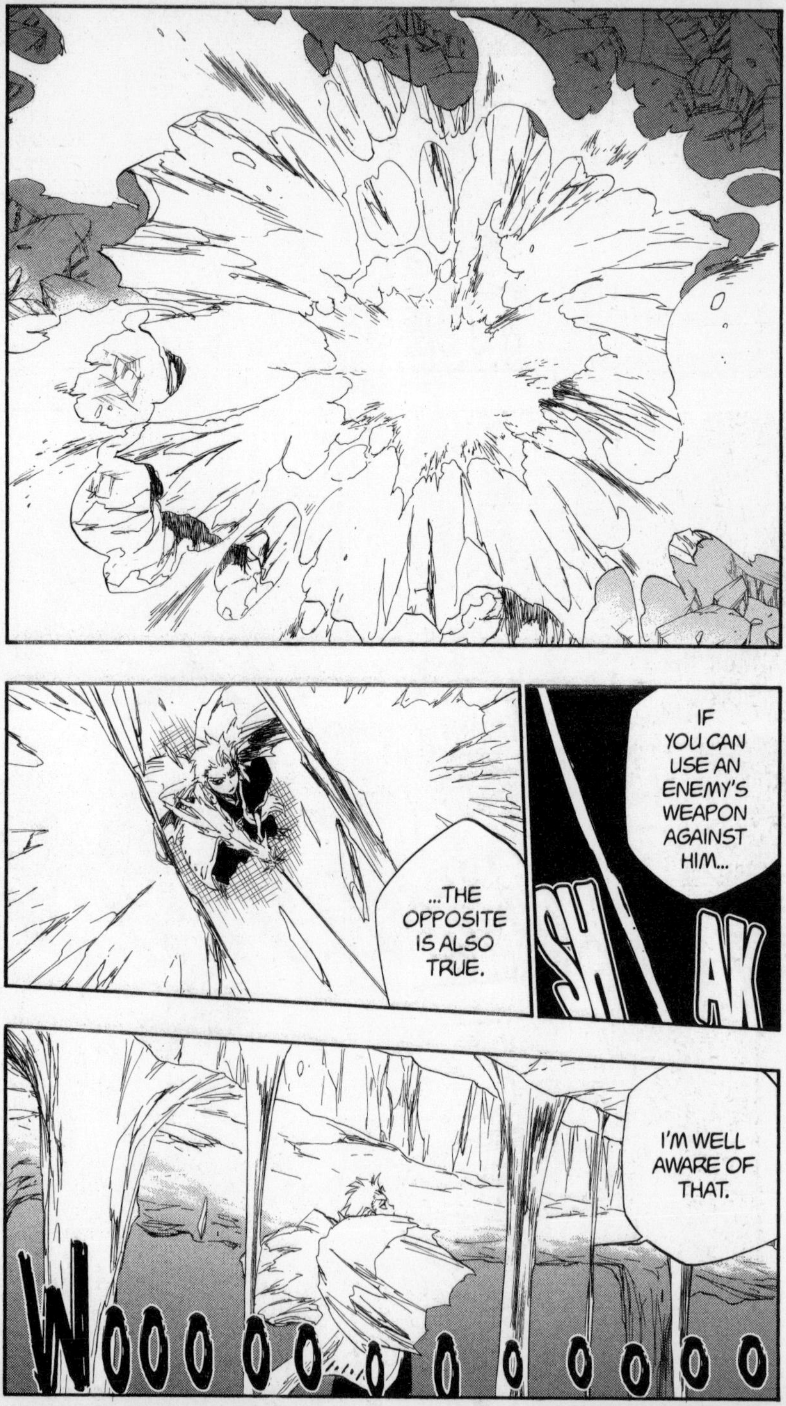
IF YOU CAN USE AN ENEMY'S WEAPON AGAINST HIM...
SHAK
...THE OPPOSITE IS ALSO TRUE.
I'M WELL AWARE OF THAT.
WOOOOOOOOOOOOO

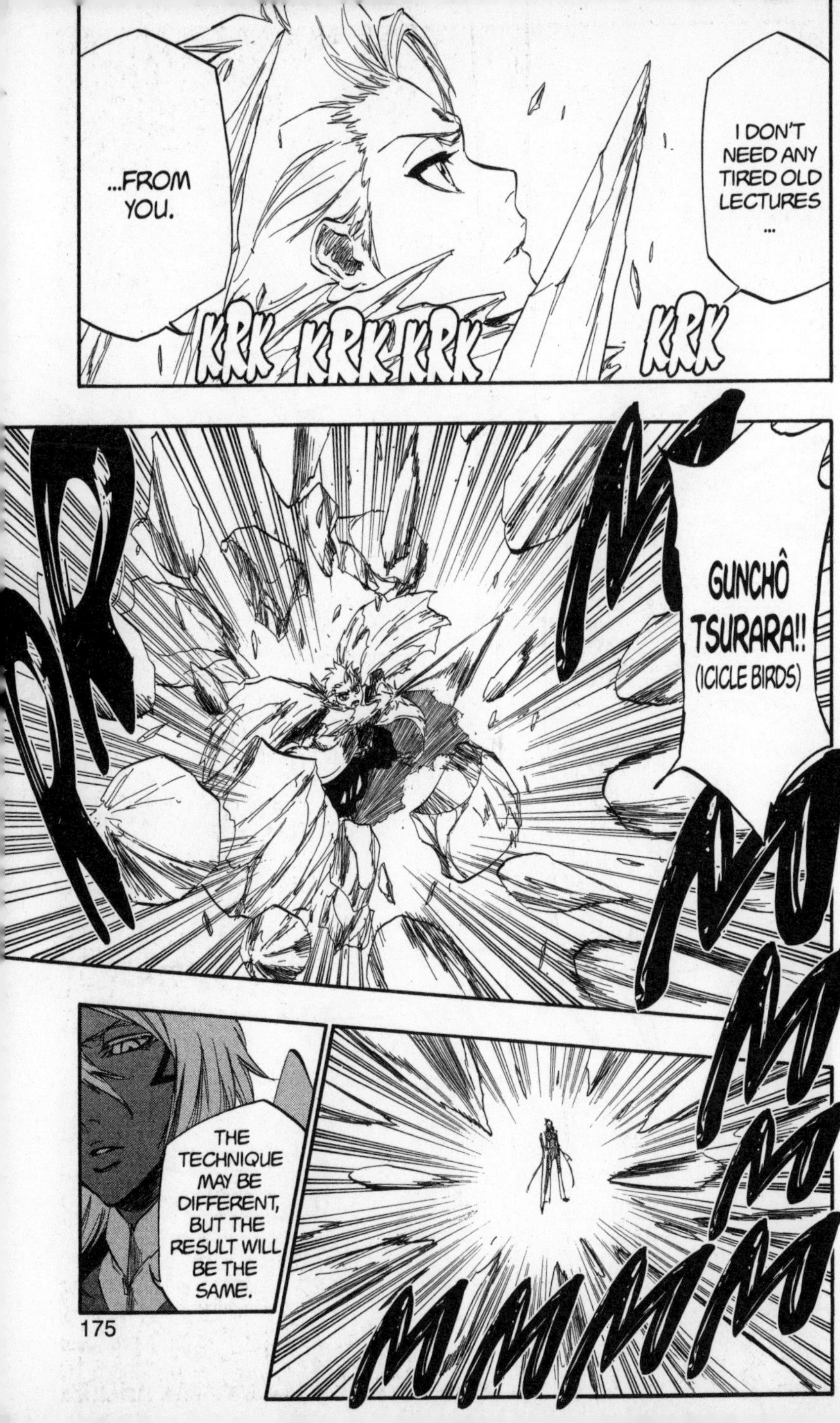
I DON'T NEED ANY TIRED OLD LECTURES ...
...FROM YOU.
KRK KRK KRK KRK
GUNCHÔ TSURARA!! (ICICLE BIRDS)
THE TECHNIQUE MAY BE DIFFERENT, BUT THE RESULT WILL BE THE SAME.

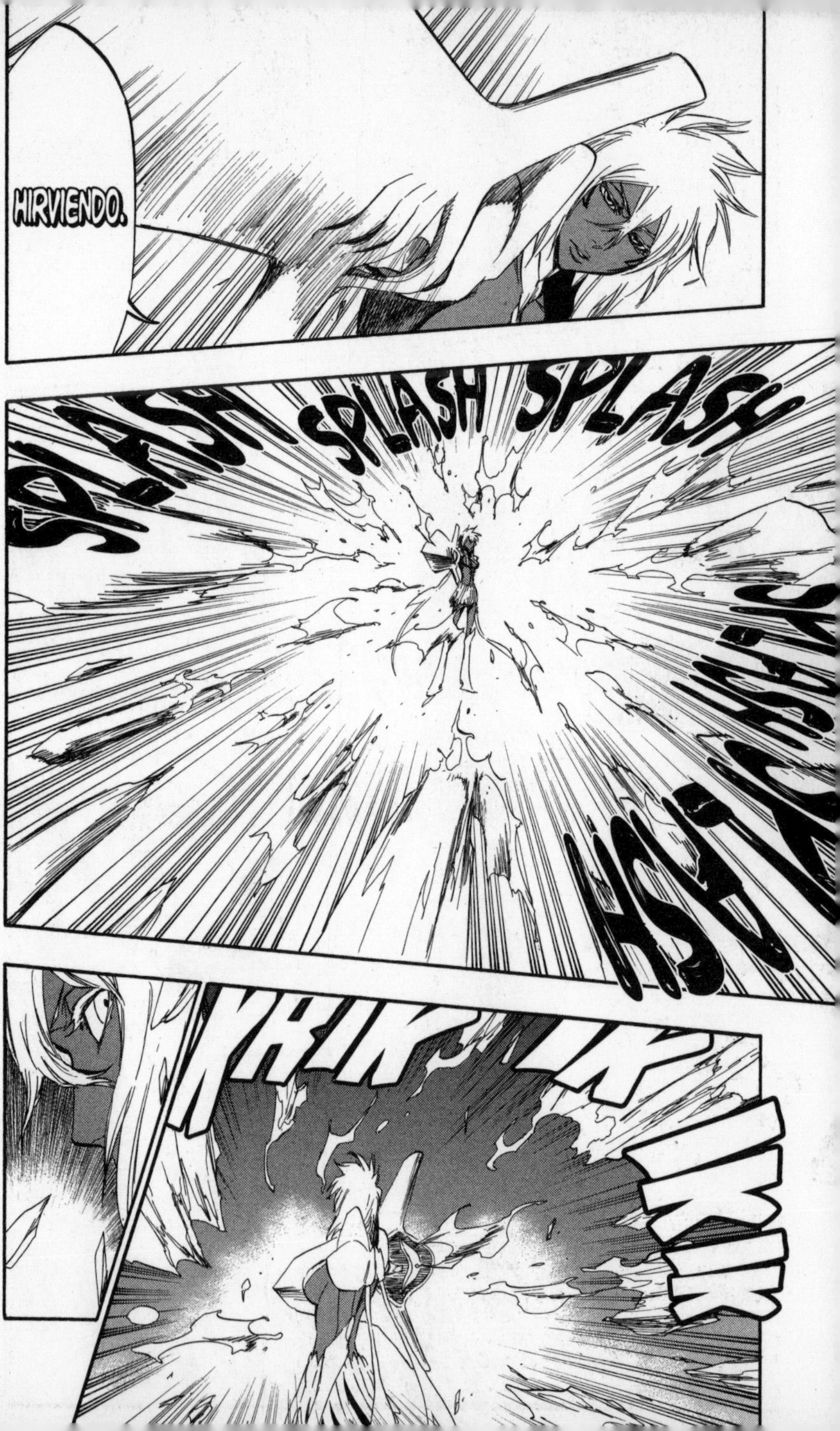
HIRVIENDO.
SPLASH SPLASH SPLASH

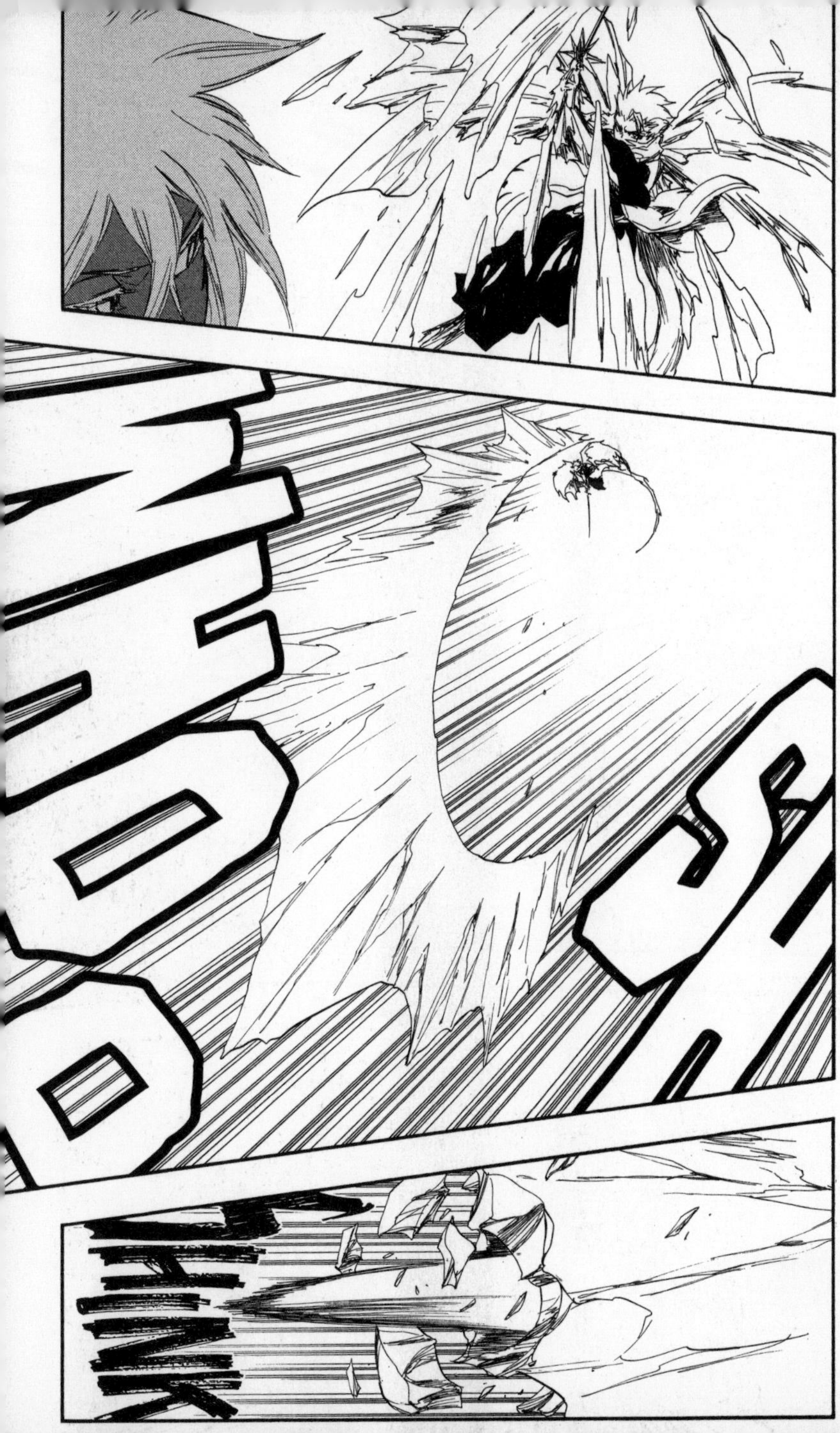
THUNK

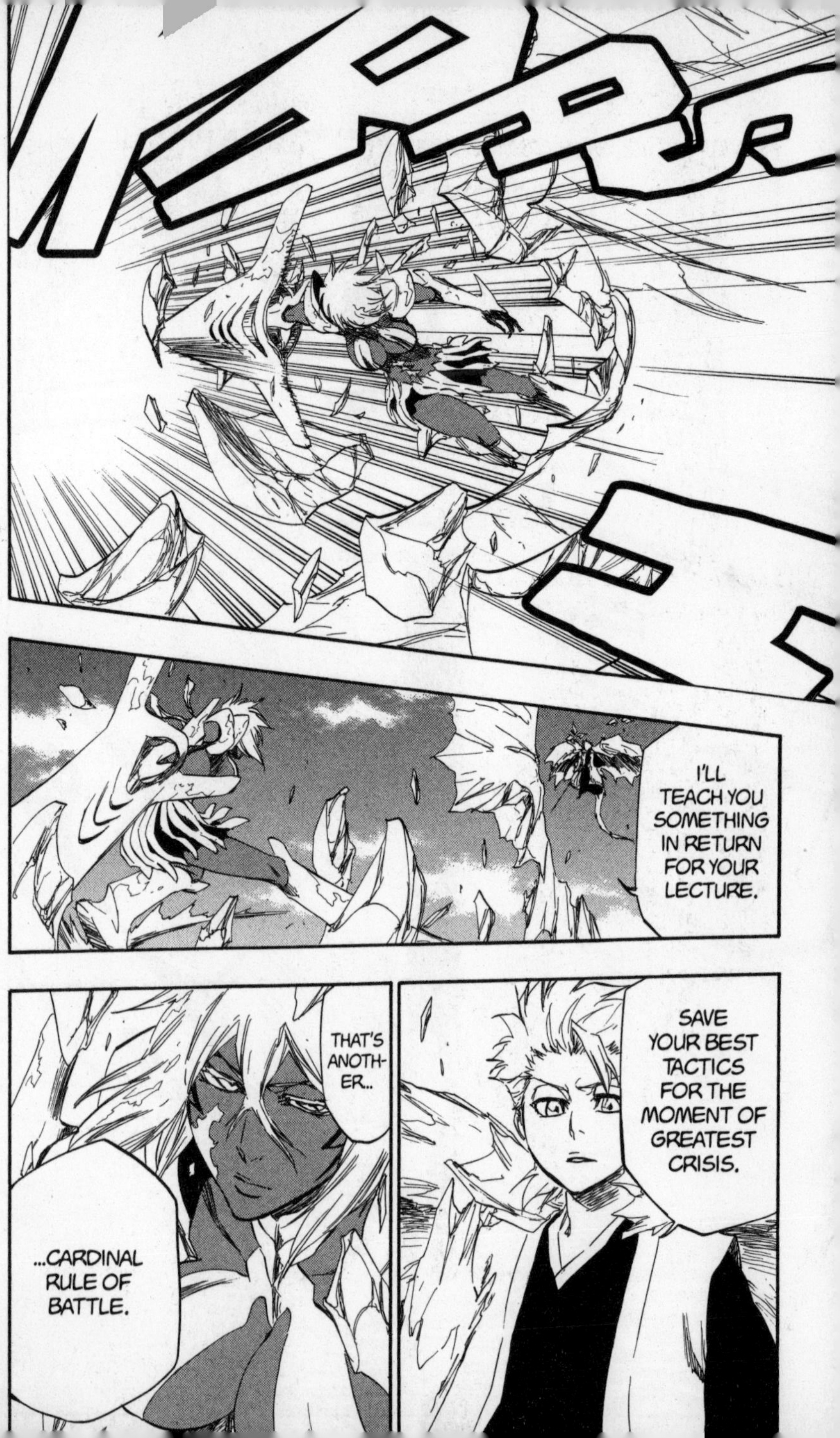
I'LL TEACH YOU SOMETHING IN RETURN FOR YOUR LECTURE.
SAVE YOUR BEST TACTICS FOR THE MOMENT OF GREATEST CRISIS.
THAT'S ANOTHER...
...CARDINAL RULE OF BATTLE.

BLEACH358. King of the Clouds

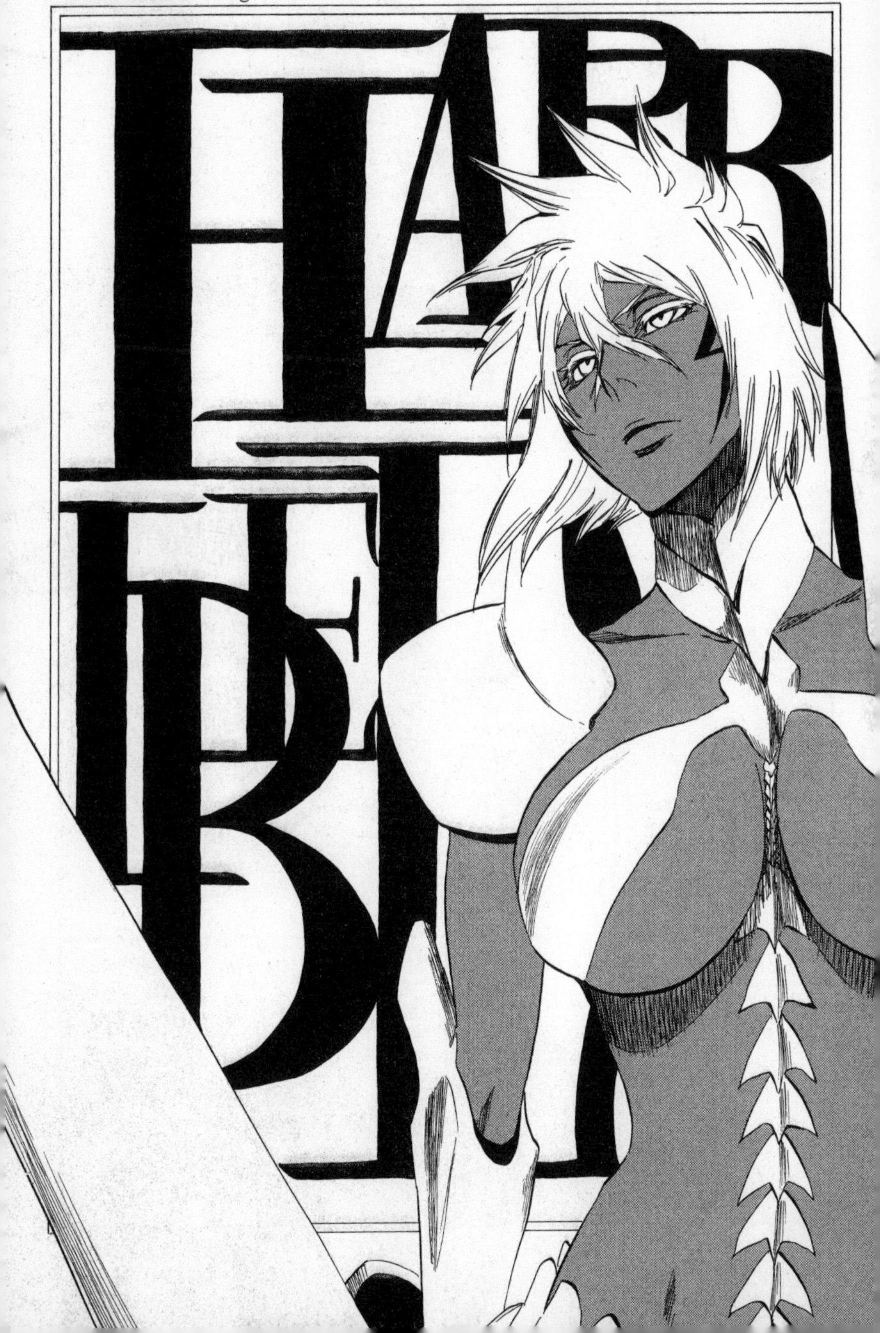

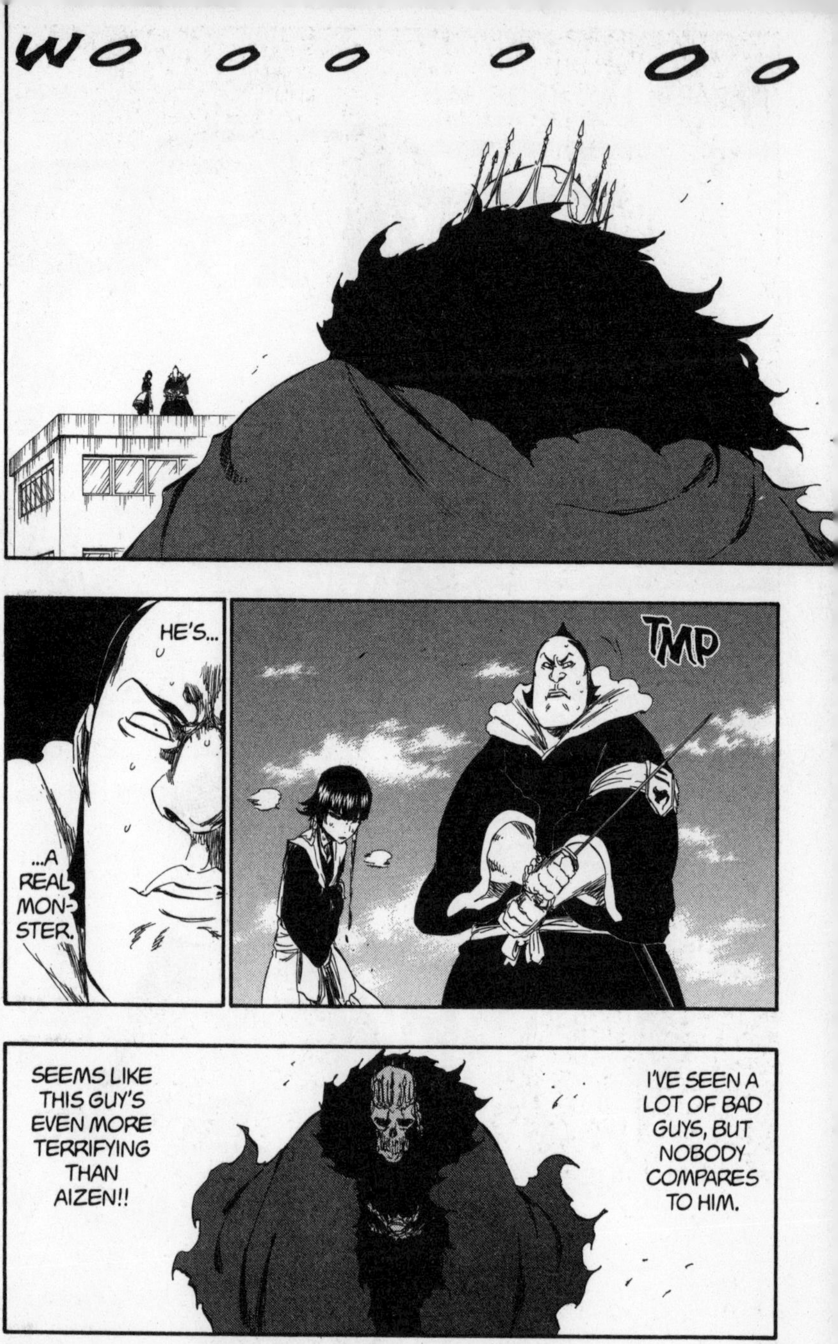
WOOOOOOO
TMP
HE'S...
...A REAL MONSTER.
I'VE SEEN A LOT OF BAD GUYS, BUT NOBODY COMPARES TO HIM.
SEEMS LIKE THIS GUY'S EVEN MORE TERRIFYING THAN AIZEN!!

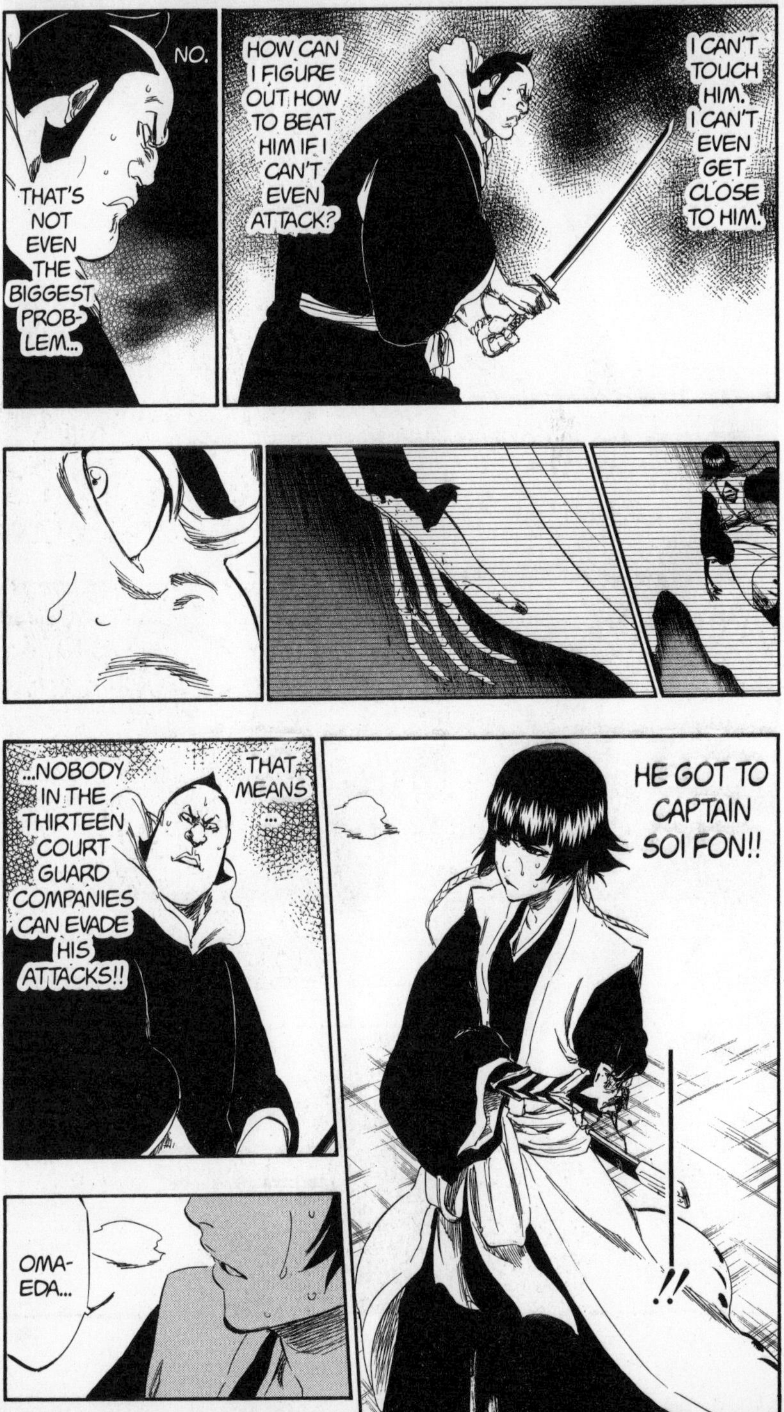
I CAN'T TOUCH HIM. I CAN'T EVEN GET CLOSE TO HIM.
HOW CAN I FIGURE OUT HOW TO BEAT HIM IF I CAN'T EVEN ATTACK?
NO.
THAT'S NOT EVEN THE BIGGEST PROB-LEM...
HE GOT TO CAPTAIN SOI FON!!
!!
THAT MEANS...
...NOBODY IN THE THIRTEEN COURT GUARD COMPANIES CAN EVADE HIS ATTACKS!!
OMA-EDA...

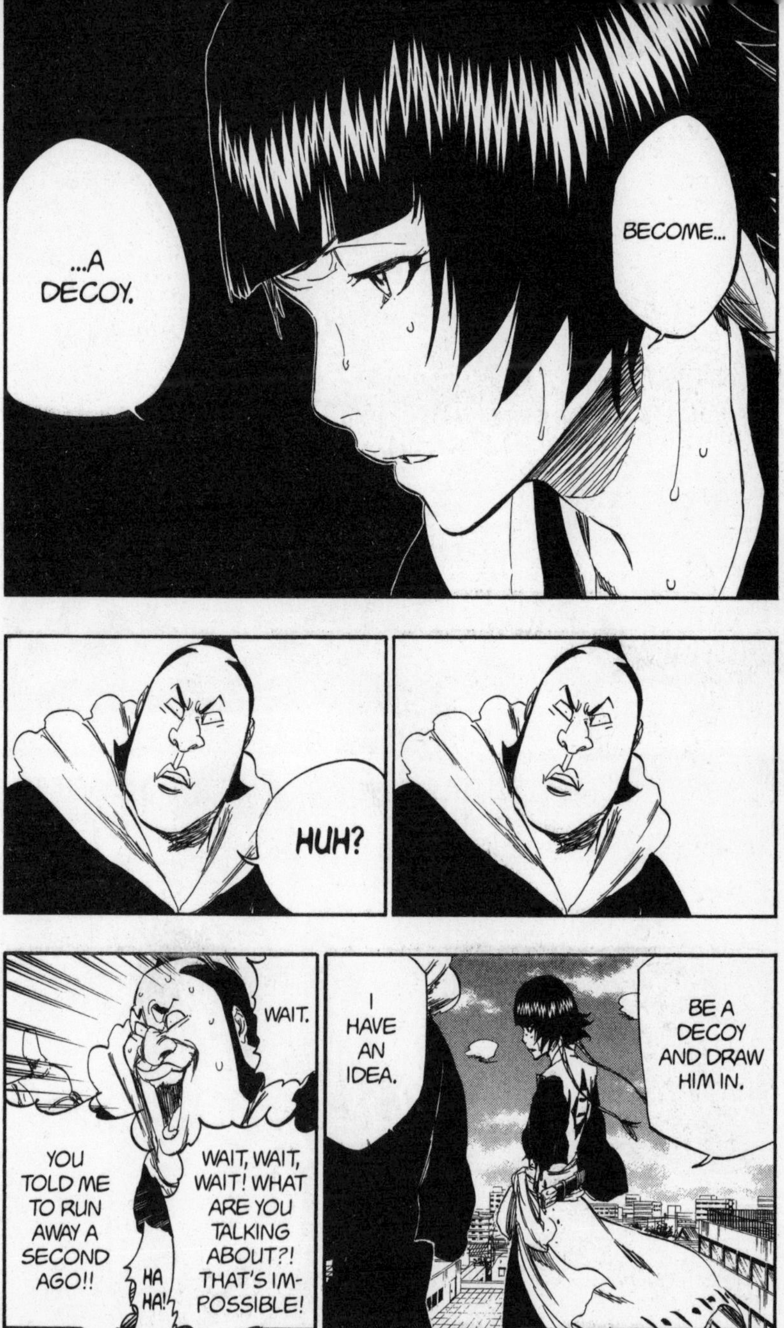
BECOME...
...A DECOY.
HUH?
BE A DECOY AND DRAW HIM IN.
I HAVE AN IDEA.
WAIT.
WAIT, WAIT, WAIT! WHAT ARE YOU TALKING ABOUT?! THAT'S IM-POSSIBLE!
HA HA!
YOU TOLD ME TO RUN AWAY A SECOND AGO!!

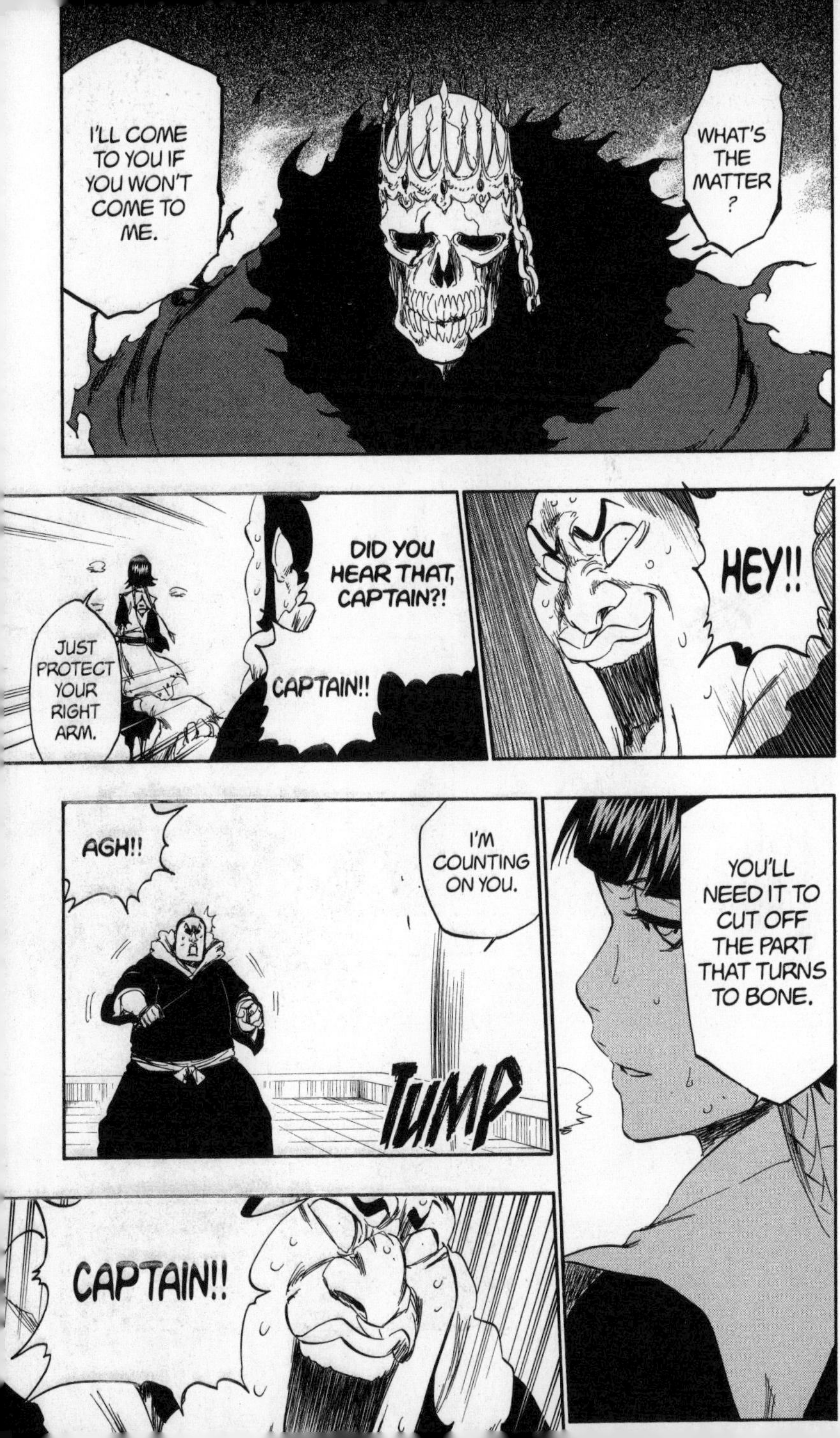
WHAT'S THE MATTER?
I'LL COME TO YOU IF YOU WON'T COME TO ME.
HEY!!
DID YOU HEAR THAT, CAPTAIN?!
CAPTAIN!!
JUST PROTECT YOUR RIGHT ARM.
YOU'LL NEED IT TO CUT OFF THE PART THAT TURNS TO BONE.
I'M COUNTING ON YOU.
AGH!!
TUMP
CAPTAIN!!

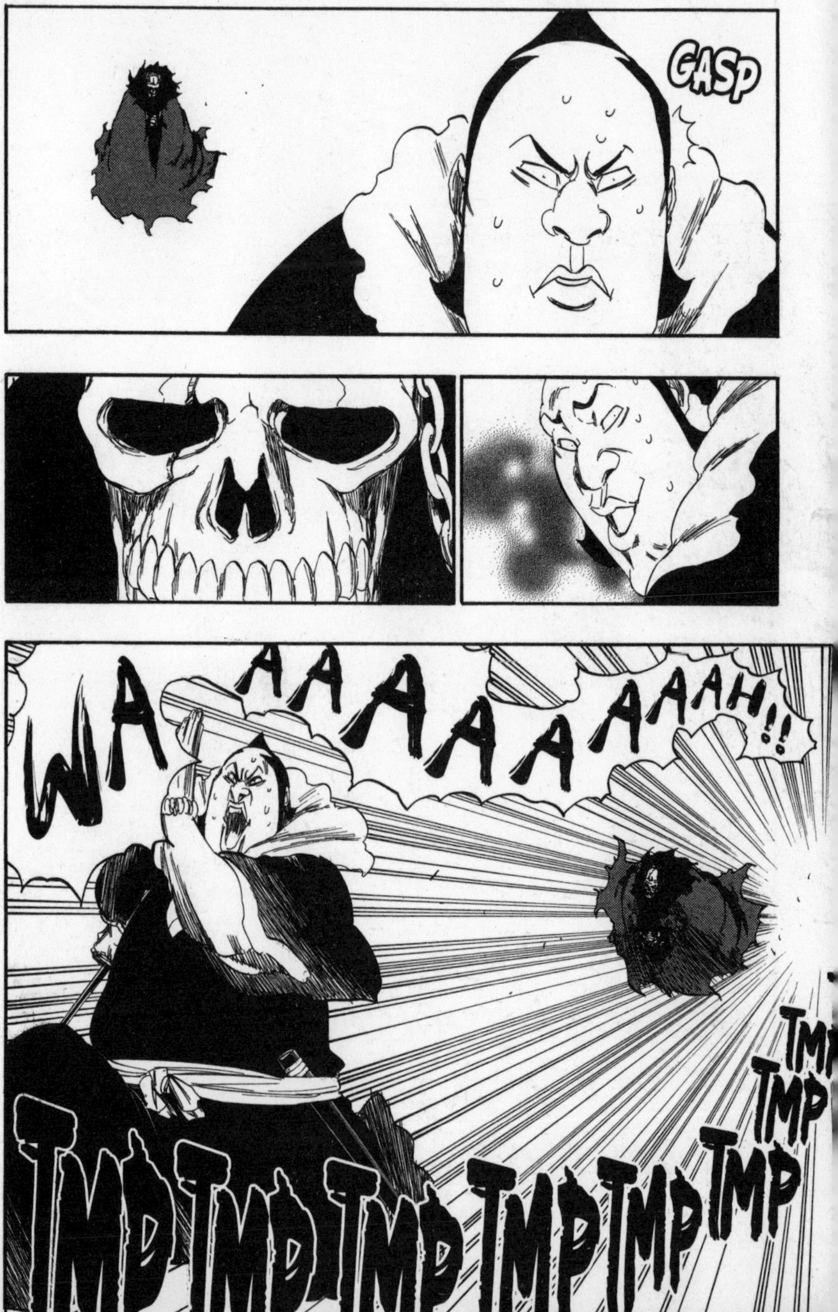
GASP
WAAAAAAAAAAAH!!
TMP TMP TMP TMP TMP TMP TMP TMP

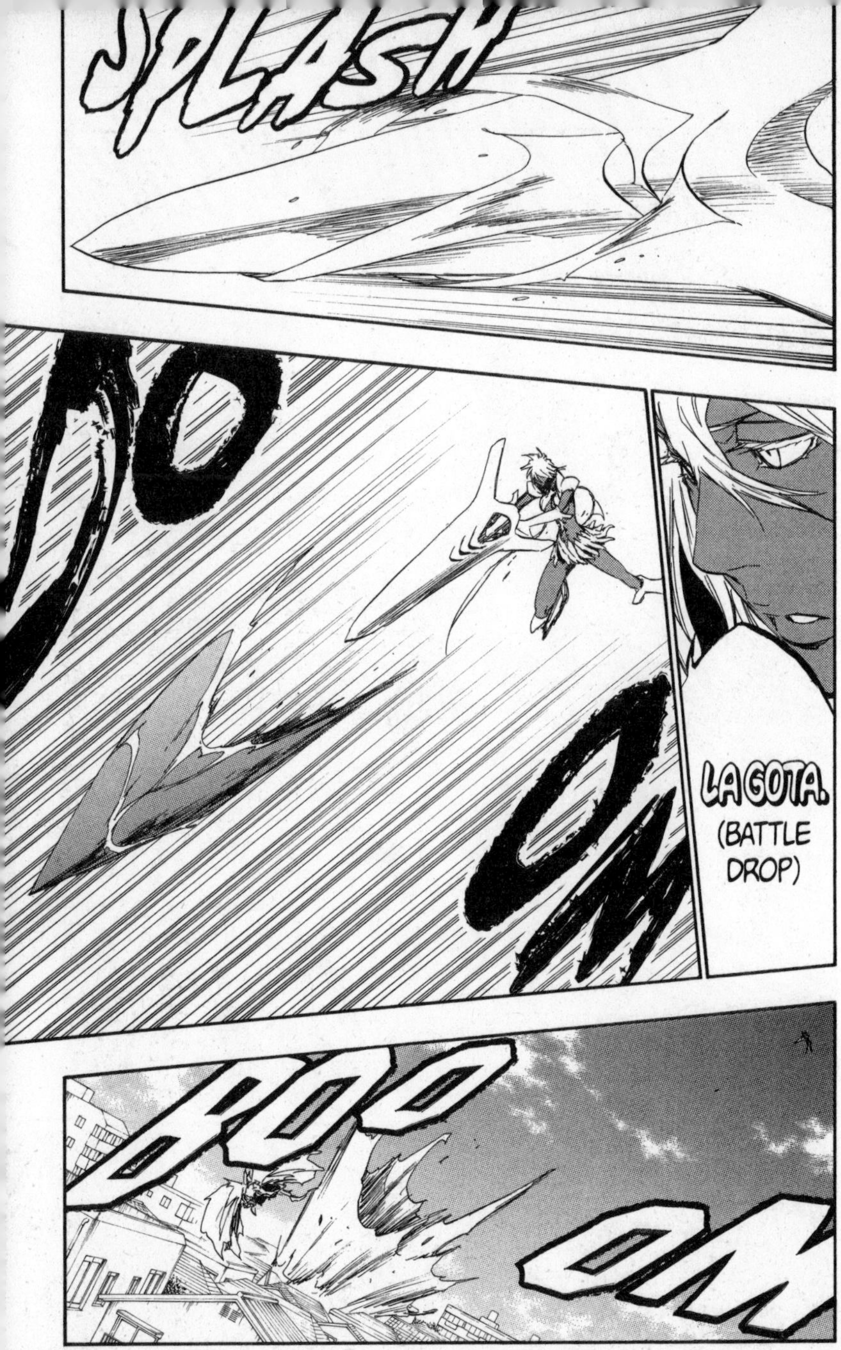
SPLASH
LA GOTA.
(BATTLE DROP)
DOOM
FOOOM

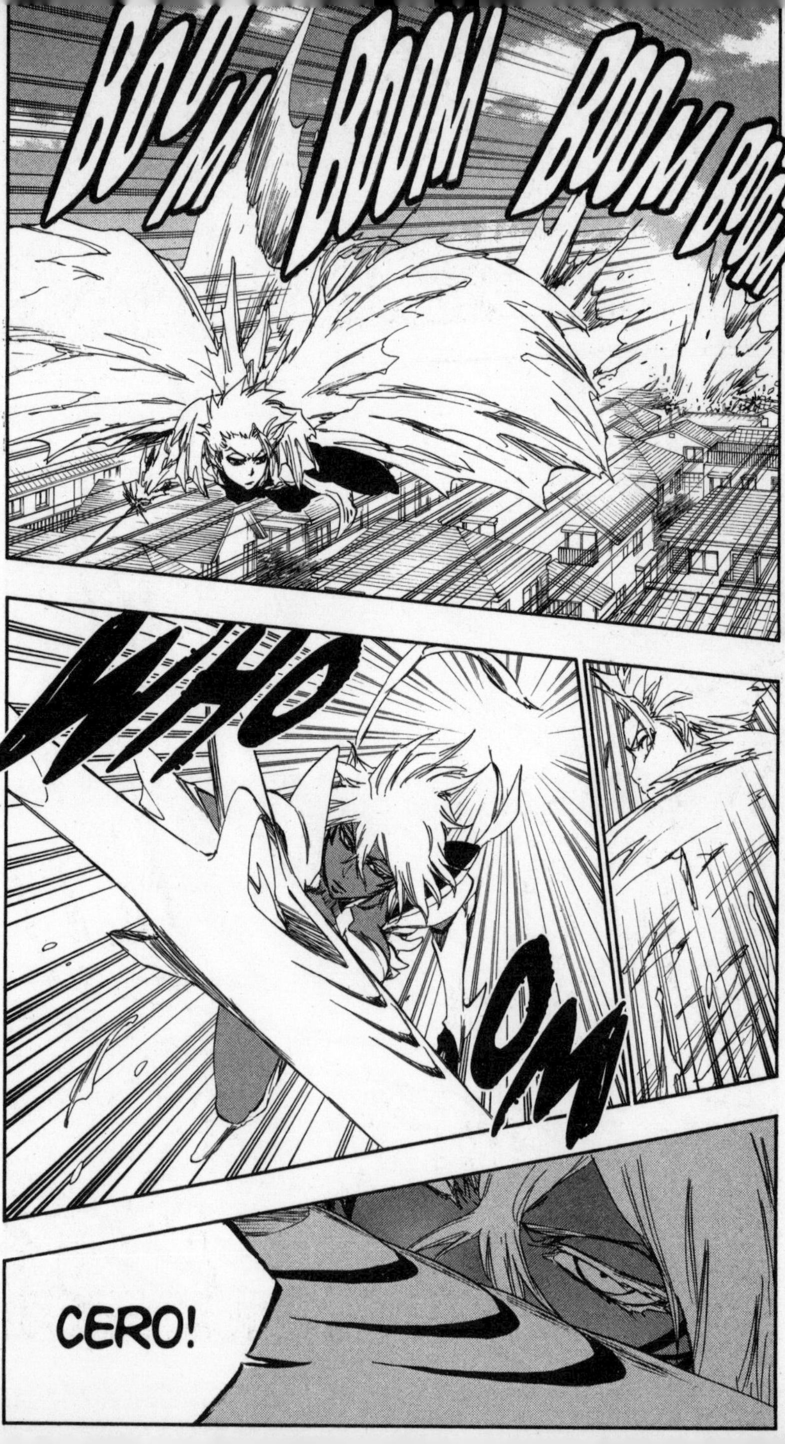
BOOM BOOM BOOM BOOM BOOM
WHOOM
CERO!

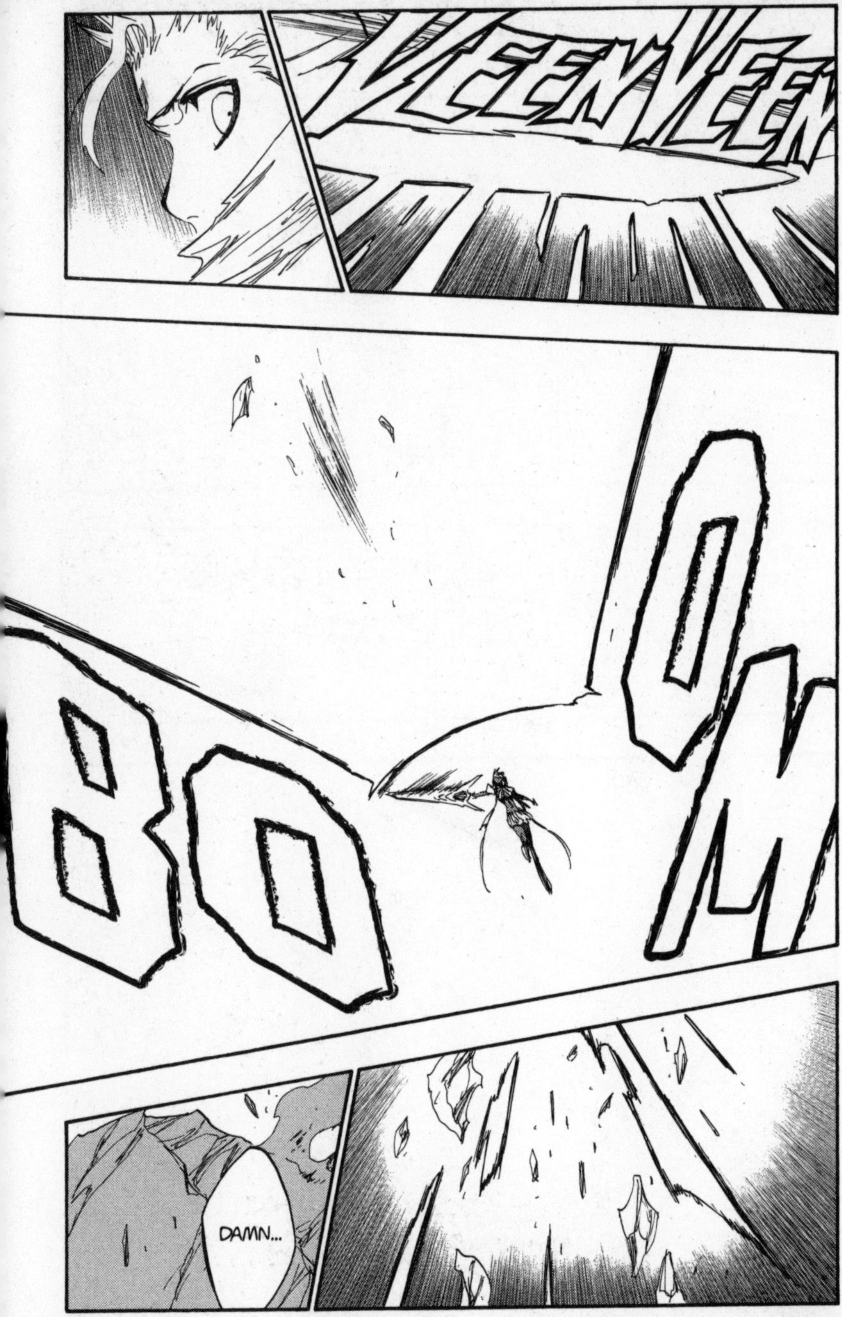
VEEN VEEN
BOOM
DAMN...

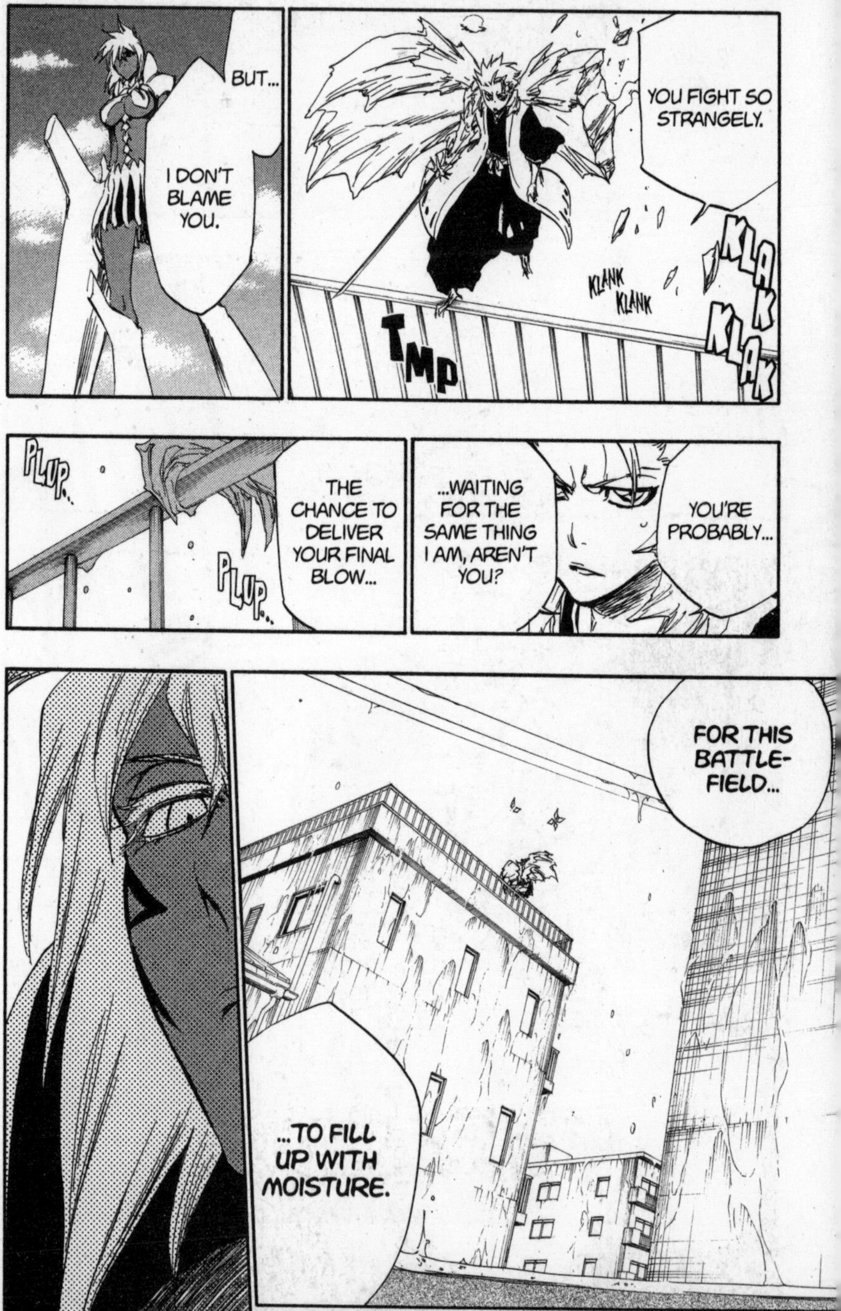
YOU FIGHT SO STRANGELY.
KLANK KLANK
KLAK KLAK
TMP
I DON'T BLAME YOU.
BUT...
YOU'RE PROBABLY...
...WAITING FOR THE SAME THING I AM, AREN'T YOU?
THE CHANCE TO DELIVER YOUR FINAL BLOW...
PLUP...
PLUP...
FOR THIS BATTLE-FIELD...
...TO FILL UP WITH MOISTURE.

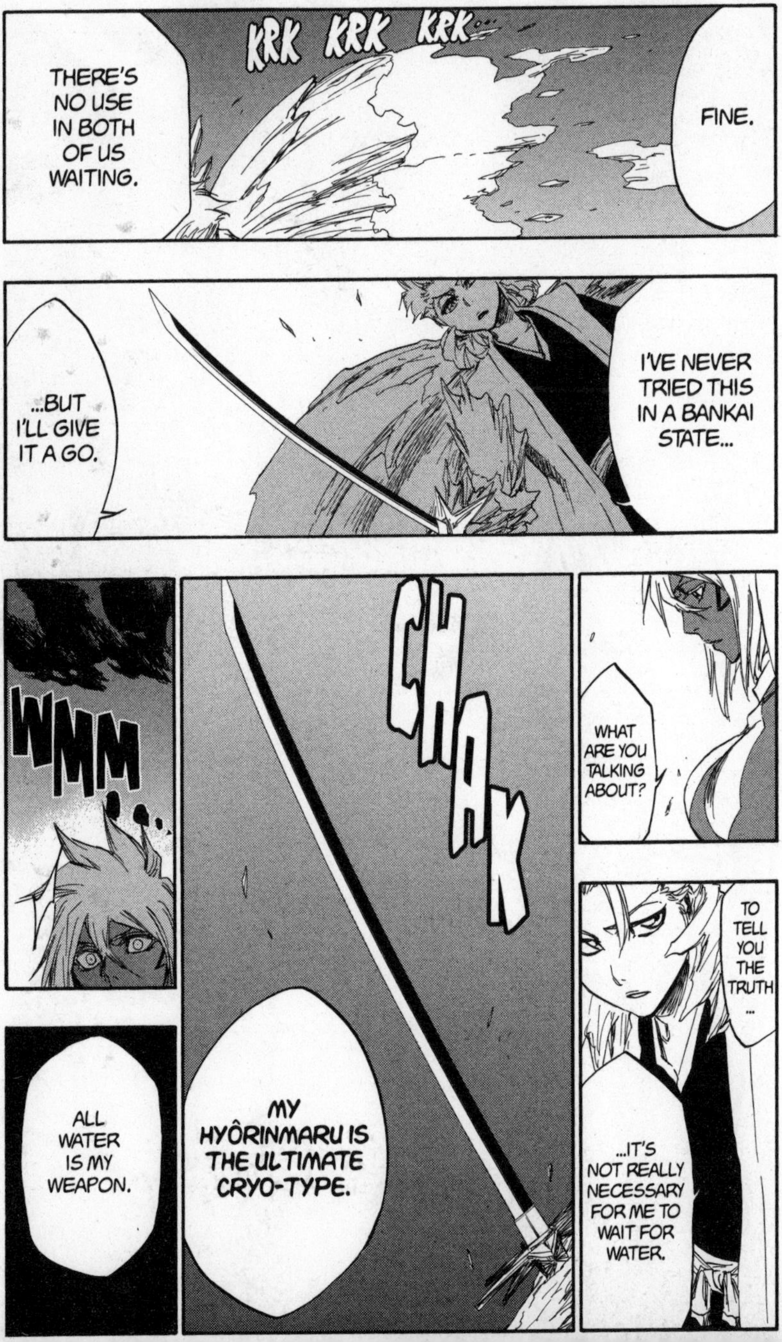
KRK KRK KRK...
FINE.
THERE'S NO USE IN BOTH OF US WAITING.
I'VE NEVER TRIED THIS IN A BANKAI STATE...
...BUT I'LL GIVE IT A GO.
WHAT ARE YOU TALKING ABOUT?
TO TELL YOU THE TRUTH...
...IT'S NOT REALLY NECESSARY FOR ME TO WAIT FOR WATER.
CHAK
MY HYÔRINMARU IS THE ULTIMATE CRYO-TYPE.
WMM...
ALL WATER IS MY WEAPON.

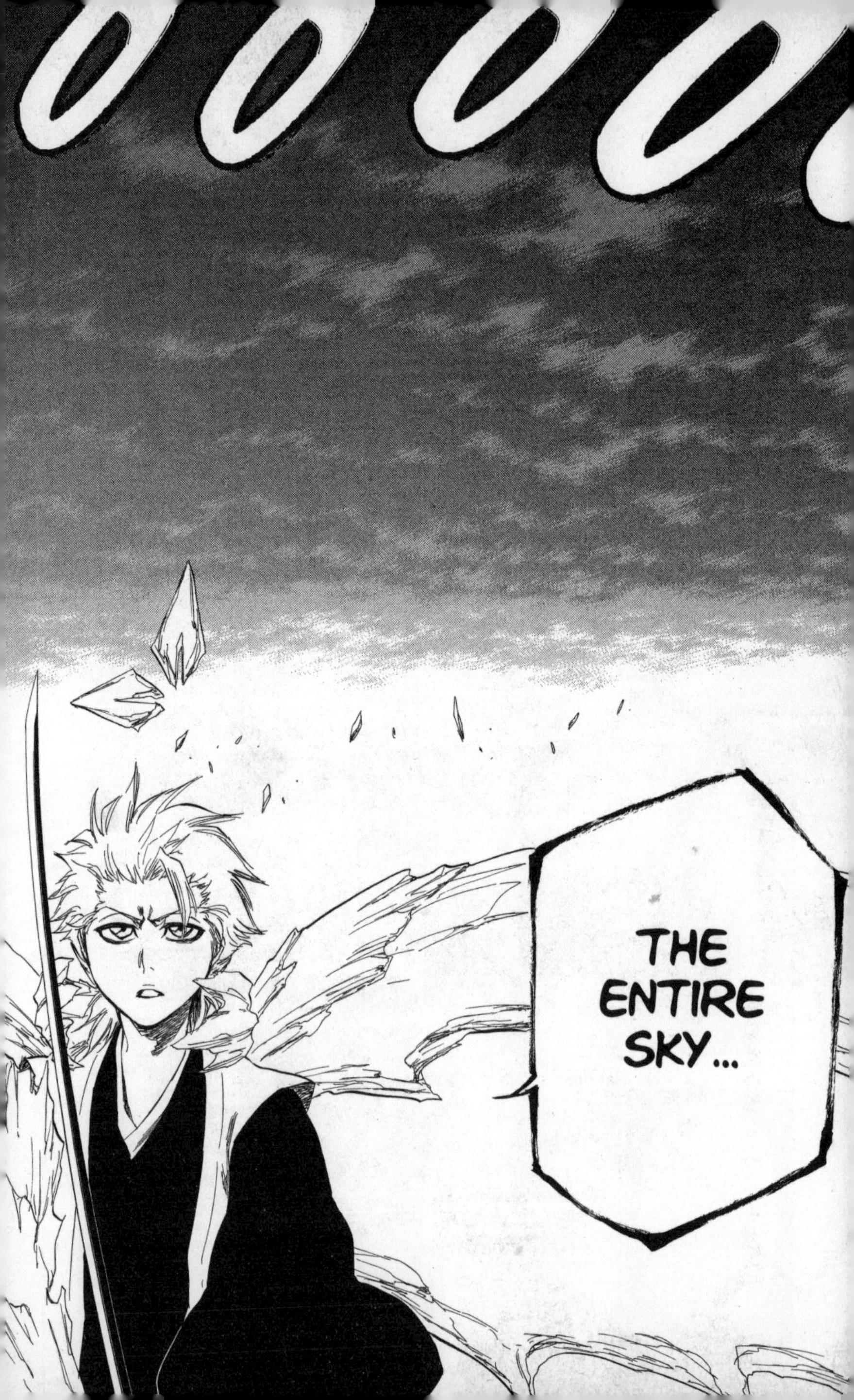
THE ENTIRE SKY...

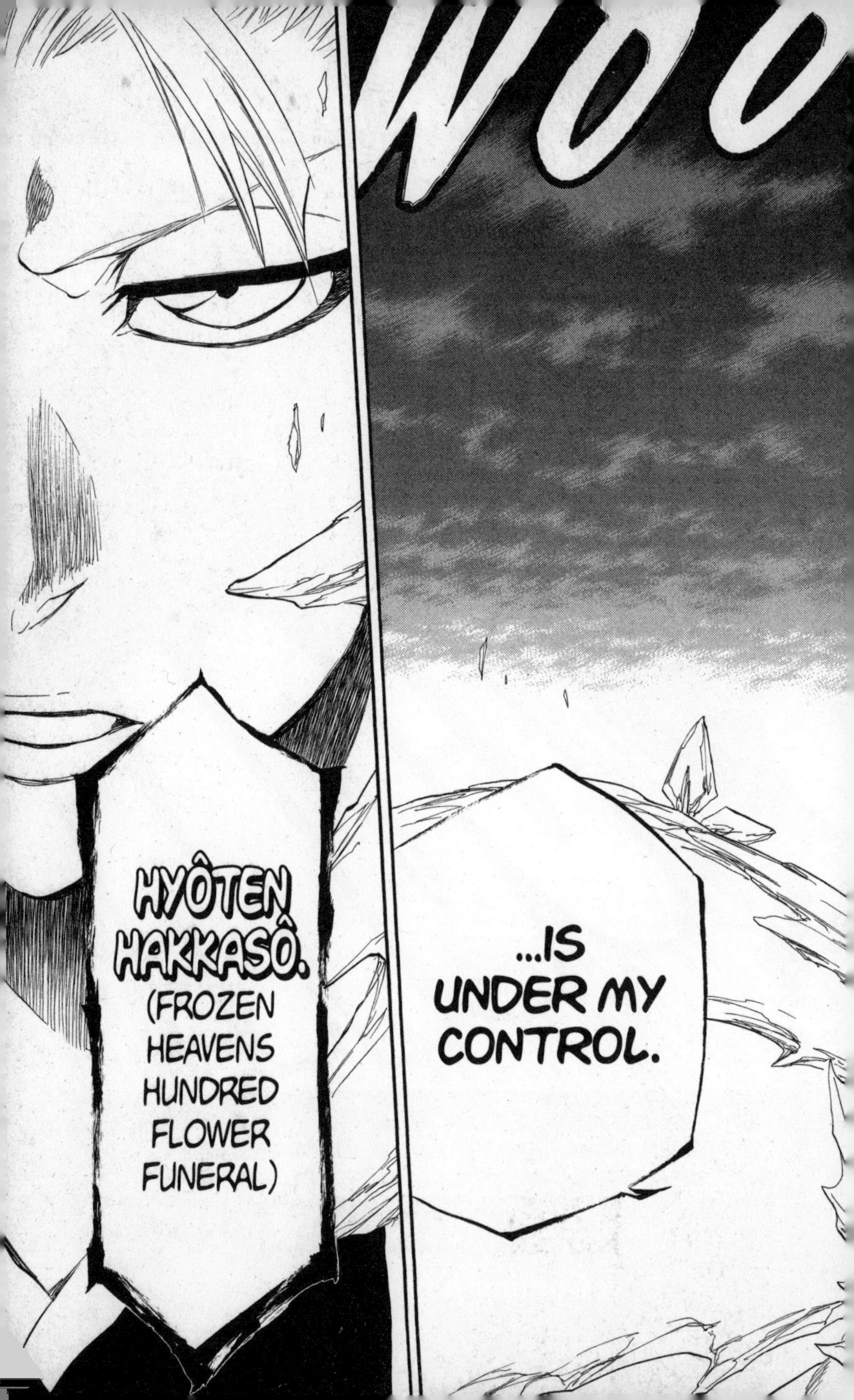
WOO
...IS UNDER MY CONTROL.
HYÔTEN HAKKASÔ. (FROZEN HEAVENS HUNDRED FLOWER FUNERAL)

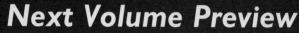

The Soul Reaper captains continue their battle with Aizen's remaining forces. Just when things look dire, surprising reinforcements arrive to turn things on their head. Will Aizen himself finally join the fight?!

Coming July 2012!!